Current Issues in Finance, Economy and Politics

Çağatay Başarır (ed.)

Current Issues in Finance, Economy and Politics

Theoretical and Empirical Finance and Economic Researches

PETER LANG

Bibliographic Information published by the Deutsche Nationalbibliothek

The Deutsche Nationalbibliothek lists this publication in the Deutsche Nationalbibliografie; detailed bibliographic data is available online at http://dnb.d-nb.de.

Library of Congress Cataloging-in-Publication Data

A CIP catalog record for this book has been applied for at the Library of Congress.

Cover illustration
© REDPIXEL.PL/shutterstock.com

Printed by CPI books GmbH, Leck

ISBN 978-3-631-80132-1 (Print)
E-ISBN 978-3-631-80410-0 (E-PDF)
E-ISBN 978-3-631-80411-7 (EPUB)
E-ISBN 978-3-631-80412-4 (MOBI)
DOI 10.3726/b16226

Peter Lang – Berlin · Bern · Bruxelles · New York · Oxford · Warszawa · Wien

This publication has been peer reviewed.

www.peterlang.com

Preface and Acknowledgments

Financial system plays an important role for the distribution and transition of idle funds into the economic system. A breakdown in the operations of financial system or a fault concerning a component of the financial system affect the real sector negatively. Banking system is the underlying structure of the financial sector in most of the economies. Banking sector performs as an intermediary to match the fund surplus and fund gaps in order to transfer the surplus to who is in the need for.

Digital applications wide-spreading with the modern technological developments affect notably the banking sector and ultimately all the financial sector together with many innovations that are difficult to compete with. Technological progress enable a more dynamical financial system as a whole. In this context, as the need for innovations required to meet the gains of today's demand, financial markets develop and intensify. At this point, academicians and practitioners contribute to the process both by following the steps in these areas closely and also by their new researches and opinions. This book can be seen as a part of this effort.

In the book, new trends both in the finance and economic structure are discussed by the academicians and practitioners who are experts in their fields from different viewpoints. The book consists of 21 parts that discuss the developments in economy, financial markets such as stock exchange market and exchange rates, theoretically and empirically.

The book consists of four main sections: Economics, Banking Sector, Stock Exchange and Financial Markets. Economics section has six subsections as monetary policy, economic growth, current deficit, international services trade, Eurasian economic union and public share. Second part of the book consists of six subsections about the banking sector that is the fundemental of economic structure and the main actor of the financial sector. This main sector discusses the efficiency and performance of the banking sector and also shadow banking. In addition, banking sector is analysed in Islamic banking area. Furthermore, the interaction of banking sector and technological developments are emphasized in a separate section in this part.

The third main section has five subsections that analyse the relationship of currency markets with various financial variables, due to the recent rising trends. Moreover, this section has two subsections discussing crowdfunding and laundering of illicit money.

The last main section of the book has four subsections about the key actor of the financial sector: stock exchange. This sections discusses the divident policies, hypothesis of overconfidence in Borsa Istanbul, long memory test in Borsa Istanbul and low pricing model in initial public offerings. This book covers almost all the topics anaylysing the dynamics of economics.

We would like to thank all the authors and researchers who are experts in their field for their devotion and diligence and hope to help our readers. We also offer our endless gratitude to the families and children who are the source of motivation for our authors with their patience and support during the conduct of these valuable works.

Yours Truly

Assoc.Prof. Çağatay Başarır

Contents

List of Contributors

Ahmet Aydın
Assoc. Prof., Bandırma Onyedi Eylul University, aaydin@bandirma.edu.tr

Alban Hetemi
Ph.D., TEB SHA Department Manager/Compliance Division at TEB Bank hetemi.alban@gmail.com

Aytaç Pekmezci
Asst. Prof., Muğla Sıtkı Koçman University, aytac0803@mu.edu.tr

A. Gamze Aytekin
Asst. Prof., Balikesir University, aysegamze@balikesir.edu.tr

A. Rutkay Ardoğan
PhD Student, Ege University, rutkay@gmail.com

Berna Serener
Asst. Prof., European University of Lefke, berna_serener@hotmail.com

Burçay Yaşar Akçalı
Asst. Prof., İstanbul University, burcayy@istanbul.edu.tr

Dilek Demirhan
Assoc. Prof., Ege University, dilek.demirhan@ege.edu.tr

Engin Kurun
Assoc. Prof., Piri Reis University, ekurun@pirireis.edu.tr

Hale Kırer Silva Lecuna
Asst. Prof., Bandırma Onyedi Eylül University, hkirer@bandirma.edu.tr

Haydar Karadağ
Asst. Prof., Recep Tayyip Erdoğan University, haydar.karadag@erdogan.edu.tr

H. Levent Korap
Asst. Prof., Kastamonu University, lkorap@kastamonu.edu.tr

Kurtuluş Bozkurt
Asst. Prof., Aydın Adnan Menderes University, kurtuluş.bozkurt@adu.edu.tr

Mehmet Güçlü
Assoc. Prof., Ege University, mehmet.guclu@ege.edu.tr

M. Kenan Terzioğlu
Assoc. Prof., Trakya University, kenanterzioglu@trakya.edu.tr

Mehmet Sabri Topak
Asst. Prof., Istanbul University, msabri@istanbul.edu.tr

Mehmet Özer
Ph.D., Expert at Capital Markets Board of Turkey, mozer@spk.gov.tr

Melike Torun
Res., Asst. Dr., Istanbul University, meliket@istanbul.edu.tr

Muhammed Mustafa Tuncer Çalışkan
Asst. Prof., Bandırma Onyedi Eylül University, mcaliskan@bandirma.edu.tr

Muhittin Tolga Özsağlam
Asst. Prof., European University of Lefke,
mozsaglam@eul.edu.tr

Mustafa Şit
Asst. Prof., Harran University, msit@harran.edu.tr.

Onur Duygu
Senior Manager at Odeabank,
onurduygu@odeabank.com.tr

Ozan Gülhan
Ph.D., TEB SHA, Head of Compliance Division, ozan.gulhan@teb-kos.com

Ömer Faruk Rençber
Asst. Prof., Gaziantep University,
ofrencber@gantep.edu.tr

Özlem Kuvat
Asst. Prof., Balikesir University,
ohasgul@balikesir.edu.tr

Sefer Uçak
Asst. Prof., Balikesir University,
seferucak@balikesir.edu.tr

Serçin Şahin
Dr., Yildız Technical University,
sesahin@yildiz.edu.tr

Serpil Altınırmak
Assoc. Prof., Anadolu University,
saltinirmak@anadolu.edu.tr
Yahye Hassan Abdi
Finance Master/Anadolu University

Yasemin Dumrul
Asst. Prof., Kayseri University,
ydumrul@erciyes.edu.tr

Zerrin Kılıçarslan
Asst. Prof., Kayseri University,
zkaan@erciyes.edu.tr

Kurtuluş Bozkurt and Aytaç Pekmezci

1 Economic Growth and Current Deficit: An Analysis for OECD Countries

Highlights: Together with globalization, especially last quarter century, one of the most discussed subjects in literature of economy is effects of unbalanced current accounts on macroeconomic variables. Integration of developing countries in process of globalization, effects of liberal economy politics applications based on balance of payments on economic growth is the subject discussed on literature of economy. In this chapter, the author will use the OECD countries' data for 2005:01–2017:04 time interval. With this, panel data set will be formed. And this study will search if there is any causation relationship between current accounts balance and economic growth and analyse that.

Keywords: Economic growth, current deficit, panel data, OECD countries

Introduction

With the globalization process, especially in the last quarter of centuries, one of the most discussed issues in the economic literature has been the effects of current account imbalances on macroeconomic variables. The effects of liberal economic policies applied in the context of the integration of developing countries into the globalization process on the economic growth processes through the balance of payments are one of the most discussed topics in the economic literature. Again, the theoretical approaches, which try to explain the economic crises and are defined as the third-generation crisis models, attach great importance to the current account balance (Üzümcü et al., 2015).

The analysis of the relationship between the current account balance and economic growth has shown that different results have been achieved for the long term using a different sample, period and method. While some studies have found a cointegration relationship in the long term, some studies have not found the same.

On the one hand, when we look at the causality analyses made for the short term, it is seen that some studies have determined a single or double causality relationship between the current account deficit and economic growth in the short term. However, in some of these analyses, a causal relationship has been determined from the current deficit to economic growth and in some from economic growth to the current deficit. On the other hand, in some studies, it is seen that no causality relationship can be determined for the short term.

The main objective of this study is to empirically analyze the theoretical relationship between economic growth and current deficit for 32 OECD countries, including Turkey within the framework of 2005:1–2017:4 period and which can be reached to accurate data. For this purpose, the relationship between economic growth and current deficit for OECD countries will be analysed empirically using time series and panel data analysis.

2 Literature

When the literature is analyzed, it is seen that the relationship between economic growth and the current deficit is tested by using different data, sample, period and method, and many studies have been done in this regard. These studies have reached different application results for different samples and periods.

A summary of applied literature on relevant studies examining the relationship between economic growth and the current account deficit is given in Tab. 1.1.

3 Material and Method

In the time series, the most important assumption that is required to obtain meaningful relationships between the variables studied is that the variables must be stable. This assumption is necessary for effective and consistent estimates (Gujarati, 2005). In addition, the long-term relationship between the series is determined by the analysis of cointegration. When X_t and Y_t are the first (I (1)) error term (u_t) I (0) obtained from the regression model of the two-time series, these two variables are called *co-integrated series*. Finally, the direction of the relationship between the variables is determined by Granger causality analysis.

Johansen developed the Largest Eigenvalue (l_{max}) and Trace (l_{trace}) tests as calculated in Equation 1 based on the maximum likelihood method with the vector autoregressive (VAR) model in estimating the multiple cointegration vector between two or more variables. The r in equality shows the maximum number of cointegration vectors among the variables. l_{trace} tests the number of cointegrated vectors, and l_{max} tests the significance of the coherent vectors (Enders, 1995).

$$\lambda_{trace} = -T\sum_{i=r+1}^{k}\ln(1-\hat{\lambda}_i) \quad \text{and} \quad \lambda_{max} = -T\ln(1-\hat{\lambda}_{r+1}) \tag{1}$$

Tab. 1.1: Summary of Applied Literature

Author/s	Sample/Term	Method	Result
Debelle and Faruqee (1996)	1971–1993/ 21 Developed Countries	Horizontal Section, Time Series and Panel Data Analysis	Economic growth increases the current account deficit.
Bagnai and Manzocchi (1999)	1965–1994/ 49 Developing Countries	Time Series and Panel Data Analysis (LSDV)	Economic growth increases the current account deficit.
Freund (2000)	1980–1997/ 25 Industrialized Countries	Time Series and Panel Data Analysis	Economic growth increases the current account deficit through consumption expenditures.
Calderon, Chong and Loayza (2000)	1966–1995/ 44 Developing Countries	Panel Data Analysis (GMM)	There is an inverse but weak relationship between the current account balance and economic growth.
Kandil and Greene (2002)	1960–2000/ USA	Cointegration Analysis	Increases in GDP increase the current account deficit through the import channel.
Chinn and Prasad (2003)	1971–1995/ 18 Developed, 71 Developing Countries	Panel EKK Analysis	There is a weak relationship between growth and current account balance in both developing countries and developed countries.
Parikh and Stirbu (2004)	1970–1999/ 42 Countries in Total from Asia, Africa and Latin America	Panel Data Analysis	Economic growth increases the current account deficit.
Dominguez (2005)	1980–1990/ Singapore	Smallest Squares (EKK)	Economic growth increases the current account deficit.
Erkılıç (2006)	Turkey/ 1980–2005	EKK and VAR	There is a one-way causality relationship from the rate of economic growth to the current account deficit.
Tunalı (2007)	Turkey/ 1980–2006	Classical Linear Multiple Regression Model and VAR	One of the most important reasons for the current account deficit in the long term is economic growth.

(*continued on next page*)

Tab. 1.1: (continued)

Author/s	Sample/Term	Method	Result
Aristovnik (2007)	1971–2005/ Middle East and North Africa (MENA) Countries	EKK, LSDV, FGLS and GMM	Economic growth increases the current account deficit.
Erbaykal (2007)	Turkey/ 1987–2016	Toda and Yamamoto Causative Analysis	Economic growth is the cause of the current account deficit, and there is a reason for economic growth in the current account deficit.
Telatar and Terzi (2009)	Turkey/ 1991–2005	Granger Causality Test and VAR	There is a one-sided causality from the growth rate to the current account balance.
Morsy (2009)	1970–2006/ 28 Oil Exporting Countries	Panel Data Analysis (GMM)	Economic growth has no effect on the current account deficit.
Yılmaz and Akıncı (2011)	Turkey/ 1980–2010	Granger Causality Test	There is a one-way causality from GDP to the current account balance.
Kostakoğlu and Dibo (2011)	Turkey/ 1991–2010	VAR	Economic growth increases the current account deficit.
Sekmen and Çalışır (2011)	Turkey/ 1998–2009	ARDL	There is a positive relationship between economic growth and current account deficit in the short term; however, there is no relation in the long term.
Bayraktutan and Demirtaş (2011)	1980–2006/ 19 Developing Countries	Panel Data Analysis	Economic growth is increasing the current account deficit.
Hepaktan and Çınar (2012)	1975–2008/ 27 OECD Countries	Panel Cointegration Analysis	There is a cointegration relationship between GDP and the current account balance.
Akçay and Erataş (2012)	1993–2011/ BRIC countries	Panel Data Analysis and Dumistrescu-Hurlin Causality Test	In the long term, a causal relationship between economic growth and current transactions has been identified.
Songur and Yaman (2013)	1981–2010/ 10 Developing Countries	Panel Cointegration and Panel VECM	In the long term, a causality relationship was determined from economic growth to current transactions and from current transactions to economic growth.

Tab. 1.1: (continued)

Author/s	Sample/Term	Method	Result
Yalçınkaya and Temelli (2014)	1992–2013/ BRICS and MINT Countries	Panel Data Analysis	Both short- and long-term economic growth has been determined to be effective in the current account.
Yurdakul and Uçar (2015)	Turkey/ 1991–2014	Granger Causality Test and VAR	There is no correlation between economic growth and the current account deficit.
Şit and Alancıoğlu (2016)	Turkey/ 1980–2014	VAR	There is a two-way causality relationship between GDP and current account balance.
Erdoğan and Acet (2016)	Turkey/ 2003–2015	Granger Causality Test and VAR	There is a two-sided causality relationship between economic growth and current account balance.
Duman (2017)	Turkey/ 2003–2017	VAR	There is a one-sided causality relationship between economic growth and current account balance.
Uçak (2017)	Turkey/ 1980–2015	Granger Causality Test and VAR	There is a one-way causality relationship from real GDP to the current balance.
Ersungur et al. (2017)	Turkey/ 1998–2014	VAR	There is a two-way causality relationship between GDP and current account balance.
İslatince (2017)	Turkey/ 2003–2016	ARDL	The current account deficit has a negative impact on economic growth in both the short and long term.

Source: Edited by authors.

Determining the direction of the relationship determined by the cointegration test among the variables is an important stage for putting the data into the correct statistical model. Statistical causality is the ability of a time series variable to obtain future prediction values by being affected by the past values of the time series variable itself or by another related time series variable. The main condition of this analysis is that the variables are stationary (Işığıçok, 1994). Granger causality analysis is the most preferred method because of its ease in application. Granger causality relationship is explained by autoregressive models obtained by displacement of dependent and independent variables of static series in Equations 2 and 3. The k and m in the equations show the most appropriate delay lengths. For this purpose, various information criteria such as AIC and SIC are used (Kadılar, 2000).

$$X_t = c_1 + \sum_{i=1}^{k} \alpha_i X_{t-i} + \sum_{i=1}^{m} \beta_i Y_{t-i} + u_t \quad (2)$$

$$Y_t = c_2 + \sum_{i=1}^{k} \chi_i Y_{t-i} + \sum_{i=1}^{m} \delta_i X_{t-i} + v_t \quad (3)$$

The aim of this study is to analyze the relationship between the current account deficit (CD) and per capita income (GDP) among the 32 OECD countries where complete data for the specified period can be reached. For this, the ADF unit root test is used to determine whether the variables are stationary or not, and to determine whether there is a long-term relationship between the dependent CD and the independent GDP variables, Johansen cointegration tests are applied (λ_{max} and λ_{trace}) and Granger and Toda-Yamamoto (1995) to understand whether there is a short-term relationship. The data used in the study are seasonal for the period 2005: Q1–2017: Q4. The data are taken from the official website of the World Bank (www.worldbank.org). In the analysis study, the original data were used because negative values were found.

In the tests used in the study, the most preferred significance level was used in the literature. The Schwarz Information Criterion (SIC) was used as an asymptotically more consistent result in selecting optimal latency length during the determination of short-term relationships (lütkepohl, 1993). After selecting the most appropriate delay length, whether the model has normal distribution, autocorrelation and changing variance problem was examined.

At the point of panel data analysis, LM test and Friedman test of Breusch-Pagan (1980) were used to determine whether there is a cross-sectional dependence between the series (Bozkurt, 2013; Bozkurt and Balmumcu, 2018). Then, the CADF test was conducted by Pesaran (2006) which tested the unit root process under the assumption of cross-sectional dependence, and panel cointegration test developed by Westerlund (2007) was applied to determine whether there is any cointegration relationship between the economic growth and the balance of current processes. In addition, panel error correction model was estimated with dynamic constant effects, and average group estimators and short- and long-term relationships between current account balance and economic growth were analyzed. On the other hand, short- and long-term relationships were tested with the mean group estimator for each unit.

4 Empirical Results

At the beginning of the study, the regression model that was established between only nine countries (Australia, Belgium, Denmark, France, Ireland, Korea, Latvia, Switzerland and Turkey) among 32 OECD countries was significant, while the model that was established among others was excluded from the analysis because it is meaningless. In order to determine whether the variables for these nine countries are stable at the same degree, the most commonly used ADF unit root test was applied in the literature. The results of the analysis are given in Tab. 1.2, the calculated test statistic values of the variables.

The ADF unit root test is used to test the H_0 hypothesis that "series is not stationary" $\alpha = 0{,}05$ at the level of significance. When the calculated test statistic values of variables belonging to countries are smaller than the tau critical value, the H_0 hypothesis is rejected and the analyzed series is stated to be stable. If the examined series is not stationary, the difference is taken. When Tab. 1.2 is examined, six countries (Belgium, France, Korea, Ireland, Latvia and Switzerland) whose levels of stability are different and stable are excluded from the analysis because they do not meet the requirements of the Johansen cointegration tests. However, Toda-Yamato causality analysis was applied to determine whether there is a short-term relationship between Ireland and Latvia with different degrees of stability.

In order to determine whether the variables have a long-term relationship with the three countries (Australia, Denmark and Turkey), the same degree of stability was applied to Johansen cointegration test (λ_{max} and λ_{trace}). According to the optimally selected SIC information criteria, the most appropriate model was selected for the Johansen test. The cointegration test statistic probability values calculated among the variables according to the most appropriate model are given in Tab. 1.3.

In the Johansen tests, λ_{trace} tests the number of cointegrated vectors, λ_{max} tests the significance of the coherent vectors. With these tests, H_0 hypothesis "There is no cointegration relationship between variables" is tested at $\alpha = 0{,}05$ significance level. The value of calculated test statistic with a probability value less than 0.05, H_0 hypothesis is rejected and the long-term relationship between the examined variables is supported. In this study, it was observed that there was a long-term relationship between the variables studied in Turkey for λ_{max} and Denmark for λ_{trace} test. No long-term relationship was found for Australia.

In order to determine the direction of the short-term relationship between variables belonging to countries, Granger causality analysis was applied to classify the variables as dependent and independent. Long-term relationships

Tab. 1.2: ADF Unit Root Test Results of Nine Countries Tested Variables

Line	**Countries**	**Variables**	**Level**	**First Difference**	**Stability Degree**
1	**Australia**	CA	-3.366482	-6,681643*	I(1)
		GDP	-2.846311	-7,04924*	I(1)
2	Belgium	CA	-4,440763*		**I(0)**
		GDP	-4,469764*		**I(0)**
3	**Denmark**	CA	-2.058093	-9,951481*	I(1)
		GDP	-2.986543	-5,063922*	I(1)
4	France	CA	-4,765989*		**I(0)**
		GDP	-3,884819*		**I(0)**
5	Ireland	CA	-3,978784*		**I(0)**
		GDP	-2.823674	-8,620356*	**I(1)**
6	Korea	CA	-4,123911*		**I(0)**
		GDP	-4,804849*		**I(0)**
7	Latvia	CA	-1.49663	-5,195328*	**I(1)**
		GDP	-3,803992*		**I(0)**
8	Switzerland	CA	-4,042928*		**I(0)**
		GDP	-3,713452*		**I(0)**
9	**Turkey**	CA	-2.318361	-5,825515*	I(1)
		GDP	-2.711104	-6,138804*	I(1)

Note: Critical values given by Eviews according to the 5 % significance level and the Fixed-term + Trend model; for the level state (-3,500495) and for the first difference (-3,502373).
* : Indicates that the corresponding series is stable.

identified countries (Denmark and Turkey) preferred restricted VAR model, and the relationship undetected countries (Australia) preferred unrestricted VAR model. In addition, Toda-Yamamoto causality analysis was applied to different levels of stable countries (Latvia and Ireland). The probability values of causality analysis between variables are given in Tab. 1.4, Tab. 1.5 and Tab. 1.6, respectively.

With causality tests, H_0 hypothesis “There is no cointegration relationship between variables” is tested at $\alpha = 0{,}05$ a significance level. Since the probability of the calculated statistical value is less than 0.05, the hypothesis H0 is rejected and a short-term relationship between the variables of the country studied is indicated. Accordingly, when examined in Tabs. 1.3–1.5, two countries (Denmark and Turkey) have causality from GDP to CAs. However, no causality relationship was found from CA to GDP. So one-way relationship was found. In Australia and Latvia, short-term relationships were not observed. In addition, there was a bi-directional causality relationship from GDP to CA and from CA to GDP.

Tab. 1.3: Cointegration Test Results of the Variables Examined in the Same OECD Countries

Countries	SIC Lag Length	Johansen Model Type	λ_{trace}	λ_{max}
Australia	1	No Deterministic (No Trend + Intercept)	0.155	0.3797
Denmark	2	No Deterministic (No Trend + Intercept)	0.1073	**0.0478***
Turkey	1	No Deterministic (No Trend + Intercept)	**0.026***	0.167

Note: According to the SIC Criteria, the maximum lag length is 8 because our data set is seasonal for optimal lag length.
*: Shows that there is a long-term relationship between the related series.

Tab. 1.4: The Results of Granger-Causal Analysis of Long-Term Relationship Countries

Countries	Lag Length	GDP → CA	CA → GDP
Denmark	2	**0,0192***	0.1091
Turkey	1	**0,0087***	0.2429

*: Shows the direction of the relationship between the countries according to the level of 5 % significance.

Tab. 1.5: Granger Causality Analysis Results of Non-long Term Relationships

Countries	Lag Length	GDP → CA	CA → GDP
Australia	5	0.5154	0,2906

Tab. 1.6: Results of Toda-Yamaoto Causality Analysis of Stable Countries at Different Levels

Countries	Maximum Stability (d_{max})	Lag Length (k)	GDP → CA	CA → GDP
Latvia	1	4	0.1383	0.1876
Ireland	1	9	**0.0000***	**0.0001***

*: Shows the direction of the relationship between the countries according to the level of 5 % significance.

In the scope of panel data analysis, the Breusch Pagan's LM test was carried out to determine whether the series included horizontal cross-section dependency. As shown in Tab. 1.7, horizontal cross-section dependency was determined in both series groups.

Tab. 1.7: Horizontal Cross-Section Dependency Test Results

Variables	Breusch-Pagan LM Test Statistic	Probability Value
GDP	641.38	0.0000
CA	14781.72	0.0000

Tab. 1.8: CADF Panel Unit Root Test Results

Variables		Z[t-bar]	Probability Value
GDP	**Level**	-6.876	0.000
CA	**Level**	-8.995	0.000

Tab. 1.9: Westerlund (2007) Panel Cointegration Test Statistics Results

Test	Value	Z-Value	Probability Value
G_t	-3.766	-12,551	0.000
G_a	-17,870	-11,136	0.000
P_t	-15,156	-6.727	0.000
P_a	-12,305	-9.800	0.000

In the second phase, since horizontal cross-section dependency was determined in both series groups, CADF Panel unit root tests of Pesaran (2006) and the second generation unit root tests were investigated to determine whether the series was stable. As a result of CADF tests for both series groups, it was concluded that the series was stable at a level as shown in Tab. 1.8.

In the third stage, panel cointegration testing was performed taking into account the structural breakdowns of Westerlund. Within the scope of the test, H_0 hypothesis was established as "there is no cointegration". Tab. 1.9 shows the statistical values of GT, Ga, PT and PA test, Z values and probability values, and H_0 hypothesis was rejected according to the results. Therefore, there is a correlation between economic growth and current account balance.

Tab. 1.10 shows the estimation of the panel error correction model by the dynamic constant effects estimator. The error correction parameter is negative and significant, and there is a long-term relationship between the two variables. About 14 % of the imbalances in one period are improved in the next period and the long-term equilibrium is approached. On the other hand, while the

Tab. 1.10: Dynamic Constant Effects Estimator Estimation Results

	D.gdp	Coefficient	z	Probability Value
ec	Ca	0.335	3.82	0.000
SR	Ec	-0.138	-10.80	0.000
	ca.D1	-0.066	-4.02	0.000
	Stationary	0.259	5.15	0.000

Tab. 1.11: Average Group Estimator Estimation Results

	D.gdp	Coefficient	z	Probability Value
ec	Ca	0.667	3.59	0.000
SR	Ec	-0.170	-9.65	0.000
	ca.D1	-0.130	-2.38	0.017
	Stationary	0.314	3.17	0.002

long-term parameter of the current account deficit series is positive and significant, the short-term parameter is negative and significant. In the long term, 1 % increase in the current account balance increased the economic growth by 0.33 %, whereas the 1 % increase in the current account balance in the short term decreased the economic growth by 0.066 %.

Tab. 1.10 shows the estimation of the panel error correction model by the dynamic constant effects estimator. The error correction parameter is negative and significant, and there is a long-term relationship between the two variables. Approximately 17 % of the imbalances in one period are improved in the next period and the long-term equilibrium is approached. On the other hand, while the long-term parameter of the current account deficit series is positive and significant, the short-term parameter is negative and significant. In the long term, 1 % increase in the current account balance increased the economic growth by 0.66 %, whereas the 1 % increase in the current account balance in the short term decreased the economic growth by 0.13 %.

Unlike the pooled average group estimator in Tab. 1.11, long-term parameters for each unit were estimated separately. According to the results, the error correction parameters of Australia, Belgium, Chile, Denmark, Finland, Germany, Iceland, Ireland, Israel, Italy, Japan, South Korea, Luxembourg, Norway, Sweden, Switzerland and Turkey are negative and significant, and there is a long-term relationship between the series (Tab. 1.12).

Tab. 1.12: Average Group Estimator Estimation Results for Each Unit

Country Code	Countries	CA	
		Long Term Parameter	Error Correction Parameter
1	**Australia**	-0.227	-0.324*
3	**Belgium**	0.856*	-0.317*
5	**Chile**	0.774	-0.174*
7	**Denmark**	0.619	-0.178**
9	**Finland**	0.641	-0.169**
11	**Germany**	0.655	-0.154**
14	**Iceland**	0.207	-0.195**
15	**Ireland**	0.427	-0.320*
16	**Israel**	1.424	-0.182**
17	**Italy**	0.895	-0.134**
18	**Japan**	1.067	-0.217**
19	**South Korea**	-0.212	-0.238**
21	**Luxembourg**	0.175	-0.210**
24	**Norway**	0.102	-0.512*
28	**Sweden**	-1.747	-0.143**
29	**Switzerland**	0.698*	-0.199*
30	**Turkey**	-1.123	-0.304*

*%1 expresses the significance in **%5 level.

Conclusion

In this study, the relationship between CA and GDP variables of OECD countries was examined with time series and panel data analysis according to seasonal data of 2005:Q1–2017:Q4. According to time series analysis, whether there is a long-term relationship between the variables is obtained by λ_{max} and λ_{trace} tests, whether the short-term relationship is obtained by Granger and Toda-Yamamoto causality analysis.

Only nine countries were included in the analysis, which established a meaningful model among the OECD countries. Six different levels of stasis (Belgium, France, Korea, Ireland, Latvia and Switzerland) were excluded from the analysis because the Johansen co-ordination tests determined did not meet the requirements. There was a long-term relationship between the variables of the countries with stasis levels i (1) in three countries, for Turkey according to

λ_{trace} and for Denmark according to λ_{max}. No long-term relationship was found for Australia.

When the restricted VAR was examined, short-term relationship between GDP and CA was found in the Granger causality analysis from two countries with long-term relationship. However, no short-term relationships were found from CA to GDP.

In Australia, where there is no long-term relationship when unconstrained VAR is examined, there is no short-term relationship between the examined variables in any direction.

When the causality analysis of Toda-Yamamoto was examined, there was a two-way causality relationship between GDP to CA and CA to GDP in Ireland. However, in Latvia there was no short-term relationship.

According to panel data analysis, a cointegration relationship between current account balance and economic growth is determined, for Australia, Belgium, Chile, Denmark, Finland, Germany, Iceland, Ireland, Israel, Italy, Japan, South Korea, Luxembourg, Norway, Sweden, Switzerland and Turkey a long-term relationship has been identified.

References

Akçay, A, Ö. and Erataş, F. (2012). Cari Açık ve Ekonomik Büyüme İlişkisinin Panel Nedensellik Analizi Ekseninde Değerlendirilmesi. *Türkiye Ekonomi Kurumu*, 1–24. Erişim adresi: http://teacongress.org/papers2012/AKCAY-ERATAS.pdf. Erişim Tarihi:16.12.2018

Aristovnik, A. (2007). Short-and Medium-Term Determinants of Current Account Balances in Middle East and North Africa Countries. *William Davidson Working Paper*, 862.

Bagnai, A. and Manzocchi, S. (1999). Current Account Reversals in Developing Countries: The Role of Development. *Open Economic Review*, 10, 143–163.

Bayraktutan, Y. and Demirtaş, I. (2011). Gelişmekte Olan Ülkelerde Cari Açığın Belirleyicileri. *Kocaeli Üniversitesi Sosyal Bilimler Dergisi*, 22, 2, 1–28.

Bozkurt, K. (2013). Dışsal Teknolojik Şokların Gelişmekte Olan Ülkelerin Büyüme Sürecine Etkileri. *Ege Stratejik Araştırmalar Dergisi*, 4, 1, 47–69.

Bozkurt, K. and Balmumcu, Ö. (2018). Beşeri Sermaye ve Ekonomik Büyüme: Gelişmekte Olan Ülkeler İçin Bir Panel Veri Analizi. *Uluslararası İktisadi ve İdari İncelemeler Dergisi*, Prof. Dr. Harun Terzi Özel Sayısı, 391–406.

Breusch, T.S. and Pagan, A. R. (1980). The Lagrange Multiplier Test and Its Applications to Model Specification Tests in Econometrics. *Review of Economic Studies*, 47, 239–53.

Calderon, C., Chong, A. and Loayza, N. (2000). Determinants of Current Account Deficits in Developing Countries. *Policy Research Working Paper*, 2398, 1–37.

Chinn, M.D. and Prasad, E.S. (2003). Medium-Term Determinants of Current Accounts in Industrial and Developing Counties: An Empirical Exploration. *Journal of International Economics*, 59, 47–76.

Debelle, G. and Faruquee, H. (1996). What Determines the Current Account? A Cross Sectional and Panel Approach. *IMF Working Paper*.

Dominguez, K. (2005). Economics Perspective in Singapore. http://www-personal.umich.edu/~kathrynd/SIngapore.2005.pdf, Erişim Tarihi:16.12.2018

Duman, Y. K. (2017). Türkiye'de Cari İşlemler Dengesi ve Ekonomik Büyüme Arasındaki İlişki. *Finans Ekonomi ve Sosyal Araştırmalar Dergisi (FESA)*, 2, 4, 231–244.

Enders, W. (1995). Applied Econometric Time Series. John Wiley and Sons. Inc., New York, 433.

Erbaykal, E. (2007). Türkiye'de Ekonomik Büyüme ve Döviz Kuru Cari Açık Üzerinde etkili midir? Bir Nedensellik Analizi. *ZKÜ Sosyal Bilimler Dergisi*, 3, 6, 81–88.

Erdoğan, S. and Acet, H. (2016). Cari İşlemler Dengesi ve Ekonomik Büyüme Arasındaki İlişki: Türkiye Örneği (2003–2015). *The Journal of Academic Social Science Studies*, 51, 3, 539–548.

Erkılıç, S. (2006). *Türkiye'de Cari Açığın Belirleyicileri*. Türkiye Cumhuriyet Merkez Bankası, Uzmanlık Yeterlilik Tezi, Ankara.

Ersungur, Ş. M., Doru, Ö., and Aslan, M. B. (2017). Türkiye'de GSYH ve Döviz Kuru Hareketlerinin Cari Denge Üzerindeki Etkisi: VAR Analizi Yaklaşımı. *Atatürk Üniversitesi İktisadi ve İdari Bilimler Dergisi*, 31, 3, 451–463.

Freund, C. L. (2000). Current Account Adjustment in Industrialized Countries. *World Bank- Development Economies Research Group International Finance Discussion Paper*, No: 69, 483–512.

Gujarati, D. N. (2005). *Temel Ekonometri*, Çev.: Ümit Şenesen ve Gülay Günlük Şenesen, Literatür Yayıncılık, İstanbul, 849.

Hepaktan, C.E. and Çınar, S. (2012). OECD ülkelerinde Büyüme-Cari İşlemler Dengesi İlişkisi: Panel Veri Analizi. *Anadolu Üniversitesi Sosyal Bilimler Dergisi*, 12, 1, 43–57.

Işığıçok, E. (1994). *Değişkenler Arasında İlişkilerin Araştırılmasında Nedensellik Testleri ve Bir Uygulama Denemesi*. Doktora Tezi, Uludağ Üniversitesi, Bursa.

İslatince, H. (2017). The Relationship among Economic Growth, Current Account Deficit, Exchange Rates and Individual Loans in Turkey: The ARDL

Approach. *Journal of Current Researches on Business and Economics*, 7, 2, 337–348.

Kadılar, C. (2000). *Uygulamalı Çok Değişkenli Zaman Serileri Analizi*. Bizim Büro Basımevi, Ankara, 186.

Kandil, M. and Greene, J. (2002). The İmpact of Cyclical Factors on the U.S. Balance of Payments. *IMF Working Paper*, 45.

Kostakoğlu, S. F. and Dibo, M. (2011). Türkiye'de Cari Açık ve Ekonomik Büyüme İlişkisinin VAR Yöntemi ile Analizi. *Anadolu International Conference in Economics II*, 15–17 Haziran 2011, Eskişehir.

Lütkepohl, H. (1993). Introduction to Multiple Time Series Analysis. Springer-Verlag, Berlin.

Morsy, H. (2009). Current Account Determinants for Oil-Exporting Countries. *IMF Working Paper*, 09/28.

Parikh, A. and Stirbu, C. (2004). Relationship Between Trade Liberalisation, Economic Growth and Trade Balance: An Econometric Investigation. *HWWA Discussion Paper*, No: 282, 1–50.

Pesaran, M. H. (2006). A Simple Panel Unit Root Test in the Presence of Cross Section Dependence. *Cambridge Working Papers in Economics*, No: 0346.

Sekmen, F., and Çalışır, M. (2011). Is There a Trade-Off Between Current Account Deficits and Economic Growth? The Case of Turkey. *International Research Journal of Finance and Economics*, 62, 166–172.

Songur, Y. and Yaman, D. (2013). "Gelişmekte Olan Ülkelerde Cari İşlemler Dengesi ve Ekonomik Büyüme Arasındaki İlişki: Panel Veri Analizi". *Maliye Dergisi*, 164.

Şit, M. and Alancıoğlu, E. (2016). Türkiye'de Cari İşlemler Dengesi ve Ekonomik Büyüme Arasındaki İlişki: VAR Analizi. *ASSAM Uluslararası Dergi*, 3, 5, 5–23.

Telatar, O. M. and Terzi, H. (2009). Türkiye'de Ekonomik Büyüme ve Cari İşlemler Dengesi İlişkisi. *Atatürk Üniversitesi İktisadi ve İdari Bilimler Dergisi*, 23, 2, 119–134.

Toda, H. Y., and Yamamoto, T. (1995). Statistical Inference in Vector Autoregressions with Possibly Integrated Processes. *Journal of Econometrics*, 66, 1, 225–250.

Tunalı, Ç. B. (2007). Türkiye Cari İşlemleri Dengesi Sorunları. *Sosyal Bilimler Dergisi*, 2, 151–175.

Uçak, S. (2017). Cari Denge ve Ekonomik Büyüme İlişkisi: Türkiye Analizi. *Manisa Celal Bayar Üniversitesi Sosyal Bilimler Dergisi*, 15, 2, 107–140.

Üzümcü, N., Pekmezci, A. and Bozkurt, K. (2015). Cari İşlemler Dengesi ve Ekonomik Büyüme İlişkisi: Gelişmekte Olan Ülkeler İçin Bir Nedensellik

Analizi. *16. Uluslararası Ekonometri, Yöneylem Araştırması ve İstatistik Sempozyumu*, Edirne/TÜRKİYE.

Westerlund, J. (2007). Testing for Error Correction in Panel Data. *Oxford Bulletin of Economics and Statistics*, 69, 6, 709–748.

www.worldbank.org Erişim Tarihi:16.12.2018

Yalçınkaya, Ö. and Temelli, F. (2014). Ekonomik Büyüme ile Cari İşlemler Dengesi Arasındaki İlişki: BRICS ve MINT (1992–2013). *Süleyman Demirel Üniversitesi İktisadi ve İdari Bilimler Fakültesi Dergisi*, 19, 4, 201–214.

Yılmaz, Ö. and Akıncı, M. (2011). İktisadi Büyüme ile Cari İşlemler Bilançosu Arasındaki İlişki: Türkiye Örneği. *Atatürk Üniversitesi Sosyal Bilimler Dergisi*, 15, 2, 363–377.

Yurdakul, F. and Uçar, B. (2015). The Relationship between Current Deficit and Economic Growth: An Empirical Study on Turkey. *Procedia Economics and Finance*, 26, 101–108.

Mehmet Güçlü

2 Determinants of Regional Economic Growth in Turkey

Highlights: This study aims to analyze the determinants of regional economic growth in Turkey for the period 2005–2014. In addition to traditional panel econometrics methods, spatial panel econometric methods are used for this analysis. It is empirically proven that human capital, exports, and agriculture positively contribute to regional economic growth. The empirical results assert that there is no statistically significant relationship between public investment and population density and growth. Through spatial econometrics, it is investigated whether the growth of a region has an impact on the growth of neighboring regions. It is observed that there is a positive and high *spatial dependency* between the regions. In other words, the growth of neighboring regions also affects the economic growth of a region. Finally, the empirical findings suggest that an explanatory variable (a determinant of growth) that belongs to a region affects not only the growth in that region (*direct effect*) but also the growth of neighboring regions (*indirect effect*).

Keywords: Regional economic growth, spatial dependence, spatial panel econometrics, SAR model, SEM model

Introduction

Economic growth is a subject that attracts a great deal of interest in the literature. Therefore, there are many theoretical and empirical studies on it. However, there is no single and definitive theoretical model to explain economic growth. Until the late 1950s, the views of Harrod (1939) and Domar (1946) were used to explain growth. Then, the neoclassical growth theory developed by Solow (1956) and Swan (1956) led to the explanation of economic growth. Since the mid-1980s, the proposals of the theory of endogenous growth pioneered by Romer (1986) and Lucas (1988) have been accepted in the explanation of growth. Growth studies have recently been1 affected by Krugman (1991)'s new economic geography theory. In these studies, a relationship was established between economic development and geographical location (Fingleton and Fischer, 2010). In other words, the theory of new economic geography drew attention to the effects of spatial factors and spatial distribution of economic activities on growth (see Fujita, Krugman and Venables, 1999; Baldwin, Forslid, Martin, Ottavianove Robert-Nicoud, 2003; Fujita and Mori, 2005). According to this view, for example, regional imbalances can occur if productive activities are concentrated more in some regions than in other regions.

These developments related to growth theories have brought us to the conclusion that the growth of a region depends not only on its own resources but also on the performance of the neighboring regions. Neighboring regions share common economic, social, and cultural structures. Administrative boundaries between regions cannot prevent this sharing. Therefore, the effects of neighboring regions should not be ignored in the growth of a region. Advances in spatial econometric techniques have made it possible to consider this effect in empirical growth analysis.

The aim of this study is to determine the factors underlying regional income disparity in Turkey during 2005–2014 through spatial panel econometric methods and to find out whether the growth of a region has an impact on the growth of neighboring regions (spatial dependency) or not. Spatial interaction was neglected in previous empirical studies which analyzed the determinants of regional growth in Turkey. Traditional regression models implicitly consider each region as an independent unit and ignore spatial interactions between regions. In empirical studies, neglecting spatial dependence leads to biased results and misleading conclusions (Anselin and Griffith, 1988; Lesage and Pace, 2009). This paper considering spatial interaction aims to present three contributions to the literature: i) the factors underlying the differences in per capita income growth rates among the regions of Turkey will be ascertained. ii) The effect of the growth of neighboring regions on the growth of a region will be determined through spatial econometric methods. iii) The impacts of factors affecting the growth of a region on the growth of neighboring regions (spillover effects) will also be revealed.

The rest of the paper is organized as follows. In the second section, the literature on economic growth is summarized. In the following section, the econometric models and data are defined. In the fourth section, the empirical results are presented. Finally, the results are summarized, and some policy implications are discussed.

2 Literature Review

Empirical studies on economic growth can be gathered under two main groups. The first group includes studies on the convergence hypothesis: they are interested in the question "Will regional economies/countries achieve the same level of income over time?". The second group is interested in the determinants of growth: They are looking for answers to the question, "What are the factors determining the growth differences between regions/countries?"

Barro and Sala-i-Martin (1991); Armstrong (1995); Neven and Gouyette (1994); Molle and Broeckhout (1995); Carlino and Mills (1993, 1996); Evans and Karras (1996); Chatterji and Dewhurst (1996); Rey and Montouri (1999); Lall and Yılmaz (2001); Rodriguez and Oreggia (2002); and Badinger, Müller, and Tondl (2004) carried out the convergence analysis for different regions and periods. Some of the studies support the income convergence hypothesis while others reject the hypothesis.

Numerous empirical studies have been carried out on the determinants of economic growth in the literature, but there has been no consensus on which variables are determinants of growth. Dollar (1992) researches the sources of economic growth for 95 developing countries for the period 1976–1986. He claims that the real exchange rate variability and real exchange rate distortion are negatively related to economic growth. Also, he finds a statistically significant relationship between investment and growth. Fischer (1992) analyzes the economic growth for various country groups (Sub-Saharan African countries, Latin American countries, and Caribbean countries) for years 1970–1985. The researcher obtains a significant empirical relationship between human capital, investment, and budget surplus and GDP growth. Besides, he alleges that there is a negative relationship between inflation and initial real GDP growth. Knight, Loayza, and Villanueva (1993) argue that human capital, physical capital, trade openness, and population are important determinants of growth. The study by Most and Vann de Berg (1996) for 11 Sub-Saharan African countries analyzes the relationship between three main funding sources (foreign aid, foreign direct investment, and domestic savings) and economic growth. They allege that domestic savings have a slightly more effective role in economic growth than the other two sources of funds. Another study analyzing economic growth in Sub-Saharan African countries is carried out by Eastern and Levine (1997). The study relates low schooling, political instability, underdeveloped financial system, distorted foreign exchange market, high budget deficits, and insufficient infrastructure investments to low growth rates in Africa. Chen and Feng (2000) investigate the resources of China's economic growth. The empirical results put forward that private and semi-private enterprises, higher education, and international trade have a positive impact on economic growth. Furthermore, this study suggests that high fertility rates, high inflation, and the presence of state-owned enterprises reduce growth rates. Freire-Seren (2002) finds a significant positive relationship between regional growth and human capital in Spain. Barro (2003) analyzes the determinants of growth in 87 countries for the period 1965 and 1995. According to the empirical results of the study, government expenditure, inflation, life expectancy, and initial income level are negatively associated with growth, while education, investment, the rule of law, openness, and terms of trade are positively associated with growth. Chang and Mendy (2012) obtain an empirical finding that there is a significant positive relationship between the trade openness and investment and economic growth of 36 African countries for the period 1980–2000. They also claim that there is a negative relationship between foreign aid and national savings and growth. Anyanwu (2014) investigates the resources of both African countries and China's growth. He argues that domestic investment, net official aid, education, government effectiveness, metal price index, and urban population positively affect Africa's economic growth. For China, he alleges that domestic investments, trade openness, initial income, and the population are the key drivers of the growth.

There are also many studies that investigate the Turkish regional growth empirically in the literature. However, a significant part of the studies tests the convergence hypothesis. Some of them reach empirical evidence supporting the convergence hypothesis, while others also reach opposite evidence (see Tansel and Güngör, 1998; Temel, Tansel and Albersen, 1999; Berber, Yamak and Artan 2000; Erk, Ateş and Direkçi, 2000; Doğruel and Doğruel, 2003; Gezici and Hewings, 2004; Karaca, 2004; Erlat and Özkan, 2006; Kırdar and Saraçoğlu, 2008; Filiztekin, (1999). Yıldırım and Öcal (2006); Yıldırım, Öcal, and Özyıldırım (2009); Güçlü (2010); and Akçagün (2017) carried out this analysis using spatial econometric methods.

There are very few empirical studies on the determinants of growth in Turkey. The study by Bayraktar (2006) examines the relationship between economic growth and various macroeconomic variables in Turkey for years 1968–1998. It claims that human capital, investment, and inflation are the determinants of growth in Turkey in the period under discussion. Mıhçı and Köksal (2010) conduct a study to explore the determinants of Turkey's regional growth for the period 1980–2000. The econometric estimation results argue that differences in physical and human capital accumulation, industrial composition of employment, and demographic variables are the main drivers of income per capita differences between regions. In the empirical literature, although there are some studies on convergence analysis using spatial econometric methods for Turkey, there are no studies that analyze the determinants of regional growth with these methods. This chapter aims to fill this gap.

3 Econometric Model and Data

For the empirical analysis, both traditional and spatial panel regression models are used comparatively in this study. Firstly, traditional models are defined, and then spatial models are specified. Traditional panel models are two types: fixed and random effects models.

Fixed Effects Panel Model (P_{FE}):

$$y_{it} = X_{it}\beta + \alpha_i + \varepsilon_{it} \quad \varepsilon_{it} \sim N\left(0, \sigma^2\right) \quad i = 1, \ldots, T \quad N\, t = 1, \ldots, T \; (1)$$

Where *i* and *t* represent in turn the index for cross-section and time dimension. y, α_i,β, X_{it}, and ε denote the dependent variable, the fixed effect parameter, the vector of unknown parameters, the matrix of the independent variables, and error term, respectively.

Random Effects Panel Model (P_{RE})

$$y_{it} = X_{it}\beta + \alpha + u_{it} \quad u_{it} = \alpha_i + \varepsilon_{it} \quad \varepsilon_{it} \sim N\left(0, \sigma^2\right) \qquad (2)$$

Where α represents the constant term.

There are two spatial models used extensively in the literature. One of them is the spatial lag model (SAR), which takes into account spatial dependence across observations on the dependent variable. Ignoring this kind of spatiality causes estimators to be biased and inconsistent. In the SAR model, spatial dependence can be obtained through the spatially lagged dependent variable. This model has two types:

Fixed Effects Spatial Lag Model (SAR_{FE}):

$$y_{it} = \rho \sum_{j=i}^{N} w_{ij} y_{jt} + X_{it}\beta + \alpha_i + u_{it} \quad u_{it} \sim N\left(0, \sigma^2\right) \qquad (3)$$

Where ρ and w represent the spatial autocorrelation coefficient and spatial weight matrix, respectively. In this study, a row normalized binary contiguity weight is preferred. This matrix is a matrix that takes 1 if the regions are adjacent, otherwise 0. $\sum_{j=i}^{N} w_{ij} y_{it}$ denotes the spatially lagged dependent variable.

Random Effects Spatial Lag model (SAR_{RE}):

$$y_{it} = \rho \sum_{j=i}^{N} w_{ij} y_{it} + X_{it}\beta + \alpha + u_{it} \quad u_{it} = \alpha_i + \varepsilon_{it} \quad \varepsilon_{it} \sim N\left(0, \sigma^2\right) \qquad (4)$$

The other model used extensively in literature is the spatial error model (SEM). This model considers the dependency across error terms. Ignoring this kind of spatiality causes estimators to become inefficient. This model is also defined in two ways as follows:

Fixed Effects Spatial Lag Model (SAR_{FE}):

$$y_{it} = X_{it}\beta + \alpha_i + u_{it} \quad u_{it} = \delta \sum_{J=1}^{N} W_{ij}u_{jt} + \varepsilon_{it} \quad u_{it} \sim N\left(0, \sigma^2\right) \tag{5}$$

Where $u_{it}$and δ denote the spatially autocorrelated error term and the spatial autocorrelation coefficient, respectively.
Random Effects Spatial Lag model (SAR_{RE}):

$$y_{it} = X_{it}\beta + u_{it} \quad u_{it} = \alpha_i + \delta \sum_{J=1}^{N} W_{ij}u_{jt} + v_{it} \quad \varepsilon_{it} \sim N\left(0, \sigma^2\right) \tag{6}$$

The absence of a single model to explain economic growth has led to use a wide range of explanatory variables in the empirical studies [see Durlauf (2005) for a broad overview of the variables used in growth regressions]. In the selection of the explanatory variables, both the empirical literature and the availability of the data are taken into consideration as well as the propositions of neoclassical and endogenous growth theories. These variables and data sources are described below.

As the dependent variable, the annual growth rate of regional real GDP per capita is used. To get real GDP, the regional nominal GDP per capita is divided by the regional inflation index. The former is obtained from TurkStat (The Turkish Statistical Institute), and the latter is from the Central Bank of the Republic of Turkey. Levine and Renelt (1992) and Sala-i-Martin (1997) argue that the level of *initial income (INIncome)* is one of the main drivers of economic growth. The logarithm of the lag of GDP per capita as a representative of initial income is employed here. Investment is expressed as the main determinant of economic growth both in neoclassical and endogenous growth theory. Therefore, this variable is used in almost all empirical studies. The log of regional public investment as *investment variable (INV)* is defined and obtained from the Turkish Presidential Strategy and Budget Directorate. One of the main variables of the endogenous growth theory is *human capital (HC).* As an indicator of human capital, the share of higher education graduates within the noninstitutional population is preferred. In many empirical studies, population is included. Following the literature, the logarithm of *population density (PD)* is taken into consideration as an explanatory variable in the paper. To measure the impact of foreign trade on growth, *the exports variable (EX)* is included in the model as an independent variable. The logarithmic value of the variable is used in the regression. It is observed that the share of agriculture in the regional economies is relatively higher in the eastern regions of Turkey and lower in the western regions. In order to determine the relationship between the production structure of a region and its economic growth, *the share of agriculture in regional GDP (AGR)* is employed in the empirical model. For controlling the effect of the 2008 global financial crisis, *a dummy variable (CRISIS)* is added to the model. Since the impact of the crisis on the Turkish economy was seen in 2009, this variable is defined as 1 for 2009, 0 for other years.

When all the explanatory variables above are inserted to equation 1, the regression model is expressed as follows:

$$\ln\left(\frac{RGDP_{i,t}}{RGDP_{i,t-1}}\right) = \beta_1 \ln(INIncome) + \beta_2 \ln(INV) + \beta_3 HC + \beta_4 \ln(PD) + \beta_5 \ln(EX) + \beta_6 AGR + \beta_7 CRISIS + \alpha_i + \varepsilon_{it} \quad (7)$$

$$i = 1, \ldots, 26 \quad t = 2005, \ldots, 2014$$

Only the model specified in Equation 1 is redefined with the explanatory variables specified above. There is no need to redefine the regressions for other panel models (from Equation 2 to 6).

3.1 Empirical Results

For an empirical analysis of regional economic growth, the nonspatial regression models (regressions in Equation 1 and 2) are initially estimated. The results of the regressions are given in Tab. 2.1. There is no significant relationship between population density and economic growth in all of the estimated models. Only public investments are statistically significant at 10 % level of significance in the fixed effects model. All the regression results claim that human capital, exports, and agriculture are positively related to regional economic growth. It is found that the crisis has a contractionary effect on growth. The Chow statistic in the second column of Tab. 2.1 indicates to the fixed effects panel model rather than the Pooled model. Since the Hausman test statistic is statistically significant, the fixed effects model (the regression in column 2) is preferred over the random effects model. The results of this regression imply that all the variables, except for the population density variable, affect regional per capita GDP growth.

The LM test is used to determine the form of spatial dependence. Since both LM_{lag} and LM_{error} statistics are statistically significant, their robust versions should be used to select the appropriate model. The statistically significant robust LM_{lag} statistic points to the SAR model.

In Tab. 2.2, the estimation results of spatial regressions are given. The results of the spatial lag models (the regressions in Equation 3 and 4) and spatial error

Tab. 2.1: The Results of the Nonspatial Regression Models (2005–2014)

Variables	1			2			3		
	Pooled OLS			**P_{FE}**			**P_{RE}**		
INIncome	**-0.052**	*0.000*	***	**-0.259**	*0.000*	***	**-0.052**	*0.000*	***
INV	**-0.003**	*0.495*		**0.013**	*0.092*	*	**-0.003**	*0.494*	
HC	**0.375**	*0.003*	***	**0.451**	*0.014*	***	**0.375**	*0.002*	***
EX	**0.006**	*0.012*	**	**0.038**	*0.000*	***	**0.006**	*0.012*	**
PD	**0.002**	*0.715*		**-0.022**	*0.778*		**0.002**	*0.715*	
AGR	**0.125**	*0.020*	***	**0.595**	*0.000*	***	**0.125**	*0.019*	**
CRISIS	**-0.092**	*0.000*	***	**-0.086**	*0.000*	***	**-0.092**	*0.000*	***
constant	**0.421**	*0.000*	***				**0.421**	*0.000*	***
R^2	0.44			0.63			0.48		
Chow Test				5.08	*0.000*	***			
Hausman				169,8	*0.000*	***			
LM_{lag}				78.6	*0.000*	***			
Robust LM_{lag}				21.6	*0.000*	***			
LM_{error}				57.1	*0.000*	***			
Robust LM_{error}				0.002	*0.960*				

Note: Italics indicate the *p*value.
***, **, and * represent significance at 1 %, 5 %, and 10 % levels, respectively.

models (the regressions in Equation 5 and 6) are presented comparatively. Unlike the nonspatial models, the investment variable, as well as the population density variable are statistically insignificant in all the spatial regressions. Exports are found to be statistically significant in all the regressions, except for the random effects spatial lag regression in column 2. We mentioned above that the LM statistic points to the SAR model. In addition to this, the Hausman test statistic in Tab. 2.2 also indicates the fixed effects model should be preferred. Therefore, for the estimation of regional economic growth, the fixed effects SAR model (column 1) must be chosen as an appropriate model.

The statistically significant ρcoefficient in column 1 in Tab. 2.2 represents the spatial autocorrelation parameter (that is, the spatial lagged economic growth parameter), and means that income growth in a region is affected by income growth in neighboring regions (spatial effect). The positive coefficient (0.53) indicates that regions with high (or low) growth rates tend to be clustered together. When the results of the nonspatial fixed effects model in Tab. 2.1 and the results of the spatial fixed effects model in Tab. 2.2 are compared, the signs

Tab. 2.2: The Results of the Spatial Regression Models: 2005–2014

Variable	**1**			**2**			**3**			**4**		
	SAR_{FE}			**SAR_{RE}**			**SEM_{FE}**			**SEM_{RE}**		
lnIncome	**-0.165**	*0.000*	***	**-0.026**	*0.004*	***	**-0.204**	*0.000*	***	**-0.104**	*0.000*	***
INV	**0.005**	*0.437*		**-0.004**	*0.138*		**-0.002**	*0.767*		**0.000**	*0.924*	
HC	**0.277**	*0.052*	*	**0.147**	*0.108*		**0.139**	*0.360*		**0.443**	*0.000*	***
EX	**0.024**	*0.000*	***	**0.003**	*0.033*		**0.022**	*0.000*	***	**0.010**	*0.001*	***
PD	**-0.020**	*0.733*		**0.001**	*0.795*		**0.010**	*0.880*		**-0.004**	*0.514*	
AGR	**0.314**	*0.004*	***	**0.037**	*0.338*	*	**0.490**	*0.000*	***	**0.034**	*0.613*	
CRISIS	**-0.040**	*0.000*	***	**-0.032**	*0.000*	***	**-0.096**	*0.000*	***	**-0.094**	*0.000*	***
constant				**0.217**	*0.005*	***				**0.869**	*0.000*	***
ρ	0.529	*0.000*	***	**0.665**	*0.000*	***						
δ							0.645	*0.000*	***	0.666	*0.000*	
R^2	0.66			0.48			0.57			0.51		
Hausman	64.2	*0.000*	***				34.6	*0.000*	***			
Log-likelihood	606,3			572,5			602,0			557,7		

Note: Italics indicate the *p*value.
***, **, and * represent significance at 1 %, 5 %, and 10 % levels, respectively.

and significance of the coefficients do not change, except for the investment variable, but it is seen that the coefficients obtained from the spatial model are lower.

In the spatial fixed effects model (SAR_{FE}), human capital variables (*HC*) is positively associated with growth. This result is compatible with the results of many studies in the literature (see Barro, 1991 and 1996; Bils and Klenow, 2000, Easterly and Levine, 1997 and Krueger and Lindahl, 2001).

There is a strong theoretical basis for the assertion that there is a positive relationship between exports (*EX*) and economic growth. Because foreign trade is expected to contribute positively to growth by increasing technology transfer, information dissemination, and competition. The statistically significant and positive coefficient is consistent with the expectations.

The regression results argue that an increase in agricultural share *(AGR)* has a positive effect on economic growth. This result reveals that agriculture is still an important factor for regional economic growth in Turkey.

Another determinant of regional economic growth in Turkey in the period under discussion is the global financial crisis. The empirical results affirm this claim. The result of the fixed effects regression reveals that the crisis has a contractionary impact on regional growth.

Tab. 2.3: Direct and Indirect Effects

Variables	*Direct Effects*			*Indirect Effects*			*Total Effects*		
lNIncome	**-0.180**	*0.000*	***	**-0.168**	*0.000*	***	**-0.348**	*0.000*	***
INV	**0.004**	*0.429*		**0.004**	*0.458*		**0.008**	*0.441*	
HC	**0.314**	*0.048*	**	**0.292**	*0.054*	**	**0.606**	*0.048*	**
EX	**0.027**	*0.000*	***	**0.025**	*0.000*	***	**0.052**	*0.000*	***
PD	**-0.035**	*0.617*		**-0.033**	*0.626*		**-0.069**	*0.620*	
AGR	**0.342**	*0.003*	***	**0.319**	*0.004*	***	**0.661**	*0.003*	***
CRISIS	**-0.044**	*0.000*	***	**-0.041**	*0.000*	***	**-0.084**	*0.000*	***

Note: Italics indicate the *p*value.
***, **, and * represent significance at 1 %, 5 %, and 10 % levels, respectively.

Lesage and Pace (2009) assert that the direct interpretation of the coefficients of explanatory variables in the spatial regressions is misleading. Instead, they suggest a partial derivative approach by which three different effects (direct effects, indirect effects, and total effects) can be calculated. Direct effect is defined as the impact of an independent variable in region A on the growth of region A. Indirect effect (spatial spillover effects) is described as the impact of an independent variable in a region A on the growth of neighboring regions. The total effect refers to the sum of the two.

Tab. 2.3 shows direct, indirect, and total effects. All the significant coefficients in column 1 in Tab. 2.3 are found to have both direct and indirect effects. For example, the contribution of an increase in human capital in region A to the growth of neighboring regions is close to the contribution to growth in region A. This result applies to almost all the variables.

Conclusion

For policymakers, knowing the determinants of economic growth is vital in economic policy design. With this purpose, many theoretical and empirical studies have been carried out. Especially in empirical studies, all kinds of economic, social, demographic, political, and cultural variables that potentially could affect growth have been investigated. Some of the studies support each other's findings, while some oppose them. Unfortunately, neither theoretical nor empirical studies have agreed upon variables that affect growth.

In particular, it is crucial to identify the determinants of growth in an emerging economy such as Turkey, where regional growth differences are high. For this purpose, the main factors underlying regional growth differences for the 2005–2014 period are analyzed in this chapter. Based on the theoretical and empirical literature, the effects of various variables on growth are investigated. Following the majority of the studies in the literature, we accepted investment, human capital, and population variables as the main determinants of growth and used these variables in the models. Besides, exports, agricultural production, and financial crisis were employed in the regressions. The results of the econometric estimations claim that human capital, exports, and agriculture positively affect regional economic growth, while the global financial crisis negatively affects it. Also, the empirical results assert that public investment and population density do not affect growth.

The recent studies argue that economic growth not only depends on a region's own resources but also the performance of neighboring regions. Nowadays, advances in econometric estimation methods allow us to detect an interaction between regions. Through spatial econometric techniques, it can be determined whether the growth of a region has an impact on the growth of other regions. According to the results obtained from the SAR model, one of the important determinants of regional growth in Turkey is the growth of neighboring regions. Another finding is that a factor that belongs to a region and has an impact on the growth of that region affects the growth of neighboring regions. In other words, the spillover effects (indirect effects) of the determinants of growth were found out in this study.

Considering the results of this study, policymakers should investigate the reasons for the ineffectiveness of public investments on growth. Moreover, it should not be ignored by policymakers that an increase in human capital, exports, and agricultural production in a region contributes positively not only to the growth of that region but also to the growth of neighboring regions.

References

Akçagün, P. (2017). Provincial Growth in Turkey: A Spatial Econometric Analysis. *Applied Spatial Analysis and Policy*, 10(2): 217–299.

Anselin, L. and Griffith, D.A. (1988). Do Spatial Effects Really Matter in Regression Analysis?. *Papers in Regional Science*, 65(1): 11–34.

Anyanwu, J. C. (2014). Factors Affecting Economic Growth in Africa: Are There Any Lessons from China?. *African Development Review*, 26 (3): 468–493.

Armstrong, H. W. (1995). *Cross-sectional Analysis of the Regional growth Process: Convergence and Divergence among European Regions.* Armstrong, H.W. and Vickerman, R.W. (eds), London: Pion Ltd,

Badinger, H., Müller, W. and G. Tondl (2004). Regional Convergence in the European Union (1985–1999) A Spatial Dynamic Panel Analysis. *Regional Studies*, 38(3): 241–253.

Baldwin, R., Forslid, R., Martin, P., Ottaviano, G. and Robert-Nicoud, F. (2003). *Economic Geography and Public Policy*. Princeton: Princeton University Press.

Barro, R. J. (1991). Economic Growth in a Cross Section of Countries. *Quarterly Journal of Economics*, 106(2): 407–443.

Barro, R. (1996). Democracy and Growth. *Journal of Economic Growth*, 1 (1): 1–27.

Barro, R. J. (2003). Determinants of Economic Growth in a Panel of Countries. *Annals of Economics and Finance*, 4: 231–274.

Barro, R. J. and Sala-i-Martin, X. (1991). *Economic Growth*, Second Edition. London: MIT Press.

Bayraktar, B. (2006). Investigation on Sources of Growth for Turkey. *Canadian Journal of Development Studies*, 27(1):25–38.

Berber, M., Yamak, R. and Artan, S. (2000). Türkiye'de Yakınlaşma Hipotezinin Bölgeler Bazında Geçerliliği Üzerine Ampirik Bir Çalışma: 1975–1997. *9. Ulusal Bölge Bilimi Kongresi-Bildiriler Kitabı*, 51–59.

Bils, M. and Klenow, P. (2000). Does Schooling Cause Growth?. *American Economic Review*, 90(5): 1160–1183.

Carlino, G.A. and Mills, L. O. (1993). Are U.S. Regional Incomes Converging?. *Journal of Monetary Economics*, 32(2): 335–346.

Carlino, G. A. and Mills, L. O. (1996). Convergence and the U.S. States: A Time-Series Analysis. *Journal of Regional Science*, 36 (4): 597–616.

Chang, C., and Mendy, M. (2012). Economic Growth and Openness in Africa: What is the empirical relationship?. *Applied Economics Letters*, 19(18): 1903–1907.

Chatterji, M. and Dewhurst, J. H. Ll. (1996). Convergence Clubs and Relative Economic Performance in Great Britain: 1977–1991. *Regional Studies*, 30(1): 31–40.

Chen, B. and Feng, Y. (2000). Determinants of Economic Growth in China: Private Enterprise, Education, and Openness. *China Economic Review*, 11(1): 1–15.

Doğruel, F. and A.S. Doğruel (2003). Türkiye'de Bölgesel Gelir Farklılıkları ve Büyüme. A. H. Köse, F. Şenses and Yeldan, E. (eds.), *İktisat Üzerine Yazılar I: Küresel Düzen, Birikim, Devlet ve Sınıflar, Korkut Boratav'a Armağan içinde.* İstanbul: İletişim Yayınları, 287–318.

Dollar, D. (1992). Outward-Oriented Developing Economies Really Do Grow More Rapidly: Evidence form 95 LDCs, 1976–1985. *Economic Development and Cultural Change*, 40 (3): 523–544.

Domar, E. D. (1946). Capital Expansion, Rate of Growth, and Employment. *Econometrica*, 14(2): 137–147.

Durlauf, S. N., Johnson, P. A. and Temple, J. R. W. (2005). Growth Econometrics. *Handbook of Economic Growth*, 1: 555–677.

Easterly, W. R., and Levine, R. (1997). Africa's Growth Tragedy: Policies and Ethnic Divisions. *The Quarterly Journal of Economics*, 112 (4): 1203–1250.

Erk, N., S. Ateş and Direkçi T. (2000). Convergence and Growth within GAP Region (South Eastern Anatolia Project) and Overall Turkey's Regions. *IV. ODTU Uluslararası Ekonomi Kongresi*, 13–16 Eylül 2000, Ankara.

Erlat, H. and Özkan, P. (2006). Absolute Convergence of the Regions and Provinces of Turkey. *26th Annual Conference of the Middle East Economic Association*, January 6 – 8, Boston, U.S.A.

Evans, P. and G. Karras (1996). Convergence Revisited. *Journal of Monetary Economics*, 37(2): 249–265.

Filiztekin, A. (1999). Convergence across Turkish Provinces. *Koç University Working Paper.*

Fingleton, B. and Fischer, M. M. (2010). Neoclassical Theory versus New Economic Geography: Competing Explanations of Cross-Regional Variation in Economic Development. *The Annals of Regional Science*, 44(3): 467–491.

Fischer, S. (1992). Macroeconomic Stability and Growth. *Cuadernos de Economía*, 29(87): 171–186.

Freire-Seren, M. J. (2002). On the Relationship between Human Capital Accumulation and Economic Growth. *Applied Economic Letters*, 9 (12): 805–808.

Fujita, M. and T. Mori (2005). Transport Development and Evolution of Economic Geography. *Portuguese Economic Journal*, 4(2): 129–156.

Fujita, M., Krugman, P. and Venables, A.J. (1999). The Spatial Economy: Cities, Regions and International Trade. Cambridge, Massachusetts: MIT Press.

Gezici, F. and Hewings, G. J. D. (2004). Regional Convergence and the Economic Performance of Peripheral Areas in Turkey. *Review of Urban and Regional Development Studies*, 16(2): 113–132.

Güçlü, M. (2010). Regional Income Convergence in Turkey: A Spatial Econometric Perspective. *The Empirical Economics Letters*, 10(10): 1047–1054.

Harrod, R. F. (1939). An Essay in Dynamic Theory. *The Economic Journal*, 49(193): 14–33

Karaca, O. (2004). Türkiye'de Bölgelerarası Gelir Farklılıkları: Yakınsama Var mı?. Tartışma Metni 2004/7, *Türkiye Ekonomi Kurumu*, Nisan 2004.

Kırdar, M. G., and Saraçoğlu, D. Ş. (2008). Migration and Regional Convergence: An Empirical Investigation for Turkey. *Papers in Regional Science*, 87(4): 545 - 567.

Knight, M., Loayza N. and Villanueva D. (1993). Testing the Neoclassical Theory of Economic Growth: A Panel Data Approach. *Staff Papers (International Monetary Fund)*, 40 (3): 512–541.

Krueger, A. and Lindahl, M. (2001). Education for Growth: Why and for Whom. *Journal of Economic Literature*, 39 (4): 1101–1136.

Krugman, P. (1991). *Geography and Trade*. London: MIT Press.

Lall, S. and Yılmaz, K. (2001). Regional Economic Convergence: Do Policy Instruments Make a Difference?. *The Annals of Regional Science*, 35(1): 153–166.

LeSage, J. P. and Pace, R. K. (2009). *Introduction to Spatial Econometrics*. Boca Raton: Taylor & Francis.

Levine, R. and Renelt, D. (1992). A Sensitivity Analysis of Cross-country Growth Regressions. *American Economic Review*, 82(4): 942–963.

Lucas, R. (1988). On the Mechanics of Economic Development. *Journal of Monetary Economics*, 22 (1): 3–42.

Mıhçı, S. and Köksal, M. Z. (2010). Determinants of Cross-Regional Income Differentials: The Case of Turkey. *H.Ü. İktisadi ve İdari Bilimler Fakültesi Dergisi*, 28(2): 71–94

Molle, W. and Boeckhout, S. (1995). Economic Disparity under Conditions of Integration - A Long Term View of the European Case. *Papers in Regional Science*, 74: 105–123.

Most, S. J., and Vann de Berg, H. 1996. Growth in Africa: Does the Source of Investment Financing Matter?. *Applied Economics*, 28 (11): 1427–1433.

Neven D.J. and Gouyette, C. (1994). Regional Convergence in the European Community. *CEPR Discussion Paper Series 914*, London.

Rey, S. J. and Montouri, B. D. (1999). US Regional Income Convergence: A Spatial Econometric Perspective. *The Journal of the Regional Studies Association*, 33(2): 143–156.

Rodriguez-Oreggia, E. (2002). Polarization of Income under Structural Changes: Winners and Losers of Regional Growth in Mexico. *Research Papers in Environmental and Spatial Analysis*, ISBN 07530.

Romer, P. (1986). Increasing Returns and Long-run Growth. *Journal of Political Economy*, 94(5): 1002–1037.

Sala-i-Martin, X. (1997). I just Ran 4 Million Regressions. *National Bureau of Economic Research Working Paper*, No. 6252.

Solow, R. M. (1956). A Contribution to the Theory of Economic Growth. *Quarterly Journal of Economics*, 70(1): 65–94.

Swan, T. (1956). Economic Growth and Capital Accumulation. *Economic Record*, 32(2): 334–361.

Tansel, A. and Güngör, N. D. (1998). Economic Growth and Convergence: An Application to the Provinces of Turkey, 1975 - 1995. *METU-ERC Working Paper*, No: 98/9.

Temel, T., Tansel, A. and Albersen, P. J. (1999). Convergence and Spatial Patterns in Labor Productivity: Nonparametric Estimations for Turkey. *Journal of Regional Analysis and Policy*, 29(1): 3–19.

Yıldırım, J. and Öcal, N. (2006). Income Inequality and Economic Convergence in Turkey. *Transition Studies Review*, 13(3): 559–568.

Yıldırım, J., Öcal, N. and Özyıldırım, S. (2009). Income Inequality and Economic Convergence in Turkey: A Spatial Effect Analysis. *International Regional Science Review*, 32(2): 221–254.

Engin Kurun

3 Determination of Public Share in the Turkish Economy and Possible Role of Wealth Fund in Investment and Financing Policies

Highlights: Can Turkey's Wealth Fund (TWF), which has a different characteristic from foreign wealth funds both structural and functional, be successful by synthesizing the implemented and successful policies of other country funds? The possible role of the TWF in the creation of low-cost and long-term financing opportunities required by the country and the establishment of investment policies are investigated and recommendations are presented.

Keywords: Wealth Fund, public sector, Turkish economy, financing, investment

Introduction

Although the reflections of the global financial crisis on the developed and developing countries since 2008 are different, one of the most important effects is the increase in share of the public sector in the economy. The growth rates contracted by the global financial crisis, the tightening credit conditions, and the negative impact of foreign trade volume on the economy caused the increase in public expenditures to promote the economy. Additionally, postcrisis asset purchases and the balance sheet expansion policies have increased the decisive role of the public sector in the economy. In retrospect, it is observed that the free market economy could be maintained with public spending in the 1930s after the crisis in the USA called the "Great Depression". Unfortunately, following the tightened fiscal policies in 1937, about 10 % economic contraction was observed. Since 2008, after a similar intervention of the public sector, especially in the balance sheets of central banks, a similar contraction of the 1930s has been discussed, and it is emphasized that the public sector should support the economy both in terms of demand and supply for the sustainable growth.

An analysis of the share of public expenditures in total GDP in developed countries and developing countries reveals that an increase has been observed in OECD countries between 2008 and 2011 according to OECD data. According to the OECD average, the share of general public expenditures increased by 4 % in the same period. Since 2011, gradual withdrawals have been made to pre-crisis averages across countries. The share of public expenditures in GDP in Turkey has shown a stable development over the years. According to the data presented comparatively in Appendix 1, the share of public expenditures in the world economy has gradually increased. Another significant point in the table is that, while the share of public expenditures in total GDP in Turkey is about half the average of OECD member countries, only the rates in Chile are close to Turkey. Especially in Europe, this rate is close to 50 %.

In the IMF Fiscal Transparency Handbook,[1] state expenditures are classified as expenditures of general government and state economic enterprises (SEE). Central government expenditures consist of budget, extra budgetary and social security expenditures, and local administrations. The SEEs are composed of financial and nonfinancial public institutions. The central bank and public deposit banks are classified under the financial institutions collecting deposits. Nonfinancial institutions operating in the industrial and service sector on behalf of the state are partially or wholly owned by the public sector.

It is foreseen that by minimizing the share of the public sector in the free market economy, productivity and production will increase in a competitive market environment and thus sustainable economic growth will be ensured. By this way, the idle resources of the public sector will be used more effectively and the impact of political interests on the economic balance will be minimized. However, the economists who are the adopters of Keynesian policies argue that the public sector can influence economic growth through government spending. Especially with policies implemented after the crisis in 2008, the share of the public sector in the economy has been questioned once again.

Other issues discussed after the 2008 crisis period are the use of wealth funds to resolve the global economic crisis, the establishment of new wealth funds, and the effectiveness of wealth funds in this process. Although a limited number of countries have wealth funds until 2008, according to Sovereign Wealth Fund Institute (SWFI) data, there are 87 wealth funds as of February 25, 2019. According to SWFI, fund size in the world increased by 59.1 % between 2008–2012.[2]

Turkey Wealth Fund Management Company (TWF) was established on August 26, 2016 as an autonomous institution under the Prime Ministry and then attached to the Presidency of the Republic of Turkey. TWF aims to contribute to economic growth by ensuring value increase of key public assets, to support the development of assets suitable for participation financing, to deepen capital markets by supporting introduction of a variety of products, to attract

1 IMF, *Fiscal Transparency Handbook*, 2018, p. 13.
2 https://www.swfinstitute.org/sovereign-wealth-fund/

further investments to Turkey, and to provide capital for new investments, to establish and manage Turkey Wealth Fund and sub-funds with the aim of further developing strategically important industries and participating in large-scale investments.[3]

The sources of TWF consist of the institutions and assets which fall within the scope and program of privatization and are decided by the High Board of Privatization to be transferred to the Turkey Wealth Fund and cash surplus decided by the High Board of Privatization Fund to the Turkey Wealth Fund; the surplus income, resources, and assets which are in the possession of public entities and institutions within the public sectors and which are decided by the Council of Ministers to be transferred to the Turkey Wealth Fund or managed by the Company; the funding and sources which are provided from national and international money and capital markets by the Turkey Wealth Fund without seeking for the permissions and approvals stated in the related legislations; and the funding and sources provided through other resources in addition to the money and capital markets. The fund portfolio was established on February 6, 2017, with the Treasury shares transferred to the fund and the shares of the companies in the privatization program. Since that date, a new company purchase, sale, investment, or borrowing has not been announced to the public yet.

The aim of this study is to examine the proportional changes in public share in Turkey after the global crisis in comparison with OECD countries. The findings are thought to be useful in determining the investment and financing policies of the wealth fund that was implemented in Turkey in 2016. In this study, which has been carried out to draw attention to the importance of this issue, the TWF portfolio value has been updated with the latest figures, but due to the data not disclosed to the public, an approximate value has been calculated. Furthermore, since the structuring of the TWF is continuing, the independent audit reports have not been disclosed to the public yet. It is expected that the share of the public sector in the economy through wealth fund will increase indirectly, except for official figures. As a matter of fact, it seems possible for the TWF to generate financing resources through leverage in addition to active management of assets.

In the second section of this chapter, the measurement of public activity, the share of public expenditures in the economy, and the effects of wealth funds on public policies have been investigated in the literature. The methodology used in determining the public share and the characteristics of the data used

3 http://turkiyevarlikfonu.com.tr/EN/icerik/51/about-us

are explained in the third section. The findings and developments in public expenditures in Turkey have been examined and the development of the share of public institutions from the economy in accordance with IMF classification has been evaluated in the fourth section by taking into consideration the indicators in the related sectors. In the fifth section, the status of the public institutions and organizations included in the portfolio of the TWF has been discussed and the issues to be considered when determining the Wealth Fund policies have been determined.

2 Literature Review

Public expenditures have often been investigated by researchers whether they contribute to economic growth and have been found to have an impact in both directions. However, when the studies are evaluated collectively, there are more findings that contribute positively to economic growth. Adam and Bevan (2005), Lamartina and Zaghini (2008), Benos (2009), and Yıldız and Sarısoy (2012) reported positive results in their study with data of about 30 years for the OECD countries, while Folster and Henrekson (2001) Gwartney, Holcombe, and Lawson (1998) concluded negative correlation.

One of the criteria that measures the government's share in the economy is the ratio of public expenditures/GDP. Tanzi and Schuknecht (2000) in their analysis between 1870 and 1996 identified this ratio as 10 % on average in the world. Accordingly, Australia, Italy, Switzerland, and France, which are in the 12–18 % range, are classified as systems that the state intervenes in economy. As a result of the effects of the First and Second World Wars, an increase was observed in this rate. The average of public expenditures after the war was 28 %, 41.9 %, 43 %, and 45 % in 1960, 1980, 1990, and 1996, respectively. The authors' proposal is that the share of public expenditure should not exceed 30 %.

The Nobelist James Buchanan, who opposes the public intervention in the economy, argues that in these cases the economy is affected more negatively. Buchanan (1975) and Buchanan and Musgrave (1999) state that even with reasonable public intervention, the solution becomes difficult, and that the public decision-makers tend to move away from rationality because of their political preferences and tendency to make decisions in the public interest. The developed and efficient markets do not require public intervention theoretically, but on the other hand, public support in specific sectors can be discussed. Vogel (1996) recommends an effective market regulation in such cases rather than public spending.

The measurement of the effectiveness of the public is often included in the literature as a comparison of public expenditures, public investments, or specifically the effectiveness of education, health, defense, social transfer's expenditures, and performance measurement. While Barro (1990) demonstrates the contribution of public infrastructure investments to growth, Romer (1990) points out the importance of public R&D expenditures for growth. In regional economic analysis, the effectiveness of the public is often questioned. Clements (2002) examined the effectiveness of education expenditures in Europe, Gupta and Verhoeven (2001) examined the effectiveness of health and education expenditures in Africa, while Afonso, Schuknecht, and Tanzi (2005) conducted studies on the performance and effectiveness of public expenditures in OECD countries. Afonso and St. Aubyn (2004) measured the effectiveness of health and education in OECD countries. As a result of this study, they found that the share of public education expenditures in European countries was 92.4 %. The OECD average was 72.2 %, while health expenditures were determined to account for more than half of total public expenditures in general. Herrera and Pang (2005) analyzed health and education expenditures in their study of 140 countries between 1996 and 2002 and concluded that the activity in countries with high wage rates was low.

The indicators used in the measurement of public activity were determined as administrative, education, health, and infrastructure expenditures by Afonso, Schuknecht, and Tanzi (2005); and macroindicators were also utilized. According to Afonso (2004), in the study conducted in OECD countries for 1990 and 2000, the efficiency was higher in countries where the public shares' of GDP ratio is 40 % and below. While Japan and the United States performed above average, the performance of European Union countries remained below average.

Megginson and Fotak (2014) discussed the development of the wealth fund and collected the research until then as a literature survey. In January 2008–November 2013, they have determined that wealth funds have been established in 25 countries or that the establishment process has begun. The authors gathered the objectives of these newly established funds under three headings. According to their initial findings, states are aiming at the protection of cash and the management of new cash flows rather than the financing of public funds or the flow of funds to existing public financial institutions. The second element is that the more transparent, accountable, and professional investment company is generally preferred to public investment tools or public banks, which are subject to political instability and corruption. The third factor is the establishment of all these newly established funds after the successful example of Norway, and the determination of the business model in line with the organizational structure, transparency principles, professional management, stock exchange, and bond investment preferences.

Schena, Braunstein, and Ali (2018) identified that wealth funds were initially established in countries with commodity supply surplus, but this time demand for new funds, for diversification, for strengthening national competition, for the substitution of foreign investment, and for the slowing down of growth in developing countries during the global crisis. The authors pointed out similar aspects of TWF because of the fact that the portfolio of the Romanian Wealth Fund, which was established in 2017, was created by the transfer of public institutions by the share transfer. Since 2016, in addition to Turkey and Romania, announced or established funds are from the following countries: Armenia, Guyana, Bangladesh, Egypt, Nigeria, Indonesia, India, South Africa, and Thailand. It is noteworthy that the authors classify funds as the only funds available for the TWF through the issuance of a debt instrument. Halland, Noel, Tordo, and Kloper-Owens (2016) studied development funds for the financing of strategic investments in the last 15 years and identified the multiplier effect of the private sector in financing as 1:12 in direct investment. They found that such funds could reach low-cost international financing when needed and in line with policymakers' objectives, and that the private sector increased its return on investment while reducing its investment risk. The authors also discussed the structural, institutional and managerial structure of these funds for the first time in the literature.

LaPorta, Lopez-de-Silanes, and Shleifer (2002) found that state banks are subject to more specific public assignments and credit conditions than private banks. According to their findings, the efficiency of the state banks is generally lower, and it is reflected to their market values as a discount comparable with their target company values.

3 Methodology

This study analyzed the period of development in selected sectors of the share of the state in the economy in 1998–2018 in Turkey. Using the Banks Association of Turkey (TBB), Participation Banks Association of Turkey (TKBB), Insurance Association of Turkey, Turkish Capital Markets Association, Capital Markets Board of Turkey (CMB), Republic of Turkey Ministry of Treasury and Finance, Central Bank, and Borsa Istanbul data, the market share of the public institutions in banking, insurance, investment, industry, and service sectors and their ranking in the sector, credit size, market value, and basic performance indicators were analyzed comparatively.

The share of the public in the economy can be measured by different methods. While the share of the public can be determined according to the income and expenditure method in terms of GDP, it can also be determined according to the public share in the value added or total labor force provided. The GDP growth data, which was announced by TurkStat in the 3-month period, was used to determine the weight of public share in the general economy during 1998–2018 period. The consolidated budget expenditures and revenue realizations included in the monthly budget bulletin of the Ministry of Treasury and Finance and the budget balance are based on the analysis of the public's share of the economy in terms of income and expenditure. The Banks Association of Turkey and the bank sector statistical data, during the period 1998–2017, is taken into account in determining the share of public banks with annual data, but for 2018, 9-month data were taken into consideration. Similarly, the Participation Banks Association of Turkey for the 2015–2017 year data were used to determine the share of public participation bank statistics, but for 2018, 9-month data were taken into consideration. The public share in non-financial sectors was evaluated with the market values for the companies traded in Borsa Istanbul. For companies that are not open to public, we used the most recent published financial reports. The monthly data for 2009–2018 of TURKSTAT is taken as a basis in determining the share of the public sector in the total labor market.

4 Findings

When the trend of government income (GI), government spending (GS), and budget deficit (BD) share in total GDP is analyzed in Fig. 3.1, it is observed that government expenditures have increased significantly after the financial crises of 2000 and 2008. Accordingly, the budget deficit and the financing requirement of the deficit are also increasing. Since 2011, it can be said that the public deficit has fallen to a rate of 1–2 % of GDP in a controlled manner and gained stability. As the increase in government income over the years shows the burden of taxation, as a result of nominal increases, the average of the last 20 years was 21 % of GDP.

A significant portion of the government spending (GS) consisted of interest expenditures (IE). The positive effect of keeping global interest rates low in the last 10 years was observed in Fig. 3.2, where the share of interest expenditures in public expenditures in Turkey fell from 22 % in 2008 to 9 % in 2018. The remaining portion of the expenditure excluding interest allowed the steady continuation of the economic growth in the last 10 years. The share of rising social security spending (SIE), which is one of the main problems of the global economy, has increased from 9 % to 18 % in total public spending by doubling in the last 20 years. Public personnel expenses (PE) were realized in the 20–25 % range of total public expenses in the same period. The share of public expenditures in

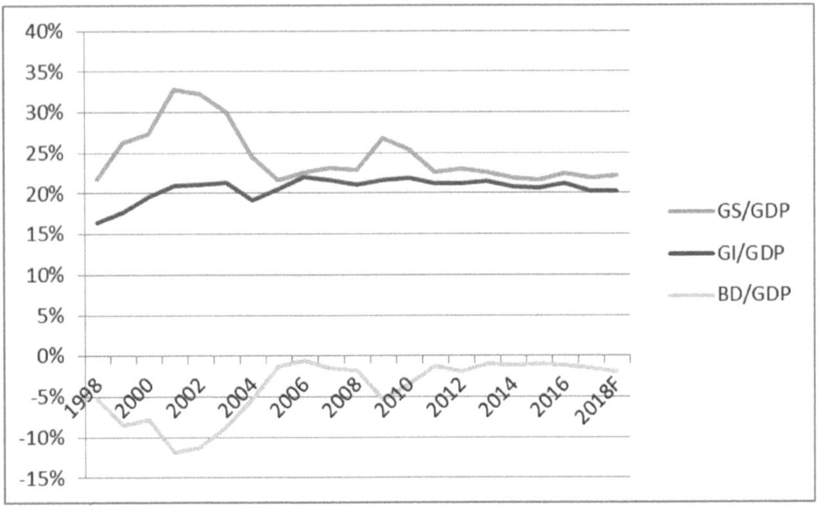

Fig. 3.1: Twenty years trend for government income/expenditure and budget deficit. Source: Monthly Budget Bulletin, June 2018. Author's own calculation.

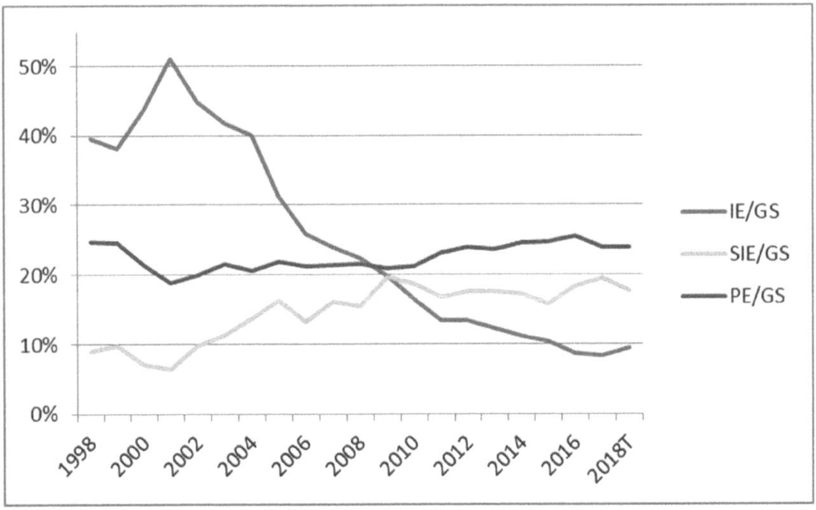

Fig. 3.2: Development of sub-items for government expenditures. Source: Monthly Budget Bulletin. Author's own calculation.

GDP has been determined as 25 % and 23 % for the last 20 years and the last 10 years. When the development of the ratio is analyzed, the share of public expenditures seems to be decreasing with the positive contribution of GDP growth. However, infrastructure investments which have been realized in the last 10 years according to the build-operate-transfer method and which are provided Treasury guarantees but reported out of public investment expenditures should also be taken into consideration. The share of public expenditures in total GDP in Turkey has improved in line with the rate proposed by Tanzi and Schuknecht (2000) to be kept below 30 %.

The share of state banks in the economy was determined by selecting three deposit banks. T.C. Ziraat Bank (TCZB) founded in 1863, Halkbank (HALKB) established in 1938, and VakifBank (VAKBN) founded in 1954 were evaluated in terms of total assets, loans, deposits, and equity in the same period. According to the four indicators mentioned above, TCZB is ranked as the first bank of the Turkish banking system. The loan growth of all three banks is particularly striking as of the years. The growth in loans, especially since 2002, has gradually increased the share of public banks and has doubled the share of the banking system. In parallel with the growth in loans, total assets increased. While 81 banks were active in 2000, the total number of banks decreased to 47 by the end of 2018 due to the consolidation by years. In the period examined in HALKB and VAKBN, they were always among the top 10 banks. As a result, the total share of the three public banks selected in the Turkish banking system as of September 2018 represents 32 % of total assets, 35 % of total loans, 36 % of total deposits, and 27 % of total equity. When the following banks were included in these three banks Turk Eximbank, Il Bank, Development and Investment Bank of Turkey, Takasbank Inc., Birlesik Fon Bank Inc., and Adabank Inc., the same rates were increased to 37 %, 41 %, 36 %, and 34 %, respectively. LaPorta, Lopez-de-Silanes, and Shleifer (2001) stated that public banks' productivity is generally lower than private banks and lower than target company values. The findings suggest that public banks may lose their equity, in case of an increase in the ratio of nonperforming loans due to the fact that the share of the public in total loans increased to 41 %; there may be additional capital requirement, and there may be a sudden decrease in market value.

As a result of the decision of the public banks to operate in participation banking in 2015, Ziraat Participation Bank Inc. and Vakif Participation Bank Inc. have been established. According to TKBB data, the share of the public sector in this system has increased gradually over the years. In 2015, the public share, which was 2 % in total assets, reached 10 % in 2016 and 17 % of total participation banks in 2017. Similarly, at the end of 2017, total loans and receivables

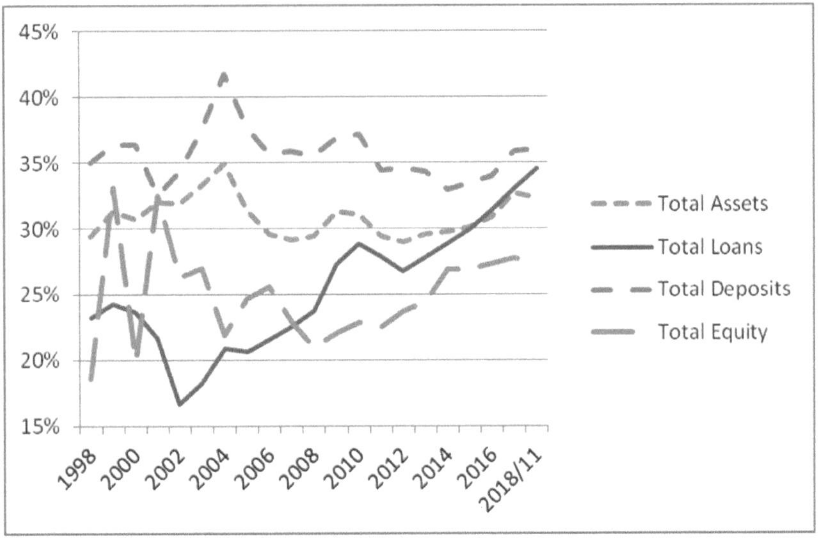

Fig. 3.3: Twenty years trend of public banks' share in the total banking system. Source: TBB. Author's own calculation.

were 19 %, collected funds 19 %, total shareholders' equity 18 %, and paid-in capital 25 % in total assets (Fig. 3.3).

The share of public banks in the total banking sector for the selected countries was analyzed comparatively in the Turkish Financial Transparency Report prepared by the IMF in 2017. In the period between the years 2008 and 2010 in Fig. 3.4, the rate of 30 % in Turkey is higher than selected 35 of the country average (15 %) and the average of OECD countries (10 %). According to this report, Turkish public deposit banks constitute 25 % of the total liability of the banking system. In addition, the share of TCZB, HALKB, and VAKBN's liabilities in total GDP in 2013 was 11 %, 7 %, and 7 %, respectively. When we add other public financial institutions to this ratio, the corresponding rate reaches 27 %.

In order to understand the share of the public sector in the industrial and service sectors other than the financial sector, 3.3.2. numbered part of the same report and the liabilities section of the public institutions whose shares are controlled by the Treasury are examined in the section. According to official authorities of IMF experts, the share of public institutions' total liabilities in GDP is approximately 23 % as of 2013. It should be considered that this ratio may be less with the offset between institutions. Potential risk increases when other

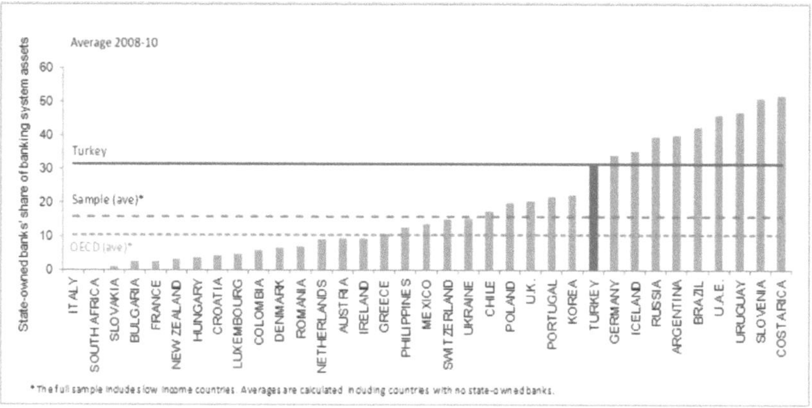

Fig. 3.4: Comparison between OECD countries and Turkey in terms of the public banks' share in total banking assets. Source: IMF, Turkey Fiscal Transparency Evaluation, Country Report No: 17, p. 64

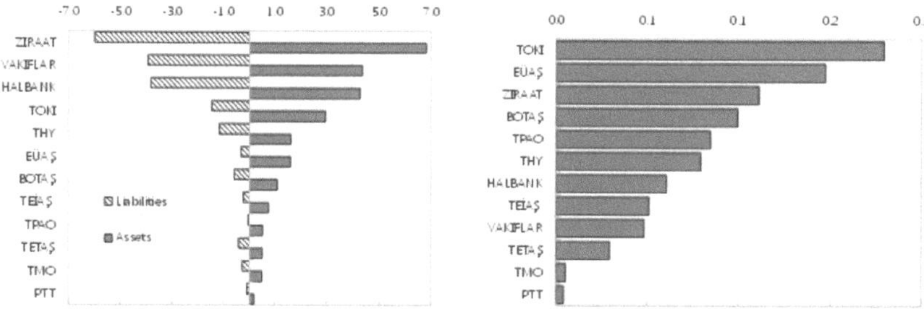

Fig. 3.5: Share in GDP in terms of the balance sheet size and net profit amount of the largest public institutions (2013). Source: IMF, Turkey Fiscal Transparency Evaluation, Country Report No: 17, p. 69

financial and non-financial companies which are not controlled by the Treasury are included. A significant portion of the public institutions listed by IMF experts was transferred to the TWF portfolio, which was established in 2016. The ratio of public institutions' balance sheet size to GDP and net profit to GDP are presented in Fig. 3.5.

The share of the public in the total labor force is another important indicator. In this context, Turkish Statistical Institute's employment data has been analyzed.[4] The share of the public sector in total employment was calculated as 12 % in the average for the last 10 years. However, particularly in 2018, the share of public employment has reached to 12.7 %, the highest level in the last 10 years. A total of 4.1 million of the 32.6 million employees are public officers. When the fundamental breakdowns are examined, it is observed that there is an increase in the Council of Higher Education and Municipalities. The number of public employees in the scope of higher education institutions reached 273 thousand in June 2018, even though the average of the last 10 years was 215 thousand. Although the average number of people employed in municipalities is 276 thousand in the last 10 years, there has been an increase especially in recent years due to the staffing of municipal economic enterprises, and in 2018 this number has reached to 371 thousand.

According to the Insurance Association of Turkey, market share of the public sector was realized approximately 34 % in life and pension business. This ratio is 9 % in the non-life elementary branch. In terms of participation insurance, no significant market share development has been observed yet. In particular, the Private Pension System (PPS) and the Automatic Enrollment System (AES) positively affected the market share of the public sector in the insurance industry. As a matter of fact, according to the data of Pension Monitoring Center, as of February 15, 2019, the market share of the public sector was observed as 17 % in PPS and 55 % in AES.

The recent steps taken to increase the effectiveness of the public sector in the financial sector are remarkable. The first is the merger of Ziraat Asset Management Inc. by purchasing other public asset management companies (Halk Asset Management Inc. and Vakif Asset management Inc.) as of January 2019. The aim is to create a strong purchasing capacity by taking advantage of the economy of scale. As a matter of fact, according to the January 2019 data of CMB, assets under the management of Ziraat Asset was calculated as TRY 34,992 million. According to this result, the market share of Ziraat Asset, which is fully controlled by the TCZB, reached to 19 % and took the first place in the Turkish asset management industry. Another step is the establishment of Real Estate Participation Bank in Turkey. As of February 27, 2019, a new bank was added to the public banks with the permission of the Banking Regulation and Supervision Agency (BRSA).

4 http://tuik.gov.tr/UstMenu.do?metod=temelist

5 Recommendations for the Turkey's Wealth Fund and Possible Strategies

Turkey Wealth Fund (TWF) was established to constitute a more powerful Turkey in 2016, to create increased resources for the financing of infrastructure investments and established principles for effective management of the strategic management of public assets. In the beginning, some public institutions with which the Treasury owns a share of Real Estate were transferred and the portfolio was formed. The portfolio content includes six public companies (Ziraat, Halkbank, THY, BOTAS, TPAO, and PTT) which were included in the analysis prepared by IMF in 2013. The composition of TWF is presented in Appendix 2 by using latest publicly available data received from TWF, Public Disclosure Platform (KAP), and the website of the related companies.

Since a consolidated financial report has not yet been published in response to the establishment of TWF in 2016, a table similar to the one in Appendix 2 has not yet been disclosed to the public. The total assets of the TWF portfolio are TRY 1,192 billion or USD 225 billion. According to the equity method, the value of assets is TRY 160 billion or USD 30 billion. However, when assessing these amounts, the value of full consolidation and real estate should also be taken into consideration. As a matter of fact, it should be taken into consideration not only the share of ownership but also of the share of TTKOM and THYAO. Furthermore, as a result of the appraisal of real estates, the total amount of shareholders' equity or total assets may be increased. With this strong portfolio, TWF has risen to an important portfolio among wealth funds, which includes the most valuable companies in Turkey. In terms of the evaluation of the role of the public sector within the economy, TWF could be expected to have a significant share in the economy both in capital market transactions (share market and debt market transactions) and venture capital and infrastructure investments.

In December 2018, TWF was first included in the periodically published report, which lists wealth funds in the world prepared by Bocconi University and Boston Consulting Group.[5] In this report, TWF ranked 18th with an asset value of USD 40 billion. TWF, which is included in the non-commodity fund category, ranks 2nd in this kind of seven funds after Australia's Future Fund. In general, the total assets under management of 37 funds is USD 6,111 billion.

Approximately one-third of the fund size and half of the total assets are composed of TCZB value. When HALKB is included, this ratio becomes 53 % and 82 %, respectively. This shows that the TWF portfolio is mainly composed of the

5 Sovereign Wealth Funds Quarterly Newsletter, December 2018.

public banks. THY is a global airline company in the TWF portfolio, but it has the largest number of flights to countries in the world and is an important institution in the transportation sector. Similarly, TTKOM is another publicly traded strategic company with a strong telecommunications infrastructure. TÜRKSAT, ÇAYKUR, ETİMADEN, PTT, which have significant value in terms of market share and effectiveness in the sector, are companies with high growth potential. In addition, BOTAS and TPAO, which are dominant players in the energy sector, have strong growth potential and cash flow opportunities.

In the world focus is on the active management of wealth funds; instead of creating resources by borrowing, natural resources (such as Norway, Saudi Arabia, Kuwait, Russia, Qatar, United Arab Emirates, Libya, Kazakhstan, Azerbaijan country – wealth funds created by natural resources such as oil, natural gas, etc.) or equity funds are provided by the sources of foreign trade surplus (China, Singapore country funds). While the amount of the assets created by Natural Resources is USD 3,838 billion, the sum of the assets created by the current account surplus is USD 1,862 billion. Other total asset funds, including TWF, are amounted to USD 413 billion.[6] In this respect, as of 2018, TWF constitutes 10 % of the other categories of wealth funds.

The Norwegian State Pension Fund, which was created in 1990 and which shows an exemplary development with both its structure and professional management principles, ranks first with its portfolio value of USD 1,054 billion. The second one is China Investment Wealth Fund which was established in 2007 and reached to USD 941 billion in a short period of time. The assets of these funds are mainly shares of local and international companies.

Despite the fact that the fund has the opportunity to create funds by borrowing, the Saudi Arabian Public Investment Fund used an international syndicated loan of USD 11 billion in 2018. According to Reuters, the fund provided a 5-year USD 11 billion resource with a base point cost of LIBOR+75 from 14–16 banks as a result of intensive demand for 6–8 billion borrowing.[7] Similarly, in 2018, the Oman Investment Fund used USD 600 million syndicated loans to purchase its subsidiary. In this process, USD 450 million of 5-year maturity loan was provided by the conventional method, and USD 150 million was provided by the Islamic method under the leadership of Citibank.[8] The loan amount is 10 %

6 Sovereign Wealth Funds Quarterly Newsletter, December 2018, p. 14.

7 https://www.reuters.com/article/us-saudi-pif-loan/saudis-public-investment-fund-says-it-closes-11-billion-debut-loan-idUSKCN1LX0JC

8 https://www.reuters.com/article/oman-investment-fund-loan/oman-investment-fund-closes-600-mln-loan-for-omantel-purchase-idUSD5N1FR00W

of the portfolio value. Both the Saudi Arabian and Oman wealth fund examples are from oil-based funds. These are the financing and investment policies that are applied to support the budget due to low oil revenues, to create new financing opportunities, and to diversify resources which are heavily depending on oil revenues.

A good example of clear and transparent disclosure of wealth fund investments is that the Saudi Arabian Wealth Fund also announced what to do with USD 11 billion. Sources of funds are government-issued energy revenues, asset transfers, returns of investments, and loans provided by the fund and the issuance of debt instrument. In line with the long-term funding strategy, the fund plans to invest in the banking sector with borrowing opportunities that are used for the first time and transfers funds to venture capital investments.[9]

According to the Bloomberg report dated February 6, 2019, TWF authorized Citibank and ICBC bank to borrow EUR 1 billion.[10]By receiving a 2-year syndicated loan with a one year grace period option, TWF will be able to transfer funds to companies in its portfolio. The details of the loan are not known since the related institutions do not make explanations on the subject and the transaction has not yet been concluded. However, this authorization shows that TWF has developed an alternative way to finance and capitalize existing companies. This kind of latest development confirms the evaluation of Schena, Braunstein, and Ali (2018) for TWF. In addition, if the financing to be provided by borrowing is used for infrastructure investments and the capitalization of the public companies in the portfolio, a result will be achieved in accordance with the function of the strategic development funds made by Halland, Noel, Tordo, and Kloper-Owens (2016). Another important issue here is the establishment of the institutional structure that the authors have set for such funds.

Conclusion

The share of public sector in the economy in Turkey has been evaluated in terms of income, expenditure, employment, public deposits, and participation banks, insurance sector, capital market, real sector, and the stock market in Istanbul. It was determined that Turkey's share of public expenditures in total GDP remained relatively low compared to OECD countries and displayed a stable outlook over

9 https://www.institutionalinvestor.com/article/b1b0164kyntbs7/Why-Would-a-Saudi-Oil-Fund-Borrow-11-Billion

10 https://www.bloomberg.com/news/articles/2019-02-06/turk-wealth-fund-said-to-hire-citi-icbc-for-1-billion-euro-loan

the last 10 years. The share of public expenditures in GDP has been determined as 25 % and 23 % for the last 20 years and the last 10 years. When the development of the ratio is analyzed, the share of public expenditures seems to be decreasing with the positive contribution of GDP growth. However, infrastructure investments which have been realized in the last 10 years according to the build-operate-transfer method and which are provided by Treasury guarantees but reported out of public investment expenditures should also be taken into consideration. According to the findings obtained, the market share of public banks reached 35 % in 2018, with nearly two times the growth in loans since 2002, especially in terms of resource and investment through public banks. According to the Financial Transparency Report prepared by the IMF in 2017, the share of public banks in Turkey, which was 30 % in 2008–2010, is quite high from the average of the 35 selected countries (15 %) and the OECD countries average (10 %). According to this report, Turkish public deposit banks constitute 25 % of the total liability of the banking system. Indeed, 82 % of the active portfolio of TWF and 52 % of the fund size is predominantly composed of state-owned banks. Since the public sector has been operating in the participation banking sector since 2015, the increase in the market share has been remarkable.

The share of the public in total employment was calculated as 12 % in the average of the last 10 years. However, particularly in 2018, the share of public employment reached 12.7 %, the highest level in the last 10 years. According to the Insurance Association of Turkey, market share of the public sector was approximately 34 % in public life and pension business. According to the data of Pension Monitoring Center, as of February 15, 2019, the share of the public sector is 17 % in PPS and 55 % in AES. One of the critical decisions of the public finance sector was taken at the end of 2018. Three public asset management companies merged under Ziraat and AUM of Ziraat Asset has reached to 19 % among the total managed assets in Turkey. Another step is the establishment of Real Estate Participation Bank as of February 27, 2019.

It was determined that the share of the public sector in the economy increased through TWF. As a matter of fact, the TWF portfolio was analyzed with the latest publicly available data, and the assets in the portfolio were examined in terms of paid-in capital, equity, and total assets. Considering the international position of the TWF, the importance of providing transparent and public disclosure information such as abroad in the evaluation of borrowing and investment opportunities is emphasized. Since there are no active operations for TWF, no performance evaluation has been made. However, the necessary data for these transactions is expected to be disclosed to the public.

Considering the determinants of the public sector's share in the economy and the risks arising from the increase in this share, it is considered important to keep the public's share in a reasonable manner in order to prevent the crowding out effect which occurred in public finance between 1990 and 2000. If TWF develops policies that support the economy, it is thought that it can make positive contributions in the export-oriented sectors. TWF may provide liquidity and make strategic investments to such selected industries. It will be possible to carry out the studies on this subject in the event that transparent public information is provided on TWF portfolio and policies.

References

Adam, C. and Bevan, D. (2005). Fiscal Deficits and Growth in Developing Countries. *Journal of Public Economics*, 89, 571–597.

Afonso, A. (2004). A Note on Public Spending Efficiency. *CE Sifo DICE Report*, 1/2004, 35–39.

Afonso, A. and Aubyn, M. S. (2005). Non-parametric Approaches to Education and Health Expenditure Efficiency in OECD Countries. *Journal of Applied Economics*, 8, 227–246.

Afonso, A., Schuknecht, L. and Tanzi, V. (2003). Public Sector Efficiency: An International Comparison. *ECB Working Paper No:242.*

Barro, R. (1990). Government Spending in a Simple Model of Endogenous Growth. *Journal of Political Economy*, *98*, 103–125.

Benos, N. (2009). Fiscal Policy and Economic Growth: Empirical Evidence from EU Countries. *Munich Personal Repec Archive*, 19174, 1–29.

Buchanan, J.M. (1975). *The Limits of Liberty: Between Anarchy and Leviathan.* Chicago: University of Chicago Press.

Buchanan, J.M. and Musgrave R.A. (1999). *Public Finance and Public Choice: Two Contrasting Visions of the State.* Cambridge, Mass: MIT Press.

Clements, B. (2002). How Efficient is Education Spending in Europe?. *European Review of Economics and Finance*, 1, 3–26.

Folster, S. and Henrekson, M. (2001). Growth Effects of Government Expenditure and Taxation in Rich Countries. *European Economic Review*, 45, 1501–1520.

Gupta, S. and Verhoeven M. (2001). The Efficiency of Government Expenditure Experiences from Africa. *Journal of Policy Modelling*, 23, 433–467.

Gwartney, J., Holcombe, R. and Lawson, R. (1998). The Scope of Government and the Wealth of Nations. *CatoJournal*, 18(2), Fall.

Halland, H., Noel, M., Tordo, S., and Kloper-Owens, J. J. (2016). Strategic İnvestment Funds: Opportunities and Challenges. *Policy Research Working Paper*, WPS7851, World Bank.

Herrera, S. and Pang, G. (2005). *Efficiency of Public Spending in Developing Countries: An Efficiency Frontier Approach*. World Bank Policy Research Working Paper Series No: 3645, Available at SSRN: httrs://ssrn.com/abstract=922917.

Lamartina, S. and Zaghini, A. (2008). Increasing Public Expenditures: Wagner's Law in OECD Countries. *Center for Financial Studies*, 13, 1–19.

La Porta, R., Lopez-De-Silanes, F. and Shleifer, A. (2002). Government Ownership of Banks. *Journal of Finance*, 57, 265–301.

Megginson, W.L. and Fotak, V. (2014). Rise of Fiduciary State: A Survey of Sovereign Wealth Fund Research, *Journal of Economic Surveys*, 29, 733–738.

Romer, P. (1990), Endogenous Technological Change. *Journal of Political Economy*, 98, 71–102.

Schena, P.,Braunstein, J. and Ali, A. (2018). The Case for Economic Development Through Sovereign Investment: A 'Paradox of Scarcity'? Global Policy, 9 (3), 365–376.

Tanzi, V. (2005). The Economic Role of the State in the 21st Century. *Cato Journal*, 25(3), 617–638.

Tanzi, V. and Schuknecht, L. (2000). *Public Spending in the 20th Century: A Global Perspective*. Cambridge: Cambridge University Press.

Vogel, S.L. (1996) *Freer Markets, More Rules, Regulatory Reform in Advanced Industrial Countries*. Ithaca, N.Y.: Cornell University Press.

Yıldız, F. and Sarısoy, S. (2012). OECD Ülkelerinde Kamu Harcamaları ve Ekonomik Büyüme İlişkisi Üzerine Ampirik Bir Çalışma. *Marmara Üniversitesi İ.İ.B.F Dergisi*, 33, 517–540.

Appendix

Appendix 3.1: Development of public expenditures in GDP in OECD countries

Countries	2008	2009	2010	2011	2012	2013	2014	2015	2016	2017
USA	40	43	43	42	40	39	38	38	38	38
England	44	47	48	46	46	44	43	42	41	-
Japan	37	41	40	41	41	41	40	39	39	-
Germany	44	48	47	45	44	45	44	44	44	44
France	53	57	57	56	57	57	57	57	57	56
Greece	51	54	52	54	55	62	50	54	49	-
Russia	-	-	-	35	35	36	39	34	-	-
Korea	32	35	31	32	33	32	32	32	32	-
Spain	41	46	46	46	48	46	45	44	42	41
Italy	48	51	50	49	51	51	51	50	49	49
Chile	-	-	-	-	-	23	24	25	25	-
Turkey	23	27	25	23	23	23	22	22	22	22
G-7 Mean	44	48	47	47	46	46	46	45	45	47
G-20 Mean	42	45	44	42	42	42	42	42	43	47
OECD Mean	43	47	47	45	45	45	44	44	43	44

Source: OECD. Author's own calculation.

Appendix 3.2: Turkey Wealth Fund Portfolio

Name of the Company	TWF Share	FFR (Free float rate)	Paid in Capital	Shareholders Equity*	Total Assets*	Listed in IMF 2013
T.C. Ziraat Bankası A.Ş. (TCZB)	%100		5,600	54,987	585,040	Y
T. Halk Bankası A.Ş. (HALKB)	%51.11	%48.89	1,250	29,541	388,222	Y
Borsa İstanbul A.Ş. (BIST)	%80.6		423	1,563	11,882	
Türk Hava Yolları A.O. (THYAO)	%49.12	%50.88	1,380	36,639	122,984	Y
Türk Telekomünikasyon A.Ş. (TTKOM)	%6.68	%13.32	3,500	7,454	36,199	

(*continued on next page*)

Appendix 3.2: (continued)

Name of the Company	TWF Share	FFR (Free float rate)	Paid in Capital	Shareholders Equity*	Total Assets*	Listed in IMF 2013
Türkiye Petrolleri A.O. (TPAO)	%100					Y
Boru Hatları ile Petrol Taşıma A.Ş. (BOTAŞ)	%100		4,625	20,052	30,292	Y
Eti Maden İşletmeleri Genel Müdürlüğü (ETIMADEN)	%100		600	2,849	3,345	
Çay İşletmeleri Genel Müdürlüğü (ÇAYKUR)	%100		1,767	2,009	4,415	
Posta ve Telgraf Teşkilatı A.Ş. (PTT)	%100		1,534	3,008	5,567	Y
Türksat Uydu Haberleşme Kablo TV ve İşletme A.Ş. (TÜRKSAT)	%100		1,955	2,211	2,697	
Milli Piyango İdaresi Genel Müdürlüğü (MPİ)	%100			3	912	
Türkiye Denizcilik İşletmeleri A.Ş. (TDİ)	%49					
Kayseri Şeker Fabrikası A.Ş.	%10		563			
TCDD İzmir Limanı	%100					
Türkiye Jokey Kulübü (TJK)	%100					
Real Estate	%100					
Total (TRY million)			**23,197**	**160,316**	**1,191,555**	
Total (USD million)			**4,377**	**30,248**	**224,822**	

*** Based on the data as of December 31, 2018 for HALKB, TTKOM, as of Septermber 30, 2018 for TCZB and THYAO, as of December 31, 2017 for BIST, BOTAS, CAYKUR, PTT, TURKSAT, MPI, as of December 31, for ETIMADEN (USD/TRY=5.30).**
Source: TWF, KAP, websites, and annual reports of portfolio companies. Author's own calculation.

Muhittin Tolga Özsağlam

4 Integration Process in Post-Soviet Eurasia: Eurasian Economic Union

Highlights: In this chapter, the functions and roles of the Eurasian Economic Union (EAEU) will be discussed by referring to its foundation treaty and its functions and roles in current affairs. In this chapter, first of all, the literature will be reminded which is related with integration theories in the international relations system. Afterwards, the foundation process of the EAEU will be described, which was derived from the Commonwealth of Independent States (CIS). The organs of the EAEU and their functions will be discussed in the main part of the chapter. The statistical data also will be at the main part of the chapter which is related with the economic indicators of the member states. The study does not neglect the trade relations among the member states, their custom union process, and free economic zone-space-sphere. Eventually, this study indicates the level of the integration by referring to the integration theories in the international political economy.

Keywords: CIS, EAEU, Eurasia, regional integration, international organization

Introduction

After the Second World War, regional organizations, subsidiary organs, and specialized agencies of the United Nations (UN) have begun to be more active within international relations system. The regional organizations have been established on the basis of alliance and cooperation. NATO and Warsaw Pact represented the alliance type of the international organizations, furthermore, European Coal and Steel Community (ECSC) was established on the basis of cooperation to enhance the regional integration rather than conflict in 1951 by Treaty of Paris. The functionalist and neo-functionalist approaches have seen the international organizations and institutions as the venues of the cooperation.

David Mitrany is a well-known representative of the functionalist approach, who analyzed the British society and underlined the importance of the cooperation among the civil institutions. Mitrany moved his analysis-perspective to the international affairs and underlined the importance of the cooperation among the communities on technical issues under the subsidiary organs of the UN. Hence, that can make contribution for the formation of international community (Archer, 2001: 136–137). Mitrany has focused on cooperation and the formation of the international organizations in related continents, Council of Europe and European Coal and Steel Community (ECSC), to enhance the cooperation and decline the possibility of the conflict (Archer, 2001: 138). In other words, his arguments were on the basis of inter-governmentalism and so, he has been identified as the representative of functionalist approach. Ernst Haas has developed the perspective and argued that technical cooperation could go further with economic and political integration processes. Haas has focused on monitoring the foundation of the European Economic Community (EEC) empirically and saw it as a laboratory for the establishment of the "supranational" body, and he argued that a supranational authority can provide the regional integration by persuading the sovereign states (Bennett, 1995: 141). However, Haas saw the emergence of sectarian movements (nationalism, external factors) in European continent as the obstacle to the federative structure in the end of 1960s (Özsağlam, 2006: 18; Ruggie, Katzenstein, Keohane and Schimtter, 2005). Haas has evaluated the relationship of the members horizontally within the regional organizations, and he did not touch the concept of the hegemonic relations within the regional organizations.

Joseph Nye and Robert Keohane as liberal institutionalists, took the comparative advantage theory of David Ricardo as the base of their complex interdependency concept for the rapprochement among the states. Keohane and Gilphin have pointed the necessity of the hegemon power to establish a new structure-regime in international relations system, and Keohane argued that regime can continue its existence by establishing institutional structure (Pease, 2000: 45–61).

John Gerrard Ruggie also has described the EU as the laboratory of the neo-functionalist approach, integration, and federative structure (Ruggie, 1998: 5). EU is still monitored by liberal institutionalists for the integration process in which faces the challenges and sectarian movements; anti liberals, nationalists and conservatives. However, the EU has provided supranational features with common visa regime (Schengen), custom union, monetary policy-common currency, agricultural policy, etc.

Certainly, the EU is currently not alone as a laboratory of the integration and supranationalism; other regional organizations also (NAFTA, OAU, EAEU) emerged as the testing entities-institutions of these concepts.

1 From the Commonwealth of Independent States to Eurasian Economic Union

After the collapse of the Soviet Union, the Commonwealth of Independent States (CIS) has been established in Minsk, Belarus, with the initiation of Russia, Belarus, and Ukraine on the basis of intergovernmentalism as a functional and multipurpose organization (Özsaglam, 2006: 64–65). Nursultan Nazarbayev reacted with other Central Asian Republics due to their exclusion from the membership of the CIS and then CIS had enlargement process by holding the meeting in Alma-Ata, Kazakhstan, on December 21, 1991. Therefore, eleven ex-Soviet republics participated in the Alma-Ata Summit (except Georgia, Moldava) and determined the political framework and institutional formation of the CIS (Voitovich, 1993: 405). However, the different perspectives of the member states in the CIS reasoned the decelerated integration process of the CIS. For instance, Azerbaijan, Georgia, Moldova, Uzbekistan, and afterwards Ukraine did not adopt themselves for an integration under the umbrella of the CIS, which are more vulnerable regarding the impact of Russia over the CIS as a "hegemonic power". On the other hand, Armenia, Belarus, Kazakhstan, Kyrgyzstan, and Tajikistan adopted more for an integration process in post-Soviet sphere in political and economic issues. Therefore, these republics tended to establish a more integrated and functional regional organization under the leadership of Russia.

2 Establishment of Eurasian Economic Union (EAEU)

Russia has adopted its foreign policy on the basis of Eurasianist perspective obviously with the Ministry of Foreign Affairs of Yevgeni Primakov. Hence, Russia tried to enhance its influence through international organizations which was mentioned in its military doctrines of 1993 and 2000. Putin has carried forward the Eurasianist policy of Primakov, when he came to the power. One of the results of this Eurasianist foreign policy orientation of Putin has resulted with establishment of the Eurasian Economic Union, which took its idea from historical Eurasianist perspective and neo-functionalist-liberal institutionalist perspective too.

Russia has begun to take steps for the foundation of the EAEU since 1996 by signing the custom union agreement with Belarus, Kazakhstan, Kyrgyzstan, and Tajikistan. However, the process developed very slowly due the lack of integration dynamics of the parties. The parties had deep economic and structural problems and so they could not adopt themselves for the custom union and other joint regulations easily.

Putin became the president of Russia in 2000 and emphasized on strengthening the economic power and relations of Russia in near abroad. Therefore, Eurasian Economic Community (EEC) was established in October, 2000, as the part of Russian Eurasianism in post-Soviet sphere. Eventually, Russia, Belarus, Kyrgyzstan, Kazakhstan, and Tajikistan became the founder members of the EEC, which formed the base of the EAEU. Certainly, the charter (foundation treaty) of the EAEU has been changed in the summits; however, basic concepts and terms have not be changed in the articles of the treaty. For instance, article 1 of the charter is still there, which underlines respecting the sovereignty and equality among the member states (Dagavorob Uçrejdanii Avraziyskom Soobştestva of 10 Oktobriya, 2000; Goda, 2000; Statya 1).

The Treaty of the EAEU describes the main roles and functions of the organization as economic integration-unification of the economics of the member states and providing the custom union (Dagavor o Avraziyskom Ekonomiçeskom Soyuze, 2014, Statya 82).

The organization was renamed in 2014 as Eurasian Economic Union, which was Eurasian Economic Community. Actually, the road map of the organization was drawn in 2011; however, it practiced in 2014 by signing the foundation treaty which was enforced in 2015. Therefore, the institutional structure of the organization was reshaped, which have ***intergovernmental*** and ***supranational*** features by forming the *Supreme Council, the Intergovernmental Council, Eurasian Economic Commission, and Court of Eurasian Economic Union* as the principal organs of the organization (Dagavor o Avraziyskom Ekonomiçeskom Soyuze, 2014, Statya 8).

Tajikistan has not joined the EAEU yet; there are different views regarding the joining of Tajikistan in the organization. One of them is that, Tajikistan can lose its sovereignty and independence, another one is Tajikistan could not fulfill its structural reforms and be ready for the custom union and other elements of the integration under the EAEU China (Panfilova, 2018). Additional to these views, there is another reality that China is the most important credit supplier of Tajiksitan and is providing the infrastructure investments of Tajikistan, and Tajikistan has currently $1.2 billion debt to China (Panfilova, 2018). Therefore, Tajikistan cannot neglect the role of China in its economy and its vulnerabilities too. Eventually, Tajikistan may try to create its special conditions and derogations for the accession to the EAEU.

2.1 Principal Organs of the EAEU

The Supreme Council is the highest organ of the organization where heads of the member states meet at least one time in a year, determine the strategy of the organization, and take the decision unanimously. The Supreme Council also solves the problems which are not solved by other organs of the organization (Dagavor o Avraziyskom Ekonomiçeskom Soyuze, 2014, Statya 11).

The Intergovernmental Council is another significant organ of the EAEU in where the head of the governments meet at least twice in a year, and it ratifies the budget of the organization and provides the orientation of the Economic

Commission (Dagavor o Avraziyskom Ekonomiçeskom Soyuze, 2014, Statya 14; Statya 16).

The Eurasian Economic Commission can be evaluated as the technical organ of the organization, which started custom union and united economic space processes as the supranational organ (Ağır, 2017: 114). The commission is located in Moscow and implies the headquarters of the organization as well. Moscow, as the headquarters of the organization, symbolizes the leadership of Russia within the organization as well.

The Court of the Eurasian Economic Union is located in Minsk and dealing with the disagreements of the parties on economic issues (Dagavor o Avraziyskom Ekonomiçeskom Soyuze, 2014, Statya 19), and showing the supranational characteristics too. The charter of the organization includes all the details regarding the regulations of international trade and trade inside of the region; tariffs, quotas, measurements, and the standards of the trade. Articles from 36 to 39 of the charter determines the trade conditions of the organization and shows its functionalist character too (Dagavor o Avraziyskom Ekonomiçeskom Soyuze, 2014, Statya 36–39).

The Eurasian Commission and the Court of Eurasian Economic Union are the basic evidences for the supranational characteristics of the organization, which they just only try to enhance the integration process and the strengthening the role of the organization in its sphere by limiting the national sovereignty of the member states. For instance, the Eurasian Commission draw the strategy and determine the economic and trade standards of the organization. On the other hand, the court is dealing with economic disputes among the parties as an international institution which is above the national courts of the member states and providing the rule of law internationally.

The current custom union regulations and proposals for expected monetary union also indicate that supranational characteristics of the EAEU will be more influential in future.

2.2 Steps for Integration

The EAEU can be identified as a new laboratory of the neo-functionalists-liberal institutionalists. Because, it has similar structural similarities with the EU in terms of intergovernmentalism and supranationalism in working procedures of the organs. Although the EAEU shows the characteristics of the EU on the legal-structural base, in addition to this, EAEU is a kind of instrument to increase the influence of Russia in the region regarding its *near abroad* policy and Eurasianist perspective too. The EAEU obviously aims to have supranational characteristics

Tab. 4.1: Mutual Trade between the EAEU states January–June 2018 USD Million and % Compared to January–June 2017

States	Armenia	Belarus	Kazakhstan	Kyrgyzstan	Russia	EAEU
Armenia	*	22.0 139.4 %	7.7 2.7 times	0.4 104.8 %	924.5 122.15	290.3 128.5 %
Belarus	22.0 139.4 %	*	424.4 140.1 %	54.7 99.5 %	17.,512.0 115.1 %	6,854.7 106.6 %
Kazakhstan	7.7 2.7 times	424.4 140.1 %	*	404.9 112.5 %	8,805.3 109.1 %	2,839.8 111.3 %
Kyrgyzstan	0.4 104.8 %	54.7 99.5 %	404.9 112.5 %	*	889.4 115.6 %	311.0 119.0 %
Russia	924.5 122.1 %	17,512.0 115.1 %	8,805.3 109.1 %	889.4 115.6 %	*	18,749.5 116.7 %

Source: The Eurasian Economic Union: Facts and Figures, Library of Eurasian Integration, Eurasian Economic Commission, http://www.eurasiancommission.org/ru/Documents/2797_1_ЕЕК_ЦИФР_англ__sait_rasv.pdf (20.2.2019).

which partially succeeded it by formation of the custom union and expects to have monetary union, and such samples are doing itself a kind of empirical-laboratory for the scholars who are interested in integration processes and who have neo-functionalist-liberal institutionalist perspectives.

Tab. 4.1 obviously illustrates the increase on mutual trade between the member states as compared to the previous year, and that can be interpreted as the impact of the custom union which provided comparative advantage to the member states on mutual trade. The member states have also emphasized on the development of the intra-trade relations by increasing their productions regarding exporting their own crude oil and manufactured raw materials as well. Currently, population of the EAEU is 183.8 million and 94.3 million is economically active population; unemployment rate is 5.4 % which is almost same with world average and less than many of the EU members (EAEU Web Page; Statista, January 2019)

2.2.1 Cooperation in Energy Sector

The EAEU is still a small regional organization regarding its population size; however, its geographical scope (geopolitical) and economic impacts are very significant, for instance, oil production of the member states totally equal to 634.2 million ton, first in the world; gas production is 744.7 million cu m2;

and steel, mineral fertilizers production, and iron production are in crucial levels in the world market (ibid). Russia and Kazakhstan are the pioneers of the integration process and so they saw the energy sector as one of the important dynamics of the organization. Therefore, additional to the custom union among Russia, Belarus, and Kazakhstan, they emphasized on creating a common energy policy to enhance the intra-trade and also to determine common energy policy on exporting to third countries. The treaty of the EAEU also underlines the importance of the cooperation and common energy policy as well. The articles from 79 to 85 provide the main framework of the energy policy of the EAEU and underline the cooperation on oil, natural gas, and electricity by forming common space within the organization (Dagavor o Avraziyskom Ekonomiçeskom Soyuze, 2014). These related articles also articulate the energy security and cooperation of the members states on transportation of the energy sources efficiently to the third countries (Dagavor o Avraziyskom Ekonomiçeskom Soyuze, 2014; Statya, 79–85). The energy policy of the EAEU makes contribution to the integration process within the organization by forming the integrated energy projects. Therefore, interdependency is enhancing inside of the organization and building the walls of the Eurasian House, which is supported strongly by Russia and Kazakhstan. Russia and Kazakhstan, rich member countries on energy sources, find new consumers inside of the organization, and also they may have new energy routes in advance to diversify their own energy routes to the third countries and provide energy security too.

On the other hand, Armenia and Belarus are certainly willing for creation of common energy space on oil, gas, and electricity as well. For instance, Belarus imports Russian crude oil and hydrocarbon, and the price for 100 cubic meters is $173 (it is $250 for Armenia and $430 for Ukraine), which is cheaper from the world market prices, and Belarus benefits from it (Zemskova, 2018: 12). Armenia also benefits the prices of energy sources obviously with cooperation under the umbrella of the EAEU due to dependency of Armenia on Russian energy (Moscow provides 75 % of energy requirements of Armenia). Such as, Armenia had price advantage on gas import, which was $271 for 1000 cubic meters in 2014 and declined to $189 in 2015 (Zemskova, 2018: 13).

The energy forms the most significant and influential component of the EAEU, and it seems like a kind of challenge to the EU's energy policy as well. Because, Georgia and Ukraine have close relationship with the EU, and they try to adopt themselves to the energy policy of the EU as well. However, geopolitical positions of Armenia and Belarus are very crucial which may create a competition among Russia and the EU's energy policies in Georgia and Ukraine in advance. Certainly, there may be another scenario too; the geopolitical positions of Armenia and Belarus may be the hub for transportation of Russian or Kazakhstan's gas to the EU or to different third countries too in advance. Even though, Belarus still is not a member of World Trade Organization and far from the Energy Charter too. On the other hand, Russia also did not ratify the Energy Charter, only Armenia has signed the EU Energy law, so it implies the complicated situation in the region regarding the energy issues.

Therefore, current affairs indicate that energy is not only an instrument of the economic integration among the member states of the EAEU, it is also a strategic instrument on the hands of the energy giant countries: Russia and Kazakhstan. Especially, since integration process in EAEU strengthens the hands of Russia to play its role in the Eurasia sphere.

3 Perspectives of the Member States for the Integration under the EAEU

Russia plays a crucial role on the integration process of the EAEU as the leader of the Eurasia region. After the demise of the USSR, Russia had lost its influence in post-Soviet sphere during the presidency of Boris Yeltsin. However, Yevgeni Primakov, the former Prime Minister of Russia, emphasized on enhancing the influence of Russia through the CIS. However, Russia could not mobilize all the members of the CIS for an economic integration and a military alliance in the post-Soviet sphere. Therefore, Vladimir Putin has focused on the creation of the EAEU with some members of the CIS, which are eager for the integration in post-Soviet Eurasia. Therefore, Putin has played crucial role for the foundation of the EAEU, and he described the demise of the USSR as a greatest geopolitical catastrophe in the century, stating that he wants to create a powerful supranational institution between Europe and Asia-Pacific regions (Mostafa and Mahmood, 2018: 164). Putin's words obviously indicate the willingness of Russia for the creation of a federative structure in post-Soviet sphere, which can maximize the role of Russia in the region as the most powerful country economically, militarily, and politically as well.

Kazakhstan is another eager country for the integration under the umbrella of EAEU. Nursultay Nazarbayev became one of the significant figures of the union of Eurasian idea in post-Soviet sphere. He always supported the integration trends under the CIS, and then he realized that intensive integration was not possible under the framework of the CIS due to the unwillingness of other members of the CIS: Azerbaijan, Georgia, Moldova, Ukraine, and Uzbekistan. Therefore, Nazarbayev has focused on cooperation with Russia and Belarus to form a new organization to provide the integration in Eurasia sphere. Kazakhstan is known with its multilateral foreign policy orientation as well as Eurasianist stance.

The rich oil and gas sources of Kazakhstan pushes itself to follow the multilateral foreign policy between the regional and global powers: Russia, China, European Union, and USA. Roman Vassilenko, Deputy Minister of Foreign Affairs of Kazakhstan, underlined the importance of the cooperation among the EAEU and the EU in the long term, who assumed the economic cooperation and integrated economic space from Europe to Asia-Pacific region. Vassilenko's words also show the functionalist-institutionalist perspective of Kazakhstan regarding the foreign policy orientation towards the integration under the framework of international organizations (Gotev, 2019). There may be concern on the future of Kazakhstan regarding the strengthening of the Kazakh nationalism and Pan-Slavism after the presidency of Nursultan Nazarbayev, who provided the national harmony and protected the multicultural structure, supporting the integration processes in Eurasia space.

Belarus always supported the integration process in post-Soviet Eurasia, for instance, Belarus became one of the founders of the CIS, and Minsk, capital city of Belarus, became the headquarters of the CIS. Belarus is the first country which formed custom union with Russia and formed confederation as well (BBC, December 8, 1999). Although Belarus supports the integration process under the framework of the EAEU, it can sometime have intergovernmental reflections and oppositions to the regulations of the union and Russia too. For instance, Alexander Lukashenko, the President of Belarus, rejected signing of the custom union codes in 2016, who believed that it is not working properly, and ordered the experts to withdraw from the custom union as well (Moscow Times, March 15, 2017). Belarus is a poor country in terms of natural resources when compared with Russia and Kazakhstan. Therefore, Belarus is dependent on Russia's energy sources and difficult to challenge to Russian leadership and its policies within the organization and integration process of the organization as well. However, after Lukashenko nobody can assume orientation of foreign policy of Belarus too.

Kyrgyzstan is another eager country which has agreed to international free trade, joined the World Trade Organization, and followed a multilateral foreign policy in international relations system. However, Kyrgyzstan is a very poor country regarding its natural resources and arable lands. Kyrgyzstan's joining to EAEU is a kind of compulsory task; it is not the best choice, even though, "it is choice of lesser of two evils" as Almazbek Atambayevsaids states (Putz, 2016). On the other hand, Kylychbek Dzhakypov, Deputy Minister of Economy, also has underlined the significance of Kyrgyzstan's joining to EAEU by referring to working of more than half million Kyrgyz in Russia, showing the benefits of EAEU (Putz, 2016). Both statements show the coexistence of social and economic rationality in Kyrgyzstan joining EAEU. Therefore, it is possible to say that Kyrgzstan is a passive country and follower of integration process in Eurasia sphere.

Armenia can be defined as the poorest country and also unstable politically within the EAEU. However, Armenia benefits by joining the EAEU, which almost doubled its export rate to the EAEU countries in 2016 (Arka News Agency, 2016). Armenia's export to Russia forms 27 % of its total export in 2017 (Trading Economics, 2019). On the other hand, Armenia has protected its relations with the EU and adopted some regulations to the EU law, following the demise of the Soviet Union. However, Armenia also saw the benefits of the EAEU by supplying cheaper energy from Russia as it is mentioned above. Therefore, Armenia preferred to have more integrated relations with Eurasian institutions and Russia too.

Conclusion

The EAEU is a result of the CIS' unsuccessful integration attempt due to the lack of the will of the CIS' some members under the umbrella of the CIS, which are Azerbaijan, Georgia, Moldova, Ukraine, and Uzbekistan. While the CIS pursues as the multipurpose organization in post-Soviet sphere, the EAEU has been established on the basis of both intergovernmental and supranational institutional structure, which represents the functionalist, neo-institutionalist perspective in the region and commits the economic, social integration and that can contribute to the political alliance in advance.

The EAEU can be identified as a laboratory of the supranationalism, and it has obvious similarities with the EU regarding its institutional structure. Although the EAEU has economic mission, it also serves the geopolitical interests of the member states, such as Russia behaves as the leader of the Eurasian region and also it considers the EAEU as an instrument to pursue its regional interests. On the other hand, other member states consider the economic benefits and as the part of the multilateral policies too.

Eventually, according to the recent data, there is an integration process under the umbrella of the EAEU. The member states increased the volume of trade among themselves and also energy importer countries benefit from the privileged low energy prices of Russia. Hence, such facts strengthen the integration under the EAEU. The EAEU also can be identified as a kind of evidence for the emerging of the multipolar world system as well.

References

Ağır, O. and Ağır, Ö. (2017). Avrupa Birliği ve Avrasya Ekonomik Birliği Kuruluş Süreçlerinin Karşılaştırılması. *Türkiye Sosyal Araştırmalar Dergisi*, Sayı:1.

Archer, C. (2001). *Internaitonal Organizations*. Third Edition. London: Routledge.

Arka News Agency. http://arka.am/en/news/economy/armenia_s_exports_to_eeu_nearly_double_since_joining_the_bloc/ (6.1.2019).

BBC News. (1999). http://news.bbc.co.uk/2/hi/europe/555384.stm (7.2.2019)

Bennett, A. L. R. (1995). *International Organizations: Principles and Issues*, Sixth Edition, Prentice Hall, New Jersey.

Dagavor o Avraziyskom Ekonomiçeskom Soyuze, 2014. (Treaty on Eurasian Economic Union, 2014)

Dagavorob Uçrejdanii Avraziyskom Soobştestva of 10 Oktobriya 2000 Goda, Foundation Treaty Eurasian Council, 10th October 2000 Year, 2000.

EAEU Web Page. (2009). http://www.eaeunion.org/?lang=en#about, (8.2.2019)

Gotev, Georgi, Kazakhstan advocates closer ties between EU and Eurasian Economic Union, Euractiv, January 17, 2019. https://www.euractiv.com/section/central-asia/news/kazakhstan-advocates-closer-ties-between-eu-and-eurasian-economic-union/ (9.2.2019)

John, G. R. (1998). *Constructing the World Polity: Essays on International Institutionalization*, London: Routledge.

Mahmood, M. and Golam M. (2018). Eurasian Economic Union: Evolution, Challenges and Possible Future Directions. *Journal of Eurasian Studies*, Volume 9, Issue:2: 163–172.

Moscow Times, March 15, 2017. https://www.themoscowtimes.com/2017/03/15/lukashenko-orders-withdrawal-of-belarusian-specialists-from-customs-union-a57434 (9.2.2019).

Özsağlam, M. T. (2006). *Bölgeselcilik ve Federalizm Arasında: Bağımsız Devletler Topluluğunun Orta Asya'daki İşlevi*, unpublished PhD Thesis, Sosyal Bilimler Enstitüsü, Marmara Üniversitesi.

Putz, C. (2016). https://thediplomat.com/2016/02/a-blurry-union-kyrgyzstan-and-the-eurasian-economic-union/ (7.2.2019).

Panfilova, V. (2018). Tajikistan takes firs steps towards EAEU. http://vestnikkavkaza.net/analysis/Tajikistan-takes-first-step-towards-EAEU.html (10.2.2019).

Rugguie, J. G., Katzenstein, P. J., Keohane, R. O., and Schmitter, C. (2005). Transformations in World Politics: The Intellectual Contributions of Ernst B. Haas. *Annual Reviews*, 8: 271–96.

Statista, The Statistics Portal, January 2019. https://www.statista.com/statistics/268830/unemployment-rate-in-eu-countries/, (7.2.2019).

The Eurasian Economic Union: Facts and Figures, Library of Eurasian Integration, Eurasian Economic Commission. http://www.eurasiancommission.org/ru/Documents/2797_1_EEK_ЦИФР_англ__sait_rasv.pdf (20.2.2019).

Trading Economics (2019). https://tradingeconomics.com/armenia/exports-by-country (7.2.2019).

Voitovich, S. A. (1993). The Commonwealth of Independent States: An Emerging Institutional Model. *European Journal of International Law*, 4(3).

Zemskova, K. (2018). The Common Energy Market of the Eurasian Economic Union: Implications for the European Union and the role of the Energy Charter Treaty (ECT). *Occasional Paper Series*, 2018.

Ahmet Aydın

5 Competitiveness of Turkey in the Context of International Services Trade with OECD Countries

Highlights: The aim of this study is to examine the competitiveness of Turkey in international services trade with OECD member countries within the framework of the Intra-Industry Trade (IIT) and the Revealed Comparative Advantages (RCA). Thus, the scope of Turkey's international services trade will demonstrate the basic features of commercial specialization. According to data for 2017, the services sector created more than half (53 %) of the Turkey's gross domestic product (GDP), and it is an extremely important sector for Turkey. However, it is known that most of the services cannot be subject to the international trade. The balance of invisible trade consisting of the income and expenses of the services subject to trade is a sub-account group of current accounts that have given positive balance for years in Turkey's balance of payments and thus contributes significantly to the reduction of the current account deficit.

Keywords: Turkey, services trade, international competitiveness, intra-industry trade, RCA index

Introduction

According to the data of 2017, the service sector accounts for more than half of Turkey's Gross Domestic Product (53.4 %) and has a much higher share than the industrial and agricultural sectors. It is known that the most of the services sector, which is ranked first in the sector ranking in terms of Turkish economy, is not subject to international trade. The balance of services consisting of the income and expenses of the services subject to trade is a subgroup of current accounts that have given positive balance for years in Turkey's balance of payments and thus contributes significantly to the reduction of the current account deficit. According to the Central Bank of Turkey (2018) data, "Foreign Trade Balance" deficit was $ 59 billion (166 billion USD exports, 225 billion USD imports) in 2017 and $ 41 billion (128 billion USD exports, 169 billion USD imports) in the January–September period. On the other hand, the "Balance of Services", also called "invisible trade", was $ 19.9 billion in 2017 ($43.6 billion in income, $ 23.7 billion in expense) and $ 18.9 billion in 2018 January–September period ($36.5 billion in income, $ 17.5 billion in expense). Considering that the current

Tab. 5.1: Invisible Trade Balance of Turkey (1996–2018, Billion $)

Years	Balance	Years	Balance	Years	Balance
1996	6.7	**2004**	12.7	**2012**	22.6
1997	10.9	**2005**	15.9	**2013**	23.7
1998	13.4	**2006**	13.9	**2014**	26.8
1999	7.4	**2007**	14.1	**2015**	24.2
2000	11.3	**2008**	18.9	**2016**	15.3
2001	9.1	**2009**	18.7	**2017**	19.9
2002	7.9	**2010**	16.7	**2018 (1–9)**	18.9
2003	10.4	**2011**	20.3		

Source: OECD (2018), Trade in services (indicator). doi: 10.1787/3796b5f0-en (Accessed on 22 November 2018).

account deficit was $ 47.3 billion in 2017 and $ 29.9 billion in 2018-September period, it is understood that the balance of invisible surplus, which was $ 19.9 billion in 2017 and $ 18.9 billion in 2018, contributed greatly to the reduction of the current account deficit.

In Turkey, the ratio of service revenues to exports of goods was 26 % in 2017 and 29 % in 2018 January–September period. These ratios show that service revenues correspond to about one-third of commercial goods exports, which is quite significant. Another important point here is that Turkey's balance of services has not to have a deficit since 1996, including the years of the crisis. Tab. 5.1 shows the development of the Invisible Trade Balance of Turkey by years. The balance has been positive since 1996.

Considering both its share in national income and its role in reducing the current account deficit, the evaluation of Turkey's competitiveness in commercial services is of great importance. In this study, the competitiveness of Turkey in international services trade, intra-industry trade, and RCA indices were evaluated. In most of the analyses in the literature, RCA calculations have been discussed in terms of international trade in goods. In addition, the evaluation of intra-industry trade rates will reveal whether intra-industry trade has increased over time, whether there has been a change in competitiveness. In terms of Turkey, the RCA values in international services trade will be calculated and whether there is a competitive advantage on the basis of specialization and division of labor, and whether intra-industrial trade rates will be calculated and whether there is a development on the basis of scale economies and service differentiation within the monopolistic competition approach. The aim of this study is to examine the competitiveness of Turkey in international services trade with OECD member countries through the intra-industry trade theory and revealed comparative advantages approaches. In the first part, general information about services trade is mentioned. In the second part, Services IIT and RCA calculations-analyses were carried out within the scope of Turkey's trade with OECD member countries. The data and findings obtained in the third section were evaluated and policy recommendations were made. The work is terminated with the result section.

2 General Information about Services Trade

The World Trade Organization General Agreement on Trade in Services (GATS) entered into force in 1995. Initially, while restrictions on services trade continued to change shape and size, a certain level of liberalization was ensured and the world trade services trade began to grow rapidly. The World Trade Organization (WTO, 2015) describes the services trade as the most dynamic segment of World Trade. Because in the last two decades, services trade has grown much faster than the trade in goods. As of 2017, exports of World Commercial Services amounted to 5.3 trillion dollars, and imports of World Commercial Services amounted to 5.1 trillion dollars (OECD, 2018). In this process, the biggest benefit is achieved by developed countries, but rising market economies have also made some gains, and they have increased their share in World Services trade over 35 %.

Considering the growth rates of world services exports by subgroups, it is striking that there was a partial recovery in 2016, while the growth rate in all groups was declining in 2015. Exports of world trade services increased by 0.4 % in 2016. Moreover, this increase occurred despite the fact that global transport exports, which are important subgroups of services trade, hit and fall by the transport and airline industries due to stagnant economic conditions and excessive capacity (WTO, 2017: 28, 64). The distribution of world services trade by selected countries and regions and information about the situation of Turkey are given in Tab. 5.2.

Turkey's exports to the world increased from \$36.5 billion in 2010 to \$43.9 billion in 2017 while the exports of OECD member countries increased from \$2.8 trillion in 2010 to \$3.7 trillion in 2017. On the other hand, Turkey's imports of services from the world increased from \$19.9 billion in 2010 to \$24 billion in 2017, while the imports of OECD member countries increased from \$2.5 trillion in 2010 to \$3.1 trillion in 2017. According to these data, as of 2017, Turkey's share in world services exports is 0.8 % and OECD members' share is around 70 %. When we look at the share of imports of services, Turkey has 0.5 % and OECD

Tab. 5.2: Services Trade, Million $, 2010–2017

	Exports			Imports		
Years	**Turkey**	**OECD**	**World**	**Turkey**	**OECD**	**World**
2010	36.524	2.806.173	3.922.258	19.903	2.514.527	3.835.750
2011	41.373	3.146.639	4.412.872	21.197	2.758.416	4.287.126
2012	43.680	3.193.263	4.544.928	21.030	2.781.839	4.458.977
2013	48.295	3.408.838	4.838.131	24.564	2.916.597	4.726.932
2014	51.835	3.658.437	5.197.742	25.080	3.100.413	5.133.008
2015	46.797	3.471.006	4.937.015	22.620	2.962.065	4.847.536
2016	37.607	3.516.472	4.962.968	22.214	3.004.938	4.870.963
2017	43.995	3.753.478	5.351.191	24.056	3.177.099	5.181.675

Source: Prepared by the author with the OECD data (2018).

member countries have 61 %. In addition, Turkey, as of 2016, is among the WTO's "Leading Exporters and Importers" according to the classification: 29th in services exports and 39th in services imports. Turkey's share in exports is higher than Norway, Finland, Brazil, Greece, Portugal, and Czech Republic (Tab. 5.3).

The group stated as "Commercial Services" accounts for more than 90 % of total EBOBS services in terms of exports and imports (98 % in exports). While "Travel" services were the most important group in Turkey's exports in 2010, they constituted 57 % of total exports in 2015 and 20 % in 2016. As a result of this sharp decline, the coup attempt in Turkey in 2016 and the reflections of problems with Russia and some other countries, especially on tourism, etc., can be shown. The "Transportation" service group ranked second in 2010 with 26 %, while in 2016, it accounted for 35 % of total service exports. The share of other groups is relatively small, and the total of travel and transportation only has a 55 % share in 2016.

While "transportation" was 41 % in 2010, this ratio was 36 % in 2016 in Turkey's services trade of export. "Travel" services had a 26 % share in 2010, while in 2016, this rate fell to 21 %. There has been an increase in the share of most service groups in the intervening period. While the country with the highest share in Turkey's exports of services was Russia in the period 2012–2015, Germany ranked first in 2016 (approximately $5 billion). The decline in exports to Russia in 2016 is very sharp. The first reason that comes to mind is the strained relations with the plane crisis. It is seen that Russia has started to become an important export service market in Turkey since 2017. These countries are closely followed by the United Kingdom, the United States, Italy, and France.

Service sectors, despite the significant weight of national economies, face international barriers to foreign trade. When foreign trade is considered, foreign trade goods come to mind. "World exports of goods and services" is also covered by both "commercial goods" and "commercial services". However, the methods used in the classification of trade in goods cannot be used in the commercial services. Services have a separate classification system. Previously, while EBOBS 2002-based data was produced and published with the balance of invisible within the balance of payments, the EBOBS 2010 system has been started since 2010. These classifications are not as detailed as trade in goods and have significant problems in data. UN Comtrade, WTO-UNCTAD-ITC Trade in Services dataset, OECD stats, IMF, and Eurostat shares and publishes data in this context. However, these data do not appear to be coherent and consistent for various reasons.

3 The Competitiveness Power of Turkey in Services Trade: RCA and IIT Analyses

3.1 Methodology

In this section, the indices of Turkey's intra-industry trade with OECD countries and revealed comparative advantage are calculated. Data on services foreign trade was obtained and used within the scope of the IMF-EBOPS service classification system. Calculations related to IIT and RCA ratios in services trade were made on the basis of these industries. The main account groups of the classification system called "Extended Balance of Payments Services Classification 2010" (EBOPS, 2010) are as follows (OECD, 2018):

S. Total EBOBS Services
SA. Manufacturing services on physical inputs owned by others
SB. Maintenance and repair services n.i.e.
SC. Transport
SD. Travel
SE. Construction
SF. Insurance and pension services
SG. Financial services
SH. Charges for the use of intellectual property n.i.e
SI. Telecommunications, computer, and information services
SJ. Other business services
SK. Personal, cultural, and recreational services
SL. Government goods and services n.i.e.

Tab. 5.3: International Trade in Services of Turkey (2010–2016, Thousands of US Dollars)

EBOPS	2010			2011			2012			2013			2014			2015			2016[b]		
Services Category[a]	Export	Import	Balance	Export	Import	Balance	Export	Import	Balance	Export	Import	Balance	Export	Import	Balance	Export	Import	Balance	Export	Import	Balance
S.	36.524	19.903	16.622	41.373	21.197	20.177	43.680	21.030	22.650	48.295	24.564	23.730	51.835	25.080	26.755	46.797	22.620	24.177	37.607	22.214	15.393
SA.	..	..	..	86	25	62	100	39	61	139	45	94	134	60	74	124	57	67	100	104	-3
SB.	..	..	..	38	123	-85	51	187	-136	41	236	-195	38	292	-254	27	343	-315	106	420	-314
SC.	9.439	8.094	1.345	11.063	8.653	2.410	12.674	8.962	3.711	14.266	10.297	3.969	15.599	10.154	5.445	14.287	8.317	5.970	13.027	7.955	5.072
SD.	22.631	5.206	17.425	25.120	4.895	20.225	25.411	4.104	21.307	28.054	4.826	23.227	29.542	5.070	24.472	26.685	5.382	21.303	7.531	4.773	2.757
SE.	1.122	263	859	1.250	410	840	1.376	342	1.034	1.201	524	677	1.282	199	1.083	784	409	375	903	414	489
SF.	722	1.265	-543	835	1.307	-472	865	1.294	-430	1.002	1.722	-720	1.165	1.686	-521	1.064	1.379	-315	1.088	1.481	-393
SG.	491	726	-235	534	1.226	-691	533	1.179	-646	780	1.337	-557	823	1.904	-1.081	661	1.783	-1.122	675	1.612	-937
SH.	..	818	-818	..	682	-682	..	744	-744	..	785	-785	..	675	-675	..	683	-683	..	763	-763
SI.	480	243	237	468	282	187	436	299	138	327	256	71	290	208	82	212	213	-1	166	197	-31
SJ.	244	1.676	-1.433	200	1.733	-1.533	262	1.989	-1.728	398	2.559	-2.161	343	2.359	-2.016	250	1.766	-1.517	623	2.347	-1.723
SK.	913	256	657	1.273	294	979	1.220	331	889	1.288	473	815	1.795	441	1.354	1.878	381	1.497	1.586	358	1.229
SL.	484	1.355	-872	505	1.568	-1.063	753	1.560	-807	801	1.504	-703	824	2.033	-1.208	827	1.907	-1.081	613	1.792	-1.179
CS	36.041	18.547	17.493	40.868	19.628	21.239	42.927	19.470	23.457	47.494	23.061	24.433	51.010	23.047	27.964	45.970	20.713	25.257	36.994	20.422	16.572
OCS	3.971	5.247	-1.277	4.560	5.933	-1.373	4.692	6.178	-1.486	4.995	7.656	-2.661	5.698	7.471	-1.772	4.847	6.614	-1.766	5.041	7.170	-2.130
OS	4.454	6.603	-2.148	5.065	7.501	-2.435	5.444	7.738	-2.294	5.796	9.159	-3.363	6.522	9.503	-2.981	5.674	8.521	-2.847	5.654	8.962	-3.308

Source: OECD (2018)

Notes:

a) EBOPS Services Groups are: S: Total EBOPS Services, SA: Manufacturing services on physical inputs owned by others, SB: Maintenance and repair services n.i.e., SC: Transport, SD: Travel, SE: Construction, SF: Insurance and pension services, SG: Financial services, SH: Charges for the use of intellectual property n.i.e, SI: Telecommunications, computer, and information services, SJ: Other business services, SK: Personal, cultural, and recreational services, SL: Government goods and services n.i.e., CS: Commercial services, OCS: Other commercial services, OS: Other services.

b) 2016 data is provisional

Services not allocated
Commercial services
Other commercial services
Other services

Turkey's services trade data retrieved from the OECD Stats, based in EBOPS 2010. However, the distribution of Turkey's export and import data by subsectors has not been achieved, and general information on Total Services trade has only been obtained. Turkey's foreign trade data were calculated by taking the opposite of the trade flows of the countries concerned. For example, the export of services to the Turkish partner of Rapporteur Russia was evaluated as Turkey's import of services to Russia.

3.1.1 Intra-Industry Trade (IIT) in Services

Services intra-industry trade means the simultaneous export and import of services included in the same service group. The high level of services intra-industry trade shows that there is a high competitive power on the basis of scale economies and service differentiation in the related service group. In this context, services intra-industrial trade calculations were made using Groubel Lloyd (GL) individual industrial index, and EBOPS 2010-based data for 2010–2016 were used. There is no reason why this index, which is proposed for trade in goods, should not be used in services trade. However, since the level of consolidation in commercial trade is high, it is useful to be cautious.

For the "i" product group, IIT's share in total trade (Grubel and Lloyd, 1971: 497; Greenaway and Milner, 1986: 62):

$$B_i = 1 - \frac{|X_i - M_i|}{X_i + M_i} \quad or \quad B_i = \frac{(X_i + M_i) - |X_i - M_i|}{X_i + M_i} \tag{1}$$

In equality, Xi and Mi, respectively, i represents exports and imports of products. This index can also be expressed in percentages.

$$0 \leq B_i \leq 1 \text{ Or, in percent} 0 \leq B_i \leq 100$$

If the value of the index is zero, there is a full inter-industry trade, and if the value of the index is one, there is a full intra-industry trade. If inter-industry trade is high, it is interpreted that there has not been any development in the relevant industry based on economies of scale and service differentiation within the scope of monopolistic competition. In this case, there is a competitiveness power based on traditional comparative advantages.

3.1.2 Revealed Comparative Advantages (RCA) in Services

Revealed Comparative Advantages (RCA) reflect the performance of the industries for foreign trade and give the country an idea for specialization in foreign trade. In order to find out which industries are more specialized for performance, export and import shares must be proportional to each other. Almost all of the analysis in the literature is related to the trade in goods. In this study, for the first time, calculations were made within the scope of exports and imports of service industries. The Balassa approach (1965,1966) has been adopted methodically in RCA calculations. Recent studies on RCA analyses include Miteva-Kacarski (2018); Javier, Banday, and Mittal (2018); Jackman, Lorde, Lowe, and Alleyne (2011); Shahab and Mahmood (2013); Startienė and Remeikienė (2014); Leromain and Orefice (2014); Levchenko and Zhang (2016); Maryam et al. (2018) and so on.

In the 2010–2016 period, the results of Turkey's trade with OECD countries were described in two different RCA indices (RCA1, RCA2). In the literature, although there are only calculations made on the basis of exports, there are also studies in which imports are taken into account. In this study, since the results will be evaluated together with the EIT ratios, imports were also taken into consideration. Methodologically, the calculation methods of indexes are as follows:

$$RCA_1 = \frac{(\sum_{OECD}^{TR,i} X / \sum_{OECD}^{TR} X)}{(\sum_{OECD}^{TR,i} M / \sum_{OECD}^{TR} M)} \tag{2}$$

$\sum_{OECD}^{TR,i} X$: Turkey's exports of i service group to OECD countries,

$\sum_{OECD}^{TR} X$: Turkey's total exports of services to OECD countries,

$\sum_{OECD}^{TR,i} M$: Turkey's imports of i services group from OECD countries,

$\sum_{OECD}^{TR} M$: Turkey's total imports of services from OECD countries.

The RCA1 index was calculated by dividing Turkey's exports of services to OECD countries by the total exports of services to OECD countries from the i service group by the total imports of services to OECD countries in the i service group by the total imports of services from OECD countries. The performance of the related service group in trade with OECD countries is measured considering both exports and imports.

$$RCA_2 = \frac{(\sum_{OECD}^{TR,i} X / \sum_{World}^{TR} X)}{(\sum_{OECD}^{TR,i} M / \sum_{World}^{TR} M)} \tag{3}$$

$\sum_{OECD}^{TR,i} X$: Turkey's exports of i service group to OECD countries,

$\sum_{World}^{TR} X$: Turkey's total exports of services to the world,

$\sum_{OECD}^{TR,i} M$: Turkey's imports of i services group from OECD countries,

$\sum_{World}^{TR} M$: The total of Turkey's imports of services from the world.

The RCA2 index was calculated as the ratio of exports from the I service group to the total service exports of Turkey to the world in the context of Turkey's trade in services with OECD countries, by dividing imports from OECD countries into Turkey's total service imports from the world in the i service group. Thus, by considering both export and import, the trade of the related service group to OECD countries is scaled to Turkey's overall total trade. RCA1 calculates the performance of the Turkey-OECD countries for the OECD of related services group of countries in the limited size of the trade, RCA2 calculates the performance for OECD countries for the relevant service groups, trade with all countries of Turkey in much larger sizes.

If the calculated index values are over 1, it is concluded that there is a specialization in the relevant industry and a comparative competitiveness advantage. If the value calculated according to the related service group is less than 1, it will be interpreted that the average of that group is below the average and the comparative advantage has not occurred. In other words, if "RCA > 1" is "comparative advantage" and "RCA < 1", there is no "comparative advantage". In order to avoid asymmetry problem in the values obtained in this way, with the help of the index called Revealed Symmetrical Comparative Advantage (RSCA), the results remain between -1 "and+1" (Dalum et al. taken, 1998; Shoohibul, 2013: 138; Widodo, 2009; Startienė and Remeikienė, 2014: 432):

$$RSCA_{ij} = (RCA_{ij}-1) / (RCA_{ij}+1) \quad (4)$$

In the RSCA indices are obtained by adding 1 (one) to the RCA values; minus values indicate that there is no comparative advantage, and the positive values indicate that there is a comparative advantage.

The high RCA values in international services trade means that they have an advantage, i.e., competitive power, on the basis of specialization and division of labor.

3.2 IIT and RCA Ratios in Turkey's Commercial Services Trade with OECD Countries

In this section, before going into intra-industrial trade and RCA analyses, information will be given about the share of EBOPS service groups in Turkey-OECD countries' foreign trade in exports and imports. The analysis and calculations to

Tab. 5.4: Exports and Imports Share of EBOPS Services in Turkey-OECD Trade (2010–2016)

EBOPS SERVICES	**Services Exports of Turkey to the OECD Countries According to the EBOPS Services (%)**		**Services Imports of Turkey from OECD Countries According to the EBOPS Services (%)**	
	2010	**2016**	**2010**	**2016**
S. Total EBOPS Services	100,00	100,00	100,00	100,00
SA. Manufacturing services on physical inputs owned by others	0,05	0,52	0,63	0,36
SB. Maintenance and repair services n.i.e.	0,08	1,04	2,55	3,82
SC. Transport	**26,25**	**31,79**	**25,53**	**18,83**
SD. Travel	**61,25**	**48,28**	**31,87**	**27,33**
SE. Construction	0,03	0,46	0,95	1,77
SF. Insurance and pension services	0,3	0,82	1,11	1,21
SG. Financial services	1,64	1,48	*8,06*	***10,61***
SH. Charges for the use of intellectual property n.i.e	0,07	0,79	8,62	6,16
SI. Telecommunications, computer, and information services	1,46	2,76	7,72	9,32
SJ. Other business services	***5,54***	***11,27***	***9,51***	***17,91***
SK. Personal, cultural, and recreational services	0,5	0,28	0,34	0,47
SL. Government goods and services n.i.e.	2,84	0,49	3,1	2,19

Source: Author's Calculations based on OECD Stats Data.

be made in the following section will be evaluated with the shares of the related service groups in trade and will provide a more healthy and accurate finding (Tab. 5.4).

Groups with the highest share in Turkey's exports of services to OECD countries are "travel" and "transportation". In 2010, travel services accounted for 61 % of total service exports and 26 % of transportation, while travel accounted for 48 % and 31 % of transportation as of 2016. Turkey's imports from OECD countries travel services was 32 % in 2010, transportation accounted for 25 % of the group, and these rates in 2016 have been realized as 27 % and 19 %, respectively. In short, travel and transportation service groups are pointed out as the two most

Tab. 5.5: IIT Indices of Turkey in the Context of Turkey-OECD Trade (2010–2016)

EBOPS SERVICES	2010	2011	2012	2013	2014	2015	2016
S. Total EBOPS Services	0,63	0,68	0,73	0,74	0,76	0,82	0,90
SA. Manufacturing services on physical inputs owned by others	0,30	0,41	0,75	0,79	0,71	0,84	0,72
SB. Maintenance and repair services n.i.e.	0,13	0,05	0,10	0,91	0,61	0,39	0,50
SC. Transport	0,61	0,68	0,70	0,66	0,63	0,65	0,65
SD. Travel	0,38	0,36	0,42	0,44	0,44	0,50	0,63
SE. Construction	0,11	0,05	0,26	0,16	0,53	0,81	0,48
SF. Insurance and pension services	0,75	0,50	0,82	0,78	0,72	0,80	0,91
SG. Financial services	0,62	0,44	0,34	0,30	0,20	0,23	0,29
SH. Charges for the use of intellectual property n.i.e	0,03	0,18	0,13	0,10	0,13	0,15	0,27
SI. Telecommunications, computer, and information services	0,59	0,77	0,52	0,57	0,61	0,76	0,53
SJ. Other business services	0,88	1,00	0,96	0,98	0,85	0,81	0,87
SK. Personal, cultural, and recreational services	0,47	0,49	0,73	0,92	0,90	0,80	0,85
SL. Government goods and services n.i.e.	0,66	0,59	0,61	0,72	0,70	0,88	0,43
Commercial Services	0,72	0,76	0,81	0,82	0,81	0,86	0,99

Source: Author's Calculations based on the OECD Stats Data.

important service groups in Turkey's commercial services foreign trade. "Other Business Services" and "Financial Services" are the third important groups following travel and transportation services. Other EBOPS service groups have relatively low shares.

3.2.1 IIT Indices of Turkey in the Context of Turkey-OECD Services Trade

Commercial services intra-industrial trade rates provide information on whether services trade is based on traditional specialization and division of labor or whether it is based on scale economies and service differentiation within the scope of monopolistic competition. According to Tab. 5.5, values close to zero mean IIT is low and values close to one mean IIT is high.

As shown in Tab. 5.5, it is observed that IIT has been increasing in terms of "Total EBOPS Services". The index value, which was 0.63 in 2010, reached 0.90 in 2016. Between 2010 and 2016, IIT rates rose every year. In more detail, IIT is high in transportation services in all years between 2010 and 2016. It has never

Tab. 5.6: RCA1 Indices of Turkey in the Context of Turkey-OECD Trade

EBOPS SERVICES	2010	2011	2012	2013	2014	2015	2016
SA. Manufacturing services on physical inputs owned by others	0,08	2,01	0,97	0,89	1,12	0,96	1,45
SB. Maintenance and repair services n.i.e.	0,03	0,01	0,03	0,49	0,27	0,17	0,27
SC. Transport	1,03	1,01	1,08	1,19	1,33	1,43	1,69
SD. Travel	1,92	2,33	2,17	2,07	2,18	2,06	1,77
SE. Construction	0,03	0,01	0,09	0,05	0,22	0,47	0,26
SF. Insurance and pension services	0,27	0,17	0,40	0,37	0,35	0,46	0,68
SG. Financial services	0,20	0,14	0,12	0,10	0,07	0,09	0,14
SH. Charges for the use of intellectual property n.i.e	0,01	0,05	0,04	0,03	0,04	0,05	0,13
SI. Telecommunications, computer, and information services	0,19	0,33	0,20	0,23	0,27	0,43	0,30
SJ. Other business services	0,58	0,52	0,53	0,56	0,46	0,47	0,63
SK. Personal, cultural, and recreational services	1,47	1,58	0,34	0,50	0,76	0,46	0,60
SL. Government goods and services n.i.e.	0,92	1,22	1,32	1,04	1,14	0,88	0,23

Source: Author's Calculations based on the OECD Stats Data.

fallen below 0.61 since 2010. In the service groups which has a very low share in OECD-Turkey services trade, "Manufacturing Services on Inputs Owned by Others", "Maintenance and Repair Services", "Construction", "Insurance and Pension," "Telecommunications, Computer and Information", "Other Business Services", "Personal, Cultural and Recreation Services", and "Government Goods and Services n.i.e.", especially after 2013, IIT is high. In the "travel" services, there has been an increase in IIT rates in 2012 and beyond, but it has not reached 0.50 index by 2015. In 2015 and 2016, it rose above 0.50 and reached 0.65.

In general, it is possible to say that Turkey is in the case of competing economies with OECD member countries in terms of open-to-export service sectors, and trade generally takes place on the basis of scale economies and service differentiation (the darkest values in the table indicate that IIT is taking place).

3.2.2 Turkey's RCA Ratios within the Scope of Commercial Services with OECD Countries

In this section, both RCA and RSCA index values were calculated in terms of trade in services between Turkey and OECD member countries and the results obtained were evaluated.

Tab. 5.7: RSCA1 Indices of Turkey in the Context of Turkey-OECD Trade

EBOPS SERVICES	2010	2011	2012	2013	2014	2015	2016
SA. Manufacturing services on physical inputs owned by others	-0,85	**0,34**	-0,02	-0,06	**0,06**	-0,02	**0,18**
SB. Maintenance and repair services n.i.e.	-0,94	-0,97	-0,94	-0,34	-0,58	-0,71	-0,57
SC. Transport	**0,01**	**0,01**	**0,04**	**0,09**	**0,14**	**0,18**	**0,26**
SD. Travel	**0,32**	**0,40**	**0,37**	**0,35**	**0,37**	**0,35**	**0,28**
SE. Construction	-0,95	-0,97	-0,84	-0,91	-0,64	-0,36	-0,59
SF. Insurance and pension services	-0,57	-0,71	-0,43	-0,46	-0,49	-0,37	-0,19
SG. Financial services	-0,66	-0,75	-0,79	-0,82	-0,87	-0,83	-0,76
SH. Charges for the use of intellectual property n.i.e	-0,98	-0,90	-0,92	-0,94	-0,92	-0,90	-0,77
SI. Telecommunications, computer, and information services	-0,68	-0,51	-0,66	-0,62	-0,57	-0,40	-0,54
SJ. Other business services	-0,26	-0,32	-0,31	-0,28	-0,37	-0,36	-0,23
SK. Personal, cultural, and recreational services	**0,19**	**0,23**	-0,50	-0,34	-0,14	-0,37	-0,25
SL. Government goods and services n.i.e.	-0,04	**0,10**	**0,14**	**0,02**	**0,07**	-0,06	-0,63

Source: Author's Calculations based on the OECD Stats Data.

The calculated RCA, RSCA1, RSCA2, and RSCA2 indices for Turkey's trade in services with OECD countries are presented below. The evaluations were made according to RSCA indices and the dark and underlined values reflect the service groups in which comparativeness superiority emerges. In other words, positive values mean that competitiveness power is high.

The competitiveness of Turkey in services trade with OECD countries, according to the RCA1 and RSCA1 indices (Tab. 5.6 and Tab. 5.7), which calculate Turkey's competitiveness in services trade with OECD countries only, shows that Turkey has a continuous comparativeness advantage over the 2010–2016 period in the "transportation" and "travel" service groups, which are two service groups that have the largest share in services trade. "Personal, Cultural, and Recreation "and" Government Goods and Services n.i.e." in service groups, it is understood that the comparativeness superiority seen in the beginning was lost in 2015 and 2016.

Turkey's competitiveness in services trade with OECD countries, according to RCA2 and RSCA2 indexes, which deal with Turkey's trade with the world in a wider context (Tab. 5.8 and Tab. 5.9), is clearly seen to have a comparative advantage in the "Travel" Group between 2010 and 2016. In "Transportation"

Tab. 5.8: RCA2 Indices of Turkey in the Context of Turkey-OECD Trade

EBOPS SERVICES	2010	2011	2012	2013	2014	2015	2016
SA. Manufacturing services on physical inputs owned by others	0,10	2,00	0,80	0,78	0,88	0,67	1,05
SB. Maintenance and repair services n.i.e.	0,04	0,01	0,03	0,43	0,21	0,12	0,20
SC. Transport	1,23	1,00	0,89	1,04	1,05	1,00	1,23
SD. Travel	2,30	2,31	1,80	1,81	1,71	1,44	1,28
SE. Construction	0,03	0,01	0,07	0,04	0,17	0,33	0,19
SF. Insurance and pension services	0,33	0,17	0,33	0,33	0,27	0,32	0,49
SG. Financial services	0,24	0,14	0,10	0,09	0,05	0,06	0,10
SH. Charges for the use of intellectual property n.i.e	0,01	0,05	0,03	0,03	0,03	0,04	0,09
SI. Telecommunications, computer, and information services	0,23	0,32	0,17	0,20	0,21	0,30	0,22
SJ. Other business services	0,70	0,52	0,44	0,49	0,36	0,33	0,46
SK. Personal, cultural, and recreational services	1,76	1,57	0,28	0,43	0,59	0,32	0,43
SL. Government goods and services n.i.e.	1,09	1,21	1,10	0,91	0,90	0,61	0,16

Source: Author's Calculations based on the OECD Stats Data.

Tab. 5.9: RSCA2 Indices of Turkey in the Context of Turkey-OECD Trade

EBOPS SERVICES	2010	2011	2012	2013	2014	2015	2016
SA. Manufacturing services on physical inputs owned by others	-0,83	0,33	-0,11	-0,13	-0,06	-0,20	0,02
SB. Maintenance and repair services n.i.e.	-0,93	-0,97	-0,95	-0,40	-0,65	-0,79	-0,67
SC. Transport	0,10	0,00	-0,06	0,02	0,02	0,00	0,10
SD. Travel	0,39	0,40	0,29	0,29	0,26	0,18	0,12
SE. Construction	-0,94	-0,97	-0,86	-0,92	-0,70	-0,51	-0,68
SF. Insurance and pension services	-0,51	-0,71	-0,50	-0,51	-0,57	-0,51	-0,34
SG. Financial services	-0,61	-0,75	-0,82	-0,84	-0,90	-0,88	-0,82
SH. Charges for the use of intellectual property n.i.e	-0,98	-0,90	-0,93	-0,95	-0,93	-0,93	-0,83
SI. Telecommunications, computer, and information services	-0,63	-0,51	-0,71	-0,66	-0,65	-0,54	-0,65
SJ. Other business services	-0,18	-0,32	-0,39	-0,34	-0,47	-0,51	-0,37
SK. Personal, cultural, and recreational services	0,28	0,22	-0,56	-0,39	-0,25	-0,52	-0,40
SL. Government goods and services n.i.e.	0,05	0,10	0,05	-0,05	-0,05	-0,24	-0,72

Source: Author's Calculations based on the OECD Stats Data.

services, comparative advantage has been determined in all years except 2012. In the "Personal, Cultural, and Recreation" and "Government Goods and Services n.i.e." service groups, the comparative superiority observed at the beginning of 2013 was lost in 2013 and beyond. In the "Manufacturing Services on Physical Inputs Owned by Others" service group, it has been determined that it has a comparative advantage in 2011 and 2016.

As a result of RCA and RSCA analysis, it can be said that Turkey is in the case of competing economies with OECD member countries in terms of overseas service sectors, and that trade in "transport" and "travel" services is generally specialization and division of labor. In the 2010–2016 period, it is clear that Turkey has a comparative advantage in the "travel services" group every year.

One of the important findings of this is that RSCA1, which deals with the competitiveness of Turkey in the services trade with OECD countries within the scope of trade in services with the OECD, and RSCA2, which deals with the competitiveness of Turkey in the services trade with OECD countries within the scope of that Turkey's world with trade in services, so much larger scale, it is observed that there is almost no difference between the findings. In other words, both indices revealed similar findings and given Turkey's trade with non-OECD countries, it is seen that there is almost no difference in the competitiveness of OECD countries, and the competitiveness of service groups remains almost the same. This situation can be interpreted as the fact that the two service groups have a competitive power based on very solid foundations.

According to IIT and RCA analyses, "Transport" and "Travel" service groups, which ranked first two places in Turkey's OECD countries and services foreign trade, have highest competitiveness. The high level of both IIT and RCA values reveals the special competitiveness and division of labor within the traditional comparative advantages, while also demonstrating the high competitiveness of scale economies and service differentiation within the scope of monopolistic competition. While this situation is extremely positive for both sectors, the rival economy structure arises among the OECD countries and by these groups. On the other hand, according to RTA and IIT analyses, the competitiveness of Turkey in terms of "Financial services", "Telecommunications, computer and information services", and "Other Business Services" that increase in total services trade as of 2016, are low and exhibit a complementary economic structure with OECD countries by these groups.

Conclusion

Intra-industry trade provides additional gains according to traditional comparative advantages and inter-industry trade. With the access to economies of scale in terms of production and service delivery, low-cost and efficient production can be made and services can be provided; it enables to benefit from wider markets, and consumers have access to a wider range of goods and services due to differentiated products and services. In this context, in Turkey's trade with OECD countries, in terms of total services trade, the IIT rate has never fallen below 0.63 since 2010. IIT structure has been observed since 2014 in all service groups except for "Financial Services "and "Charges for the Use of Intellectual Property n.i.e.". As of 2016, IIT was not observed in the "Official Goods and Services" group, which had a high IIT structure until 2016. It is possible to say that Turkey is in the case of competing economies with OECD countries in terms of Foreign Service sectors, and trade is generally realized on the basis of scale economies and service differentiation.

RCA, also called comparative advantage, is important in terms of reflecting the export performance and specialization trend. In terms of basic service groups in Turkey's trade with OECD countries, export performance and the direction of specialization were measured with two different indices that suggested whether comparative advantages emerged. As well as service groups remaining for specialization, weak performance groups have also been identified. While a comparative advantage is observed in transportation, travel group, it has been understood that the comparative advantage of "Personal, Culture and Recreation" and "Government Goods and Services n.i.e." groups have disappeared in recent years. Turkey's advantages in trade with OECD countries does not change when it is based on Turkey's trade with the world.

In this context, as the main policy recommendations, the sub-service groups "transportation" and "travel", which are very high in the services trade with OECD countries and which contribute greatly to the reduction of Turkey's current deficit problem, should be supported by all kinds of incentives. It is recommended to facilitate the transportation of related services, to develop new service delivery strategies and techniques, to continue continuous improvement and development efforts in service delivery quality by taking into consideration the inability to store and consume where service sectors are the most important disadvantages. In other sub-service groups where the competitive power of Turkey is relatively low in terms of both intra-industry trade and revealed comparative advantages, i.e., where competition power is low, service delivery strategies based on scale efficiency, new and competitive service delivery, division of labor and specialization, etc., development is essential. Considering that the share of these service groups in Turkey's services trade has increased in recent years albeit slowly, there is a risk that Turkey will lose its competitive edge in services trade unless necessary measures are taken in the medium and long term.

References

Balassa, B. (1965). Trade Liberalisation and 'Revealed' Comparative Advantage. *The Manchester School Journal*, 33(2): 99–204.

Balassa, B. (1966). Tariff Reductions and Trade in Manufactures among the Industrial Countries. *American Economic Review*, 56: 466–473. (Herbert G. Grubel and P.J. Lloyd (Eds.), Intra-Industry Trade. Edward Elgar Publishing, Cheltenham: 2003, 28–35).

Dalum, B., Laursen, K. and Villumsen, G. (1998). Structural Change in OECD Export Specialisation Patterns: De-Specialisation and Stickiness. *International Review of Applied Economics*, 12: 447–467.

Greenaway, D. and Milner, C. (1986). The Economics of Intra-Industry Trade. Basil Blackwell, Oxford.

Grubel, H. and Lloyd, P.J. (1971). The Empirical Measurement of Intra-Industry Trade. *Economic Record*, 47: 494–517.

Jackman, M., Lorde, T., Lowe, S. and Alleyne A. (2011). Evaluating Tourism Competitiveness of Small Island Developing States: A Revealed Comparative Advantage Approach. *Anatolia - An International Journal of Tourism and Hospitality Research*, 22(3): 350–360.

Maryam, J., Banday, U. J. and Mittal, A. (2018). Trade Intensity and Revealed Comparative Advantage: An Analysis of Intra-BRICS Trade. *International Journal of Emerging Markets*, 13(5): 1182–1195.

Levchenko, A. A. and Zhang J. (2016). The Evolution of Comparative Advantage: Measurement and Welfare Implications. *Journal of Monetary Economics*, 78: 96–111.

Leromain, E. and Orefice, G. (2014). New Revealed Comparative Advantage İndex: Dataset and Empirical Distribution. *International Economics*, 139: 48–70.

Miteva-Kacarski, E. (2018). Revealed Comparative Advantage in Trade Between the Republic of Macedonia and CEFTA 2006. Economic Review, *Journal of Economics and Business*, 16 (1): 59–70. ISSN 1512-8962

OECD. (2018). Trade in Services (indicator). doi: 10.1787/3796b5f0-en (Accessed on 22 November 2018).

OECD.(2018). https://www.oecd.org/sdd/its/EBOPS-2010.pdf

Shahab, S. and Mahmood, M. T. (2013). Comparative Advantage of Leather Industry in Pakistan with Selected Asian Economies. *International Journal of Economics and Financial Issues*, 3(1): 133–139

Shohibul, A. (2013). Revealed Comparative Advantage Measure: ASEAN-China Trade Flows. *Journal of Economics and Sustainable Development*, 4(7): 136–145

Startienė, G. and Remeikienė, R. (2014). Evaluation of Revealed Comparative Advantage of Lithuanian Industry in global Markets. *Procedia - Social and Behavioral Sciences*, 110: 428–438

TCMB (The Central Bank of the Republic of Turkey). (2018). *Electronical Data Distribution System*. https://www.tcmb.gov.tr/

Widodo, T. (2009). Comparative Advantage: Theory, Empirical Measures and Case Studies. *Review of Economic and Business Studies*, 4: 57–82

WTO. (2015). Services Trade. https://www.wto.org/english/thewto_e/20y_e/services_brochure2015_e.pdf (accessed: 11.11.2018)

WTO. (2017). World Trade Statistical Review 2017. https://www.wto.org/english/res_e/statis_e/wts2017_e/wts2017_e.pdf (erişim: 24/11/2018)

Haydar Karadağ and Mustafa Şit

6 Does The Monetary Policy of the Central Bank Lead to a Housing Bubble? Empirical Analysis for Turkish Economy

Highlights: Valuing housing prices above the required level causes a housing bubble. In this study, the effect of the monetary policy implemented by CBRT (Central Bank of the Republic of Turkey) on housing prices was investigated. Phillips and Ouliaris cointegration and Canonical Cointegration Regression (CCR) estimation methods were selected as the research method. Unlike the studies in the literature, the hedonic housing price index, bank rates, different econometric tests, and up-to-date data were used. As a result of the study, it was determined that increasing CBRT's money supply and decreasing rediscount rates could result in a housing bubble.

Keywords: Housing Bubble, Hedonic Housing Price Index, Monetary Policy, CCR Test

Introduction

Real estate prices are influenced by macroeconomic variables as well as geographical location (Dilber and Sertkaya, 2016: 11). While real estate prices affect the banking sector, they also play an important role in macroeconomic stability (Kulalı, 2016: 49). However, the banking sector is also affected by the monetary policies implemented by Central Banks (Uysal and Yiğit, 2016: 190).

The decline in interest rates in developed countries in the 2000s has significantly increased the return on investment instruments in developing countries. This situation caused capital flows to developing countries. Increasing foreign capital inflows, while increasing liquidity in these countries, also reduced interest rates. The banking sector started to provide loans for the housing market with falling interest rates (Uysal and Yiğit, 2016: 189). The demand for the real estate sector has expanded with the loans granted to the housing sector. Thus, real estate prices increase and housing bubble is formed (Dilber and Sertkaya, 2016: 12).

Roubini (2006) indicated that a moderate interest rate could be effective in responding to the economic distortions caused by bubbles. The central banks can influence asset prices through nominal interest rates or changes in money supply over credit and stock prices (Darıcı, 2018: 223).

In this study, the impact of the monetary policy implemented by the Central Bank on housing prices in the Turkish economy was investigated with monthly data from 2010–2018. In the first part of the study, the relationship between housing bubble and monetary policy was introduced. After that, the relevant literature review was included. In the third part, the impact of the monetary policy implemented by the CBRT on housing prices was tested econometrically.

2 Housing Bubble and Monetary Policy Relation

With credit expansion, financial liberalization led to liquidity flow into real estate markets. Nevertheless, falling interest rates increased consumer spending by supporting credit utilization. This also supplied economic growth. The decrease in interest rates and the prolongation of maturities played an important role in the increase in housing credit. With the increasing demand, housing prices increased. However, this process increased the risk of the formation of the real estate bubble and then the collapse of the bubble (Mutluer, 2008: 240–241). Unexpected changes in money supply and interest rates affected real estate prices according to the rate of spread mechanism (Coşkun, 2016: 208).

The mortgage crisis in 2008 occurred in a period when markets were efficient and investors were rational (Kulalı, 2016: 49). Thus, a relationship emerged between the real estate bubble and the banking crises (Mutluer, 2008: 240).

The main reasons for the mortgage crisis are the high credit policy provided to the real estate sector in an uncontrolled manner and the loose monetary policy pursued by the FED by lowering policy interest rates in the 2001-2005 period. The expansionary monetary policy pursued by the FED in this period led to an excessive increase in real estate prices (bubbles) by increasing the demand for real estate in the USA (Erarslan and Bayraktar, 2012: 38, 40).

The 2008 crisis required both the central banks to maintain price stability and the monetary policy-asset prices relationship to be taken into account in terms of financial stability. In the traditional central bank approach, monetary policy was thought to respond to changes in asset prices when inflationary pressure was occurring. However, it was believed that the bubble formed by the excessive rise in asset prices was not the direct target of monetary policy. However, with the recent crisis, this view seems to have been replaced by an interventionist approach (Darici, 2018: 222).

In the Turkish economy, with the impact of the mortgage crisis, the central objective of CBRT was determined to provide price stability and financial stability. In this context, money supply, rediscount rates, and the adjustment of credit and liquidity ratios of the banking sector and short-term interest rates are present (Oktar and Dalyancı, 2011: 7).

3 Literature

Kolcu and Yamak (2018) tested the monthly data for 2010:01–2017:09 in the Turkish economy with Autoregressive Distributed Lag (ARDL) border test developed by Pesaran and Shin (1999). According to the test results, the long-term relationship between housing prices, income, and housing credit interest rate was determined. Williams (2011) explained that many factors contributed to the contraction in the housing sector in many countries and the subsequent global financial crisis. He determined that the monetary policies to be implemented could affect the development of housing price bubbles. McDonald and Stokes (2013) examined the causes of the housing bubble in the 1987–2010/8 period in the United States using Granger causality analysis and VAR modeling methods. In the study, the Federal Reserve's interest rate policy, which keeps the federal fund rate low, was determined to be a reason for the housing price bubble. Darıcı (2018) revealed that expansionary monetary policy for the Turkish economy created pressure to increase housing prices. In this process, increasing housing prices as a result of the creation of more credits by banks can cause the formation of a bubble. The emergence of such a situation in the economy may cause financial instability. Eickmeier and Hofmann (2010) examined the interaction between monetary policy and more than 200 financial and asset variables in the United States. In the 1987–2007 period, they investigated the factor-augmented vector autoregressive model (FAVAR) with three-month data. As a result of the analysis, they found that the monetary policy shocks had a strong and lasting effect on the money market, with real estate prices, real estate asset, and private sector debts.

In addition, Central Banks can prevent excessive price increases in housing and real estate prices by applying monetary policy. Feinman (2010), using VAR analysis, found that the monetary policy applied until 2003–2006 had very little effect on housing prices under the current economic conditions. According to Feinman, central banks can prevent bubbles that may occur in housing prices by using monetary policy more effectively. Limjaroenrat (2017) examined the effect of monetary policy on the formation of housing bubbles using the time-varying coefficient structural vector autoregression (TVC-SVAR) method. In his study, he predicted that the asset price bubble would fall due to strict monetary policy. Under the assumption of sticky asset prices, Gali (2017) predicts that the asset price bubble will fall due to the strict monetary policy. Thus, he found that the housing price, unlike the flexible stock price, decreased as a result of the high rate of the interest rate.

Coşkun and Jadevicius (2017) examined whether there was a bubble in the Turkish housing market in the period 2010 January–December 2014. They tested the interdependence between housing prices and a set of explanatory variables by an extended Case-Shiller (2003) model and Dickey-Fuller (Rtadf). According to the regression estimates, they could not detect the presence of the bubble in housing prices in Turkey. In general, the researchers found that monetary policy could affect the development of housing price bubbles. Unlike the studies in the literature, the hedonic housing price index, bank rates, different econometric tests, and up-to-date data were used.

4 Econometric Analysis

In this part of the study, the effects of the monetary policy implemented by CBRT on housing prices were analyzed using KPSS unit root, Phillips and Ouliaris cointegration, and Canonical Congruence (CCR) tests.

4.1 Data Set

In this study, the impact of the monetary policy implemented by the CBRT on housing prices was analyzed through the following variables. The appropriate time interval for the data was 2010: M1 and 2018: M12. The hedonic housing price index and money supply data were analyzed in a logarithmic form. Due to the fact that the data related to the Interest Rates Applied to the Reserve Requirements are not available in the given time frame, it could not be included in the analysis. Data were obtained from the CBRT electronic data distribution system.

Hedonic Housing Price Index was chosen as the dependent variable. Because this index is different from other housing price indices. It has been purified from the quality effect dependent on the observable properties of the residences. Also it represents housing prices across Turkey. This price index is created using the hedonic regression method. Shown with HHPI icon.

Money Supply (M2): money supply was chosen because it was the main policy tool to determine inflation. It was shown with the MS icon.

Rediscount rate: the interest rate applied by the CBRT for rediscount credits. The central bank's increase in the rediscount rate causes the money supply to decrease, the money supply curve to the left, and interest rates to increase. The

Central Bank determines the interest rate of credits granted to commercial banks through this policy instrument. Thus, this affects the market interest rate and determination of short-term interest rates. In addition, increasing or decreasing the rediscount rate by the central bank affects the credit volume. All these effects are considered to have an impact on housing credits and prices. This variable is shown with the REDISCOUNT symbol.

Housing Credit Interest: interest rates applied to housing credits by banks. Shown with HCI icon. In the study, the model showing the factors determining the real estate prices is as in Equation 1:

$$hhpi_t = f(ms_t, rediscount_t\ ,\ hci_t) \tag{1}$$

4.2 Methods and Findings

In the study, KPSS unit root test was applied to determine the stasis of the series. Traditional unit root tests test the zero hypothesis that the time series is y_t I(1). On the contrary, the alternative hypothesis in the KPSS unit root test tests the unit root in the series and tests that it is not stationary. The purpose of the KPSS (Kwiatkowski-Phillips-Schmidt-Shin) test is to purify the deterministic trend in the observed series and to ensure that the series is stable (Kwiatkowski, Phillips, Schmidt and Shin, 1992).

The hypotheses in the KPSS test are different from the other unit root tests.

H_0: The series is stable;

H_1: The series is not stable; it is.

The results of the KPSS unit root test are presented in Tab. 6.1. The results indicate that all series are stationary in the first-degree difference. As a result, the stability of all variables is I (1). For this reason, the variables were analyzed by taking the first-degree differences.

Since the series I (1) was found as a result of the KPSS unit root test, the model was estimated using Phillips and Ouliaris and CCR methods. In this analysis, Philips and Ouliaris cointegration test was used because the number of observations was greater.

The Phillips and Ouliaris cointegration test is highly dependent on the specification in two variable models and is performed better with other procedures (Reimers, 1992: 335). The Phillips and Ouliaris cointegration test includes procedures designed to detect the presence of a unit root in the residues of (together) regressions between economic time series levels (Phillips-Ouliaris, 1990: 165).

Tab. 6.1: KPSS Unit Root Test Results

Variables		KPSS LM Test Statistic			
		Level I (0)		First Difference I(1)	
		Intercept	Trend and Intercept	Intercept	Trend and Intercept
LNHHPI		1,181 (9)	0,195 (8)	0.262 (6)	0.091 (0)
LNMS		1.(9)	0,144 (8)	0.056 (9)	0,046 (10)
REDISCOUNT		0,527 (8)	0,193 (8)	0,291 (0)	0,106 (3)
HCI		0,602 (7)	0,151 (7)	0.309 (13)	0,101 (12)
Critical	*%1*	*0.739*	0.2160	*0.739*	0.2160
Values.	*5 %*	*0.463*	0.1460	*0.463*	0.1460
	10 %	*0.347*	0.1190	*0.347*	0.1190

Note: The values in parentheses are latency lengths. The optimal latency parameter, The Bartlett kernel (default) spectral estimation method, and the Newey-West Bandwidth (automatic selection) criteria were used in the KPSS test.

Tab. 6.2: Results of Phillips and Ouliaris Cointegration Test

Equation	Test Statistics	Chance	Z-Statistic	Chance	Delay Length
DLNHHPI= β_0+ β_1DLNMS+ β_2*DREDISCOUNT*+ β_3DHCI	-5,046*	0.005	-47,419*	0.001	5

The critical values obtained by Phillips-Ouliaris (1990) using Monte Carlo method are 1 %, 5 %, and 10 % for -4.06927, -3.43163, and -3.1016. *,**, and *** indicate the existence of a cointegration relationship at 1.5 and 10 percent and significance level.

In Tab. 6.2, the results of Phillips and Ouliaris cointegration were given. According to the results in Tab. 6.2, because the test statistics at 1 % significance level were greater than the critical values, the null hypothesis without cointegration was rejected statistically. As a result of this test, the variables are cointegrated. Therefore, there was a long-term relationship between variables.

One of the methods developed for estimating and testing coefficients of variables in the cointegration model is the CCR (Park, 1992: 119). In the CCR method, stationary transforms of series are used to solve the long-term correlation problem between the cointegration equation and Stochastic shocks (Stock and Watson, 1993: 783).

Tab. 6.3: CCR Results

Variable	CCR	
	Coefficient	Prob.
DLNMS	0.098811*	**0.0225**
DREDISCOUNT	-19.88559*	**0.0100**
DHCI	-0.004938*	**0.0000**
Observations	106	
R-squared	0.864	
Adjusted R-squared	0.919	
Jarque-Bera	5,827** (0,054)	

*, ** and *** denote significance at 1 %, 5 %, and 10 %. The results of CCR based on 5 lags.

In Tab. 6.3, the results of the CCR prediction were presented. The CCR test shows 91.9 % highly adjusted R-squared values. According to the findings, while the coefficients of the rediscount and housing credit interest rates are negative, the coefficient of the money supply variable is positive. The coefficients of variables are statistically significant at the 1 % significance level. According to Jarque-Bera value, series are normal distributions.

Conclusions

In this study, it was investigated whether the monetary policy instruments implemented by the CBRT lead to a housing bubble. In order to test the stability of variables, KPSS unit root test was applied. According to the test results, it was determined that the first differences of the series were stabilized. In this analysis, Phillips and Ouliaris cointegration test were used because the number of observations was greater. According to the results of this test, long-term relationship between the variables was determined.

The coefficients of money supply, rediscount rate, and housing credit interest rates were determined by the CCR estimation method. According to the results, a 1 % increase in the supply of money in the Turkish economy leads to a 9.88 % increase in housing prices. The value of the national currency decreases with the increase in the supply of money and an inflationary environment occurs. This leads to an increase in housing prices. Accordingly, it can be said that increases in money supply negatively affect housing demand. Because housing prices are increasing, housing demand is adversely affected.

A 1 % increase in rediscount rates reduces housing prices by 19.88 %. Rediscount rates determine short-term interest rates. The increase in the rediscount rate causes a decrease in the money supply and an increase in interest rates. The increase in interest rates reduces the demand for housing credits and thus the housing demand. The decrease in housing demand leads to a decrease in housing prices. It also supports the result of the money supply. While the increase in money supply increases prices, the increase in rediscount rates and the decrease in money supply have a negative impact on prices. In the same way, a 1 % increase in housing credit interest causes a 0.4 % decrease in housing prices. The results are appropriate for theory, because the increase in interest rates in the determined variables leads to downward pressure on housing demand and prices.

As a result, it can be said that the monetary policies implemented by the CBRT may be effective in determining the housing prices. Increasing the CBRT's money supply and reducing rediscount rates could result in a housing bubble. According to the findings, the most effective tool in policy tools is the rediscount ratios. Because it has more effect on housing prices. For subsequent studies, research can be developed by adding the variable of interest rates applied to reserve requirements for analysis.

References

Case, K. E., & Shiller, R. J. (2003). Is there a bubble in the housing market?. Brookings papers on economic activity, 2003(2), 299–362.

Coşkun, Y. (2016). Konut Fiyatları ve Yatırımı: Türkiye İçin Bir Analiz. *Niğde Üniversitesi İktisadi ve İdari Bilimler Fakültesi Dergisi*, Vol. 9, No. 2, pp. 201–217.

Coşkun, Y. and Jadevicius, A. (2017). Is There a Housing Bubble in Turkey?, *Real Estate Management and Valuation*, Vol. 25, No. 1, pp. 48–73.

Darıcı, B. (2018). Para Politikası ve Konut Fiyatları İlişkisi: Türkiye Ekonomisi için Ampirik Bir Analiz. *Anemon Muş Alparslan Üniversitesi Sosyal Bilimler Dergisi*, Special Issue, pp. 221–228.

Dilber, İ. and Sertkaya, Y. (2016). 2008 Finansal Krizi Sonrası Türkiye'de Konut Fiyatlarının Belirleyicilerine Yönelik Analiz. Muş *Alparslan Üniversitesi Sosyal Bilimler Dergisi*, Vol. 4, No. 1, pp. 11–30.

Eickmeier, S and Hofmann, B. (2010). Monetary Policy, Housing Booms and Financial (Im)Balances. *European Central Bank Working Paper Series*, No. 1178.

Erarslan, C. and Bayraktar, Y. (2012). Konut Balonlarının Oluşumunda Fed'in Rolü ve Küresel Krizden Çıkartılacak Bazı Dersler. *İstanbul Üniversitesi İktisat Fakültesi Mecmuası*, Vol. 62, No. 2, pp. 38–59.

Feinman, J. N. (2010). Did Monetary Policy Cause the Housing Bubble?. https://institutional.dws.com/content/_media/DAM458_CloserLook0210.pdf, (01.03.2019).

Gali, J. (2017). Monetary Policy and Bubbles in a New Keynesian Model with Overlapping Generations. http://www.crei.cat/wp-content/uploads/2018/01/nk_bubbles_dec2017.pdf, (03.03.2019).

Kolcu, F. and Yamak, N. (2018). Gelir ve Faiz Oranlarının Konut Fiyatları Üzerindeki Kısa ve Uzun Dönem Etkileri. *Uluslararası İktisadi ve İdari İncelemeler Dergisi*, Special Issue, pp. 141–152.

Kulalı, İ. (2016). Etkin Piyasalar Hipotezi ve Davranışsal Finans Çatışması. *Finans ve Bankacılık Çalışmaları Dergisi*, Vol. 5, No. 2, pp. 46–57.

Kwiatkowski, D., Phillips, P. C. B., Schmidt, P. and Shin, Y. (1992). Testing the Null Hypothesis of Stationarity Against the Alternative of a Unit Root, How Sure Are We That Economic Time Series Have a Unit Root?. *Journal of Econometrics*, Vol. 54, pp. 159–178.

Limjaroenrat, V. (2017). Monetary Policy and Housing Bubbles: Some Evidence when House Price is Sticky. https://cepr.org/sites/default/files/40006_LIMJAROENRAT%20-%20Monetary%20Policy%20and%20Housing%20Bubbles.pdf, (02.03.2019).

McDonald, J. F. and Stokes, H. H. (2013). Monetary Policy and the Housing Bubble. *Journal of Real Estate Finance and Economics*, Vol. 46, No. 3, pp. 437–451.

Mutluer, D. (2008). Gayrimenkul Fiyatlarının Derlenmesi Ülke Örnekleri ve Türkiye İçin Bir Uygulama. *TİSK Akademi*, Vol. 2008/2, pp. 240–278.

Oktar, S. and Dalyancı, L. (2011). Türkiye Ekonomisinde Para Politikası ve Enflasyon Arasındaki İlişkinin Analizi, *Marmara Üniversitesi İktisadi ve İdari Bilimler Fakültesi Dergisi*. Vol. 31, No. 3, pp. 1–20.

Park, J. Y. (1992), Canonical Cointegrating Regressions. *Econometrica*, Vol. 60, No. 1, pp. 119–143.

Pesaran, M.H. and Shin, Y. (1999). "An Autoregressive Distributed Lag Modelling Approach to Cointegration Analysis." Econometrics and Economic Theory in the 20th Century: The Ragnar Frisch Centennial Symposium, Strom, S. (ed.) Cambridge University Press.

Phillips, P.C.B. and Ouliaris, B. (1990). Asymptotic Properties of Residual Based Tests For Cointegration. *Econometrica*, Vol. 58, No. 1, pp. 165–193.

Reimers, H. E. (1992). Comparisons of Tests for Multivariate Cointegration. *Statistical Papers*, Vol. 33, pp. 335–359.

Roubini, N. (2006). Why central banks should burst bubbles. *International Finance*, 9(1), 87-107.

Stock, J. H. and Watson, M. W. (1993). A Simple Estimator of Cointegrating Vectors in Higher Order Integrated Systems. *Econometrica*, Vol. 61, No. 4, pp. 783–820.

Uysal, D. and Yiğit, M. (2016). Türkiye'de Konut Talebinin Belirleyicileri (1970–2015): Ampirik Bir Çalışma. *Selçuk Üniversitesi Sosyal Bilimler Meslek Yüksekokulu Dergisi*, Vol. 19, No. 1, pp. 185–209.

Williams, J. C. (2011). Monetary Policy and Housing Booms. *International Journal of Central Banking*, Vol. 7, No. 1, pp. 345–355.

Hale Kırer Silva L. and M. M. Tuncer Çalışkan

7 The Efficiency and Profitability of the Turkish Banking Sector

Highlights: The aim of this study is to evaluate the efficiency of the Turkish banking system and its relationship with banks' profitability for the years between 2005Q1 and 2018Q2 on a quarterly basis. We gather the data from The Banks Association of Turkey. In this context, we employ a widely used nonparametric approach, which is called Data Envelopment Analysis (DEA) to calculate efficiency scores. The input and output variables are elected in accordance with an intermediation approach. Accordingly, total loans and net interest income are used as output measures; while total assets, total deposits, number of employees, and the number of branches are used as input measures. After determining the efficiency, our ultimate purpose is to show if there is a connection between efficiency and profitability by taking the return on assets (ROA) and returns on equity (ROE) as bank profitability indicators. In this context, our findings show that banks in Turkey have relatively higher efficiency scores in the first three quarters of the year but not in the last quarters. When we examine the relationship between efficiency and profitability, the results does not give a robust relationship. However, there is a moderate relationship for the last periods of the years.

Keywords: Turkish banking sector, profitability, efficiency, ROA, ROE

Introduction

According to the Cambridge dictionary, industrial efficiency is defined as "the ability of a manufacturer to produce a product at as low a cost as possible and still make a profit". From this point, it is seen that efficiency and profit are directly related to each other. So as a manufacturer, if your company's efficiency is better than your opponents', your company's profitability could be better than the others. As a manufacturer in a complex economic system, you try to reduce your costs to make a profit. For this reason, when you need to borrow money from a bank, you try to sing with the lowest interest rate bank credit. If you cannot find the credit on time, your company would easily find itself in a liquidity crisis.

Therefore, it can be easily understood that banks are one of the most important actors in this complex system. If you imagine economy as a human body, from all of the body parts, banks can be imagined as the heart of the body for pumping money from lenders to borrowers. If some problems occur in the banking system, all of the economy can be easily affected from this crisis just the same way as when human body has heart problems. For this reason, the banking sector must be powerful in an economic system.

Then, how can we have a powerful banking sector? Here is important to ask what we understand as a powerful banking sector. If you have a blocked artery that fails to carry blood to your heart, you will be under a high risk to have a heart attack. So there should be sufficient blood flow to prevent from heart attacks. Just as blood flows in our body, money flows in the economy. Thus, powerful economy and banking sector must not have money flow problems.

In many different times, local or global, many economies had crises. In Turkey, one of the most important economic crises happened in February 2001. Macroeconomic instability, high fiscal imbalances, high and volatile inflation, increased concerns about current account deficit, and liquidity problems were the most important reasons of that crisis. Most of the banks were funding Turkish Government, and the assets of the banks were filled with Turkish treasury bonds. With the increase of current account deficit, like everybody, banks demanded for more liquidity. Interest rates took place respectively 39 %, 95 %, and 183 % after September 2000. In this period, banks were trying to sidestep the harmful effects of inflation.

These macroeconomic and structural problems in the banking sector, with the negative discourse of politicians, turned into a systemic banking crisis. With the high economic and political uncertainty, interbank overnights rose to %6500, where the average was %4018. Turkish lira lost over 70 % of its value within a few days. The increase in interest rates deteriorated the money flow and financial statements of banks. By the deterioration of money flow, many banks and enterprises could not continue their trades and had to shut down.

After this crisis, the capital adequacy of the banks was discussed, and banking regulation and supervision agency implemented the Basel criterions. Basel criteria are focused on an effective system of banking supervision and capital requirements under Basel standards. Many countries have failed to meet the requirements of the first two Basel criteria but Turkey was forced to implement criteria with the IMF agreement. Reforms applied after February 2001 crisis, the political stability ensured after 2002, more efficient and independent supervision system, and unbalancing and preserving market stability led to the banking sector to have better assets quality, higher capital levels, high capital adequacy ratio, and strong financial statements. Thus, Turkey has become one of the most successful countries that has been applying the Basel criteria on banking system. As a result, in 2016, Turkish banks were declared as an "equivalent country" by the European Union Commission that confirmed the Turkish banking sector's full compatibility with Basel Standards (The Banks Association of Turkey, 2017).

Within this framework, our aim in this study is to examine the efficiency of Turkish Banking System and to reveal its relationship with profitability for the years between 2005Q1 and 2018Q2 on quarterly basis. In this context, we will review the literature in the following section. Then we will give information about the methodology and data. Finally, we will explain the empirical findings and conclude the chapter.

2 Literature

Deposits banks have a crucial role in the Turkish financial system since they have an intermediation function. Banks provide loans to the ones who have a fund deficit with the money they collect from the ones who have a fund surplus. Nowadays, individual and corporate investors, financial regulators, and policymakers all around the world have been concerned about how efficiently banks use their resources. Correspondingly, the number of researches has increased considerably, particularly since the beginning of the 2000s.

There are several methods in the literature to measure the efficiency. However, DEA is one of the most applied methods. It is a nonparametric technic based on mathematical programming and aims to measure the relative efficiency of one firm over another firm in the same sector. The method has been used for many sector analyses such as airline, transport, banking, healthcare, etc. Among those, there are significant numbers of studies examining the banking sector. Within this context, different types of efficiency analysis applying DEA were made for Turkish banking sector by Cingi and Tarım (2000), Isik and Hassan (2002), Çolak and Altan (2002), Behdioglu and Özcan (2009), Savaş (2009), Seyrek and Ata (2010), Akbalık and Sırma (2013), Kırer (2013), Yayar and Karaca (2014), Torun and Özdemir (2015), Bozdağ et al. (2016), Bayram (2016), Özel vd. (2017), and Öner ve Demirel Arıcı (2018).

Another important subject is the relationship between efficiency and profitability. Oral and Yolalan (1990) conducted a research to investigate the relationship between efficiency and profitability of bank branches and found that more profitability was related to more service efficiency for bank branches. Abbasoğlu et al. (2007) did not obtain a robust relationship between efficiency and profitability in Turkey for the postcrisis years from 2001 to 2005. However, Danışoğlu (2013) pointed out that the efficiency affected profitability of the banks in a positive direction in Turkey for the period between 1960 and 2009. Tazhenova (2013) and Palečková (2014) had also an unfavorable relationship, respectively, for Kazakhstan and Czech Republic. On the contrary, Priya and Velnampy (2013) pointed out a significant relationship for Sri Lanka.

3 Methodology and Data

There are three main efficiency measurement methods in the literature. The most basic method is ratio analysis that is the ratio of an output to an input. The other one is a parametric approach and includes Stochastic Frontier Approach (SFA), Distribution Free Approach (DFA), and Thick Front Approach (TFA). The main assumption of these approaches is that the ones with best performance in the observation set are on the efficiency frontier and the biased ones from the frontier are inefficient. Finally, nonparametric approaches consist of Free-Disposal Hull (FDH) and Data Envelopment Analysis (DEA). In fact, FDH is a special condition of DEA with fewer constraints. No random error is a general assumption for nonparametric approaches. In this chapter, we employ DEA.

DEA measures the relative efficiency of decision-making units (DMUs), which produces multiple outputs by using similar type of multiple inputs. It examines this relative efficiency in two steps. In this context, first DMUs that form the efficiency frontier are determined. After that, the stated frontier is accepted as a reference and efficiency scores are calculated by measuring the distance of nonefficient DMUs to this frontier. In this context, a basic DEA model can be expressed as follows:

$$E = Min\left(\sum_{i=1}^{m} v_i\right),$$

$$\sum_{r=1}^{p} u_r Y_{rk} = 1$$

$$\sum_{r=1}^{p} u_r Y_{rj} - \sum_{i=1}^{m} v_i X_{ij} \leq 0$$

$$u_r \geq \varepsilon,\ v_i \geq \varepsilon,\ j = 1,\ldots,n\ r = 1,\ldots,p\ i = 1,\ldots,m$$

In the linear programming model u_r indicates output; v_i input, X_{ik} observed amount of input of the ith type of kth DMU, Y_{rj} observed amount of output of the rth type of kth DMU, and ε positive small number.

Standard DEA models involve input- and output-oriented approaches under constant returns to scale (CRS) or variable returns to scale (VRS). Input-oriented approaches aim to produce the given output with minimum input, whereas output approaches focus on producing maximum output with given input. Standard DEA models are performed for cross-sectional data; however, Malmquist DEA Models are applied panel data (Coelli, 1996). In this study, we employ the Malmquist Productivity Index Models to analyze the Turkish banking sector efficiency.

MPI was first introduced by Sten Malmquist in 1953. The Malmquist Index examines the efficiency change between two time periods and separates the index into two, namely "catch-up effect" and "frontier-shift effect". The first one shows if the DMUs improve or worsen their efficiency, and the second one compares the efficiency between two periods. $\delta^2\left(\left(x_0, y_0\right)^2\right)$ and $\delta^1\left(\left(x_0, y_0\right)^1\right)$ show DMU_0 at the time period two and one, respectively. Then catch-up (C) and frontier-shift (F) effects and MPI are measured as following formulas:

$$C = \frac{\delta^2\left(\left(x_0, y_0\right)^2\right)}{\delta^1\left(\left(x_0, y_0\right)^1\right)}$$

$$F = \left[\frac{\delta^1\left(\left(x_0, y_0\right)^1\right)}{\delta^2\left(\left(x_0, y_0\right)^1\right.} \times \frac{\delta^1\left(\left(x_0, y_0\right)^2\right)}{\delta^2\left(\left(x_0, y_0\right)^2\right.}\right]^{\frac{1}{2}}$$

$$MPI = C \times F$$

These formulas have three kinds of information. If the C is greater than 1, there is a progress in relative efficiency from period one to two, while equal to 1 and less than 1 indicate no change and regress in efficiency. If the F is greater than 1, this shows progress in the frontier technology around DMU_0 from period one to two, while equal to 1 and less than 1 show the status quo and regress in the frontier technology. And finally if MI is greater than 1, this indicates a progress in the total factor productivity, whereas equal to 1 and less than 1 reveal, respectively, status quo and deterioration in the total factor productivity (Cooper et al., 2007: 329, 330, 331).

In this chapter, we analyze the efficiency of the Turkish banking sector by running Input-Oriented Malmquist DEA Model under Variable Returns Scale for the period between 2005–1 and 2018–2 on a quarterly basis. To calculate the efficiency scores, we use the DEA-Solver_PRO software.

The financial statements in Turkey were prepared according to Inflation Accounting System (Serial XI, No: 20) until the end of 2004. Since then International Financial Reporting Standards (Serial XI, No: 25) have been started to be applied. Because of this reason we choose the year 2015 as starting year of our analysis.

The selection of the variables is one of the most crucial steps in DEA. However, there is not a consensus in the literature regarding this issue. Yet there are two mostly used approaches for the banking sector analysis, namely "production approach" (PA) and "intermediation approach" (IA). PA considers banks as firms that use capital and labor to produce different types of deposits and loans, while IA sees banks as intermediate funds between depositors and borrowers, and interprets deposits as inputs (Boďa and Zimková, 2015:436). To model the bank behavior, IA is more preferable than PA in the banking sector (Elyesiani and Mehdian, 1990:543), and we determine our variables in that vein. Accordingly, we use total assets, total deposits, number of employees, and number of branches as input measures; while total loans and net interest income as output measures to evaluate the efficiency. To analyze the Turkish banking sector, we include the biggest twenty banks in the second quarter of 2018 in terms of their size of assets that represents 95 % of total assets. We also exclude the banks with negative interest income.

As profitability indicators, we use ROA and ROE that are formulized, respectively: $\frac{Net\ Profit}{Total\ Assets}$ and $\frac{Net\ Profit}{Total\ Equity}$. We gather all the data from the web page of the Banks Association of Turkey.

4 Empirical Results

DEA-Solver software results show Malmquist Indices separately respect to the time period pairs: 2005Q1->2005Q2, 2005Q2->2005Q3, and so on for time interval 1, or 2005Q1->2018Q2 for time interval 53. In this context, we have 53 different analyses regarding time interval from 1 to 53.

Tab. 7.1 shows the three indices for the time interval 53 as evaluated by the Malmquist I-V Model. According to these estimations, the analyzed banks display on average a progress in relative efficiency, in the frontier technology, and in total factor productivity from period 2005Q1 to 2018Q2.

When each quarter for all the banks is analyzed, in general total factor productivity increases in the first quarter of the years and decreases in the last quarter of the years. Fig. 7.1 shows the average Malmquist Indices of each year by quarters and Q_i, i=1,2,3,4 indicates each quarter of the year. As it is seen in the figure, banks have a progress in their total factor productivity except in last quarters. Only in 2007 first quarter's average index sharply rises because of the two small-scale banks namely Bank Mellat and Arap Türk Bankası A.Ş.

In Turkey, banks are grouped under four categories. These are state-owned deposit banks, privately owned deposit banks, banks under the Savings Deposit Insurance Fund (TMSF/SDIF), and foreign banks that are divided in two as the ones founded in Turkey and the ones having branches in Turkey (See Appendix

Tab. 7.1: Efficiency Scores for Time Interval 53

2005Q1=>2018Q2	**Catch-up**	**Frontier**	**Malmquist**
Türkiye Cumhuriyeti Ziraat Bankası A.Ş.	2.466	0.649	1.599
Türkiye İş Bankası A.Ş.	1.014	1.007	1.022
Türkiye Garanti Bankası A.Ş.	0.899	1.076	0.968
Akbank T.A.Ş.	1.040	0.988	1.027
Yapı ve Kredi Bankası A.Ş.	1.002	1.009	1.011
Türkiye Halk Bankası A.Ş.	1.290	0.889	1.147
Türkiye Vakıflar Bankası T.A.O.	2.136	0.697	1.488
Finans Bank A.Ş.	0.839	1.196	1.003
Türk Ekonomi Bankası A.Ş.	0.775	1.313	1.018
Denizbank A.Ş.	1.099	1.045	1.148

Tab. 7.2: (Continued)

2005Q1=>2018Q2	**Catch-up**	**Frontier**	**Malmquist**
HSBC Bank A.Ş.	0.789	1.814	1.431
ING Bank A.Ş.	1.551	1.060	1.644
Şekerbank T.A.Ş.	1.422	1.281	1.822
Citibank A.Ş.	3.300	1.405	4.636
Alternatif Bank A.Ş.	1.123	1.647	1.849
Anadolubank A.Ş.	1.531	1.655	2.534
Burgan Bank A.Ş.	2.978	0.274	0.816
Bank Mellat	1.156	0.597	0.690
ICBC Turkey Bank A.Ş.	1.253	2.045	2.563
Arap Türk Bankası A.Ş.	0.693	0.765	0.530
Average	**1.418**	**1.121**	**1.497**

Source: Authors' own calculations

A). Fig. 7.2 shows that state-owned banks have higher efficiency scores until 2008. However, since then the scenario changes in favor of the foreign and private banks. The main reason of this situation could be related to decreasing interest rates. Up to this period, private and foreign banks were funding public treasury with high interest rates. Hence there was no motivation to be efficient. However, decreasing interest rates urged foreign and private banks to hold concern about efficiency more than the state-owned banks. Although there has been more concern about efficiency, the achievement has been decreasing in the recent years.

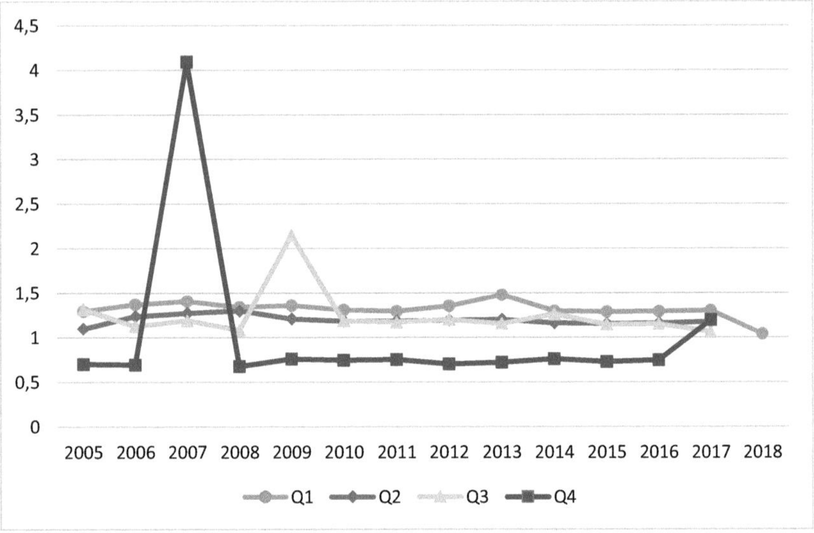

Fig. 7.1: Average Malmquist Indices. Source: Authors' own calculations

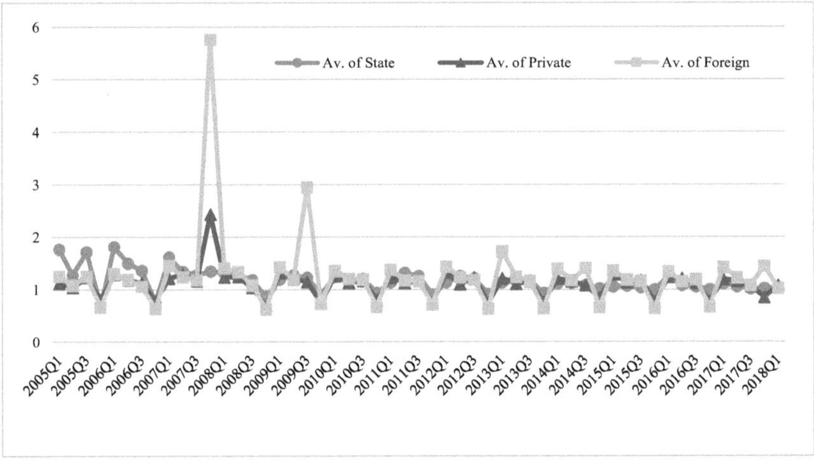

Fig. 7.2: Malmquist Indices by the Shareholder Structure. Source: Authors' own calculation

Tab. 7.3: Pearson Correlation Test Results

	MIQ1	roaq1	roeq1		MIQ2	roaq2	roeq2
MIQ1	1			**MIQ2**	1		
roaq1	0.16	1		**roaq2**	0.388	1	
roeq1	0.05	0.96	1	**roeq2**	0.534	0.962	1
	MIQ3	**roaq3**	**roeq3**		**MIQ4**	**roaq4**	**roeq4**
MIQ3	1			**MIQ4**	1		
roaq3	0.406	1		**roaq4**	0.497	1	
roeq3	0.254	0.942	1	**roeq4**	0.515	0.881	1

Source: Authors' own calculations

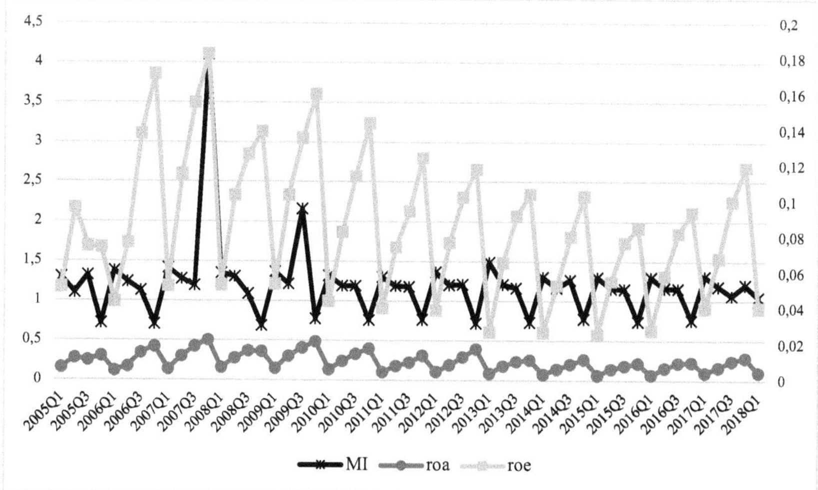

Fig. 7.3: Efficiency and Profitability Scores of the Turkish Banking System.
Source: Authors' own calculations

To see the relationship between profitability indicators and MI, we employ Pearson Correlation Test. Tab. 7.2 shows the results for each quarter. In the last quarters of the year, we see a moderate positive linear relationship between efficiency and profitability. In the first quarter, the relationship is quite weak.

Graphs have an important function to visualize and develop the trends in a series. In this regard, Fig. 7.3 illustrates the average Malmquist Indices and average profitability scores of the sample data. In the figure MIs are depicted according to primary axis, while ROA and ROE are plotted according to secondary axis. As it is seen in the figure, both ROE and ROA constantly declined until 2016. This situation could be explained by the decreases of interest rates. However, increasing economic uncertainty in Turkey after 2016 caused a rise in risk premium or Credit Default Swap (CDS), etc. Therefore, interest rates started to increase once again, and this change affected positively both ROA and ROE. Fig. 7.3 also displays efficiency decreases in the last quarters. The reason of this low efficiency could be the result of the low increase rate of ROE and ROA.

Conclusion

The aim of this study is to investigate how efficiently Turkish banks are operated and to discover if there is a relationship between banks' efficiency and profitability. For this purpose first of all we employ the Malmquist DEA model to calculate the efficiency scores. When the analysis is made according to the time interval 53, the Turkish Banking Sector shows a progress in relative efficiency, in the frontier technology, and in total factor productivity from first quarter of the year 2005 to the second quarter of the year 2018. The regulations, which were implemented after two severe banking crises in 2000 and 2001 in Turkey, compelled the banking system for taking some substantial steps.

The positive effects of these regulations are still perceived in Turkish financial system, although there is a relative decline in efficiency in recent years.

The method allows seeing the efficiency in each quarter for every bank. Accordingly, our empirical findings show that banks in Turkey have relatively higher efficiency scores in the first three quarters of the year but not in the last quarters. The Malmquist Index scores are less than one in the last quarters, which indicates deterioration in the total factor productivity. This could be the result of the low increase rate of ROE and ROA.

At this point, we focus on if the terms efficiency and profitability are related. We all know that although they seem to be related, those two terms are pretty different from each other. Profitability displays how much profit a bank is generating, while efficiency scores show that how efficiently a bank uses its resources to make profit. In this context, to see relationship we employ the Pearson Correlation Test and run the test for three variables, which are MI, ROA, and ROE. According to the results, it is hard to talk about a robust relationship between MI and both ROA and ROE. As it is expected ROA and ROE are strongly correlated. Nevertheless, results give a moderate relationship between MI and profitability indicators for the last periods.

We also examine the efficiency according to bank's shareholders structure. Therefore, banks are grouped under four categories in Turkey: state-owned deposit banks, privately owned deposit banks, banks under the Savings Deposit Insurance Fund (TMSF/SDIF), and foreign banks that are divided in two as the ones founded in Turkey and the ones having branches in Turkey. Our findings indicate that state-owned banks have higher efficiency scores until 2008, and lower efficiency scores after this period. We believe that decreasing interest rates urged foreign and private banks to be concerned about efficiency more than the state-owned banks. Although there has been more concern about efficiency, the achievement has been decreasing in the recent years. This situation requires banks to take precautions for diminishing efficiency.

References

Abbasoğlu, O.F., Aysan, A. F. & Gunes, A. (2007). Concentration, Competition, Efficiency and Profitability of the Turkish Banking Sector in the Post-crises Period. Retrieved from http://mpra.ub.uni-muenchen.de/5494/mpra

Akbalik & Sırma (2013). Türkiye'de yabancı bankaların etkinliği, veri zarflama analizi uygulaması, *Finansal Araştırmalar Ve Çalışmalar Dergisi*, 4(8), 1–16.

Bayram N. (2016). Veri zarflama analizi ve toplam faktör verimliliği: aracı kurumlar üzerine bir uygulama, *Verimlilik Dergisi*, 2, 7–44.

Behdioğlu S. & Özcan G. (2009). Veri zarflama analizi ve bankacılık sektöründe bir uygulama, *Süleyman Demirel Üniversitesi I.I.B.F. Dergisi*, 14(3), 301–326.

Boďa, M. & Zimková, E. (2015). Efficiency in the Slovak banking industry: a comparison of three approaches, *Prague Economic Papers*, 24(04), 434–451.

Bozdağ E. G., Altan M. S. & Bozdağ A.E. (2016). Bankacılık sisteminde etkinlik ve verimlilik (veri zarflama analizi ile bir uygulama), Aksaray Üniversitesi I.I.B.F. Dergisi, 2(1), 33–47.

Cingi S. & Tarim A. (2000). Türk Banka Sisteminde Performans Ölçümü Dea-Malmquist TFP Endeksi Uygulaması, *Türkiye Bankalar Birliği, Araştırma Tebliğleri Serisi*, 1, 1–34.

Coelli, T. (1996). *A Guide to Deap Version 2.1: Data Envelopment Analysis (Computer) Program* (Cepa Working Papers, No. 8/96, ISBN:1 86389 4969). Retrieved from https://www.researchgate.net/profile/Lall_Ramrattan/post/Data_envelope_analysis/attachment/59d6486f79197b80779a31a3/AS%3A466830453153794%401488312461596/download/Deap.pdf (17.02.2019)

Çolak Ö. F. & Altan, Ş. (2002). Toplam etkinlik ölçümü: Türkiye'deki özel ve kamu bankaları için bir uygulama, *Iktisat Işletme ve Finans Dergisi*, 17(196), 45–55.

Cooper, W. W., Seiford, L. M., & Tone, K. (2007). *Data Envelopment Analysis: A Comprehensive Text with Models, Applications, References and Dea-Solver Software*, Second Edition, USA: Springer.

Danişoğlu, S. (2013). An Analysis Of Efficiency And Profitability In The Turkish Banking System. Retrieved from http://www.aidea2013.It/docs/368_aidea2013_banking-and-finance.pdf. (Access Date: 10.01.2019)

Elyasiani E. & Mehdian S. (1990). Efficiency in the commercial banking industry, a production frontier approach, *Applied Economics*, 22(4), 539–551. doi: 10.1080/00036849000000010

Isik, I. & Hassan, M. K. (2002). Technical, scale and allocative efficiencies of Turkish banking industry, *Journal of Banking & Finance*, 26(4), 719–766. Retrieved from https://doi.org/10.1016/S0378-4266(01)00167-4.(Access Date: 02.02.2019)

Kirer, H. (2013). Malmquist indices of productivity change in Turkish banking sector for the period between 2002–2011, *Journal of Social Policy Conferences*, 64–65(1–2), 75–86.

Oral, M. & Yolalan, R. (1990). An empirical study on measuring operating efficiency and profitability of bank branches, *European Journal of Operational Research*, 46(3), 282–294, Issn 0377–2217. Retrieved from https://doi.org/10.1016/0377-2217(90)90002-S. .(Access Date: 02.02.2019)

Öner, M. & Demirel Arici, N. (2018). Türk bankacılık sektörünün etkinlik ve verimlilik analizi: 2012–2017 VZA ve malmquist TFV endeksi uygulaması, *Bankacılar Dergisi*, 106, 18–36.

Özel, N. G., Şahin, I.E. & Göral, R. (2017). Türk Bankacilik Sektöründe Etkinlik Ve Verimlilik Analizinin Veri Zarflama Yöntemi Ile Incelenmesi: 2013–2015 Dönemi Uygulamasi, *Sosyal Ekonomik Araştırmalar Dergisi (The Journal of Social Economic Research)*, 17(30th year special edition), 85–100

Palečková, I. (2014). Relationship between Profitability and Efficiency in the Czech Banking Sector. Retrieved from http://icfb.rs.opf.slu.cz/sites/icfb.rs.opf.slu.cz/files/paleckova.pdf.(Access Date: 03.02.2019)

Priya, K. & Velnampy, T. (2013). Efficiency and profitability: a case study of banking sector in Sri Lanka, *Global Journal of Management and Business Research Accounting and Auditing*, 13(5). Retrieved from https://globaljournals.org/gjmbr_volume13/6-efficiency-and-profitability-a-case.pdf .(Access Date: 11.01.2019)

Savaş, F., (2009). *Veri zarflama analizi ve bankacılık sektöründe etkinlik ölçümü uygulaması* (Master's Thesis, Yıldız Teknik Üniversitesi Sosyal Bilimler Enstitüsü).

Seyrek, I. & Ata, H. A. (2010). Veri zarflama analizi ve veri madenciliği ile mevduat bankalarında etkinlik ölçümü, *BDDK Bankacılık ve Finansal Piyasalar*, 4(2),

67–84. Retrieved from https://core.ac.uk/download/pdf/6603197.pdf.(Access Date: 15.03.2019)

Tazhenova, M. (2013). *Evaluating profitability and efficiency of bank performance: The case of Kazakhstan banks* (Master Of Science Dissertation, Eastern Mediterranean University). Retrieved from http://i-rep.emu.edu.tr:8080/xmlui/bitstream/handle/11129/1478/tazhenova.pdf?sequence=1. (Access Date: 18.03.2019)

The Banks Association of Turkey. Retrieved from https://www.tbb.org.tr/en/banks-and-banking-sector-information/statistical-reports/20

The Banks Association of Turkey (2017). *Banks in Turkey 2016*, Retrieved from https://www.tbb.org.tr/en/content/upload/dokuman/150/banks_in_turkey_2016.pdf

Torun, N. K. & Özdemir, A. (2015). Türk bankacılık sektörünün 2008 küresel finansal krizi sürecinde veri zarflama analizi ile etkinlik analizi, *Selçuk Üniversitesi Sosyal Bilimler Enstitüsü Dergisi*, 33, 129–142.

Yayar R. & Karaca S. (2014). Efficiency analysis in Turkish banking sector, *Niğde Üniversitesi İİBF Dergisi*, 7(2), 1–15.

Appendix A. Bank List

Deposit Banks

State-owned Banks

Türkiye Cumhuriyeti Ziraat Bankası A.Ş.
Türkiye Halk Bankası A.Ş.
Türkiye Vakıflar Bankası T.A.O.

Privately-owned Banks

Adabank A.Ş.
Akbank T.A.Ş.
Anadolubank A.Ş.
Fibabanka A.Ş.
Şekerbank T.A.Ş.
Turkish Bank A.Ş.
Türk Ekonomi Bankası A.Ş.
Türkiye İş Bankası A.Ş.
Yapı ve Kredi Bankası A.Ş.

Banks Under the Deposit Insurance Fund

Birleşik Fon Bankası A.Ş.

Foreign Banks

Foreign Banks Founded in Turkey

Alternatifbank A.Ş.
Arap Türk Bankası A.Ş.
Bank of China Turkey A.Ş.
Burgan Bank A.Ş.
Citibank A.Ş.
Denizbank A.Ş.
Deutsche Bank A.Ş.
HSBC Bank A.Ş.
ICBC Turkey Bank A.Ş.
ING Bank A.Ş.
MUFG Bank Turkey A.Ş.
Odea Bank A.Ş.
QNB Finansbank A.Ş.
Rabobank A.Ş.

Deposit Banks	
	Turkland Bank A.Ş.
	Türkiye Garanti Bankası A.Ş.
	Foreign Banks Having Branches in Turkey
	Bank Mellat
	Habib Bank Limited
	Intesa Sanpaolo S.p.A.
	JPMorgan Chase Bank N.A.
	Société Générale (SA)

Source: The Banks Association of Turkey, https://www.tbb.org.tr/en/modules/banka-bilgileri/banka_Listesi.asp?tarih=17/2/2019

Ömer Faruk Rençber

8 A Research on the Factors Affecting Profitability in Banks with Ridge Regression Analysis

Highlights: This chapter aims to investigate the factors affecting the profitability of banks by using ridge regression (RR) analysis. Linear regression analysis is a method that is used as an alternative to linear or panel regression analysis in multiple linear connections and is a biased estimation tool. The study covers 27 banks with public, private, and foreign capital operating in Turkey and the period after 2008. In the study, CAMELS ratios which are frequently used in evaluating the performance of banks are taken into consideration. Accordingly, capital adequacy, asset quality, quality of management, liquidity and sensitivity to capital risk, and profitability ratios [ROA, equity profitability ratio (ROE), ratio of pre-tax profit to total assets (PBCO/TA), and ratio of total income to total expense (TI/TE)] were taken as dependent variables. In this study, four regression models were developed according to each rate of return. As a result of the study, it has been concluded that the amount of nonperforming loans has a significant effect on all profitability ratios of interest income, other operating expenses, and net profit per branch.

Keywords: Banks, profitability, ridge regression analysis, ROA, ROE

Introduction

The position and importance of the banking sector in the financial system are significant. Banks are financial institutions that bring together those in need of funds and those in excess of funds. Banks directly contribute to employment in the country, as well as functions such as fund transfers, services, and economic and fiscal policies (Yazıcı, 2016: 85). The proper functioning of the banking system is closely related to everyone in the economic system (Erdoğan, 2018: 22).

According to September 2017 data in the Turkish banking system, there are 51 banks, of which 33 are deposits, 13 are development and investment, and 5 are participation banks. According to a report published by the Banks Association in 2017 comparing 13 countries, the profitability of the banking sector in Turkey is low. The Turkish banking sector has the lowest return difference after the Russian capital between the return on equity (ROE) and government borrowing paper returns (BAT, 2018: 5).

The profitability of banks can be measured by factors such as asset profitability, net interest margin, equity margin, wages and commissions, quality of loans, and control of costs. The profitability indicator is an important factor in assessing the market situation of a bank in terms of establishing resources from national and international markets and competing with its competitors (Staikours et al., 2004).

In this study, it was aimed to investigate the factors affecting the profitability of banks by using the ridge regression method. Banks are evaluated according to the performance criteria expressed as CAMELS. In this study, E:profitability ratios (asset profitability, equity capital profitability, ratio of net before interest to total assets, and ratio of total income to total expenditure) are dependent variables; C: capital adequacy, A: asset quality, M: Management Quality, L: liquidity; and S: Market Risk rates are independent variables.

In the literature, in some studies on the profitability of banks, the methods they use and the variables they use are as in Tab. 8.1.

As seen in Tab. 8.1, there are many studies examining the profitability of banks. However, these are similar because of the financial ratios and methods they use. However, the data set for variables is obtained by ratio analysis and has a high-level relationship with each other. This results in a problem called a multilinear connection problem. In similar studies, researchers have taken different variables from each other or have solved this problem by making transformations. In this study, unlike the studies in the literature, ridge regression analysis which is the biased estimator of the regression analysis, which is calculated according to the linear least squares method, is applied. Therefore, it aims to show the applicability of the method in this field as well as to evaluate the factors affecting the profitability of the banks.

The study covers 27 banks with public, private, and foreign capital operating in Turkey and the post-2008 period. Accordingly, the method was first theoretically studied and then the variables were briefly introduced. Then, the results obtained from the regression analysis according to four different dependent variables were examined and compared.

2 Method: Ridge Regression Analysis

Regression analysis is a type of analysis that explores the causal relationship between continuous dependent variables and independent variables that are not related to each other. If independent variables are associated with each other, a problem called a multiple linear connections or a multiple linear connection

Tab. 8.1: Some Studies Examining the Profitability of Banks in the Literature

Author (Year)	**Year and Country Covered by the Study**	**Variables Used**	**Method**
Sufian (2009)	2000–2007; China	ROA, ROE, Net Interest Margin, Loans/ Total Asset, Total Assets (ln), Loan Loss/ Total Loans, Non-interest Income/Total Assets, Inflation, GDP (ln)	Panel Data Analysis
Yılmaz (2013)	2005–2010; Brazil, Czech Republic, Hungary, Malaysia, Mexico, Poland, South Africa, Taiwan, and Turkey	ROA, ROE, Interest Margin, Liquidity, Capital Adequacy, Expenses Management, Bank Size	Panel Data Analysis
Albulescu (2015)	2005–2013; Six South and Middle USA Countries (Chile, Colombia, El Salvador, Honduras, Mexico, and Paraguay)	ROA, ROE, Nonperforming Loans to Total Gross Loans, Regulatory Capital to Risk-Weighted Assets, Liquid Assets to Total Assets, Non-interest Expenses to Gross Income, Interest Margin to Gross Income	Panel Data Analysis
Reis, Kılıç and Buğan (2016)	2009–2013; Türkiye	İçsel (Profitability of Assets, Net Interest Margin, Leverage Ratio, Liquidity Ratio, Ratio of Operation Expenses and Loan Deposit Rate) External (Inflation, GDP, Market Capitalization)	Panel Data Analysis
Knezevic and Dobromirov (2016)	2004–2011; Sırbistan	ROA, Size of Bank, Cost to İncome Ratio, Capitalization of a Bank, Liquidity, Market Concentration, Total Assets of Commercial Bank Divided by GDP, Market Capitalization to Total Assets, Annual Inflation Rate, GDP	Panel Data Analysis
Basarır and Sarıhan (2017)	1989–2015; Turkey	Total Credits/Total Assets, Non-performing Loans/Total Credits, ROA, GDPG, Inflation	Panel Data Analysis (ARDL)
Taş and Duramaz (2018)	2006–2016; Türkiye	ROA, ROE, Capital Adequacy Ratio, Total Deposits/Total Assets, Equity/Total Assets, Nonperforming Loans/Total Loans and Receivables, Net Interest Income after Specific Provisions/Total Assets, Non-interest Income/Total Assets, Growth Rate, Inflation	Panel Data Analysis

(*continued on next page*)

Appendix (continued)

Author (Year)	Year and Country Covered by the Study	Variables Used	Method
Hasanov, Bayramli, Musehel (2018)	2012–2017; Azerbaycan	ROA, Capital, Size, Loans, Deposits, Cyclical Non-oil GDP, Cyclical Total GDP, Inflation Expectation, Change in Exchange Rate, TL/USD Exchange Rate	Dynamic Panel Data Analysis
Almaqtari, Homaidi, Tabash and Farhan (2019)	2008–2017; India	Gross Domestic Product, Inflation Rate, Interest Rate, Exchange Rate, Financial Crisis, and Demonetization	Panel Data Analysis

occurs. Therefore, it is not possible to create a lower false regression model according to the linear least squares method (Charnes et al., 1986).

In literature, the RR method is often used in the case of multiple linear connection problems. Some of the areas of application are: cargo transportation demand estimation (Çekerol and Nalchakan, 2011), airport non-aviation income analysis (Fasone vd, 2016), corporate failure estimation (Pereira VD, 2016). The multiple linear connection problem is the case where independent variables used in the analysis are highly correlated with each other. This is an assumption that the least squares method (LS) should be checked before the analysis is started in the applications of linear regression analysis (Albayrak, 2005: 119).

The sign of partial regression coefficients in a multiple linear connections may be different from the theory and from what is expected. According to the RR technique, it is aimed to minimize linear errors by adding a small bias constant to the estimates. In general, except for adding a small k constant to the diagonal values of the variance-covariance matrix, the operation of RR and LS techniques is the same. Accordingly, on the one hand, the variance of the estimates is reduced with RR, and on the other hand, biased estimates are made with the k ratio (Albayrak, 2005:119). As an example, the mathematical representation of an LS regression model that contains a dependent and an independent variable is as follows:

$$y = \beta x + \varepsilon \quad (1)$$

Here, y is the dependent variable, x is the independent variable, β is the regression coefficients of the independent variable, and $\varepsilon$is the error term. Here, the β coefficient is calculated as follows:

$$\beta = (x\prime x)^{-1} x\prime y \tag{2}$$

According to the LS method, the expected value of the estimates is equal to the value of the principal mass, so the estimates are non-biased. Accordingly, since the variables are standardized, it is$x\prime x = R$the number R indicates the correlation coefficient of the model obtained by taking each x variable as dependent and the other independent. As this value approaches 1, there is a multiple linear connection problem. The regression coefficients of the multiple linear linkages increase the variance and covariance, and although the R2 of the model is high, t test is not significant for most of the independent variables (Bager et al., 2017).

In the model, if the VIF value is above 10, the correlation coefficient between the independent variables is above 0.8, or the condition index number is above 30, the multiple linear connection problem is mentioned. Although RR analysis is a biased method, it is a method that aims to minimize the effects of independent variables on each other for estimation of regression coefficients and to obtain stable coefficient estimates (Çekerol and Nalçakan, 2011). Accordingly, the standardized partial correlation values by adding a small constant to the diagonal of the matrix bias of the regression coefficients are calculated as follows:

$$\beta = (x\prime x + kI)^{-1} x\prime y \tag{3}$$

Where k parameter is 0, the method is the classical linear regression analysis. However, this value is a positive number less than 1, and there is no specific calculation method. Usually, the regression model is generated by giving random values between 0 and 1 for the k parameter. Accordingly, the k parameter can be determined according to the value of R^2 or β numbers. In the literature, it is generally observed that the k parameter is taken as a value below 0.3 (Pereira et al., 2016).

3 Variables Used in the Study

This study aims to examine the factors affecting the profitability of the banks operating in Turkey by using the RR method. Therefore, CAMELS rates were taken into consideration and E: Earnings were taken as dependent variables. At this point, as an indicator of profitability in banks, profitability, equity, profit before tax, and total income/total expenses are used. In this study, four different RR analyses were applied and four regression models were developed. However, other CAMLS ratios (C: Capital adequate, A: Asset quality, M: Management quality, L: Liquidity, S: Sensitivity to market risk) were considered as independent variables. The dependent and independent variables used in the study and their short definitions are presented in Tab. 8.2.

Tab. 8.2: Dependent and Independent Variables Used in the Study

Type	Abbreviation	Variable Name	Short Description
Dependent Variables	**ROA**	Asset Profitability Ratio	It measures whether or not the bank's gains and assets are used effectively as a result of the investment in its assets.
	ROE	Return on Equity	This ratio, which shows the earnings obtained by the bank's shareholders in return for the capital they put in the bank, is expressed as a return on equity.
	PBCO/TA	Profit Before Continuing Operations/ Total Assets	It shows the sectoral profitability in general. In other words, it is an indicator of how much profit an enterprise does without the cost of foreign resources.
	TI/TE	Total Income/ Total Expenses	This is an indicator of the income and expense balance. It is also considered as a profitability ratio.
Independent Variables	**CA_1**	Capital Adequacy Ratio	This is calculated by the ratio of banks' own resources to the credit, market, and operational risk amounts. It is a ratio that measures capital adequacy in general.
	CA_2	Equity/Total Assets	This is the rate at which a percentage of the bank's assets is financed by its own resources. In particular, banks that use loans want this ratio to be high in order to avoid a problem in collecting their receivables.
Independent Variables	**AQ_1**	Nonperforming Loans (gross)/ Total Loans and Receivables	There is a high risk of non-payment of a nonperforming loan. High share of nonperforming loans and total loans and receivables in banks is negative for banks.
	AQ_2	Total Loans and Receivables/ Total Assets	This indicates the ratio of the loans and receivables given by the banks in the total assets. Although this rate is not expected to fall below 50 %, it can be said that the banks have not fulfilled their primary lending obligations, if they fall.
	AQ_3	Total Loans and Receivables/ Total Deposits	This indicates the ratio of loans and receivables given by banks to total deposits.

Tab. 8.2: (continued)

Type	Abbreviation	Variable Name	Short Description
	AQ_4	Fixed Assets/ Total Assets	This is the percentage of what percentage of the bank's assets depend on fixed assets.
	MQ_1	Nonperforming Loans (gross)/ Total Loans and Receivables	This may be considered as an indicator of risk management in the share of nonperforming loans in total loans and receivables. It is desirable to be low.
	MQ_2	Net Profit Per Branch	This is a branch-based profit measurement and is a ratio of administrative quality.
	MQ_3	Other Operating Expenses/Total Assets	This is the rate of operating expense in total assets. It is desirable to be low.
	LQ_1	Liquid Assets/ Total Assets	This is the rate at which the bank's resources are invested in liquid assets.
	LQ_2	YP Liquid Assets/YP Passive	This ratio should be 80 % and above. This is the rate that indicates that the foreign currency assets of the banks should have sufficient or insufficient liquidity to meet their foreign currency liabilities.
	LQ_3	Liquid Assets/ Short-Term Liabilities	Short-term liabilities include the short-term loans received by banks from banks in Turkey and abroad, as well as the debt to money markets.
	SMR_1	YP Assets/YP Liabilities	This is an indication of the foreign exchange position for the banks. The low rate is a positive situation.
	SMR_2	Interest Income/ Total Assets	It is desirable to be high.
	SMR_3	Balance Sheet Foreign Currency Position/Equity	Its low rate is considered a positive situation.

Source: Erdogan (2018)

The good or bad profitability of a bank is a sign of its financial strength. The success of banks in profitability is closely related to their capital adequacy. Because a bank must maintain its capital at the necessary level in order to maintain its activities and obtain the necessary profit. A bank with a high profit expectancy should have a strong capital structure. Capital adequacy refers to the need to have adequate resources against losses due to the risks that banks face. Asset quality is a component that shows the financial stability of a bank and the risks it carries. In general, the corporate governance of banks is an important issue in terms of their activity and financial stability. Therefore, management quality has a significant impact on the profitability of banks. Liquidity ratios are ratios that show how much of the short-term debt payment power and resources are kept in cash. Changes in market prices, exchange rates, interest rates, or stock prices are evaluated to affect the financial position of the banks or the existing capital levels (Erdoğan, 2018).

4 Application

4.1 Purpose and Scope of the Study

This study aims to investigate the factors affecting the profitability of banks by using the RR method. Profitability (ROA), return on equity (ROE), pre-tax profit (PBCO), and total income/total expense (TI/TE) ratios as an indicator of banks' profitability are dependent variables; the other 15 ratios given in Tab. 8.3 are taken as independent variables.

In the study, 2008 period were examined post-financial crisis era, located in the capital of Turkey and showing active operations, 27 banks listed in Tab. 8.3 constitute the scope of the study.

As can be seen in Tab. 8.3, public, private, and foreign-owned banks are all included in the scope of the study. State-owned banks are banks that consist of all or more than half of the state-owned, government-elected representatives of government. Banks with private capital are banks owned by resident real and legal persons in the country other than the public institutions and institutions of more than half of their capital. Banks with foreign capital are banks belonging to real persons and legal entities whose capital is abroad. The descriptive statistics for the data set of the study are as follows:

As can be seen in Tab. 8.4, the data of the variables contain extreme values and follow an image away from the normal distribution. However, the variables in the table are obtained by calculating the same financial ratios with four transactions. For example, the ratio coded MQ_1 is calculated by dividing the total loans and receivables with nonperforming loans while the ratio of AQ_1 is calculated by

Tab. 8.3: Banks within the Scope of Work

	Depositary Banks with Public Capital		Depositary Banks with Foreign Capital
1	Ziraat Bank	13	Alternative bank
2	Halkbank of Turkey	14	Arab Turkish Bank Inc.
3	Vakifbank of Turkey T.A.O	15	Burgan Bank Inc.
	Depositary Banks with Private Capital	16	Citibank Inc.
4	Adabank Inc.	17	Denizbank Inc.
5	Akbank Inc.	18	Deutsche Bank Inc.
6	Anadolubank Inc.	19	HSBC Bank Inc.
7	Fibabanka Inc.	20	ICBC Turkey Inc.
8	Şekerbank Inc.	21	ING Bank Inc.
9	Turkish Bank Inc.	22	MUFG Bank Turkey Inc.
10	Turkish Economy Bank Inc.	23	Odea Bank Inc.
11	Turkiye İş Bankası Inc.	24	QNB Finansbank Inc.
12	Yapı ve Kredi Bankası Inc.	25	Rabobank Inc.
		26	Turkland Bank Inc.
		27	Turkiye Garanti Bankası Inc.

dividing the total amount of loans and receivables by nonperforming loans. In this case, there is a high correlation between independent variables, in other words, multiple linear connection problems.

As a result of the analysis, it was observed that the correlation coefficient between some variables was above 0.8 and that some of the VI values were above 10, and the condition index number was between 1 and 350. It is expected that the VIF value will be below 10 and Condition Index value will be below 30 for all dimensions in order to avoid multiple linear connection problems between the independent variables (Albayrak, 2005: 111). Due to the fact that assumptions cannot be obtained for all these reasons, the application of linear or panel regression analyses is considered as a statistical error. Therefore, in this study, RR analysis, which is a biased estimator of linear regression, was applied. In this phase, the regression coefficients were analyzed with different values between 0 and 1 for the determination of k constant and the regression coefficients after the k=0,2 point were stagnated for the four regression analyses. For this reason, regression coefficients were calculated accordingly, considering that the k constant should be taken as 0.2 in the analyses.

Tab. 8.4: Descriptive Statistics

CA_1		**CA_2**		**AQ_1**		**AQ_2**		**AQ_3**	
Maximum	595,37	Maximum	89,72	Maximum	19,26	Maximum	84,72	Maximum	646.933,91
Minimum	12,19	Minimum	4,20	Minimum	0,00	Minimum	1,87	Minimum	9,42
Mean	21,96	Mean	13,64	Mean	3,64	Mean	58,79	Mean	3.362,29
S. Deviation	41,55	S. Deviation	10,10	S. Deviation	2,61	S. Deviation	14,90	S. Deviation	41.749,01
VIF	*3,67*	*VIF*	*6,55*	*VIF*	*3,98*	*VIF*	*16,22*	*VIF*	*15,4*
AQ_ 4		**MQ_1**		**MQ_2**		**MQ_3**		**LQ_1**	
Maximum	19,96	Maximum	6,82	Maximum	105,70	Maximum	9,14	Maximum	91,30
Minimum	0,18	Minimum	0,00	Minimum	0,00	Minimum	0,66	Minimum	8,59
Mean	3,16	Mean	1,05	Mean	5,68	Mean	3,01	Mean	32,06
S. Deviation	1,98	S. Deviation	0,99	S. Deviation	15,19	S. Deviation	1,22	S. Deviation	14,90
VIF	*11,74*	*VIF*	*3,63*	*VIF*	*18,59*	*VIF*	*12,1*	*VIF*	*10,2*
LQ_ 2		**LQ_ 3**		**SMR_1**		**SMR_2**		**SMR_3**	
Maximum	90,79	Maximum	43.449,68	Maximum	156,73	Maximum	23,24	Maximum	427,49
Minimum	2,33	Minimum	15,81	Minimum	15,21	Minimum	1,92	Minimum	0,03
Mean	33,06	Mean	319,98	Mean	77,19	Mean	8,48	Mean	85,74
S. Deviation	13,84	S. Deviation	2.951,04	S. Deviation	18,53	S. Deviation	2,63	S. Deviation	75,06
VIF	*4,24*	*VIF*	*8,15*	*VIF*	*15,2*	*VIF*	*12,2*	*VIF*	*5,15*
ROA		**PBCO/TA**		**ROE**		**TI/TE**			
Maximum	8,15	Maximum	10,07	Maximum	39,64	Maximum	320,57		
Minimum	0,00	Minimum	0,00	Minimum	0,03	Minimum	84,07		
Mean	1,45	Mean	1,66	Mean	11,49	Mean	138,69		
S. Deviation	1,03	S. Deviation	1,21	S.Deviation	6,84	S.Deviation	25,94		

Source: Calculated by the author

Tab. 8.5: Active Profitability Dependent Variable Results

Code	Variable	Regression Coefficient	Absolute Ranking
CA_1	Capital Adequacy Ratio	0,004	11
CA_2	Equity/Total Assets	0,012	10
AQ_1	Nonperforming Loans (gross)/Total Loans and Receivables	0,080	3
AQ_2	Total Loans and Receivables/Total Assets	-0,021	8
AQ_3	Total Loans and Receivables/Total Deposits	0,001	14
AQ_4	Fixed Assets/Total Assets	0,038	5
MQ_1	Nonperforming Loans (gross)/Total Loans and Receivables	-0,409	1
MQ_2	Net Profit Per Branch	0,034	6
MQ_3	Other Operating Expenses/Total Assets	-0,162	2
LQ_1	Liquid Assets/Total Assets	-0,026	7
LQ_2	FC Liquid Assets/FC Passive	0,001	15
LQ_3	Liquid Assets/Short-Term Liabilities	-0,001	13
SMR_1	YP Assets/YP Liabilities	-0,016	9
SMR_2	Interest Income/Total Assets	0,078	4
SMR_3	Balance Sheet Foreign Currency Position/Equity	-0,004	12
Constant		4,520	

4.2 Examination of Factors Affecting Active Profitability

Asset profitability represents the net profitability of the investment in assets. Methodologically, the rate of active profitability is calculated by dividing net profit by the total assets. The ratio shows the ability to manage the returns from the bank's assets. The results obtained according to the RR analysis applied by taking the active profitability ratio as the dependent variable and the other 15 ratio as independent variable are as in the following table:

The regression coefficient in Tab. 8.5 corresponds to the beta value in classical regression analysis, while the absolute rank represents the absolute rank of the regression coefficients. Accordingly, the three most important factors affecting the asset profitability of banks are: the share of gross and net nonperforming loans (MQ_1 and AQ_1) and total operating expenses (MQ_3) within total assets. MQ_1 and MQ_3 have negative effects and AQ_1 have positive effects. In general, the highest positive effect rates are AQ_1, SMR_2, and AQ_4. The lowest effect ratios are LQ_2, AQ_3, and LQ_3. In general, the rates that have the greatest negative effect are MQ_1, MQ_3, and LQ_1. The regression equation obtained according to these results is as follows:

$$ROA = 0,04CA_1 + 0,012CA_2 + 0,08AQ_1 - 0,021AQ_2 + 0,001AQ_3 + 0,038AQ_4 \\ -0,409MQ_1 + 0,034MQ_2 - 0,162MQ_3 - 0,026LQ_1 + 0,001LQ_2 \\ -0,001LQ_3 - 0,016SMR_1 + 0,078SMR_2 - 0,004SMR_3 + 4,52$$

When the ROA values calculated by this equation are compared with the actual values, it was found that the ratios used accounted for 63 % of the assets' profitability of the banks.

4.3 Examining the Factors Affecting Pre-tax Profitability of Continuing Operations

The result of the regression analysis, which examines the dependent variable obtained with the ratio of total assets and the ratio of pre-tax profitability of continuing operations, and other ratios are in the following table.

In Tab. 8.6 according to the results of sorting as a result of the absolute value of the regression coefficients, PBCO/TA ratios have the most significant impact in the rate of return on total loans and receivables, net of nonperforming loans share is (MQ_1), the ratio of operating expenses to total assets are (MQ_3), and the ratio of interest income to total assets are (SMR_2). According to the positive effect, SMR_2, AQ_1, and MQ_2 rates are the most important; according to the negative effect, MQ_1, MQ_3, and LQ_1 ratios were the most important results. The regression equation, which contains dependent variables and independent variables, is as follows according to the results obtained in Tab. 8.6:

$$\frac{PBCO}{TA} = -0,002CA_1 + 0,028CA_2 + 0,075AQ_1 - 0,019AQ_2 \\ +0,001AQ_3 + 0,036AQ_4 - 0,456MQ_1 + 0,038MQ_2 \\ -0,195MQ_3 - 0,021LQ_1 + 0,001LQ_2 - 0,002LQ_3 \\ -0,012SMR_1 + 0,164SMR_2 - 0,004SMR_3 + 3,513$$

The correlation coefficient is 0.83 between the estimated values and the actual values calculated according to the obtained regression equation. In this case, the dependent variable of independent variables is expressed as the explanatory rate of R^2 is found to be 68 %. In this case, it is possible to comment that 32 % of the dependent variable is explained with other financial ratios.

Tab. 8.6: Results Obtained According to PBCO/TA-Dependent Variable

Code	Variable	Regression Coefficient	Absolute Ranking
CA_1	Capital Adequacy Ratio	-0,002	12
CA_2	Equity/Total Assets	0,028	7
AQ_1	Nonperforming Loans (gross)/Total Loans and Receivables	0,075	4
AQ_2	Total Loans and Receivables/Total Assets	-0,019	9
AQ_3	Total Loans and Receivables/Total Deposits	0,001	15
AQ_4	Fixed Assets/Total Assets	0,036	6
MQ_1	Nonperforming Loans (gross)/Total Loans and Receivables	-0,456	1
MQ_2	Net Profit Per Branch	0,038	5
MQ_3	Other Operating Expenses/Total Assets	-0,195	2
LQ_1	Liquid Assets/Total Assets	-0,021	8
LQ_2	FC Liquid Assets/FC Passive	0,001	14
LQ_3	Liquid Assets/Short-Term Liabilities	-0,002	13
SMR_1	YP Assets/YP Liabilities	-0,012	10
SMR_2	Interest Income/Total Assets	0,164	3
SMR_3	Balance Sheet Foreign Currency Position/Equity	-0,004	11
Constant		3,513	

4.4 Examination of Factors Affecting ROE

ROE indicates the rate of profit that corresponds to a unit of the capital of the bank owner or its shareholders. The ratio is calculated by dividing the annual net profit by the number of shares. The regression coefficient values obtained as a result of the application are as follows:

According to Tab. 8.7, the most important effect ratios are on the ROE-dependent variable according to the absolute value; the ratio of net nonperforming loans (MQ_1) within the total loans is the ratio of operating expenses (MQ_3) in total assets and the ratio of interest income (SMR_2) in total assets. However, the most effective rates were SMR_2, AK1, and MQ_2; and the most effective rates were MQ_1, MQ_3, and LQ_1. The regression equation obtained according to these results is as follows:

Tab. 8.7: Results Obtained According to ROE-Dependent Variable

Code	Variable	Regression Coefficient	Absolute Ranking
CA_1	Capital Adequacy Ratio	0,036	12
CA_2	Equity/Total Assets	-0,251	6
AQ_1	Nonperforming Loans (gross)/Total Loans and Receivables	0,635	4
AQ_2	Total Loans and Receivables/Total Assets	-0,236	7
AQ_3	Total Loans and Receivables/Total Deposits	0,007	15
AQ_4	Fixed Assets/Total Assets	-0,069	10
MQ_1	Nonperforming Loans (gross)/Total Loans and Receivables	-3,134	1
MQ_2	Net Profit Per Branch	0,132	8
MQ_3	Other Operating Expenses/Total Assets	-1,790	2
LQ_1	Liquid Assets/Total Assets	-0,280	5
LQ_2	FC Liquid Assets/FC Passive	0,052	11
LQ_3	Liquid Assets/Short-Term Liabilities	-0,009	14
SMR_1	YP Assets/YP Liabilities	-0,078	9
SMR_2	Interest Income/Total Assets	0,876	3
SMR_3	Balance Sheet Foreign Currency Position/Equity	-0,019	13
Constant		41,510	

$$
\begin{aligned}
ROE = {} & 0,036CA_1 - 0,251CA_2 + 0,635AQ_1 - 0,236AQ_2 + 0,007AQ_3 \\
& -0,069AQ_4 - 3,134MQ_1 + 0,132MQ_2 - 1,79MQ_3 - 0,28LQ_1 \\
& +0,052LQ_2 - 0,009LQ_3 - 0,078SMR_1 + 0,876SMR_2 - 0,019SMR_3 + 41,51
\end{aligned}
$$

As a result of regression analysis, it was found that the independent variables explained the dependent variable $R^2 = 53$ %. Accordingly, 47 % of the ROE is explained in different proportions.

4.5 Investigation of Factors Affecting Profitability by Total Income and Total Expense

The ratio of total income to total expense is an indication of the profit-loss status of the enterprise. In order to increase their profits, banks must either increase their incomes or reduce their expenses. Therefore, this ratio is of great importance for banks and the regression coefficient values obtained as a result of the regression analysis applied as the dependent variable is as in Tab. 8.8.

Tab. 8.8: Results of Regression Analysis Based on TI-/TE-Dependent Variable

Code	Variable	Regression Coefficient	Absolute Ranking
CA_1	Capital Adequacy Ratio	-0,148	11
CA_2	Equity/Total Assets	1,654	4
AQ_1	Nonperforming Loans (gross)/Total Loans and Receivables	3,932	3
AQ_2	Total Loans and Receivables/Total Assets	-0,283	9
AQ_3	Total Loans and Receivables/Total Deposits	0,001	15
AQ_4	Fixed Assets/Total Assets	-1,303	5
MQ_1	Nonperforming Loans (gross)/Total Loans and Receivables	-8,277	2
MQ_2	Net Profit Per Branch	0,688	6
MQ_3	Other Operating Expenses/Total Assets	-9,603	1
LQ_1	Liquid Assets/Total Assets	-0,516	7
LQ_2	FC Liquid Assets/FC Passive	0,139	12
LQ_3	Liquid Assets/Short-Term Liabilities	-0,060	13
SMR_1	YP Assets/YP Liabilities	-0,168	10
SMR_2	Interest Income/Total Assets	-0,423	8
SMR_3	Balance Sheet Foreign Currency Position/Equity	-0,043	14
Constant		197,855	

As can be seen in Tab. 8.8, the independent variables affect the profitability level according to the ratio of total income to total expense, which has the most significant effect on absolute value, respectively; the share of other operating expenses to total assets, the ratio of non-performing gross and net loans (MQ_1 and AQ_1) in total loans and receivables. The least influencing factors are AQ_3, SMR_3 and LQ_3 coded ratios. Variables that positively affect profitability most; AQ_1, CA_2, and MQ_2 are the coded variables however MQ_3 is MQ_1 and AQ_4 coded variables are negatively affect the profitability. The regression equation obtained according to these results is as follows:

$$\frac{TI}{TE} = -0,148CA_1 + 1,654CA_2 + 3,932AQ_1 - 0,283AQ_2 + 0,001AQ_3$$
$$-1,303AQ_4 - 8,277MQ_1 + 0,688MQ_2 - 9,603MQ_3 - 0,516LQ_1$$
$$+0,139LQ_2 - 0,06LQ_3 - 0,168SMR_1 - 0,423SMR_2 - 0,043SMR_3 + 197,86$$

Tab. 8.9: Three Ratios with Positive and Negative Direction of Banks' Profitability

ROA	*SPBCO/AK*	*ROE*	*TI/TE*
Three Ratios Most Affecting Positive Directional Profitability			
AQ_1	SMR_2	SMR_2	AQ_1
SMR_2	AQ_1	AQ_1	CA_2
AQ_4	MQ_2	MQ_2	MQ_2
Three Ratios Most Affecting Negative Directional Profitability			
MQ_1	MQ_1	MQ_1	MQ_3
MQ_3	MQ_3	MQ_3	MQ_1
LQ_1	LQ_1	LQ_1	AQ_4

Accordingly, it was concluded that banks should reduce other operating expenses and subsequent loans in order to increase their profitability according to TI/TE ratio. In the case where the estimated values obtained by the equation and the actual values are compared, R^2 level is found as 59 %. In this case, it is concluded that the independent variable describes the dependent variable by 59 %.

Conclusion

Banks have great importance for countries at national and international level. As in other businesses, profitability is also an important factor for banks. In the literature, profitability of banks is measured by variables having many internal and external effects. However, in most of these applications, statistically, panel data analysis, quantitative decision methods, or ratio analysis were used in financial terms; a small number and high-level non-correlated ratios were used. The reason for this is that the financial ratios are highly correlated with each other and cannot provide the assumptions of multivariate statistical techniques.

This study aimed to investigate the profitability of banks by considering the CAMELS ratios with RR. In this context, the ratio of 15 independent and four-factor ratios in Tab. 8.3 were taken as a dependent variable and analyzed. As a result, four regression models were developed according to four different profitability ratios.

According to the results obtained, the three ratios that affect the profitability which are considered as positive and negative are the same as in Tab. 8.9.

As can be seen in Tab. 8.9, the ratio of AQ_1 and SMR_2, that is, the ratio of gross loans in total loans and receivables and the share of interest income in total assets, were found to be positively effective for three types of profitability. The most remarkable point here is: the increase in the share of gross loans in nonperforming loans and receivables and the increase in the profitability of the bank. Similar results were obtained in the 2009 study by Sufian and Habibullah. In this study, it was stated that this situation was compatible with Berger and DeYoung's (1997) *skimping hypothesis. The skimping hypothesis* states that a bank that maximizes profit in the long term is due to the fact that it does not want to bear the cost for monitoring the loan payments because it wants to reduce the costs in the short term. This shows that banks in Turkey focus on reducing costs in order to increase their profitability. On the other hand, the increase in interest income and the increase in the profitability of banks is already expected. Similarly, net profit per branch is another important ratio for profitability ratios. In terms of management quality, it is still expected that profitability can be increased by active work of branches.

When paying attention to the ratios that affect the profitability rates in the negative sense, the share of net nonperforming loans in total loans and receivables, the share of operating expenses in total assets, and the share of liquid assets in total assets are the variables that affect the profitability rates in the negative direction. The most striking issue here is that the share of liquid assets in total assets negatively affects the bank's profitability. At this point, Graham and Bordeleau (2010) concluded that liquid assets reduced the profitability of banks. They have shown as the reason for this the depreciation of the money after the financial crises. They also suggested that the banks' liquid assets were neither too much nor too little, they were not useful for the banks, and they should be balanced in an intermediate point. Therefore, the findings are supported by similar studies in the literature.

In future studies, the RR analysis in terms of the method is applied in different subjects in which there are multiple linear connection problems; in terms of banks, it can be suggested to examine the issue at international level.

References

Albayrak, A. S. (2005). Çoklu Doğrusal Bağlantı Halinde En Küçük Kareler Tekniğinin Alternatifi Yanlı Tahmin Teknikleri ve Bir Uygulama. *Zonguldak Karaelmas Üniversitesi Sosyal Bilimler Dergisi*, 1(1), 105–126.

Albulescu, C.T. (2015). Banks' Profitability and Financial Soundness Indicators: A Macro-Level Investigation in Emerging Countries. *Procedia Economics and Finance*, 23, 203–209.

Almaqtari, F. A., Al-Homaidi, E. A., Tabash, M. I. and Farhan, N. H. (2019). The Determinants of Profitability of Indian Commercial Banks: A Panel Data Approach. *International Journal of Finance & Economics*, 24(1), 168–185.

Bager, A., Roman, M., Algedih, M. and Mohammed, B. (2017). Addressing Multicollinearity in Regression Models: A Ridge Regression Application. *Journal of Social and Economic Statistics*, vol. 6, no. 1

Basarır C. and Sarıhan A. Y. (2017). The Relationship Between Profitability of Banking Sector and Macroeconomic and Financial Variables: Panel ARDL Application. *Journal of Business Research Turk*, 9(3), pp: 16–24

Berger, A. N. and DeYoung, R. (1997). Problem Loans and Cost Efficiency in Commercial Banks. *Journal of Banking & Finance*, 21(6), 849–870.

Charnes, A., Cooper, W. W. and Sueyoshi, T. (1986). Least Squares/Ridge Regression and Goal Programming/Constrained Regression Alternatives. *European Journal of Operational Research*, 27(2), 146–157.

Çekerol, G. and Nalçakan, M. (2011). Lojistik Sektörü İçerisinde Türkiye Demiryolu Yurtiçi Yük Taşıma Talebinin Ridge Regresyonla Analizi. *MU Iktisadi ve Idari Bilimler Dergisi*, 31(2), 321–344.

Erdoğan, S. (2018). Türk Bankacılık Sektörünün 2009–2016 Dönemi CAMELS Derecelendirme Sistemi İle Performans Analizi. Tokat: Gaziosmanpaşa Üniversitesi, Social Sciences Institute, *Unpublished Master Thesis*, Tokat.

Fasone, V., Kofler, L. and Scuderi, R. (2016). Business Performance of Airports: Non-Aviation Revenues and Their Determinants. *Journal of Air Transport Management*, 53, 35–45.

Fasone, V., Kofler, L. and Scuderi, R. (2016). Business Performance of Airports: Non-Aviation Revenues and Their Determinants. *Journal of Air Transport Management*, 53, 35–45.

Hasanov, F., Bayramli, N. and Al-Musehel, N. (2018). Bank-Specific and Macroeconomic Determinants of Bank Profitability: Evidence from an Oil-Dependent Economy. *International Journal of Financial Studies*, 6(3), 78.

Knezevıc, A. V. and Dobrovırov, D. (2016). The Determinants of Serbian Banking Industry Profitability. Economic *Research-Ekonomska Istraživanja*, 29:1, 459–474. DOI: 10.1080/1331677X.2016.1174390

Reis, Ş.G., Kılıç, Y. and Buğan, M. F. (2016). Banka Karlılığını Etkileyen Faktörler: Türkiye Örneği. *Muhasebe ve Finansman Dergisi*, Ekim, 21–36.

Staikouras, C. K. and Wood, G.E. (2004). The Determinants of European Bank Profitability. *International Business-Economics Research Journal*, 3 (6), ss. 57–68.

Sufian, F. (2009). Determinants of Bank Profitability in a Developing Economy: Empirical Evidence from the China Banking Sector. *Journal of Asia-Pacific Business*, 10 (4), 281–307.

BAT (2018). *Araştırmalar ve Sunumlar.* "Bankalarımız" Erişim Tarihi: 12.12.2018 https://www.tbb.org.tr/tr/bankacilik/arastirma-ve-yayinlar/kitaplar/kitaplar/55?year=

Yazıcı, M. (2016). *Bankacılığa Giriş*, Beta Yayınevi, İstanbul, Türkiye.

Serpil Altınırmak and Yahye Hassan Abdi

9 Examination of Islamic Banks Operating in Turkey in Terms of Efficiency and Productivity According to Multi-criteria Decision-Making Methods

Highlights: The Islamic Banks in Turkey were initially founded with the name "Private Financial Institutions" in a law enacted in 1983. In 2001, the Private Financial Institutions had become subject to the Banking Law and got equal rights with commercial banks. With a recent amendment made in 2005, the name of the Private Financial Institutions has been changed to "Participation Banks" because of its insufficiency to explain Islamic Banking transactions. In this study, it is aimed to make performance ranking of Participation Banks operating in Turkey based upon their efficiency and productivity rates between the period 2007 and 2016 by using Multi-criteria Decision-Making Method's Fuzzy TOPSİS Method and Shannon Entropy. Albaraka Türk, Türkiye Finans, and Kuveyt Türk which operated continuously in the respective period were taken into evaluation. The Ziraat Participation Bank and Vakif Participation Bank, started their operations in 2015 and 2016, respectively, hence their data is not analyzed in the study.

Keywords: Islamic banking, participation banks, Fuzzy TOPSIS method, Shannon entropy, Multi-criteria Decision-Making Method's

Introduction

The concept of Islamic Banking is recognized throughout the world in the 19th century. Because of the expansion of classical banking in Western countries and the avoidance of classical banking transactions by Muslim societies, this system was introduced by the Muslim scholars in the 19th century in order to evaluate the economy of the Muslim community outside the economic system.

We can define the Islamic Banking or interest-free banking system as an economic system that operates in fund collection and utilization activities based on the principle of profit-loss shareholding (Tenekeci, 2017: 9). The main difference between classical banking and Islamic banking is interest. Therefore, Islamic Banking is a banking system that maintains fund-raising and utilization activities on the basis of profit-loss partnership instead of interest. As for banking services, they offer their customers similar services to classical banking.

The aim of the Islamic banking system is to develop economic activities in line with the economic principles accepted by Islam. In particular, it is desirable to ensure that the masses who do not want to evaluate their savings in interest-backed banks participate effectively in capital formation. Therefore, as far as possible, the primary purpose of Islamic Banks, which adopts the principle of interest-free banking in the existing legal system, is expressed as the creation of a market where the interest rate is not included, the risk is shared, and the trade types which are not contrary to the Islamic Rules are dominant (Özulucan and Deran, 2009: 89). Islamic banks have contributed to the participation of Muslims in the economic system that cannot evaluate their own capital in the economy by realizing these objectives. Islamic banks provide services to their customers by avoiding not only interest but also anti-Semitism, drugs, and all things that are prohibited in the Islamic religion.

2 Development of Islamic Banking in Turkey

Islamic banks operate in Turkey as in other countries. The Turkish government, one of the founding members of the Islamic Development Bank (IsDB), established in 1975, increased its capital share in 1984 and became one of the largest shareholders of this bank and gained the right to become a permanent member of the IsDB Board of directors. Thus, the Turkish government played a major role in the development of Economic Cooperation programs among 56 Muslim countries, increase foreign trade, support infrastructure projects, encourage the private sector and develop various financing techniques, and increased its effectiveness within the IsDB, one of the world's leading financial institutions. From now on, The States Industrial Workers Investment Bank was established in 1975 as the first application of interest-free banking in Turkey in order to serve the citizens who want to evaluate their savings in accordance with the interest-free system and small- and medium-sized enterprises. It continues to operate until 1978 is known to give significant experience in Turkey. In the establishment of the bank, the Board of Directors has been authorized to choose to work with interest rates. In 1978, the bank started working as an interest in DESIYAB (State Industry and Workers Investment Bank) with the decision of the Board of Directors. In 1988, DESIYAB's name (State Industry and Workers Investment Bank) was changed to Development Bank of Turkey. Furthermore, another important development in Turkey related to interest-free financing was the "Profit/Loss Sharing Certificate (KZOB)" in the same decree as the establishment decree of DESIYAB (Ustaoglu, 2014: 4).

In spite of all these developments, the institutions working with the Islamic Banking System in Turkey have entered the Turkish Banking System in accordance with the decision of the Council of Ministers dated 16.12.1983 and numbered 83/7506 and the decree of the Private Financial Institution. On 24.02.1984, Undersecretariat of Treasury and Foreign Trade and the same year in March of the Republic of Turkey, the details of the system were arranged with the notifications issued by the Central Bank (Canbaz, 2012: 169). After this decree in Turkey, Islamic banks continued their activities under the name of Private Finance Institutions.

Although the legal structures of Private Finance Institutions were completed on 25.02.1985, their establishment and activities were realized by law numbered 83/7506 until 19.12.1999. Since 1999, Private Finance Institutions have been subject to the Banking Law No. 4389 by Law No. 4491. After being subject to this law, the Law No. 4672 of May 12, 2001 amending the Law on Banks, with the aim of guaranteeing the savings collected in these institutions, within the framework of the Association of Private Finance Institutions and the Regulation prepared by this Union and to be administered within the scope of the Regulation 21 Assurance Fund (transferred to the SDIF by Law no. 5411) was established (Tenekecioğlu, 2017: 21).

The number of Islamic banks established in Turkey from 1984 to 1996 has reached six and the establishment of these banks has become as follows; Al Baraka Turk and Faisal Finance Private Finance Institutions were established in 1984. Both banks started their operations one year later in 1985. Kuveyt Turk Private Finance Institution was established in 1989. After that, Anadolu Financial Institution was established in 1991, Ihlas Financial Institution was established in 1995, and the Asian Private Financial Institution was established in 1996. In the first three of these banks, the foreign capital is high, while in the last three banks the share of domestic capital is high (Canbaz, 2014: 208). Interest in Islamic Banking products and services in Turkey is increasing day by day. In 2014, Ziraat Participation Bank and Vakıfbank Participation Bank entered the Turkish Participation banking sector again as participation banks. In addition, the Asian Bank was closed in 2016. Thus, the number of Participation Banks in Turkey has already been five. Since the future of Islamic finance is bright in Turkey, this number is expected to increase further in the coming years.

Founded under the name of Private Finance Institution, İhlas Finance Institution has failed financially due to the crises experienced in 2001 and was put into liquidation process by BRSA (Canbaz, 2014: 208). When the Ihlas Finance Institution was bankrupt, it was taken over by Ulker Group and its name was changed to Family Finance. In 2005, Family Finance merged with

Tab. 9.1: Participation Banks' Share in the Banking Sector (2015–2016) %

Sector Share	**2015**	**2016**
1-Funds Collected	5.9 %	5.6 %
2-Funds Used	5.2 %	4.8 %
3-Total Assets	5.1 %	4.9 %
4–Equities	4.1 %	3.8 %
5-Net Profit	1.6 %	2.9 %

Source: Yurttadur and Demirbaş, 2017: 95.

Anadolu Finance with Turkey Finance Participation bank (Sumer and Onan, 2016: 299–300).

Although Islamic Banking in Turkey continues until 2005 with the name of the Private Finance Institution, this name has failed to explain the full meaning of Islamic Banking. Islamic banking has been tested against the crisis that started in 1990 and became global in 2008 and its contribution to the real sector and then it is called "Participation Bank" which explains Islamic Banking in full understanding (Canbaz, 2014: 207). The amendment of the name "Private Financial Institution" as "Participation Bank" was made on the grounds of Banking Law No. 5411 dated 19.09.2005.

The main objective of the establishment of Participation Banks in Turkey is to attract funds from oil-rich Islamic countries to Turkey, to strengthen economic relations between Islamic countries, and to bring the passive funds of Muslim societies that cannot relate to traditional banks into the real economy (Aras and Öztürk, 2011: 170). The Participation Banks established for this purpose have contributed to the revitalization of the Turkish economy by attracting funds from both oil-rich countries and those in Turkey who cannot evaluate their savings in the economy.

Participation Banks' share in the banking sector between 2015 and 2016 is shown in Tab. 9.1. While Participation Banks had a decline in funds collected and disbursed in 2016, they increased profitability. The decline in funds, assets, and equity funds used in 2016 could be due to the closure of a Participation Bank.

As of July 2017, the asset size of Participation Banks in the total banking sector in Turkey is 4.7 %, and this is a very low rate. This ratio shows that Participation Banks have many steps to be taken in terms of development potential. In addition, the total number of branches of the Participation Bank, operating in July 2017, is 959, of which 3 are foreign branches, and the total number of employees is 14.465 (Atar, 2017: 1053).

3 Efficiency and Productivity Analysis of Islamic Banks in Turkey According to Multi-criteria Decision-Making Method

3.1 Aim and Importance of Research

The aim of the study is to arrange the Participation Banks operating in Turkey according to their efficiency and productivity using fuzzy TOPSIS Shannon entropy methods from Optimal Decision-Making Methods. For this purpose, the efficiency and productivity of banks are calculated with accepted rates in the literature. According to the results of the ratio analysis, fuzzy TOPSIS and Shannon entropy methods will be sorted to arrange. Three of the five banks that the Bank's operations in Turkey, Albaraka Turk, Kuveyt Turk, Turkey Finance Institution have been taken into the study. Since Ziraat Participation Bank and Vakıf Participation Bank have three-year histories, they have not been included in the ten-year analysis.

3.2 Literature Review

Akın and Ece (2010) study the performance between 2003 and 2009 years of Participation Banks operating in Turkey, and the increasing share of the Bank is evaluated in the Turkish Financial sector. In this study, the basic principles of Islamic Finance System, its increasing importance, and the comparison of Islamic banking and traditional banking were discussed. Moreover, the development of Participation Banks as of the years and the increasing share of the Turkish Financial System were presented using various banking indicators.

In his (2013) study, Sırrım attempted to determine whether they were successful by providing information about the development process, legal infrastructure, and implementation phases of Participation Banks in Turkey. He also dealt with the success and failure of these banks and the reasons. In the last part of the study, recommendations were given to increase the success and productivity of Participation Banks.

Ergeç et al. (2014) in their studies evaluated the bank's customers' approach to traditional banks and the provision of Islamic banking products and services in the Turkey Participation Bank. In this study, banking system usage data of 500 Participation Bank customers in Eskişehir province were used. As a result of the study, it was seen that Participation Bank customers were highly supported by traditional banks in Islamic banking.

In Ada and Dalkılıç (2014)'s studies, using the set of indicators formed by the balance sheet data of 22 Islamic Banks, they examined the effect of scale efficiency, efficiency changes, and total factor productivity change. The study benefited from data of four Islamic banks operating in Turkey and 18 Islamic banks operating in Malaysia for the period 2009–2011. Data envelopment analysis, efficiency changes, and total factor were used in the measurement of efficiency, while Malmquist Total Factor Productivity Index was used in the productivity change. As a result of the study, it was observed that Participation Banks in Turkey had a high average of scale activity compared to banks in Malaysia in 2009 and a low rate in 2010–2011. The change in total productivity was realized as low for Turkey in the period of 2009–2010 compared to 2010–2011, and in Malaysia, there was an increase in banks except for three banks.

In the studies of Toraman et al. (2015), current and potential customer's perceptions of Islamic Banking activities were investigated by the survey method. In the survey, significant differences were determined between the answers of all participants who preferred to work with an Islamic bank, who did not prefer and were unstable. As a result, Islamic banking activities were not sufficiently known by the customers and the perception of Islamic finance of potential bank customers was very weak. They analyzed the performance of Traditional and Participation Banks by comparing method. Within the scope of the study, the financial ratios of the Traditional and Participation Banks operating in Turkey have been utilized in the financial statements for the period 2006–2014. Using independent samples through the T-test method, it was found that the total assets and liquid assets of traditional banks were higher than Participation Banks, and they were stronger than Participation Banks in terms of capital adequacy. In addition, the two-stage generalized moments' method has been used to influence bank profitability. As a result of the analysis, it is concluded that bank profitability is positively positive with operational efficiency and capital adequacy and that there is a negative correlation with the ratio of nonperforming loans to total loans, which is an indicator of credit quality.

Aktan et al. (2014) examined the factors that led to the growth of Islamic banks. During the study, some statistical techniques have found significant findings regarding the stability and growth of these banks. In this study, it was found that relatively small banks were more stable than banks with higher Z-points, and on the other hand, regression results were found indicating that large banks had a higher income range than small banks.

Bayramoğlu and Başarır (2018) in their studies they using the CAMELS-based TOPSIS Model developed by the head Participation Bank operating in Turkey and the risk ratings were made to use banks' financial ratios in 2016. As a result, Vakıf Participation Bank was identified as the Participation Bank with the lowest risk compared to other Participation Banks. However, considering that the Vakıf Participation Bank has just started its activities, it has been determined that Kuveyt Türk performs more in terms of risk management.

Samad (1999) examined by comparing the relative performances of full-fledged Islamic banks and Conventional Banks in Malaysia during 1992–1996. As a result of this study, the administrative efficiency of Conventional Banks was higher than that of full-fledged Islamic Banks.

In the study, Hussien (2001) investigated the cost-effectiveness of Islamic banks in Sudan during the 1990–2000 period. In the study, the cost-effectiveness of 17 banks was investigated by applying the Stochastic Frointer Approach. As a result, it has been determined that small banks are more efficient than large banks.

Hamim et al. (2006) compared the activities of Islamic Banks operating in Malaysia between 1997 and 2003 using the Stochastic Frointer Approach. In this study, it was concluded that the assets, deposits, and financing bases of Islamic Banks were rapidly growing compared to Conventional Banks and that Islamic Banks were more efficient than local banks in this period.

Srari (2011) examined the impact of financial liberalization on the increase in banking productivity in the Gulf Cooperation Council countries during the 1990–2007 period. In the study, DEA and Malmquist Total Factor Productivity Index was applied by taking into consideration the Islamic and Conventional Banks. The results showed that Gulf countries' banks during the liberalization period had a change in productivity, rather than a rise in productivity. It was also concluded that Conventional Banks performed better in productivity than Islamic Banks.

4 Method

4.1 Effectiveness and Productivity Analysis of Participation Banks in 2007–2016 Period

While determining the ratios we use for efficiency and productivity, Yolalan's (2001) "Productivity Conference in Banking", Dönek and Özdemir's (2000) "Performance Measurement of the Turkish Commercial Banking Sector", and Baykara's (2012) "Analysis of Efficiency and Productivity in Participation Banks" were used in the studies.

4.2 Efficiency and Productivity Ratios of Participation Banks

In the study, six efficiency and six productivity ratios used in the determination of their efficiency and productivity in Participation Banks were determined and shown in Tab. 9.2.

Tab. 9.2: Efficiency and Productivity Ratios

Efficiency	**Rates**	
Efficiency 1	Non-performing Loans/Loans + Leasing	$NPL/(L_o + Le)$
Efficiency 2	Loans + Financial Leasing/Total Assets	$(L_o + FL)/TA_s$
Efficiency 3	Profit Share Expenses/Collected Funds + Credits Obtained	PE/(CF+C)
Efficiency 4	Profit Sharing Yields/Profit Sharing Expenses	PY/PE
Efficiency 5	Equities/Total Risk Weighted Assets	$E_q/TRWA_s$
Efficiency 6	Profit Sharing Yield/Equity	PY/E_q
Productivity	**Rates**	
Productivity 1	Profit Before Taxes/Total Assets	PT_x/TA_s
Productivity 2	Net Income of the Period/Equities	NIP/E_q
Productivity 3	Loans + Financial Leasing/Branch Number	$L_{o/}BN$
Productivity 4	Loans + Financial Leasing/Funds Collected + Credits Obtained + Equities	$(L_o+FL)/(Fc+CO+E_{q})$
Efficiency 5	Net Pay and Commissions Income/Total Assets	$NPCI/TA_s$
Efficiency 6	Total Assets/Number Of Employees	TA_s/NE

Source: Created by the Author

In order to convert the data which is in absolute number format related to efficiency and productivity to be used in the ranking of Participation Banks in terms of performances, the approach proposed by Wang (2007) was used. According to this approach, in the period of d, the value of the alternative i according to the j criterion is indicated by $y_{ij}(d)$. In addition, the performance ranking according to the J criteria of the I alternative is $PS_{ij} = \left(ps_{1ij}, ps_{2ij}, ps_{3ij}\right)$ under the $i = 1, 2, \ldots, k; j = 1, 2, \ldots, l; d = 1, 2, \ldots, s$ conditions.

$$ps_{1ij} = \min_{1 \leq d \leq s} \{y_{ij}(d)\}, \quad ps_{2ij} = \frac{1}{s}\sum_{d=1}^{s} y_{ij}(d), \quad ps_{3ij} = \max_{1 \leq d \leq s} \{y_{ij}(d)\} \tag{1}$$

Taking into account the Equation 1, the values$[PS_{i1}, PS_{i2}, \ldots, PS_{il}]$ constitute the performance matrix according to all criteria of the alternative $A_i \ (i = 1, 2, \ldots, k)$.

After determining the efficiency and productivity ratios to be used in the analysis, the fuzzy evaluation matrix was first formed as in Tab. 9.3 for weighting them.

Tab. 9.3: The Matrix of Fuzzy Evaluation for Efficiency Ratios

	NPL/ $(L_o + Le)$	$(L_o + FL)$ $/TA_s$	PE/(CF+C)	Kprevenue/ Kpexpense	ö/ravt	Kpg/ö
Albaraka Türk	(0.01,0.02, 0.04)	(0.66,0.72, 0.78)	(0.03,0.05, 0.05)	(1.84,1.92, 2.18)	(0.12,0.15, 0.21)	(0.61,0.75, 0.92)
Kuveyt Türk	(0.01,0.03, 0.05)	(0.62,0.69, 0.82)	(0.02,0.04, 0.04)	(1.88,2.17, 2.36)	(0.13,0.15, 0.18)	(0.53,0.69, 1.02)
Türkiye Finans	(0.02,0.03, 0.05)	(0.71,0.76, 0.84)	(0.03,0.05, 0.05)	(1.95,2.09, 2.28)	(0.12,0.14, 0.17)	(0.62,0.73, 1.12)

Source: Created by the Author

Tab. 9.4: Normalized Intermittent Decision Matrix for Activity Ratios $(\alpha = 0.5)$

	NPL/ $(L_o + Le)$	$(L_o + FL)/$ TA_s	PE/(CF+C)	Kprevenue/ Kpexpense	ö/ravt	Kpg/ö
Albaraka Türk	[0.17, 0.305]	[0.299, 0.326]	[0.297, 0.347]	[0.289, 0.315]	[0.27, 0.36]	[0.26, 0.319]
Kuveyt Türk	[0.191, 0.363]	[0.28, 0.326]	[0.237, 0.283]	[0.311, 0.348]	[0.285, 0.326]	[0.233, 0.326]
Türkiye Finans	[0.218, 0.33]	[0.318, 0.347]	[0.307, 0.368]	[0.31, 0.336]	[0.266, 0.312]	[0.259, 0.354]

Source: Created by the Author

After the fuzzy evaluation matrix was created, fuzzy data $\alpha = 0.5$(neutral) was taken into consideration and converted into intermittent data. Then, by using normalization, the intermittent decision matrix is obtained as in Tab. 9.4.

After the normalized intermittent decision matrix is obtained, the lower and upper limit values of intermittent entropy and intermittent differentiation are obtained as in Tab. 9.5.

The weights for the efficiency ratios were obtained as in Tab. 9.6.

According to the efficiency ratio weights, NPL/$(L_o$+ Le) was the most important with 0.346527 value, $(L_o$+ FL)/TA_s with the value of 0.042658.

The Participation Banks are listed within the scope of the efficiency ratios by taking advantage of Fuzzy TOPSIS from the provision of weights for efficiency ratios. In this context, the first normalized Fuzzy Decision Matrix is obtained as shown in Tab. 9.7.

Subsequently, the weighted normalized Fuzzy Decision Matrix was found as in Tab. 9.8 by using the benchmark weights.

Tab. 9.5: e_i^L, e_i^R, d_i^Lve d_i^R Values for Efficiency Ratios

Ratios	$[e_i^L, e_i^R]$	$[d_i^L, d_i^R]$
NPL/(L_o+ Le)	[0.865, 0.997]	[0.002, 0.134]
(L_o+ FL)/TA_s	[0.985, 0.999]	[0.0003, 0.014]
PE/(CF+C)	[0.969, 0.994]	[0.005, 0.03]
Kpprevenue/kpexpense	[0.987, 0.999]	[0.0007, 0.01
ö/ravt	[0.968, 0.998]	[0.001, 0.031]
Kpg/ö	[0.947, 0.999]	[0.0009, 0.052]

Source: Created by the Author

Tab. 9.6: Weight of Efficiency Ratios

Ratios	**Weights**
NPL/(L_o+ Le)	0.346527
(L_o+ FL)/TA_s	0.042658
PE/(CF+C)	0.292698
Kpprevenue/kpexpense	0.055002
ö/ravt	0.12697
Kpg/ö	0.136144

Source: Created by the Author

Following this, each Participation Bank's positive ideal solution (A^* and its distance from negative ideal solution (A^- are found as in Tab. 9.9.

In the last step of the fuzzy TOPSIS,CC_i values of each Participation Bank were found and the rank from bigger to smaller. The example of this relationship is shown in Tab. 9.10.

According to Tab. 9.11 in terms of efficiency ratios, while Turkey Finance ranks first with 0.322093CC_i values, then come Kuveyt Turk with 0.30806 and Albaraka Turk with 0.312295 values.

After the fuzzy evaluation matrix was created, fuzzy data $\alpha = 0.5$(neutral) was taken into consideration and converted into intermittent data. Then, by using normalization, the intermittent decision matrix is obtained as in Tab. 9.12.

After obtaining the normalized intermittent decision matrix, the lower and upper limit values of intermittent entropy and intermittent differentiation are obtained as in Tab. 9.13.

The weights for the productivity ratios were obtained as in Tab. 9.14.

Tab. 9.7: Normalized Fuzzy Decision Matrix for Efficiency Ratios

	NPL/(L_o+ Le)	(L_o+ FL)/TA_s	PE/(CF+C)	Kprevenue/ Kpexpense	ö/ravt	Kpg/ö
Albaraka Türk	(0.31,0.55,1)	(0.78,0.86,0.9)	(0.55,0.55,0.77)	(0.78,0.81, 0.92)	(0.57,0.7,1)	(0.54,0.67, 0.82)
Kuveyt Türk	(0.25,0.48,0.92)	(0.73,0.82,0.9)	(0.67,0.67,1)	(0.79,0.92,1)	(0.64,0.7,0.8)	(0.47,0.61, 0.91)
Türkiye Finans	(0.29,0.47,0.66)	(0.84,0.9,1)	(0.52,0.52,0.78)	(0.82, 0.88,0.96)	(0.57,0.68, 0.79)	(0.55,0.65,1)

Source: Created by the Author

Tab. 9.8: Weighted Normalized Fuzzy Decision Matrix for Efficiency Ratios

	NPL/(L_o+ Le)	(L_o+ FL)/TA_s	PE/(CF+C)	Kprevenue/ Kpexpense	ö/ravt	Kpg/ö
Albaraka Türk	(0.1,0.19, 0.34)	(0.033,0.036, 0.039)	(0.16,0.16, 0.22)	(0.04,0.04, 0.05)	(0.07,0.08, 0.12)	(0.07,0.09, 0.11)
Kuveyt Türk	(0.08,0.16, 0.31)	(0.031,0.0035, 0.041)	(0.19,0.19, 0.29)	(0.04,0.05, 0.05)	(0.08,0.08, 0.1)	(0.06,0.08, 0.12)
Türkiye Finans	(0.1,0.16, 0.23)	(0.03,0.03, 0.04)	(0.15,0.15, 0.22)	(0.04,0.04, 0.05)	(0.07,0.08, 0.1)	(0.07,0.08, 0.13)

Source: Created by the Author

Tab. 9.9: Distances of each Alternative $\mathbf{A}^*$and $\mathbf{A}^-$ for Efficiency Ratios

Participation Banks	d_i^*	d_i^-
Albaraka Türk	4.150737	1.8849
Kuveyt Türk	4.178375	1.860266
Türkiye Finans	4.080042	1.938545

Source: Created by the Author

The efficiency ratio was found to be the most significant NPCI/TA_s with the value of 0.232693, and (Lo+FL)/(Fc+C+Eq) with the value of 0.057269.

Subsequently, the weighted normalized Fuzzy Decision Matrix was found as in Tab. 9.16 by using the benchmark weights.

Following this, each Participation Bank's positive ideal solution (A^* and its distance from negative ideal solution($A^-$are found as in Tab. 9.17.

Tab. 9.10: $\mathbf{CC_i}$ Values for Efficiency Ratios and Ranking of Participation Banks

Participation Banks	CC_i	Rank
Albaraka Türk	0.312295	2
Kuveyt Türk	0.30806	3
Türkiye Finans	0.322093	1

Source: Created by the Author

Tab. 9.11: Fuzzy Evaluation Matrix for Productivity Ratios

	PT_x/TA_s	NTP/E_q	L_o/BN	$(L_o+FL)/(F_c+C+E_q)$	$NPCI/TA_s$	TA_s/NE
Albaraka Türk	(0.008,0.0, 0.03)	(0.07,0.14, 0.21)	(35973225, 65602525 ,107226671)	(0.71,0.75, 0.81)	(0.004,0.008, 0.01)	(2489898, 4958985 ,8654040)
Kuveyt Türk	(0.01,0.01, 0.02)	(0.09,0.13, 0.19)	(36583115 ,56817081 ,78331509)	(0.65,0.73, 0.85)	(0.003,0.005, 0.01)	(2150260, 4887364, 8675188)
Türkiye Finans	(0.008,0.0, 0.03)	(0.06,0.13, 0.25)	(32450402, 62829073, 102254489)	(0.8,0.86, 0.95)	(0.003,0.006, 0.01)	(2151632 ,5184760, 9717193)

Source: Created by the Author

Tab. 9.12: Normalized Fuzzy Decision Matrix for Productivity Ratios ($\alpha = \mathbf{0.5}$)

	PT_x/TA_s	NTP/E_q	L_o/BN	$(L_o+FL)/(F_c+C+E_q)$	$NPCI/TA_s$	TA_s/NE
Albaraka Türk	[0.18, 0.372]	[0.199, 0.333]	[0.214, 0.365]	[0.295, 0.316]	[0.23, 0.382]	[0.177, 0.323]
Kuveyt Türk	[0.209, 0.282]	[0.212, 0.304]	[0.197, 0.285]	[0.28, 0.318]	[0.163, 0.29]	[0.167, 0.322]
Türkiye Finans	[0.191, 0.344]	[0.187, 0.361]	[0.201, 0.348]	[0.336, 0.365]	[0.191, 0.327]	[0.174, 0.354]

Source: Created by the Author

Tab. 9.13: Values for Productivity e_i^L, e_i^R, d_i^Lve d_i^R Ratios

Ratios	$[e_i^L, e_i^R]$	$[d_i^L, d_i^R]$
PT_x/TA_s	[0.87, 0.994]	[0.005, 0.129]
NTP/E_q	[0.878, 0.997]	[0.002, 0.121]
L_o/BN	[0.886, 0.995]	[0.004, 0.113]
$(L_o+FL)/(F_c+C+E_q)$	[0.985, 0.997]	[0.002, 0.014]
$NPCI/TA_s$	[0.865, 0.994]	[0.005, 0.134]
TA_s/NE	[0.828, 0.999]	[0.0008, 0.171]

Source: Created by the Author

Tab. 9.14: Weights of Productivity Ratio

Ratios	Weights
PT_x/TA_s	0.228967
NTP/E_q	0.140729
L_o/BN	0.195187
$(L_o+FL)/(F_c+C+E_q)$	0.057269
$NPCI/TA_s$	0.232693
TA_s/NE	0.145155

Source: Created by the Author

Tab. 9.15: Normalized Fuzzy Decision Matrix for Productivity Ratios

	PT_x/TA_s	NTP/E_q	L_o/BN	$(L_o+FL)/(F_c+C+E_q)$	$NPCI/TA_s$	TA_s/NE
Albaraka Türk	(0.22,0.55, 1)	(0.28,0.56, 0.85)	(0.33,0.61, 1)	(0.80,0.86, 0.92)	(0.34,0.63, 1)	(0.25,0.51, 0.89)
Kuveyt Türk	(0.36,0.5, 0.67)	(0.37,0.52, 0.76)	(0.34,0.52, 0.73)	(0.77,0.89, 1)	(0.25,0.44, 0.79)	(0.22,0.5, 0.89)
Türkiye Finans	(0.24,0.55, 0.87)	(0.25,0.53, 1)	(0.3,0.58, 0.95)	(0.69,0.75, 0.81)	(0.29,0.52, 0.87)	(0.22,0.53, 1)

Source: Created by the Author

In the last step of the fuzzy TOPSIS,CC_i values of each Participation Bank were found and the rank from bigger to smaller. This is as shown in Tab. 9.18.

According to Tab. 9.18, Albaraka Türk ranks first with 0.260953 CC_ivalues, followed by Kuveyt Turk with 0.2444 and Turkey Finance with 0.257572 values.

Tab. 9.16: Normalized Fuzzy Decision Matrix for Productivity Ratios

	PT_x/TA_s	NTP/E_q	L_o/BN	$(L_o+FL)/(F_c+C+E_q)$	$NPCI/TA_s$	TA_s/NE
Albaraka Türk	(0.05,0.12, 0.22)	(0.03,0.07, 0.12)	(0.06,0.11, 0.19)	(0.04,0.04, 0.05)	(0.08,0.14, 0.23)	(0.03,0.07, 0.12)
Kuveyt Türk	(0.08,0.11, 0.15)	(0.05,0.07, 0.1)	(0.06,0.1, 0.14)	(0.04,0.05, 0.05)	(0.05,0.1, 0.18)	(0.03,0.07, 0.12)
Türkiye Finans	(0.05,0.12, 0.2)	(0.03,0.07, 0.14)	(0.05,0.11, 0.18)	(0.03,0.04, 0.04)	(0.06,0.12, 0.2)	(0.03,0.07, 0.14)

Source: Created by the Author

Tab. 9.17: Distances of each Alternative $\mathbf{A}^*$ and $\mathbf{A}^-$ for Productivity Ratios

Participation Banks	d_i^*	d_i^-
Albaraka Türk	4.481879	1.582524
Kuveyt Türk	4.560639	1.475144
Türkiye Finans	4.502892	1.562199

Source: Created by the Author

Tab. 9.18: $\mathbf{CC_i}$ Values for Productivity Ratios and Ranking of Participation Banks

Participation Banks	CC_i	**Rank**
Albaraka Türk	0.260953	1
Kuveyt Türk	0.2444	3
Türkiye Finans	0.257572	2

Source: Created by the Author

Considering the ranking of Participation Banks in terms of efficiency and productivity ratios, the banks in the first two have changed their positions, while the last one has always been Kuveyt Turk. This indicates that Kuveyt's Turk Participation Bank performs less in terms of efficiency and productivity than the other two banks.

Conclusion

Financial indicators announced to the public as of certain periods are important for Performing Performance Analysis in the banking sector.

There are five Participation Banks operating in Turkey as of 2017. These are, Albaraka Turk Participation Bank INC, Kuveyt Turk Participation Bank INC, Turkey Finance Participation Bank INC, Vakıf Participation Bank INC, and Ziraat Participation Bank INC.

The study covers the period 2007–2016. During this period, three Participation Banks with uninterrupted activity (Albaraka Turk, Kuveyt Turk, and Turkey Finance) were included in the analysis. Since Ziraat Participation Bank INC and Vakıf Participation Bank INC started to operate in 2015 and 2016, respectively, they could not be included in the study. Islamic Banking operations are growing rapidly in Turkey, as in the whole world. However, they do not yet have the expected level of transaction volume.

The effective and productive work of the Participation Banks operating in the intense competition in the banking sector has gained importance. For this reason, six efficiency and six productivity ratios of three Participation Banks operating in 2007–2016 were calculated by a literature review. Performance scores were determined according to fuzzy TOPSIS and Shannon entropy methods of Multi-criteria Decision-Making Models of Participation Banks, whose efficiency and productivity ratios were calculated. According to the results of the analysis, in terms of efficiency and productivity ratios, the first two Participation Banks have changed their positions, while the last one has always been Kuveyt Turk. This indicates that the Kuveyt Turk Participation Bank performs less in terms of efficiency and productivity than the other two banks.

When the literature is analyzed, performance analysis studies for the banking sector are frequently seen. There are also studies in which Multi-criteria Decision-Making models are used to measure the performance of Participation Banks. However, no studies have been conducted to measure the performance of Participation Banks by using fuzzy TOPSIS and Shannon entropy method.

References

Ada, A. A. & Dalkılıç, N. (2014). "Efficiency Analysis İn Islamic Banks: A Study For Malaysia and Turkey", *BDDK Bankacılık ve Finansal Piyasalar*, 8(1), 9–33.

Akın, F. & Ece, N. (2010). "İslami Finans Sistemi İçerisinde İslami Bankacılığın Yeri ve Türkiye'de Katılım Bankacılığının Gelişimi", *Mevzuat Degisi*, 13, 151.

Aktan, B., Masood, O. & ve Ashraf, M. (2014). "Stability Estimation of Islamic Banks: An Empirical Analysis", *Journal of Academic Studies*, 16(62), 21–39.

Altan, M. (2001). *Fonksiyonlar ve İşlemler Açısından Bankacılık.* (1. Baskı). İstanbul: Beta Basım Yayım Dağıtım.

Aras, O. N. & Öztürk, M. (2011). "Reel Ekonomiye Katkıları Bakımından Katılım Bankalarının Kullandırdığı Fonların Analizi", *Ekonomik Bilimler Dergisi*, 3(2), 167–179.

Atar, A. (2017). "Başlangıcından Günümüze Dünyada ve Türkiye'de İslami Bankacılığın Genel Durumu", *Tarih Kültür ve Sanat Araştırmaları Dergisi*, 6(4), 1029–1062.

Baykara, H. V. (2012). "*Katılım Bankalarında Etkinlik ve Verimlilik Analizi*", Yüksek Lisans Tezi. Tokat: Gazi Osmanpaşa Üniversitesi, Sosyal Bilimler Enstitüsü. Türkiye Katılım Bankalar Birliği.

Bayramoğlu, M. F. & Başarır, Ç. (2018). "Türk Katılım Bankalarının Risk Derecelendirmesi: CAMELS Tabanlı TOPSİS Modeli Uygulaması", *İşletme & Ekonomi Yazıları* (Ed.Nurhan Şakar), s. 390–399.

Canbaz, M. (2012). Katılım Bankacılığı ve Türkiye'deki Gelişimi. F. Kaya (Ed.). *Bankacılık Giriş Ve İlkeler İçinde* (s. 137–198). (1. Baskı). İstanbul: Beta Basım Yayım Dağıtımı.

Dönek, E. & ve Özdemir, A. İ. (2000). "Türk Ticari Bankalarının Performans Değerlendirilmesi", *Verimlilik Dergisi*, 2000(3), 93–112.

Ergeç, E. H., Kaytancı, B. G. & Toprak, M. (2014). "Katılım Bankası Müşterilerinin Bankacılık Sistemi Kullanım Tercihleri: Mevduat Bankaları İçin İslami Bankacılık Pencerisi", *Tüketici ve Tüketim Araştırmaları Dergisi*, 6(2), 53–90.

Hamim, M., Naziruddin, A. & Syed, H. (2006). "Efficiency of Islamic Banking in Malaysia: A Stochastic Frontier Approach", *Journal of Economic Cooperation*, 27(2), 37–70

Hussein, K. A. (2001). *Operational Efficiency İn Islamic Banking: The Sudenese Experience*, Islamic Research and Training Institute, Islamic Development Bank, 1–42.

Özulucan, A. & Deran, A. (2009). "Katılım Bankacılığı İle Geleneksel Bankaların Bankacılık Hizmetler ve Muhasebe Uygulamaları Açısından Karşılaştırılma sı", *Mustafa Kemal Üniversitesi Sosyal Bilimler Enstitüsü Dergisi*, 6(11), 85–108.

Samad, A. (1999). "Comparative Efficiencyof the Islamic Bank Vis- A – Vis Conventional Banks in Malaysia", *IIUM Journal of Economics and Management*, 7(1), 1–27.

Srairi, S. A. (2011). "Productivity Growth İn GCC Banking İndustry: Conventional Versus Islamic Banks", *Journal of Knowledge Globalization*, 4(2), 59–90.

Sümer, G. & Onan, F. (2016). "Dünya'da Faizsiz Bankacılığının Doğuşu, Türkiye'deki Katılım Bankacılığının Gelişme Süreci ve Konvansiyonel Bankacılıktan Farkları", *Gazı Üniversitesi İktisadi ve İdare Bilimler Fakültesi Dergisi*, 17(3), 296–308.

Tenekeci, M. (2017). *Katılım Bankacılığın Finansal İstikrara Etkisi: Türkiye Örneği*, Yüksek Lisans Tezi. Konya: Karatay Üniversitesi, Sosyal Bilimler Enstitüsü. Türkiye Katılım Bankalar Birliği.

Toraman, C., Ata, H. A. & Buğan, M. F. (2015). "İslami Bankacılık Faaliyetlerine Yönelik Müşteri Algısı Üzerine Bir Araştırma", *Gaziantep University Journal of Social Sciences*, 14(4), 761–779.

Ustaoğlu, D. (2014). *Türkiye'de Katılım Bankacılığı Sektördeki Yeri ve Önemi*, Yüksek Lisans Tezi. Aydın: Adnan Menderes Üniversitesi, Sosyal Bilimler Enstitüsü.

Wang, T. C. & Chang, T. H. (2007). "Application Of TOPSIS İn Evaluating İnitial Training Aircraft Under A Fuzzy Environment", *Expert Systems with Applications*, 3(4), 870–880.

Yolalan, R. (2001). *Bankacılıkta Verimlilik Konferansı*, Türkiye Katılım Bankaları Birliği. İstanbul.

Mehmet Sabri Topak

10 Credit Risk in the Turkish Banking Sector: A Study on 1990–2017 Period

Highlights: Having a robust banking system is relevant for all agents of the economy. The vitality of risk management is as becoming more vivid for banking sector considering the role of the sector in the economy and the sector's influence on other sectors. There are three types of risks in banking sector: credit risk, market risk, and operational risk. Credit risk is the type of risk that has the highest rate in total risk. This chapter aims to analyze credit risk in the Turkish banking sector for the period of 1990–2017. Loans/Total Assets ratio is used to analyze the change in credit items, and Assets/GDP and Loans/GDP ratios are used to analyze the development level of the sector. Non-performing Loans (NPL/Total Loans) is used to analyze the credit risk of the sector. In the period following the economic crisis of 2001, structural reforms regarding risk management in banking sector and auditing initiated profound affects in the operations of banks. The study exhibits the reforms implemented in 2001 has directly affected the credit risk in the Turkish banking sector.

Keywords: Banking sector, risk, credit risk, Basel

Introduction

Banks are financial institutions that collect funds through deposits and dispense the funds in the form of loans. Banking sector acts as an intermediary between those who save and those who are in need of funds. This makes banking a vital function in the realization of investments in the economy and in meeting needs of individuals and institutions. Having a robust banking sector in this sense concerns all the agents in the economy.

The main function of banks in the economy is to provide the liquidity of funds through credit mechanism. Banks provide the deposited funds to the financial system and ensure that those funds are used effectively. One of the important functions of banking is to help reduce development differences between the regions by providing funds. Banks contribute to funding of fixed assets by converting short-term funds into long-term funds. Due to deficiencies of the capital markets in developing countries the role of banking sector is much more critical. The fact that banks collect small savings as deposits and provide loans for large investment projects is another critical function of the banking sector. The sector also contributes to the development of national and international trade through various credit products and payment methods. In addition to all these, banks also play an active role in the implementation of the monetary policies (Akgüç, 1987).

One of the most important conditions of having a healthy economy is to have a developed banking sector. There is no doubt that a crisis in the banking sector will effect both the financial sector and the real sector. Given the global level of international trade and capital flows, a financial crisis in any part of the world can become infectious. Therefore, the importance of risk management in the banking sector is becoming a more vital topic at a global scale.

The chapter consists of four sections. Following the introduction section, the second section provides information about the concept of risk and Basel criteria. The third section is devoted to the banking sector in Turkey. The fourth section analyzes the credit risk in the Turkish banking sector for the period 1990–2017.

2 The Concept of Risk and Basel Criteria in Banking

Banks are institutions that carry out their activities on the relationship of trust in the economy. At the core of banking activities are taking various risks, managing these risks, and making them profitable. It is very important for the banks to correctly manage the risk they take on, the functioning of the financial system, and the economies of the country. While the crisis experienced in a company operating in any sector in the real sector adversely affects only that company or its sector, the failure of a bank to fulfill its obligations can affect both the banking sector and the country's economy deeply. Therefore, risk management in banking is an important issue for the healthy functioning of the economy.

Risk management is not a complete elimination of risk. Banking activities are intrinsically risky and therefore cannot be eliminated. To predict the source of the risks that are important in risk management, to accurately calculate the risk and to adjust the capital adequacy to the risk by increasing the return. However, with globalization, the issue of risk management in banking has gained a new dimension. The end of the Bretton Woods system is a milestone in terms of the current shape of the banking sector's activities today when the financial markets are connected to each other on a global scale. The collapse of the Bretton Woods system in the early 1970s and the decrease in international capital flows and barriers to trade caused significant changes in the variety and structure of the services offered in the banking sector (Smith et al., 2011. In the following years, especially the developments in information technology and the facilities provided in the communication, the entire financial system and the banking sector have been reshaped. The start of the local banks operating in the international arena has revealed new opportunities and new risks for the banking sector. The fact that the regulations regulating banking activities remained at the local level during this period also revealed a significant need for the functioning of the financial system in the global sense (Grote and Marauhn, 2006).

The oil crisis in 1974 caused significant fluctuations in international financial markets and caused serious disagreements and problems in the banking sector. In 1974, the abrupt bankruptcy of the German bank Herstadt and the panic in international financial markets showed that a banking crisis in one country could have a negative impact on the entire world economy. The global crisis emerging in financial markets and affecting all economies has shown that the banking sector needs regulatory authority at an international level and international standards in terms of risk management. For this purpose, the Basel Committee was established by the central banks of the USA, England, France, Switzerland, Germany, Italy, Sweden, Canada, Japan, and Benelux countries at the end of 1974 (Lambrecht, 2017).

Basel's Banking Committee published the "Capital Adequacy Agreement" in 1988 in order to ensure an international minimum standard in the banking sector and to eliminate differences in the calculation of capital adequacy ratio on a country basis. The main objective of the so-called Basel I settlement is to take measures against credit risk (Torun, 2017). For this purpose, a minimum capital adequacy ratio of 8 % was determined, effective from the end of 1992. The minimum capital adequacy ratio is calculated by the ratio of the total assets weighted at risk. While weighted by risk, only credit risk was taken into consideration in Basel I. In order to ensure the simplicity of calculation of the standard, Basel I applied the minimum capital ratio of 8 % to all loans regardless of the maturity, size, and value of the lending institution (Saunders, 2002: 4).

After the implementation of Basel I, the rapid increase in capital movements at the international level, the emergence of new instruments such as credit derivatives, and the low level of performance of the banks on loans, led to the need to revise the capital adequacy ratio determined in Basel I. The works, which started in 1999, were published under the name Basel I in June 2004. With the new regulation, the Basel Committee provides information on how to manage the risks encountered in banking and how to calculate the capital adequacy ratio and provides statements on the implementation of Basel II criteria (BRSA, 2005: 27).

In Basel II, there are three types of risks defined when calculating the minimum capital adequacy ratio. These are credit risk, market risk, and operational risk.

- Credit Risk is the possibility of loss that the bank may be exposed to due to the fact that the customer who uses the bank does not comply with the contractual requirements and cannot fulfill its obligations completely or partially on time (BRSA, 2006).
- Market risk is the risk caused by the possibility of a decrease in the asset prices of banks due to changes in market prices or rates.
- Operational risk covers all risks other than credit risk and market risk and is due to errors in the processes and controls related to the operations of the banks (Candoğan and Altan, 2014).

In September 2008, with the collapse of the Lehmann Brothers investment bank in the United States of America and rapidly spreading to other countries in the process of economic crisis, taking lessons in the process of economic crisis provides to begin work on Basel III. The regulation, called the Basel III criteria, strengthened the regulations regarding the current capital requirement and was announced in 2010. The aim of Basel III is to increase the resilience of financial and economic shocks, regardless of the source of the banking system. In order to achieve this, principles have been adopted to increase the transparency and the ability of the banks to inform the public, to expand the enforcement of risk management and corporate governance principles in banking, and to increase the resilience of the banks on an individual basis (Cangürel, et al., 2010).

Banks are credit institutions. Credit risk is the type of risk that has the largest share in total risk in banking. In this phase of the study, general information about the banking sector in Turkey will be given first, and then the evaluation of the credit risk related to the 1990–2017 periods will be made in the Turkish banking sector.

3 The Banking Sector in Turkey

Banking in Turkey began in the Ottoman Empire period before 1923, the founding year of the Republic, and 18 banks established during this period continued to exist in the Republic period (Akgüç, 2007). With the establishment of the Republic of Turkey, abolishing capitulations and giving priority to economic development paved the way for the development of national banking. In this process, the establishment of the Central Bank of the Republic of Turkey (CBRT) in 1931 is an important development both in terms of the country's economy and banking sector (Yıldırım, 2004).

With a series of decisions taken on January 24, 1980 regarding the economy, significant developments have been made in the banking sector in Turkey since 1980. In this period, there has been a number of radical changes in the financial markets and banking sector with liberal policies that have been implemented for the first time in Turkey. Some of these changes include the determination of foreign exchange rates by the market, the release of credit and deposit rates, the efforts to harmonize the banking sector legislation with international norms, and the reduction of barriers to entry into the sector. As a result of these developments, the number of banks which were 43 in 1980 increased to 64 in 1990 and 81 in 1999. Despite these positive developments in banking, the ratio of total credit and receivables of the sector to total assets fell significantly between 1990 and 2001. In 1990, the rate of 47 % was as 25 % in 2001. The main reason for the decrease in the ratio of loans to total assets, which is the main function of banks as the banking sector grows, is that the financing needs of the public sector are met by banks with a high real interest rate during this period. The high levels of budget deficits in the country's economy and the use of public banks for different purposes in the period 1990–2001 caused significant competition disparities in the sector due to the increasing financing needs of the public sector. In this period, the inadequacy of equity, low asset quality, high sensitivity to market risks, risk management, and weaknesses in the internal control system are important problems.

In addition to the tight fiscal policy applied in the economy in 2000, the foreign exchange nudity (and the pre-disclosure of foreign exchange rates in the context of this policy) applied to break the inflationary expectations caused significant changes in banks' strategies compared to the 1990s. In this period, banks provided short-term foreign currency resources and started to lend long-term Turkish lira. This change made banks with a weak financial outlook more vulnerable to exchange rate, interest rate, and liquidity risk. As a result of the economic crises experienced in November 2000 and February 2001, the economic management had to give up its policy of nudging the exchange rate. In 2001, which was the most severe economic crisis in the history of the Republic, the government of the time had to make important structural reforms under the name of "Transition to Strong Economy Program". The basis of this program is the strengthening of the Turkish banking system (Bumin, 2016).

By the year 2000, the structural problems of the banking sector in Turkey and its risks were beyond the scope of consideration. The establishment of Banking Regulation and Supervision of Agency (BRSA), which was established in August 2000 as an independent institution in this process, is an important development in terms of risk management and auditing in the

Tab. 10.1: The Top 10 Biggest Banks in the Turkish Banking Sector as of 31.12.2017

Bank	Foundation Year	Share of Assets%	Share of Credits (%)	Share of Deposits (%)
T.C. Ziraat Bankası A.Ş.	1863	14.09 %	14.88 %	15.57 %
Türkiye İş Bankası A.Ş.	1924	11.75 %	12.03 %	11.91 %
Akbank T.A.Ş.	1948	10.25 %	9.58 %	10.81 %
Türkiye Halk Bankası A.Ş.	1938	9.90 %	10.24 %	11.29 %
Türkiye Garanti Bankası A.Ş.	1946	9.22 %	10.52 %	10.59 %
Yapı ve Kredi Bankası A.Ş.	1944	9.66 %	9.92 %	9.90 %
Türkiye Vakıflar Bankası	1954	8.78 %	9.37 %	9.08 %
QNB Finansbank A.Ş.	1987	4.08 %	4.24 %	3.95 %
Denizbank A.Ş.	1997	3.93 %	3.88 %	4.40 %
Türk Ekonomi Bankası A.Ş.	1927	2.78 %	3.17 %	3.25 %
Total		**84.44 %**	**87.83 %**	**90.75 %**

Source: Turkish Banking Association, 2017,(https://www.tbb.org.tr/tr/bankacilik/banka-ve-sektor-bilgileri/banka-bilgileri/bankalar/64)

Turkish banking sector. A significant step has been taken for the Turkish banking sector with the "Regulation on the Establishment and Operation of Internal Audit and Risk Management Systems in Banks" published by the BRSA in February 2001. The implementation of Basel criteria in addition to the configuration studies on risk management and internal audit in banks has changed the financial outlook of the Turkish banking sector and has increased its resilience to crises.

There are 51 banks in the Turkish banking sector as of the end of 2017. Of these banks, 33 are deposit banks, 13 are participation banks, and 5 are participation banks. Of the 33 deposit banks, 3 consists of banks with public participation, 9 with private capital, 20 with foreign capital, and 1 with the transfer to the Saving Deposit Insurance Fund (BRSA, 2017). As of the end of 2017, the banks in the top 10 in the Turkish banking system and their ratios in the total sector are listed in Tab. 10.1.

The largest 10 banks in the sector are the deposit banks. T.C. Ziraat Bank and Halkbank of Turkey and Vakıflar Bank of Turkey are public-owned banks in the top 10 banks. The total assets of these three banks constitute 32.77 % of the sector. This figure shows that public banks have an important place in the banking sector. There are 11,585 branches in the sector by the end of 2017, and 208,280 people are employed (BRSA, 2017).

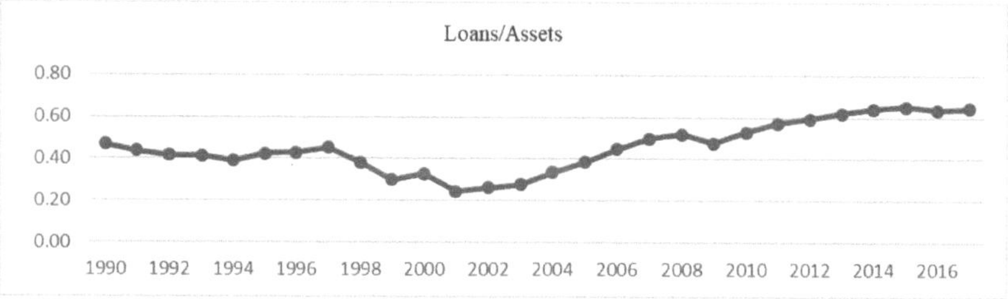

Fig. 10.1: The Turkish Banking Sector (1990–2017) Total Loans/Total Assets. Source: Monthly Banking Sector Data, BRSA (www.bddk.org.tr/BultenAylik/)

4 Credit Risk in the Turkish Banking Sector

In Turkey, 2001 has distinct importance when evaluating the banking sector data. As a result of the lessons learned from the 2000 November and 2001 February crises, within the framework of the macroeconomic reforms in Turkey, arrangements were made to significantly reduce the risks that the financial sector and banking sector carry. The strengthening of the Turkish banking system is the basis of the government's program of transition to a strong economy announced in 2001. While the inflation rate in Turkey was approximately 75 % on average annually during the 11-year period (1990–2001) before the implementation of this program, the inflation rate in the 2002–2017 period was below 9 % on average annually as a result of the decisions and reforms made in the economy. The rapid drop in inflation in the period after 2001 directly affected all macroeconomic indicators and the activities and financial structure of the banking sector in Turkey. For this reason, there are significant differences between 1990–2001 and 2002–2017 in the development of the Turkish banking sector and the credit risk in the sector.

In this section of the study, first of all, the course of the credit item in the Turkish banking sector in 1990–2017 will be examined and then the credit risk assessment of the sector will be made.

4.1 Development of Credits in Turkish Banking Sector

The ratio of the loans to the total assets of the Turkish banking sector for the period 1990–2017 is in Fig. 10.1. In this period, it is observed that the rate of decline from 1990 to 1994 fell from 47 % to 39 %. After the economic crisis in 1994, the ratio of loans in total assets increased in 1995–1997 period when the economy was relatively good. The rate, which began to decline in 1998

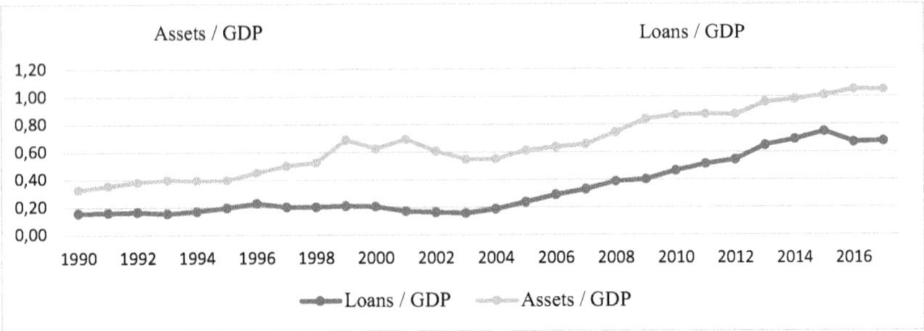

Fig. 10.2: The Turkish Banking Sector (1990–2017)Assets/GDP and Loans/GDP. Source: The Banks Association of Turkey, (https://www.tbb.org.tr/tr/bankacilik/banka-ve-sektor-bilgileri/istatistiki-raporlar/59)

with the impact of Russia and Far East crises, also tended to decline between 1998 and 2001. The ratio of loans to total assets was 24.6 % in 2001, one of the most severe economic crises in the Turkish economy. This figure is the lowest level that took place in this 40-year period since 1980 when Turkey entered the market economy. The main reason why the ratio of loans to total assets in the sector tends to decline until 2001 is that banks finance the high public financing deficit with a high real interest rate in the Turkish economy during the period 1990–2001. During this period, the public financing deficit was financed by printing substantial amounts of money and issuance of government debt securities (GDDS). On the one hand, while this situation caused high inflation, on the other hand, the uncertainties caused by inflation in the economy and the high real interest rates and the continuous increase in the public finance deficit prevented the growth of the loans item. While the high real interest rates negatively affect the credit usage of individuals and companies, it is observed that the savings in the economy were transferred to the funding of the public sector through banks during this period.

As a result of the reforms implemented in 2001, which are a milestone in terms of the banking sector, the ratio of loans to total assets in the following years tends to increase. The ratio, which was 24.6 % in 2001, rose to 64.5 % in 2017. Due to the global economic crisis that started in 2008, the ratio of loans to total assets in the sector fell only in 2009 in the period 2001–2017.

The development period of the Turkish banking sector in 1990–2017 is in Fig. 10.2. In an economy, there are basically two ratios (total assets/GDP and total credits/GDP) that reflect the level of development of the banking sector. As the total assets/GDP increase in the chart during the 1996–2001 period, the reason for the decrease in credits/GDP is that banks have to assume the public financing deficit due to the macroeconomic conditions in the Turkish economy during this period as stated above. It is observed that there is an upward trend in the Turkish banking sector in the following periods after 2002. In other words, after 2002, the banking sector entered into a rapid development process in Turkey.

4.2 Credit Risk in the Turkish Banking Sector

As a measure of credit risk, the most widely used variable in academic studies is NPL (non-performing loans/total loans). Ahmad and Ariff (2007), Espinoza and Prasad (2010), Nkusu (2011), Ben Ameur and Mhiri (2013), Makri et al. (2014), Brighi and Venturelli (2014), Owoputi and Kayode and Adeyefa (2014), Topak and Talu (2017), and Gila-Gourgoura and Nikolaidou (2017) are some of the studies used by the NPL as a measure of credit risk. In this section of the study, while analyzing the credit risk in the Turkish banking sector, NPL was used as a measure of credit risk in the sector as in many studies in the literature.

The rise in credit risk in the banking sector is due to the failure of borrowers to meet their obligations in the economy. When individuals or institutions use credit, they plan to pay off their credit debt with the proceeds they expect to achieve in the future. Similarly, the banks that extend the loan make a loan and evaluate the risk situation of the country's economy and the sector in which the company conducts its activities and makes a loan agreement. The rise of NPL in the banking sector shows that the real incomes of individuals or institutions are insufficient compared to the expected incomes and therefore the economy is in a negative position compared to the expectations. In this sense, the increase of NPL in the sector is an important indicator of the decision-makers in the economy.

The course of the NPL in the Turkish banking sector in the 1990–2017 period is presented in Fig. 10.3. In the years 1994, 1998, 1999, 2000, 2001, and 2009, which are the years of crisis in terms of the Turkish economy, it is observed that NPL has increased significantly compared to the previous year. In 2001, which was one of the biggest economic crises in the history of the Republic, the NPL was at the highest level of all time with 37.4 %. Immediately after the crisis of February 2001, BRSA published a series of Regulations on the Establishment and Operation of Internal Audit and Risk Management Systems in Banks and a number of structural reforms in the field of internal audit and risk management in banking. As a result of the "transition to strong economy" program implemented by the economic management in 2001 and the arrangements made in the banking sector, credit risk in the Turkish banking sector has started to

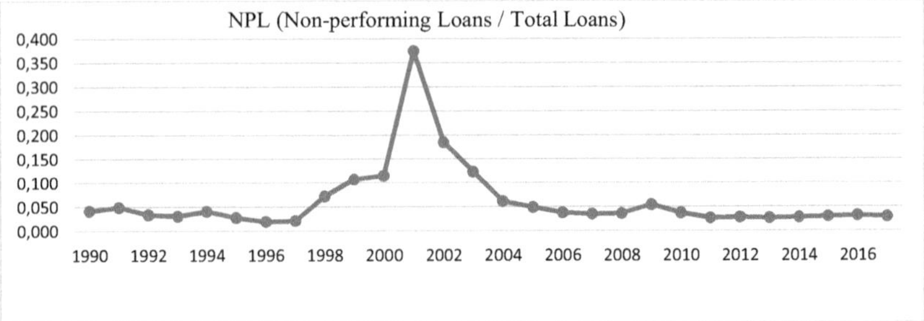

Fig. 10.3: Credit Risk in the Turkish Banking Sector (1990–2017). Source: Monthly Banking Sector Data, BRSA (www.bddk.org.tr/BultenAylik/)

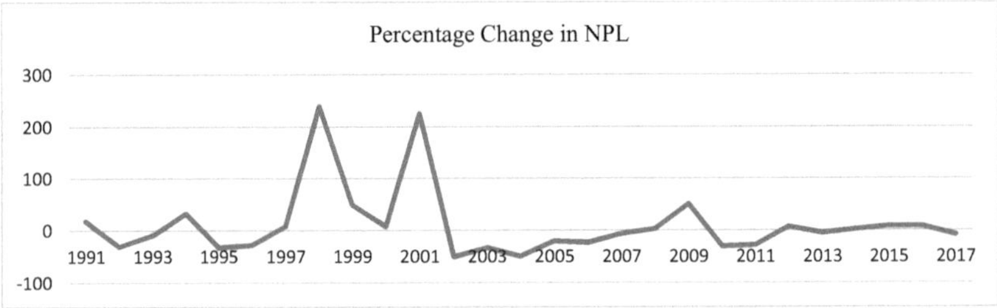

Fig. 10.4: Percentage Change in Credit Risk in the Turkish Banking Sector (1991–2017). Source: Monthly Banking Sector Data, BRSA (www.bddk.org.tr/BultenAylik/)

fall sharply in line with the positive developments experienced in the general economy since 2002. The NPL, which dropped to 18.5 % in 2002, decreased to 12.3 % and 6.2 % in 2003 and 2004, respectively. The NPL, which fell below 5 % in 2005 with the exit from the crisis, was realized below 4 % in all years other than 2009 in the 12-year period until 2017. The global economic crisis began in the United States in 2008 due to the negative impact on Turkey's economy; the NPL has risen to 5.4 % in 2009.

In order to better analyze the change in credit risk in the Turkish banking sector, the annual percentage change in the NPL is given in Fig. 10.4. As per the figure, the NPL decreased by 31 % and 9 % in 1992 and 1993 compared to the previous year, while it increased by 33 % in 1994. While the Turkish economy grew by 5 % and 7.7 % respectively in real terms, it contracted by 4.7 % in 1994. In this period, it is observed that there is a negative and strong relationship between the NPL and the real economic growth rate.

The ratio of NPL, which decreased by 32 % and 29 % in 1995 and 1996, followed a horizontal course in 1997. The years 1995, 1996, and the rate of real economic growth in Turkey's economy in 1997 and 7.9 %, respectively, was realized as 7.4 % and 7.6 %. During these periods when economic growth was high, credit risk in the sector declined significantly. The NPL, which increased by 239 % in 1998, increased by 49 % in 1999 to 10.7 %. The reason for the increase in credit risk during this period is that the Far East and Russia crises have a negative impact on the Turkish economy. The Turkish economy contracted 3.4 % in 1999. In 2000, the existing high credit risk in the sector increased further and the NPL increased to 11.5 %.

In the 2001 economic crisis, NPL increased by 225 % to 37.4 %, the highest level of all times. The most severe crisis in Turkey in terms of the general economy and banking sector occurred in 2001. In 2001, the Turkish economy shrank by about 6 % in real terms. As a result of the arrangements made in the economy and banking sector in 2001, credit risk in the Turkish banking sector began to decline rapidly. In the 6-year period between 2002 and 2007, while the Turkish economy grew by 7.1 % on average annually, NPL has been decreasing steadily compared to the previous year. The NPL, which was 37.4 % in 2001, decreased to 3.5 % in 2007 as a result of positive developments in the economy and the sector. The NPL, which remained at the same level as 2007 in 2008, increased by 50 % in 2009, when the Turkish economy shrank by 4.7 %. In the Turkish economy, which grew by 8.5 % and 11.1 % in 2010 and 2011 after the 2009 economic crisis period, NPL decreased by 31.6 % and 28.1 %. In this period, where the rate of economic growth is relatively high, it is observed that the rate of loans in follow-up has also decreased significantly.

The credit risk in the Turkish banking sector was lower in 2011–2017 than in previous periods. The NPL had a maximum of 3.2 % in this eight-year period. The positive developments in macroindicators in the Turkish economy positively affected the credit risk during this period.

Conclusion

In order to have a strong economy today, it is necessary to have an advanced financial system. Banks are credit institutions that are at the center of the financial system in terms of their functions. While the minimum capital adequacy ratio is calculated in banking, there are three types of risks defined in Basel II regulation. These are credit risk, market risk, and operational risk.

This chapter was written for the purpose of examining credit risk in the banking sector in Turkey. In order to analyze the tendency of the loans item in the banking sector, by calculating the Loans/Total Assets ratio of the sector, the Assets/GDP and Loans/GDP ratios of the banking sector are calculated in order to analyze the level of development of the sector, and in order to examine the credit risk in the sector, NPL (Non-performing Loans/Total Loans) was calculated and analyzed for 1990–2017 period. Findings obtained as a result of analysis:

1. In the context of the establishment of Banking Regulation and Supervision Agency (BRSA) in 2000 and the "Transition to Strong Economy" program implemented during the 2001 economic crisis, the Regulation on the Establishment and Operation of Internal Audit and Risk Management Systems in banks has changed the risk management and control in the Turkish banking sector considerably. The Turkish banking sector, which has been restructured in this process, has been very positive in all of the ratios used in the analysis since 2002.
2. The loans/total assets ratio in the sector tends to decrease in the 1990–2001 period and increase in the 2002–2017 period. While the ratio of 47 % in 1990 fell to 24.6 % in 2001, it rose to 65 % in 2017. The decrease in the ratio until 2001 was due to the fact that the public sector's ever-growing financing gap was the funding of the banks with high real interest rates. As inflation and interest rates fell rapidly in the country after 2001, banks started to perform their basic function in the economy and the ratio of loans in total assets started to increase rapidly.
3. While the assets/GDP ratio of the sector had a tendency to increase from 1990 to 2001, there was no significant change in the Loans/GDP ratio in the same period. While the banking sector grew during this period, the ratio of loans to GDP remained horizontal because banks were unable to perform their basic functions due to the conditions of the economy. After 2003, the trend was rising at both rates. The loan/GDP ratio, which was about 15 % in 2002 and 2003, rose to 75 % in 2014.
4. There is a strong negative relationship between the ratio of NPL and real economic growth rate of the sector. While the economy contracted in 1994, 1998, 2000, 2001, and 2009, which we could see as crisis years in terms of the Turkish economy, the rate of continued loans increased significantly. Compared to the previous period, the nonperforming loans, which increased by 33 % in 1994, 239 % in 1998, 225 % in 2001, and 51 % in 2009, reached the highest level of all time in 2001 with 37.4 %. In the period in which high real growth rate was realized in the economy, the rate of nonperforming loans decreased.

5. The ratio of NPL started to decline rapidly after 2001. The significant decrease in credit risk in the sector in the post-2001 period compared to the pre-2001 period shows that the regulations related to banking have been successful within the framework of the transition to a strong economy program. In nearly 20 years after 2001 did not lead to a crisis for the banking sector in Turkey reinforces our opinion.

References

Ahmad, N. H. and Ariff, M. (2007). Multi-Country Study of Bank Credit Risk Determinants. *International Journal of Banking and Finance*, Vol. 5, No. 1, pp. 135–152.

Akgüç, Ö. (1987). *100 Soruda Türkiye'de Bankacılık*. Vol. 54, Gerçek Yayınevi. İstanbul.

Akgüç, Ö. (2007). Türkiye'de Yabancı Bankalar. *Muhasebe ve Finansman Dergisi*, (36), pp.6–17.

Ameur, I. G. B. and Mhiri, S. M. (2013). Explanatory Factors of Bank Performance: Evidence from Tunisia. *International Journal*, Vol. 2, No. 1, pp. 1–11.

Banks Association of Turkey (2018). *Banka ve Sektör Bilgileri*. (https://www.tbb.org.tr/tr/bankacilik/banka-ve-sektor-bilgileri/istatistiki-raporlar/59).

BRSA (2005). 10 Soruda Yeni Basel Sermaye Uzlaşısı (Basel II).

BRSA (2006). *Bankalarin İç Sistemleri Hakkında Yönetmelik*, 26333 Sayılı Resmi Gazete.

BRSA (2017). *Türk Bankacılık Sektörü Temel Göstergeler Raporu*, Aralık 2017.

BRSA (2018). *Monthly Banking Sector Data*. (www.bddk.org.tr/BultenAylik/).

Brighi, P. and Venturelli, V. (2014). How Do Income Diversification, Firm Size and Capital Ratio Affect Performance? Evidence for Bank Holding Companies. *Applied Financial Economics*, Vol. 24, No. (21), pp. 1375–1392.

Bumin, M. (2016). Yeniden Yapılandırma Sonrası 2004–2014 Döneminde Türk Bankacılık Sektörü. *Maliye ve Finans Yazıları*, No.105, pp.177–222.

Candoğan, M. A. and Altan, M. (2014). Basel Kriterleri Çerçevesinde Operasyonel Risk Ölçüm Yöntemlerinin Karşılaştırılması: Örnek Bir Uygulama. *Selçuk Üniversitesi Sosyal Bilimler Enstitüsü Dergisi*, No.31, pp.265–276.

Cangürel, O., Güngör, S., Sevinç, V.U., Kayci, İ. and Atalay, S. (2010). Sorularla Basel III. Risk Yönetim Dairesi. BRSA.

Espinoza, R. A. and Prasad, A. (2010). Nonperforming Loans in the GCC Banking System and Their Macroeconomic Effects. No.224, *International Monetary Fund*.

Gila-Gourgoura, E. and Nikolaidou, E. (2017). Credit Risk Determinants in the Vulnerable Economies of Europe: Evidence from the Spanish Banking System. *International Journal of Business and Economic Sciences Applied Research*, No.1, pp.60–71.

Grote, R. and Marauhn, T. (Eds.). (2006). *The Regulation of International Financial Markets: Perspectives for Reform*. Cambridge University Press. Cambridge

Lambrecht, M. B. (2017). *The Basel II Rating: Insuring Access to Finance for Your Business*. Routledge, London.

Makri, V., Tsagkanos, A. and Bellas, A. (2014). Determinants of Non-Performing Loans: The case of Eurozone. *Panoeconomicus*, Vol. 61, No. 2, pp. 193–206.

Nkusu, M. M. (2011). Nonperforming Loans and Macrofinancial Vulnerabilities in Advanced Economies (No. 11–161). *International Monetary Fund.*

Owoputi, J. A., Kayode, O. F. and Adeyefa, F. A. (2014). Bank Specific, Industry Specific and Macroeconomic Determinants of Bank Profitability in Nigeria. *European Scientific Journal*, ESJ, Vol. 10, No. 25, pp. 408–423.

Saunders, A. (2002). *Credit Risk Measurement: New Approaches to Value at Risk and Other Paradigms*. John Wiley & Sons.New York

Smith, R. C., Walter, I. and DeLong, G. (2011). *Global Banking*, 3rd ed. Oxford University Press, New York.

Topak, M. S. and Talu, N. H. (2017). Bank Specific and Macroeconomic Determinants of Bank Profitability: Evidence from Turkey. *International Journal of Economics and Financial Issues*, Vol. 7, No. 2, pp. 574–584.

Torun, M. (2017). Basel II Uygulamalarının Bankacılık Sektörüne Etkileri. *Uygulamalı Sosyal Bilimler Dergisi*, Vol. 1, No. 1, pp. 1–19.

Yıldırım, O. (2004). Türk Bankacılık Sektörünün Temel Sorunları ve Sektörde Yaşanan Mali Riskler. *Dış Ticaret Dergisi*, No. 30, pp. 1–13.

Serçin Şahin

11 Shadow Banking, Leverage Cycles, and the Great Recession

Highlights: The shadow banking system, the role of which in the global financial crisis has been widely debated, has increased its share in the financial system over the last 40 years. Although this system supported the real economy by rapidly increasing the total credit supply in the run-up to the crisis, it also made the financial system, and the economy as a whole, more vulnerable due to its inherent fragilities. In this study, we compare the shadow banking system with traditional banking and examine the primary feedback mechanisms with which they amplify the leverage cycles. Finally, as Geanakoplos (2010a,b), we argue that the Great Recession was a deleveraging phase of a leverage cycle, but the significant share of shadow banks in the financial system increased its amplitude and caused it to be much severe than the previous crises.

Keywords: Shadow banking, leverage cycles, haircuts, the Great Recession

Introduction

It would not be wrong to say that the global financial crisis that started in the USA in 2007–2008 and spread all over the world, *The Great Recession*, is the biggest crisis in the world since the Great Depression in 1929. In discussions on the crisis, mostly "Shadow Banking" is accounted for the gravity of the crisis.

The "shadow banking" term was first used by economist Paul McCulley in a speech he made at the annual financial symposium at Jackson Hole in 2007, and has been widely adopted by economists since then (Adrian and Ashcraft, 2012; Gallin, 2015; Adrian, Moench and Shin, 2010). Although its name was coined recently, actually, shadow banking is not a new phenomenon. It started in 1932 with the establishment of the Federal Home Bank System (FHBS) by the US government to boost the housing market as a part of the measures taken to stimulate the economy following the Great Depression (Flannery and Frame, 2006). Later, Fannie Mae (1932), Ginnie Mae (1968), and Freddie Mac (1970) were also established to serve for the same purpose. These "Government-sponsored Enterprises" (GSEs) created securities backed by mortgage loans and funded themselves by selling these securities in the capital markets. Thus, they developed a funding method different from traditional commercial banks, which funded themselves with retail deposits, and laid the foundation of today's shadow banking system (Pozsar, Adrian, Ashcraft and Boesy, 2010; Adrian and Ashcraft, 2012).

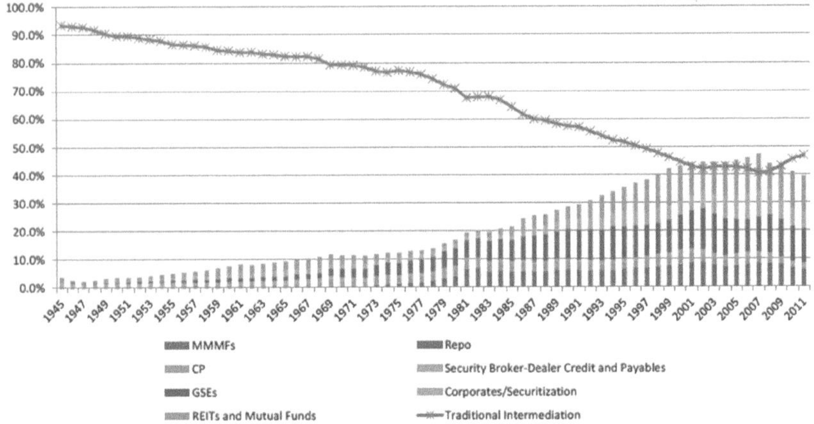

Fig. 11.1: The Share of Shadow Banking Sector in Total Financial Sector Liabilities. Source: Adrian & Ashcraft, 2012

As seen in Fig. 11.1, the share of shadow banking in total financial sector liabilities increased continuously, but traditional banks continued to be the primary credit provider in the economy until the 1980s. However, since the late 1970s, shadow banking's share has increased rapidly, and it caught up with the traditional banking sector just before the global financial crisis (Adrian et al., 2010; Adrian and Shin, 2009).

In the historical development of shadow banking, we see that both supply- and demand-side factors mutually reinforce each other. Probably the most important factor on the supply side was the minimum capital adequacy regulation brought by the Basel agreement that entered into force in 1988. This regulation required the banks to hold a minimum level of capital equal to a risk-weighted ratio of the assets on their balance sheets. As the risk of the assets increased, the amount of capital to be held increased accordingly (Brunnermeier and Pedersen, 2009). In order to evade this regulation and reduce their cost of capital, traditional banks securitized and transferred the long-term and risky loans on their balance sheets such as mortgages to off-balance sheet vehicles that operate outside the mandate of regulatory agencies and funded them in large repo markets (Pozsar, 2008). With this method called "regulatory arbitrage", banks had the opportunity to provide loans as much as they are willing to, without being subject to any capital restrictions (Gennaioli, Shleifer and Vishny, 2013; Bernanke, 2012). Secondly, the entrance of independent broker-dealers and individual non-bank financial institutions into the securitization business after witnessing that traditional banks obtained high profits from lending, securitizing, and selling loans, added momentum to the expansion of shadow banking (Pozsar et al., 2010).

On the other hand, the most important factor on the demand side was the development and growth of the repo market. After Regulation Q which set an upper limit to deposit rates in 1971, money market mutual funds (MMMFs) emerged as an alternative to banks (Adrian and Ashcraft, 2012; Krishnamurthy, 2010). MMMFs were legally restricted to invest in short-term, low-risk assets; therefore, the "shares" they issued were regarded as a close substitute to retail bank deposits and often provided higher rates of return. Short-term lending against collateral in the repo market constituted a significant part of their investment, and as the share of MMMFs increased in the financial landscape, the repo market has grown accordingly. In repo transactions, MMMFs also accepted long-term, risky, high return securities as collateral, which they are not allowed to buy legally. Therefore, MMMF's participation in the repo market increased the funding possibilities for long-term, risky securities (Rosengren, 2014).

Another factor effective in the growth of the repo market was the turn of institutional investors with vast amounts of funds, such as corporate treasury managers, pension funds, central and local governments into this market. Due to the existence of an upper limit for the deposit insurance, bank deposits were not safe enough for these investors, but, the repo market provided a secure way of investment by enabling them to lend against collateral for short-term (Gorton and Metrick, 2010, 2012).

Finally, in the years before the global financial crisis, we see that large cash pools from Asia and particularly the petrodollars from the Middle East were looking for safe and high-yield investment opportunities all over the world, but safe instruments such as government bonds had low rates of return due to the loose monetary policy in that period. Therefore, the shadow banking system has produced exactly what these funds are looking for: they transformed risky loans into securities which were – seemingly – as risk-free as government bonds, money-like, high-yield instruments. Hence, this phenomenon called "global savings glut" has also been effective in increasing the share of shadow banking in the financial system (Geanakoplos, 2010a).

The growth of the shadow banking system supported the economy by increasing the total credit supply with its flexibility. However, this was not without a price; it also caused an accumulation of risk in the financial system. In the following sections, we will examine the fragilities of shadow banks comparing to traditional banks and their crucial role in the Great Recession of 2007–2008.

2 Shadow vs. Traditional Banking

Traditional banking is the business of intermediation between suppliers and demanders of funds. Lending through intermediaries increases efficiency compared to direct funding by providing economies of scale in terms of information and risk. Credit intermediation mainly involves credit quality, maturity, and liquidity transformation. Credit quality transformation is the adjustment of default risk by changing the order in which lenders are paid. Maturity transformation and liquidity transformation occur when loans granted, and the sources used to fund them have different maturities, and liquidities, respectively (Gorton and Metrick, 2012; Pozsar et al., 2010; Adrian, 2014). Traditional banks carry out all these transformations and absorb all the risks arising from them within their balance sheets. However, they are immune to these risks due to their direct access to explicit government guarantees such as deposit insurance and the central bank liquidity facilities (Bernanke, 2012). In return for these guarantees, they are subject to regulations such as the reserve requirement ratio and the minimum capital adequacy ratio and are monitored continuously by regulatory authorities.

Traditional banks keep the loans they granted on their balance sheets until their maturities, and in this process, the spread between credit and deposit interest rates constitutes the major part of their profits. For this reason, the business model of traditional banks is called "originate-to-hold" (Gorton and Metrick, 2012; Pozsar et al., 2010; Adrian, 2014).

On the other hand, shadow banking can be defined as any credit intermediation activity that is carried out outside the regulated traditional banking system without an explicit government guarantee (Adrian, 2014; FSB, 2011; Gennaioli et al., 2013). Shadow banking slices the credit intermediation process into sequential stages and each step is carried out independently by different organizations that are specialized based on comparative advantages. The shadow banking process begins with the issuance of loans by traditional banks or specialized financial institutions. In the second stage, these loans are transferred to single- and multi-seller conduits for storage while waiting to be securitized. In the third stage, the ABS syndicate desks of broker-dealers pool these loans and slice into tranches to create asset-based securities (ABSs). ABSs are legally structured as bankruptcy-remote special purpose vehicles (SPVs). Most of the time, numerous tranches are generated in the creation of ABSs, but, roughly, tranches can be classified into three categories. The senior tranches are at the top being the most liquid and safest of all. Mezzanine tranches follow the senior tranches and lose value only in case of a major shock. Since the probability of such shocks is deemed to be extremely low, mezzanine tranches are also liquid and regarded as safe in normal times. Finally, the equity tranches are at the bottom and function as a buffer against losses for the tranches above them. Senior tranches are highly demanded by traditional banks due to their high ratings, and equity tranches are highly demanded by hedge funds due to their high rates of return. On the other hand, the demand for mezzanine tranches is limited compared to the other tranches. The mezzanine tranches that cannot be sold are transferred to other SPVs for storage. As they accumulate in these pools, broker-dealers slice them into tranches to produce ABS Collateralized Debt Obligations (ABS-CDOs, or CDOs for short). Just like ABS tranches, CDO tranches also have different ratings and different levels of demand for them. Again, unsold CDO tranches can be accumulated and sliced to form CDO-*squared*, CDO-*cubed*, and so forth. Finally, the shadow credit intermediation process is completed when these securities are wholesale-funded by money market investors such as MMMFs or pension funds. Not all shadow credit intermediation processes include each of these steps, but in general, the lower the quality of the loans to be securitized, the longer is the process (Pozsar et al., 2010; Moreira and Savov, 2016; Adrian and Asccraft, 2012; Gorton and Metrick, 2012; Hull, 2018).

During this process, shadow banks interact via market mechanism and transform long-term, risky loans into liquid instruments via securitization. For this reason, the shadow credit intermediation process is also referred to as "market-based credit intermediation" (Adrian, 2014; Pozsar et al., 2010; Adrian and Shin, 2008).

The majority of shadow bank profits comes from fees for granting and securitizing loans, and for trading these securities; not from the spread between the credit and deposit interest rates like traditional banks. Hence, with the development of shadow baking, the business model in credit intermediation has changed from *originate-to-hold* to *originate-to-distribute*. In the new model, credit and maturity risks are transferred to markets; however, because of the dependence on markets for funding securities, the market risk increased. Accordingly, credit intermediation has transformed from a high-credit-risk, low-profit business into a high-market-risk, high-profit one (Pozsar, 2008; Pozsar et al., 2010).

The repo market is the primary funding source for shadow banks in the credit intermediation process (Fig. 11.2). Because it is cheap compared to alternative funding sources, at the same time, it is safe as it is a short-term, collateralized funding instrument (Bernanke, 2012; King, 2008; Geanakoplos, 2010a). The downside of repo funding is the fact that it has to be rolled over frequently,

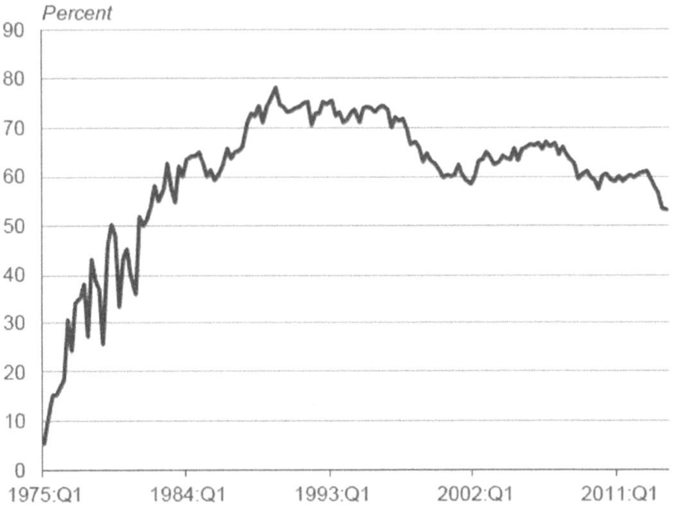

Fig. 11.2: The Share of Repo in the Funding of Securities Brokers and Investment Banks. Source: Rosengren, 2014

mostly overnight. Thus, as the dependence of a financial institution on repo funding increases, its sensitivity to changes in funding conditions, and, accordingly, its liquidity risk rises (Gorton and Metrick, 2010). Although traditional banks use the repo market as a funding source as well, shadow banks depend on it at a much higher rate (Rosengren, 2014).

As stated in the introduction, one of the essential factors in the development of shadow banking was the fact that they are operating outside the oversight of regulatory agencies without being subject to the regulations imposed on traditional financial institutions. However, the price of this exemption is, not being able to access the explicit government guarantees that regulated financial institutions have access. For this reason, shadow banks try to access these guarantees indirectly through the traditional banks' credit lines. However, these credit lines are under full discretion of traditional banks, and shadow banks' access to them in times of financial distress is entirely dependent on the decision of these banks. In this sense, the circumstances of the shadow banking system before the Great Recession was looking very similar to that of the US traditional banking system in the 19th century before the establishment of Fed and the FDIC, which was vulnerable to external shocks and bank panics (Gallin, 2015; Adrian, 2014; Rosengren, 2014).

3 Shadow Banking and Leverage Cycles

In addition to the fragilities of shadow banks mentioned above, another factor that increases their sensitivity to external shocks was the use of high leverage while borrowing from the repo market (Sunderam, 2015; Duffie, 2010). Although it has various definitions, leverage is defined as the ratio of total assets to capital in this study (Adrian and Shin, 2013).

The maximum amount of funding that financial institutions can get in the repo market, therefore the maximum leverage that can be taken is determined by haircuts or margins. The haircut is the difference between the market value and the collateral value of an asset. Since financial institutions have to finance "haircuts" with their own capital, the total amount of haircut over all of their positions cannot exceed their capital (Adrian and Shin, 2009; Brunnermeier and Pedersen, 2009). Therefore, the inverse of haircut ratio gives the maximum leverage, and the multiplication of maximum leverage with a financial institution's capital amounts to its balance sheet capacity (Adrian and Shin, 2010; Geanakoplos, 2010b).

There are several arguments for explaining the existence of haircuts. Holmstrom and Tirole (1997) emphasize the moral hazard problem that arises due to asymmetric information between the borrower and the lender. Lenders want to ensure that borrowers take risks by putting their own capital at stake and exert the maximum effort to pay their debts back. Haircuts are the reflection of this idea in the repo market (Geanakoplos, 2010a; Adrian and Shin, 2008). Geanakoplos (2010a) argues that haircuts are the result of the uncertainty about the future and asset price volatility. In this sense, the primary function of haircuts is to act as a buffer and protect lenders from unexpected drops in the market price of the collateral (Duffie, 2010). Therefore, the haircut in a repo transaction must be at the level that provides the incentive to the borrower to make the repayment and get its collateral back at the maturity, and at the same time, that ensures the lender to recover its money in case the borrower defaults and the lender has to sell the security in the market.

In practice, the haircut of an asset is determined according to the Value-at-Risk (VaR) at a certain level of confidence (Brunnermeier and Pedersen, 2009). VaR is the expected maximum loss within a specified period of time, with a certain level of confidence. For instance, if a financial institution calculates the 5 % VaR for one year as $1000 for an investment position, then there is a 5 % risk of losing more than $1000 within one year on this position. VaR of an asset is usually calculated based on the past price volatility of that asset (Linsmeier and Pearson, 2000). Therefore, the more volatile the price of an asset, the higher is

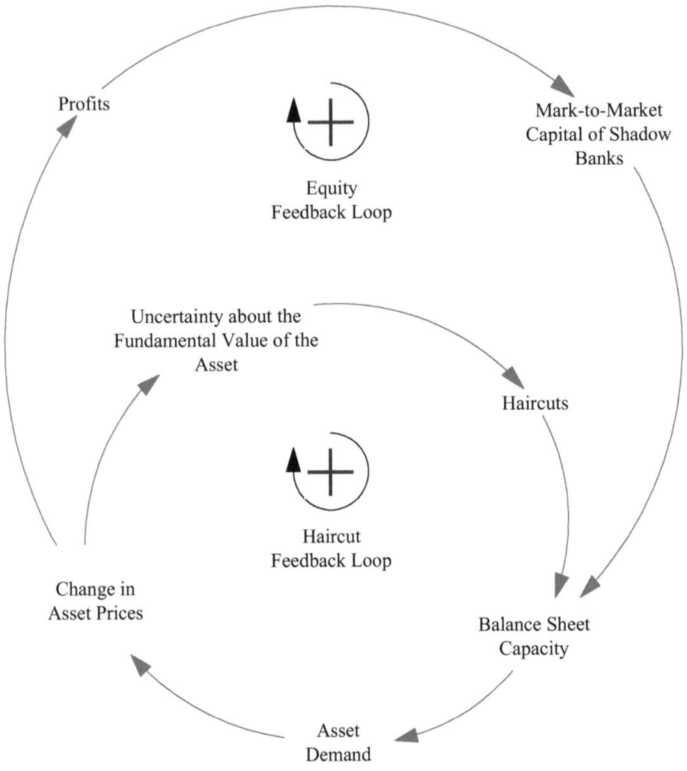

Fig. 11.3: Haircut and Capital Feedback Loops

the haircut. This fact results in the emergence of two positive feedback loops between asset prices and leverage (Fig. 11.3).

The first one is the *haircut feedback loop*. The stability of asset prices for some time causes haircuts to fall. Hence, the maximum leverage and balance sheet capacity of shadow banks increase. In order to use their capacity as much as possible, shadow banks demand more assets, and increased asset demand causes asset prices to rise accordingly. As asset prices increase, market participants become more optimistic about the future. The demand for assets increase, and asset prices rise further. However, this loop may also work the other way around. If uncertainty in financial markets increases for any reason, haircuts increase. The maximum leverage and balance sheet capacity of shadow banks decrease accordingly. Since they cannot fund the haircuts with the current level of their capital, they have to fire-sale some of the assets they hold. As they sell the assets, asset prices fall, uncertainty in the market rises and haircuts increase further (Brunnermeier and Pedersen, 2009; Krishnamurthy, 2010; Adrian and Shin, 2010).

The second loop is the *capital feedback loop*. Since the assets that shadow banks hold are overwhelmingly subject to mark-to-market accounting, an increase in the prices of the assets causes a direct increase in their capital levels. Accordingly, the amount of haircuts they can meet with their capital and their balance sheet capacity increases. In order to use their capacity efficiently, shadow banks demand more assets, causing asset prices and their capital levels to increase further. This loop can work the other way around like the previous one. If the prices of assets on the balance sheets of shadow banks for any reason, the capitals of these institutions erode. In the face of declining balance sheet capacity, they have to dispose of assets that are more than the level that their current capitals can support, and, therefore, asset prices fall further (Brunnermeier and Pedersen, 2009; Krishnamurthy, 2010).

It should be noted that the change in asset prices in both loops occurs as a result of changes in funding liquidity conditions, rather than a change in market fundamentals (Brunnermeier and Pedersen, 2009; Geanakoplos, 2010b). These two positive feedback loops interact and reinforce each other. Hence, their effect is greater than the case they would have acted separately (Brunnermeier and Pedersen, 2009).

These mechanisms lead the shadow bank leverage to be procyclical (Adrian and Shin, 2008, 2010, 2013). Namely, the prolonged stability in the financial markets leads to optimism about the future and neglection of risks. Financial institutions demand assets and increase their leverages, which causes an increase in asset prices. However, if some bad news flows into the market, the landscape changes abruptly. This time, financial institutions rapidly reduce their leverages and asset prices fall accordingly. Geneakoplos (2010a, 2010b) refers to this phenomenon as *leverage cycles*.

4 Leverage Cycles and the Great Recession

Geanakoplos (2010a, 2010b) claims that leverage cycles are a perpetual phenomenon in economies. As the argument goes, all the crises in the 20th century correspond to the deleveraging phase of a leverage cycle, and the recent global financial crisis is no exception to this (Fig. 11.4).

Indeed, optimism prevailed in financial markets for a prolonged period before the global financial crisis. Coupled with the fact that interest rates were

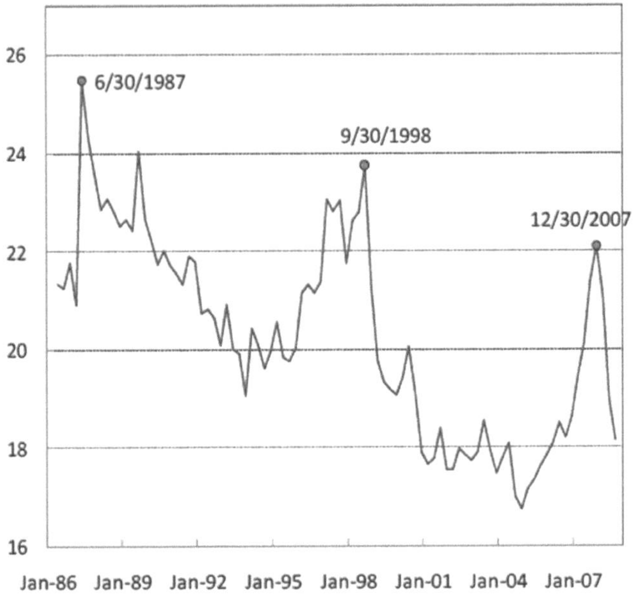

Fig. 11.4: Average Leverages of the Primary Dealers in the USA (Adrian & Shin, 2009). *Although there seems to be a decreasing trend in leverages in the figure, this is due to the fact that the sample includes the traditional banks. However, if investment banks are taken into consideration in isolation, a horizontal trend is observed (Adrian & Shin, 2009).*

so low, this optimism revealed itself as high demand for asset-backed shadow bank securities, because they provided high yields and seemed to be as riskless as treasury bonds. In order to meet the hiked demand for securities, financial intermediaries increased the supply of all kinds of loans, but particularly mortgage loans, the quality of which is sensitive to macroeconomic conditions. The increase in shadow credit intermediation resulted in an abundance of credit, and the real economy, especially the housing market, boomed in this period (Moreira and Savov, 2016).

However, the process did not function as smoothly as it seems at first sight. Shadow banks' incentives for securitization was so big that society's credit demand could not keep up with the pace. In order to increase the credit demand as rapidly as the supply, credit standards had been significantly deteriorated. Firstly, mortgage loans are started to be given to people with subprime credit scores, which could not have received loans under normal conditions. Indeed, some of the loans granted during this period were called "NINJA (No Income,

No Job, and No Assets) loans", namely, the loans that are given to individuals who do not have any income, job, or assets. Secondly, variable interest rate mortgage loans are granted. These loans started with a fixed, low "teaser rate" at first few years of their repayment period; then the interest rate was adjusted to the market rates. The rationale behind these loans was the assumption that home prices would increase, accordingly, homeowners would accumulate some net equity, and they would be able to refinance these loans in more favorable conditions before the teaser rate period ends. Finally, mortgages with very low or no down payment were given. In other words, haircuts that households have to pay when buying houses were reduced (Gorton and Metrick, 2012).

The shadow banking system produced significant amounts of residential mortgage-backed securities (RMBSs) backed by the subprime loans, and these securities are funded widely in the repo market. The senior tranches of these securities had the highest AAA rating. Since haircuts for such highly rated, "safe" securities were very low, shadow banks worked with high levels of leverage (Gorton and Metrick, 2010).

Besides, the emergence of the derivatives market called "Credit Default Swap" (CDS) for RMBS backed by subprime mortgage loans in 2005, when the leverage was already high, caused the leverages to increase even more. Because those who bought long positions in CDSs were not the ones with long positions in these instruments, but investors who were pessimistic about them. Therefore, CDSs provided the opportunity to pessimists to bet against subprime RMBSs with leverage, and optimists took the other side of CDSs to increase their leverage more (Geanakoplos, 2010a).

Housing supply boomed, as the housing demand increased with the support of loose credit conditions. However, the increase in demand could not keep up with the pace of supply in time. Therefore, after reaching a peak in the second quarter of 2006, housing prices fell slightly in the following two quarters. In the meantime, delinquencies in mortgage loans had also increased, and financial intermediaries retightened the credit standards by increasing down payment requirements and credit score thresholds to increase the quality of loans. As access to new mortgage loans became difficult, housing demand decreased, and housing prices fell further. As a result of this, homeowners with variable interest rate mortgage loans could not accumulate enough net equity to refinance their mortgages, nor could they make the repayments in the face of increased interest rates. Banks foreclosed these mortgages and tried to sell the houses to recover their losses. However, this led to a further increase in supply in the housing market, while the demand for houses was already low. Hence, housing prices decreased further (Geanakoplos, 2010a).

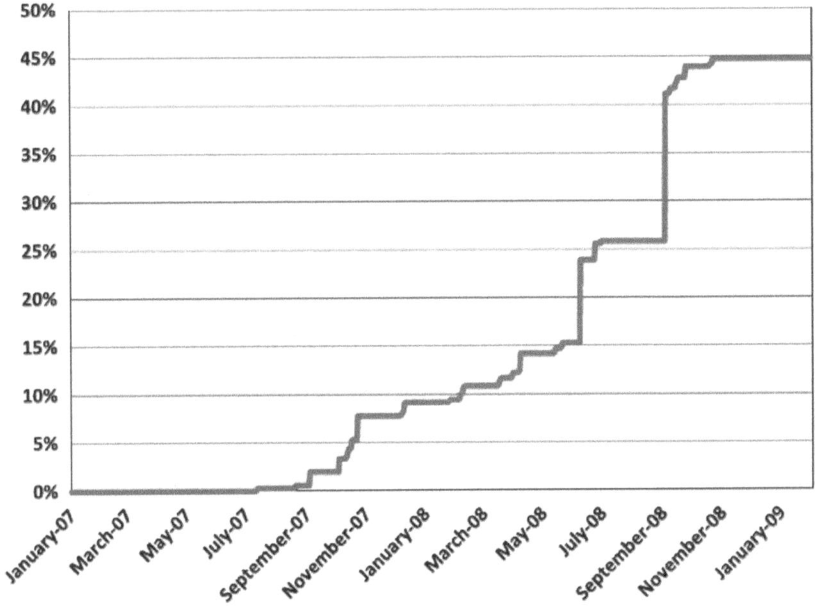

Fig. 11.5: Repo Haircut Index in the USA before the Global Financial Crisis.
Source: Gorton and Metrick, 2012

With these developments in the housing market, uncertainty about the quality of assets backed by subprime mortgage loans rose. This resulted in a decrease in security prices and an increase in their haircuts (Fig. 11.5). In the fall of 2008, haircuts for these securities rose to 100 %, meaning that these securities are no longer accepted as collateral in the repo market. Even for the assets with an investment grade, haircuts increased to the level of 20% (Duffie, 2010). Therefore, financial institutions had to fire-sell the assets that were beyond the level that can be supported by their capital and deleveraged rapidly. In fact, this could be described as a panic in the repo market, similar to the bank panics that occurred in the traditional banking system. Since the shadow banks did not have direct access to government guarantees, there was not any mechanism to stop this panic from spreading over the entire financial system. With the deleveraging of the financial system, many financial institutions went bankrupt, and many developed economies entered into recession (Gorton and Metrick, 2010).

In fact, the total amount of subprime mortgage loans was very small compared to the total size of the financial system. To be specific, the total losses in these loans amounted to a few hundred billions of dollars, which was equal to 5% of the total stock market value (Bernanke, 2012; Brunnermeier and Pedersen, 2009). However, this relatively small amount of losses led to a systemic crisis that halted the functioning of the entire financial system. The first reason for this was the fact that the shadow banking system had a large share in the financial system. With the haircut and capital feedback mechanisms we mentioned in the previous section, shadow banks first escalated the overall leverage of the financial system in the run-up to the crisis and then amplified and propagated losses in the deleveraging phase. The second reason was that another leverage cycle in the real sector, which functions through the haircuts in mortgage loans and net equity of homeowners, reinforced the leverage cycle in the financial sector. As mentioned above, with the over-optimism prevailed in the pre-crisis period, down payments (haircuts) for mortgage loans had been reduced. With the rise in demand, house prices increased, which in turn led to an increase in housing supply. However, when the demand could not keep up the pace with the supply, house prices started to fall. As a result of this, uncertainty regarding the housing market increased, which led to a rise in down payments (haircuts) of mortgage loans. The fall in house prices also led to a decrease in the net equity of homeowners. It became impossible for homeowners to refinance or repay their mortgage loans, and foreclosures soared. Sale of foreclosed houses caused to house prices to decrease further. Uncertainty and down payment rates increased accordingly (Geanakoplos, 2010a). Therefore, Geanakoplos (2010a) describes the Great Recession as a "double leverage cycle".

Conclusion

The shadow banking system has grown over the past 40 years and has become an important component of the financial system before the global financial crisis. However, shadow banks' high dependence on short-term repo funding, the absence of direct government guarantees, and their excessive use of leverage increased the vulnerabilities in the financial system. Notably, the fact that haircuts for assets used as collateral are calculated based on past volatility of the asset prices led to the emergence of the haircut and capital feedback loops, which amplified the effects of external shocks to the system.

In fact, leverage cycles are a phenomenon that has long existed before the emergence of the shadow banking system. Previous crises can also be described as a deleveraging phase of a leverage cycle. However, the shadow banks' high share in the financial system before the last global financial crisis led to an amplification of the leverage cycle. For this reason, the Great Recession has been much more severe than the previous crises. In order to prevent the emergence of a crisis of this size in the future, it is crucial to make regulations and establish the liquidity and capital guarantee mechanisms that will reduce the fragilities of the shadow banking system and the systemic risk it poses on the global financial system.

References

Adrian, T. (2014). *Financial Stability Policies for Shadow Banking*. Staff Report. Federal Reserve Bank of New York.

Adrian, T., & Ashcraft, A. (2012). *Shadow Banking: A Review of the Literature*. Staff Report. Federal Reserve Bank of New York, No. 580.

Adrian, T., & Boyarchenko, N. (2012). *Intermediary Leverage Cycles and Financial Stability*. Staff Report. Federal Reserve Bank of New York, No. 567.

Adrian, T., & Shin, H. (2008). *Financial Intermediary Leverage and Value-at-Risk*. Staff Report. Federal Reserve Bank of New York, No. 338.

Adrian, T., & Shin, H. (2009). *Money, Liquidity, and Monetary Policy*. Staff Report. Federal Reserve Bank of New York, No. 360.

Adrian, T., & Shin, H. (2010). Liquidity and Leverage. *Journal of Financial Intermediation* (19), 418–437.

Adrian, T., & Shin, H. (2013, September). Procyclical Leverage and Value-at-Risk.

Adrian, T., Covitz, D., & Liang, N. (2014). *Financial Stability Monitoring*. Staff Report. Federal Reserve Bank of New York, No. 601.

Adrian, T., Moench, E., & Shin, H. (2010). *Financial Intermediation, Asset Prices, and Macroeconomic Dynamics*. Staff Report. Federal Reserve Bank of New York, No. 422.

Bernanke, B. (2012, April 13). Some Reflections on the Crisis and the Policy Response. *Conference on "Rethinking Finance: Perspectives on the Crisis"*, New York.

Brunnermeier, M., & Pedersen, L. (2009). Market Liquidity and Funding Liquidity. *The Review of Financial Studies*, 22 (6), 2201–2238.

Duffie, D. (2010). The Failure Mechanics of Dealer Banks.

Financial Stability Board (FSB). (2011). Shadow Banking: Strengthening Oversight and Regulation- Recommendations of the Financial Stability Board.

Flannery, M., & Frame, W. (2006, Third Quarter). The Federal Loan Bank System: The "Other" Housing GSE. *Economic Review*, pp. 33–54.

Gallin, J. (2015). Shadow Banking and the Funding of the Nonfinancial Sector. In C. Hulten, & M. Reinsdorf (Eds.), *Measuring Wealthand Financial*

Intermediation and Their Links to the Real Economy (pp. 89–123). University of Chicago Press.

Geanakoplos, J. (2010a, August). Solving the Present Crisis and Managing the Leverage Cycle. *Economic Policy Review*, pp. 101–131.

Geanakoplos, J. (2010b). The Leverage Cycle. In D. Acemoglu, K. Rogoff, & M. Woodford (Eds.), *NBER Macroeconomics Annual 2009* (Vol. 24, pp. 1–65). University of Chicago Press.

Gennaioli, N., Shleifer, A., & Vishny, R. (2013). A Model of Shadow Banking. *The Journal of Finance*, 68 (4).

Gorton, G., & Metrick, A. (2010, May 12). Haircuts.

Gorton, G., & Metrick, A. (2012). Securitized Banking and the Run on Repo. *Journal of Financial Economics* (104), 425–451.

Holmstrom, B., & Tirole, J. (1997). Financial Intermediation, Loanable Funds, and the Real Sector. *The Quarterly Journal of Economics*, 112 (3), 663–691.

Hull, J. (2018). *Options, Futures and Other Derivatives* (10th Edition). New York: Pearson Education.

King, M. (2008). *Are the Brokers Broken?* Citi Group.

Krishnamurthy, A. (2010). Amplification Mechanisms in Liquidity Crises. *Americal Economic Journal: Macroeconomics*, 2 (3), 1–30.

Linsmeier, T., & Pearson, N. (2000). Value at Risk. *Financial Analyst Journal*, 56 (2), 47–67.

Moreira, A., & Savov, A. (2016, April 29). The Macroecoonomics of Shadow Banking.

Pozsar, Z. (2008, July). The Rise and Fall of the Shadow Banking System. *Regiaonal Finance Review*, pp. 13–25.

Pozsar, Z., Adrian, T., Ashcraft, A., & Boesy, H. (2010). *Shadow Banking*. Staff Report. Federal Reserve Bank of New York, No. 458.

Rosengren, E. (2014, August 13). Broker-Dealer Finance and Financial Stability. *Conference on the Risks of Wholesale Funding*, New York.

Sunderam, A. (2015). Money Creation and the Shadow Banking System. *Review of Financial Studies*, 28 (4), 939–977.

Melike Torun and Onur Duygu

12 Globalization 4.0 and Banking Sector

Highlights: This chapter explores the importance of globalization 4.0 and its effects on banking sector focusing on the scope of the digital banking trends, which reflect the developments in technology in the banking sector; mobile banking, bank and fintech collaborations, chatbot, artificial intelligence, data usage, application programming interface (API) and open banking, blockchain, and advanced technologies such as advanced trends will be examined. In addition, how mobile banking applications will shape the strategies of the customers according to their needs and spending habits, how the banks need to process the data in order to reveal the products that the customers need, and how the customer data at the hands of banks meet with open banking will be discussed. A wide range of project research will be conducted as well as dealing with transactions such as shopping, the blockchain, which the banks give importance to and still continue to work on, is not only about the transfer of money, but also how the blockchain can be used in many areas of finance such as smart contracts, credit, and insurance are investigated.

Keywords: Globalization 4.0, banking, digital banking, artificial intelligence, fintechs

Introduction

Globalization and technology have changed the existing fields of business in every period and brought new opportunities for the labor force. Looking back, globalization periods are seen in three main periods. To summarize, the first wave of globalization that began with the discovery of new trade routes and continents by Christopher Columbus in 1492, in the period of globalization 1.0, a transformation from an agricultural society to a trade and colonial-oriented society took place. The period of globalization 2.0 covers approximately the beginning of the 19th century until the beginning of the Second World War. With four major technological developments known as steam machines, train, telegraph, and mail systems have been transformed into an industrial society. The blue-collar works were also formed during this period. There are different views in the literature for the period of globalization 3.0, also known as the formation period of the information society. While advocates of the first opinion approach to the new world order after the 1945 Second World War and the development of trade as the period of globalization 3.0, the advocates of the second opinion approach Friedman (2000)'s globalization 3.0. The emergence of the internet has made the world a global information platform (Sharma and

Sheth, 2004) and the transition from the production society to the information society. International companies and new business areas based on the internet network have been formed. The transfer of knowledge and the development of technology have laid the foundations of globalization 4.0, by making a significant contribution in the context of innovation. The period of globalization 4.0 includes the developments in the future with the concepts of artificial intelligence, robot, sharing economy, and 3D printing. Schwab (2018) stated that globalization 4.0 has started and that countries and institutions should be ready. It is stated that the transformation of health, transportation/transmittal, and production, distribution, and energy issues started with the developing technology and that the institutions of the old should be renewed from head to toe along with this transformation. It is foreseen that artificial intelligence and robots will provide the transition from a production economy to the sharing economy.

2 Yields of Globalization 4.0 and Its Effects on Banking

In order to examine the effects of globalization on the banking sector, it is necessary to mention the concept of digital banking and its development.

2.1 The Development of Digital Banking

It can be said that the economic relations of technology with innovative products and services and convenience in all areas of life are also digitized. In a digitalized economy, you can own a hotel without a hotel, you can be a bookseller without a bookstore. At this point, the banker, who wants to be a banker, still has to comply with a number of regulatory rules that are arranged on behalf of more traditional banking services. The common point of innovations in the digital economy is that they have platform-based business models. These platforms, which act as intermediaries, in one sense have become the meeting point of demand and supply. In terms of customers, through these platforms, friction can be reduced by mobile vehicles, and better services can be obtained from more affordable prices (Ernst and Young, 2018). The benefits of digitalization and the change in banking take effects as day by day. Transactions are now more mobile and the interaction with branches is decreasing day by day. With the digitization of banking transactions, the productivity of the bank employees increases, while the bank customers can save time. The use and development of digital banking services and products are widely seen today (Joshi and Parihar, 2017; Ernst and Young, 2018).

As a result of the expansion of the digital economy and the reflection of platform-based business models to retail banking, platforms are mediating between retail customers with a wide range of financial products and services (including fintech providers). The subject of digitalization in retail banking, which focuses on the banking transactions of individuals, is the main topic in the World Retail Banking Report (2018). As the main reasons for the digital change in the banking sector:

- Change in customer expectations and needs,
- Legislative pressure,
- Demand for digital channels,
- Up and Coming technologies (Artificial Intelligence, Blockchain),
- Fintech and Bigtech's (Google, Amazon, Facebook, Apple, Alibaba, Tencent) banking product/service presentations are indicated in the report.

It can be said that the most important point of digital change in the banking sector is the change in customer expectations and needs (Zeybek, 2018). If technology and digitalization are defined as a tool, it is possible to observe that customer expectations change according to the solutions created by these tools. In this context, the most important trend in banking is how banks can respond more effectively to their customer needs by using digitalization rather than digitalization. The necessity of this is to determine the needs of the customer before the need arises or when it is needed, and the most important tool for this is the big data and the artificial intelligence that can process and understand this data. According to Marous (2017), the three most important trends that will affect banking in the near future are artificial intelligence, machine learning, and real-time data integration and processing with advanced data analytics. As a secondary trend, it is stated that friction should be eliminated on the customer's journey. In the third trend, the APIs as an interface created to allow functions belonging to an application to be used in another application were created on the Open Banking Platform, and the banking products and services were opened to non-bank third-party developers. With this trend, which we will examine under the heading of open banking, banks will not have to produce the best product or service but will be able to take this service from third-party developers and present it to their customers. As a result of this situation, the customer will be directed to the banking platforms where the customer can find the best service and the customer experience will be maximized in return for the service he/she receives.

2.2 The Elements of Digital Banking

In order to understand the future changes in the banking sector, we need to take a good look at current innovations and make a well-prepared roadmap. As stated in the World Retail Banking Report (2018), it is possible to explain the elements of the banking sector in terms of digitalization as follows:

- *Although digital channels of banks have developed, branches remain important as they have insufficient customer experience.*

A survey was conducted to measure customers' experience on a channel-based. Looking at the survey results without discriminating the age group, while overall satisfaction level is highest in internet banking, the level of satisfaction in mobile use is lowest. In the Y generation, known as those born after 1980, the satisfaction level in the digital banking field was highest in the branch channel. In other words, the present experience is not enough to make people who are prone to technology happy. Branch and human touch still appear in front of digitalization (World Retail Banking Report, 2018).

As customers can buy products and services from branch channels and all channels outside the branch, they want to experience the same experience in all channels. With the development of technology, the applications developed for smartphones have led to the formation of many companies. In the financial world, this development has emerged as the birth of fintechs, known as financial technology companies. Fintechs have developed applications in a wide range of fields, from artificial intelligence to portfolio management, even if they start developed applications on payment systems (Zeybek, 2018). Since the main focus of fintechs is the creation of experience, this situation has increased the expectation of service from banks. According to the survey report, the top five factors affecting customers' decision to stay in the bank in the next year are: ease of process and compliance, brand confidence, quick and timely solution creation, price/interest rate, and digital channel ease of use.

- *In the field of digital banking, personal product service delivery is important, and the use of big data of banks is very valuable.*

Analyzing the data trail left by customers for proactive product delivery is crucial. By analyzing these data, the needs of the customer are determined and personalized product presentation can be realized. According to the World Retail Banking Report (2018), nearly half of the customers who are offered personalized products by their banks feel positive about their banks. On the other hand, it was observed that the satisfaction rate decreased to 39 % when the personal product was not offered to the customers. In the report, it is exemplified the Bank of Ireland's customer data analysis tools, such as Amazon, Google, and Facebook, as well as personalized mail and omnichannel services. Thanks to the personalized presentation, 278 % annual application increase were achieved in all channels. Another example is the location-based data analysis developed jointly with Foursquare and Capital One to determine the location of the customers and offer product offerings with push notifications according to their spending habits.

- *Customers can purchase products/services in retail sectors with digitalization 7/24 and demand similar situation for banking services. It has become necessary for banks to take examples of the applications of digitization in other sectors and find solutions for their clients.*

It is known that three billion people in the world use social media and that two-third of the world's population have a cell phone. These statistics show that mobile is very important today (Cuesta et al., 2015). When we look at it in terms of banks, it is seen that banks cannot offer all their products and services as mobile.

- *Fintechs and banks need to create a new banking model by creating the eco-system (Lee and Shin, 2018).*

Two different banking models are mentioned in the World Retail Banking Report (2018). The first is the Netflix-like platform model. In this model, while different types of companies offer their services, the bank will create a platform for accessing these services. The other will be banks focused on niche customer segments (high asset balance customers, athletes, movie stars, etc.). Considering that the platform bank model will be much wider, it is inevitable that banks will create a new ecosystem with fintech companies that specialize in certain processes. In the survey conducted in the World Retail Banking Report (2018), it was stated that fintechs had a higher impact on mobile wallets/cards and payments. In this context, the most important step for banks is to integrate standard banking services such as payment/transfer/current account management with fintech solutions and reduce the costs and become the platforms that provide more value-added services to its customers. Organizational restructuring is essential in both banking models.

In the banking sector, new principles, data, technology, agile and digital-oriented organizational structure are required. Therefore, it is an unavoidable fact that banks which want to survive in this wave of transformation should internalize these principles and review their processes in line with these principles.

3 Technological Trends in Digital Banking

With technological developments, the development of money has also been affected over time. With the widespread use of the internet, the use of internet banking has increased, and later on, there have been developments in the field of mobile banking through smartphone applications. The developments in the system of payments through innovation; the changes in the financial, political, and legal structures in this field; and the trends that include new technological products and services have started to emerge in the present and future finance world. The use of digital banking and the follow-up of new technological trends are necessary in order to maintain competition in the financial sector (Ketterer and Andrade, 2016: 15). The most important technological trends with the digitalization of the banking sector are: open banking, API, machine learning with artificial intelligence, blockchain, and fintechs.

3.1 Open Banking and APIs

The APIs, which have been qualified as the smart channel that has been used by the banking sector for many years, have also been used by fintechs, which are financial technology companies. With the development of APIs, the concept of open banking has been used today (Brodsky and Oakes, 2017). In short, open banking can be defined as a collaborative model in which banking data is shared between two or more independent parties through APIs (Brodsky and Oakes, 2017). Through open banking, banks help customers make the best possible financial and commercial decisions by choosing the right services. Thanks to open banking, banks are more easily adopting products and services provided by fintech startups. In addition, banks are more competitive in adopting open banking, providing improved customer experience and new revenue streams, enabling them to closely follow current practices and survive in the digitized economy (Brodsky and Oakes, 2017).

3.2 Artificial Intelligence and Machine Learning

One of the most important focus of digitization in the context of globalization 4.0 is artificial intelligence and machine learning. The leading role of artificial intelligence in globalization 4.0 would be to automate repetitive labor-intensive tasks that may be subject to automation. The impact of this will be the acceleration and simplification of many of the tasks already carried out by intense manpower, but the impact on the workforce will be beneficial for others while ravaging for others. Although there are studies in banking and finance that examine this, it is generally based on projections. In this part of the book, firstly, after the definition of artificial intelligence and the determination of usage areas, the effects of the labor force will be examined within the scope of the estimation work of BCG (Boston Consulting Group) (Huerta and Anand, 2018).

Artificial intelligence refers mainly to the ability of computers to perform human-specific tasks such as thinking, analyzing, inference, and identification. When the usage areas are examined, the definition and function of artificial intelligence can be understood more clearly. According to BCG, artificial intelligence now has ten different areas of usage. They can be summarized as follows:

1. Machine vision
2. Speech recognition
3. Natural Language Processing (NLP)
4. Information processing
5. Data learning
6. Planning and identification
7. Speech
8. Visualization
9. Control
10. Navigation and movement.

The most important ones we have seen up to now have been learning through data through natural language processing, which leads to visual identification, voice recognition, and[1]chatbot formation. One of the best indicators of artificial intelligence in every area of our lives is the self-driving driverless cars that are expected to become widespread in the near future (Cummings, 2017). At this point, the effect of artificial intelligence on labor force has been the subject of debate. Due to the fact that artificial intelligence will simplify many routine jobs thanks to automation, it is inevitable to have a positive/negative effect on the workforce doing this routine work (Acemoglu and Restrepo, 2018).

On the other hand, with the development of artificial intelligence, it is known that the concept of the internet of objects has evolved and thus collects data by connecting objects to the internet. It is seen that the human power is insufficient

1 Chatbots, also known as virtual customer representative, are applications that simulate verbal or written human speech to customers. There is a limit to the capacity of chatbots to understand and respond. Not being able to answer more than one question at the same time, and especially the use of different accents and languages in international companies, are the parts chatbots have difficulties in. It is thought that these limits will be removed with developing software.

in the process of processing this data of magnitude, and artificial intelligence is activated at this stage as a savior. The learning process is involved in understanding and interpreting the information required by the data. The process of processing and interpreting the data of artificial intelligence is now expected to be manifested in many fields such as health, marketing, and finance (Dobrescu and Dobrescu, 2017).

While the issue of artificial intelligence and robot technologies will lead both white- and blue-collar workers to a big and deep unemployment today, according to the association of Leonard and Eczacıbaşı, it is stated that Schumpeter's (2010) theory of creative destruction will be valid and that there will be opportunities with the workforce that technology can adapt to and breed new. An example of Schumpeter's theory of creative destruction could be the announcement of the British Lloyd Bank in October 2018 that it would fire 6,000 employees from bank and would hire 8,000 skilled in large data and digitization. Today's widespread belief is that the impact of the change on the workforce will be seen after 2030, so it is possible to say that there is still time to prepare for creative destruction.

The World Economic Forum (2018) reports that in the next five years, 75 million people will be unemployed and new job opportunities will be able to be created for 133 million people. It is stated that the artificial intelligence and robots will acquire 42 % of the works by 2022, and these will be the works of the employees who mostly do the work and do not take the initiative. On the contrary, it is emphasized in the report that the work of the people who are questioning and searching for the new cannot be taken by artificial intelligence. As of 2025, 40 % of job descriptions are expected to be related to jobs that are not today.

3.3 Blockchain

In today's digitized world, we see that currencies are digitized as well. The most commonly used cryptocurrencies are decentralized currencies that use cryptography to secure transactions and verify balances. Blockchains are activated during the follow-up phase of cryptocurrencies. The blockchain, which is defined as a universal distributed account book, allows the approval of transactions and makes it possible to keep the balances of each cryptocurrency (Smith and Gamble, 2018). In other words, the blockchain is defined as a public or private encrypted distributed database. Every computer included in the network is part of the chain and contains a copy of the whole memory, so the integrity of the data is provided by many people (Smith and Kumar, 2018). When a new data is entered into the system, it must be confirmed by other users, so duplication or fake records can be blocked. There is no need for a central authority or an affirmation.

According to McKinsey (Carson et al., 2018), blockchain usage can be summarized as record keeping and operations in two main categories and six subheadings in these categories. The subheadings of the first category of record keeping are:

a) Registry Information Retention: Land Registry record save as static information.
b) Credentials Retention: It can also be used for jobs that require identities, such as registering credentials and voting.
c) Smart Contracts: Block-chain-based contracts that automatically generate results after certain conditions have occurred. As an example, the automatic occurrence of compensation can be described as the result of the occurrence of events that give rise to compensation in insurance contracts.

In the second category of transactions:

a) Dynamic Registry: Purchase/sale of assets through digital platforms.
b) Payment Infrastructures: Use in transactions such as foreign trade payments, insurance payments.
c) It can be summarized as other operations.

The term "platform" is a set of online digital editing algorithms for organizing economic and social activities. The common point of the platforms is that they offer a range of common techniques, technologies, and interfaces to a wide range of users. Digital platforms can be defined as mixed software, hardware, process, and network mix. Android and iOS operating systems are examples of digital platforms (Kenney and Zysman, 2016).

It is seen that digital platforms are also involved in blockchain technology. It is possible to summarize the benefits of blockchain technology as follows (Fanning and Centers, 2016):

- The short-term contribution of the blockchain is mainly seen as cost savings. It is expected that the impact of business models and adaptation of processes will emerge more clearly in the future. In addition, widespread use in general is expected to be in the next 3–5 years.
- According to the views of the meeting in Davos (World Economic Forum, 2018), in 2027, it was stated that 10 % of the world's GDP would be kept on the blockchain and the blockchain could contribute 1 trillion dollars to the world trade.

- Both banks and non-bank players in the banking sector saw this potential and intensified their investments in this direction.
- One of the key features of the blockchain is that it provides banks with fast and cost-effective solutions to the problem of foreign money transfers that produce huge financial gains.
- Although blockchain technology is mostly used by fintech and start-ups, banks also develop themselves to benefit from this technology. For example, with smart contracts, banks will be able to trade faster in exchange for lower costs in a wide range of areas, from letters of guarantee to foreign financing loans and insurance policies (World Economic Forum, 2018).
- All blockchain documentation is digital and can be used in many different applications. Thanks to the benefits of blockchain technology, third parties are eliminated and transaction costs are reduced and transformed into many sectors (Fanning and Centers, 2016).

3.4 New Performers in Banking – Fintechs

Along with the development of artificial intelligence and machine learning, it has become possible for banks to carry out their operational transactions without being involved in the decision-making process of bank employees. For example, banking transactions such as payment systems, robot consultants, and digitization of credit processes are performed by start-ups. Most banks have predicted that artificial intelligence helps customers automate their decision-making and personal digital assistant. With the widespread use of artificial intelligence, it is seen that the neo-banks in the form of fintech are also included in the banking sector. N26, Monzo, and Revolut are examples of these banks (Dobrescu and Dobrescu, 2017).

In the financial sector, the development of digital innovations and technology and the emergence of new business models are supported by fintechs. Thanks to fintechs, access to financial services has become easier. In addition, it has brought significant privacy, regulatory and legal obligations to the markets. Cryptocurrencies, blockchains, artificial intelligence and machine learning, mobile payment systems, and digital consulting and trading systems are examples of innovations that are at the center of the fintechs (Philippon, 2016). Although fintechs played a role in payment systems as the first usage area, it started to take place in the field of portfolio management with artificial intelligence. From this point of view, there is a perception that fintechs are in competition with banks or that there is a new threat to the decrease in bank branches and employees. On the other hand, it will be possible to say that a new ecosystem is in the financial world, with the cooperation of banks and fintechs, with the participation of customers who are financial service and product users (Guo and Liang, 2016).

Financial innovations developed on the basis that fintech is perceived as a competitor to banks are included. Traditional banking services (Ernst and Young, 2018) are made through branch offices and internet, customers are usually X generation and customer service is made through branch-oriented and communication centers. In traditional banks, data is the only resource based on internal data. The development of banks is slow due to intensive bureaucracy, length of approval periods, and budget cycles. However, in the fintechs, mobile priority has customer acquisition. Most of the customers belong to the Y generation and customer service is self-service and investing in chatboats. In fintechs, data is collected with the use of multiple resources supported by social sharing and customer interactions. The development of fintechs is fast thanks to its small organizational structures and R&D partners, with clear measurements and direct investor oversight.

It is useful to compare all three systems in order to see the advantages of internet-based enterprises, which are defined as Fintech 1 and Fintech 2.0, which are defined as bank blockchain cooperation compared to traditional banks, and to evaluate the financial benefits of cooperating with banks. In Tab. 12.1, a comparative summary is included.

Tab. 12.1: Comparison of Traditional Banks and Fintechs

Properties	Traditional Banks	Internet-Based Businesses (Fintech 1.0)	Blockchain and Banks (Fintech 2.0)
Customer Experience	Single-type scenarios	Rich scenarios	Rich scenarios
	Same service to everyone	Personalized service	Personalized service
	Poor customer experience	Good customer experience	Good customer experience
Efficiency	There are many interconnections	There are many interconnections	Point-to-point transmission – without using tool
	The tradeoff process is complicated	The tradeoff process is complicated	The transaction is made with the distributed notebook in the tradeoff
	Low efficiency	Low efficiency	High efficiency

(*continued on next page*)

Tab. 12.1: (continued)

Properties	Traditional Banks	Internet-Based Businesses (Fintech 1.0)	Blockchain and Banks (Fintech 2.0)
Costing	High level of manual control	Low level of manual control	Fully automatic
	There are many interconnections	There are many interconnections	No use of an intermediary
	High cost	High cost	Low cost
Security	Centralized data storage, can be falsified	Centralized data storage, can be falsified	Distributed data storage, protected
	Easy to leak users' personal information	Easy to leak users' personal information	With asymmetric encryption, users' personal information is more secure
	Low security	Low security	Good security

Source: Guo and Liang (2016).

Conclusion

In this study, the digital banking concept, which is digitalized with globalization 4.0, trying to keep up with the innovations brought by the economy, and new trends are mentioned. Research on the digitalization of banking transactions in both financial and academic fields has been made more recently. In this sense, this study is intended to provide preliminary information to the finance and academic circles who want to conduct research in this field.

With globalization 4.0, digitalization in the economy, and in particular with the increase of digitalization in banking and finance sector, new job descriptions in the future and the redefinition and regulation of some job descriptions or developments that are expected to disappear will be resulted (Kenney and Zysman, 2016). In line with the developments, those who want to work in this field should also have the knowledge and ability to interpret data in the fields of artificial intelligence, machine learning, fintechs, blockchain technology, and to become a good data analyst by learning to programme.

The daily and routine work which was done by the employees in the bank can be done more efficiently and quickly by machines and robots, in digital economies, where digitalization is accelerated through algorithms, digitalization can be achieved through globalization. Unlike the front-end mobile development efforts of banks and various financial institutions in the ongoing competitive environment, it is necessary for them to transform with digital strategy in order to maintain their lives in the competitive environment in return for fintech and digital platforms. In a world where data is a source of wealth, banks must effectively use the big data they obtain in order to survive in competition.

References

Boston Consulting Group (2018). The Impact of Artificial Intelligence on Financial Job Market, (http://image-src.bcg.com/Images/BCG-CDRF-The-Impact-of-AI-on-the-Financial-Job-Market_Mar%202018_ENG_tcm9-187843.pdf)

Brodsky, L. and Oakes, L. (2017). Data Sharing and Open Banking. McKinsey&Company. https://www.mckinsey.com/industries/financial-services/our-insights/data-sharing-and-open-banking.

Carson, B., Romanelli, G., Walsh, P. and Zhumaev, A. (2018). Blockchain Beyond the Hype: What is the Strategic Business Value?. McKinsey and Company.

Cuesta, C., Ruesta, M., Tuesta, D. and Urbiola, P. (2015). The Digital Transformation of the Banking İndustry. *BBVA Research (available at* https:// www. bbvaresearch.com/wp-content/uploads/2015/08/EN_Observatorio_ Banca_Digital_vf3. pdf). (Accessed date: 18.04.2019)

Cummings, M. (2017). *Artificial Intelligence and the Future of Warfare*. Chatham House for the Royal Institute of International Affairs.

Dobrescu, E. M. and Dobrescu, E. M. (2017). The Future of the Artificial Intelligence in Economics and Management. *Review of General Management*, *26*(2).

Ernst and Young (2018). A Vision for Platform Based Banking. Available at: https://www.ey.com/Publication/vwLUAssets/ey-a-vision-for-platform-based-banking /$File / ey-a-visionfor-platform-based-banking.pdf(Accessed date: 14.03.2019)

Fanning, K. and Centers, D. P. (2016). Blockchain and İts Coming İmpact on Financial Services. *Journal of Corporate Accounting & Finance*, *27*(5), 53–57.

Friedman, T. L. (2000). *The Lexus and the Olivetree: Understanding Globalization*. Farrar: Strausand Giroux.

Guo, Y. and Liang, C. (2016). Blockchain Application and Outlook in the Banking Industry. *Financial Innovation*, *2*(1), 24.

Huerta, J. M. and Anand, A. (2018). Machine Learning and Artificial İntelligence in Consumerbanking. *Journal of Digital Banking*, *3*(1), 22–32.

Joshi, D. and Parihar, S. (2017). Digitalization and Customer Perception towards the Banking Services. *Aweshkar Research Journal, 23*(2), 133–141.

Kenney, M., and Zysman, J. (2016). The Rise of the Platform Economy. *Issues in Science and Technology, 32*(3), 61.

Ketterer, J. A. and Andrade, G. (2016). Digital Central Bank Money and the Unbundling of the Banking Function. *Inter-American Development Bank.*

Lee, I. and Shin, Y. J. (2018). Fintech: Ecosystem, Business Models, İnvestment Decisions, and Challenges. *Business Horizons, 61*(1), 35–46.

Marous, J. (2017). The Use of All in Banking is Set to Explode. *The Financial Brand.*

Philippon, T. (2016). The Fintech Opportunity (No. w22476). National Bureau of Economic Research.

Schumpeter, J. (2010). *Kapitalizm, Sosyalizm ve Demokrasi* (Çev. H, İlhan.). Ankara: Alter.

Schwab, K. (2018). Globalization 4.0 – What it Means and How It Could Benefit Us All. *In World Economic Forum.*

Sharma, A. and Sheth, J. N. (2004). Web-Based Marketing: The Coming Revolution in Marketing Thought and Strategy. *Journal of Business Research, 57*(7), 696–702.

Smith, C. and Kumar, A. (2018). Crypto-Currencies–an Introduction to Not-So-Funny Moneys. *Journal of Economic Surveys, 32*(5), 1531–1559.

World Economic Forum (2018). The Future of Jobs Report 2018. Retrieved December 3, 2018 from http://www3.weforum.org/docs/WEF_Future_of_Jobs_2018.pdf

World Retail Banking Report (2018). https://worldretailbankingreport.com/wp-content/uploads/sites/3/2018/09/World_Retail_Banking_Report_2018.pdf

Zeybek, H. (2018). Dijital Bankacılık. *Mali Cözüm Dergisi, 28*, 79–107.

Dilek Demirhan and A. Rutkay Ardoğan

13 An Alternative Way of Financing for Entrepreneurs: Crowdfunding

Highlights: Increasing the level of entrepreneurial activity has been acknowledged as one of the necessary tools for economic development. Thus, solving the problems of entrepreneurs has become a priority for policy makers in almost all countries. One of the most important problems challenging entrepreneurs is raising capital to finance their businesses, and crowdfunding has emerged as an alternative to solve this problem. Distinctively from traditional financing options, crowdfunding offers raising capital from a vast majority of investors through the internet. Development of crowdfunding has accelerated especially after 2008 financial crisis, and crowdfunding volume has reached a remarkable level up to now. Although developed countries seem to have an important progress in crowdfunding until now, this alternative financing model also offers promising opportunities for entrepreneurs in developing countries. Therefore, policy makers in developing countries should pay attention to open the way for the development of crowdfunding, especially by regulating the legal infrastructure. Having considered the potential of crowdfunding in entrepreneurial activities, this chapter aims to explain its essentials by explaining different types of crowdfunding and how they function. Comparison is also made with traditional financing alternatives. Moreover, information and statistical data about crowdfunding activities are also given in the chapter.

Keywords: Entrepreneurial finance, investment-based crowdfunding, lending-based crowdfunding, reward-based crowdfunding

Introduction

One of the most important challenges encountered by entrepreneurs is raising capital. Although private equity investors, business angels, and venture capitalists have been providing a valuable source of finance for entrepreneurs especially for the last twenty years, fundraising problems of them are still unsolved. Together with the effects of 2008 global financial crisis, the demand for cheap funds especially at early stage of entrepreneurial businesses has grown tremendously (Turan, 2015). Technological developments and the rise of internet also gave hand to a new solution for the financing problem of entrepreneurs' projects, called as "crowdfunding". According to Belleflamme et al. (2011), crowdfunding may be defined as "an open call, mostly through the Internet, for the provision of financial resources either in form of donation or in exchange for the future product or some form of reward and/or voting rights".

Instead of collecting money from a small number of professional investors as in traditional financing, in crowdfunding individuals and start-ups obtain the essential financing from large audiences, called the crowd, through online social networks. In this sense, it can be argued that crowdfunding is actually a specified version of crowdsourcing. Bayus (2013) defines crowdsourcing as using the crowd to obtain ideas, feedback, and solutions to develop corporate activities. During a crowdfunding process, the creators of the project follow a similar path to crowdsourcing, by making an "open call" on internet. Despite sharing similar characteristics, crowdfunding differs from open-source practices in some angles. In an open-source practice, the crowd owns the resource, and exploits it on an individual basis. Thus, there is no restriction about who can use it. However, the main idea cannot be shared during a crowdfunding process. In an economic sense, it is not a public good, assuming non-rivalness and non-excludability (Fershtman and Gandal, 2011).

As the financial crisis in 2008 dried supply of many financial sources, artisans, philanthropists, entrepreneurs, and start-ups got the worst hit in terms of reaching crucial financial resources. This has led to crowdfunding to emerge as an alternative financial resource for them. Nowadays, most of the projects (owners of the projects are called as founders) are published on online portals, such as Kickstarter (founded in 2009), Indiegogo (founded in 2008), Rocket Hub (founded in 2010), and the crowd (called as funders) examine them to decide whether to finance these projects. Interestingly, funding may not be the only motivation for founders. According to Mollick (2014), crowdfunding is used by some founders for marketing purposes to create interest in new projects. Also, they have an opportunity to observe the demand for a proposed product, so that they can decide not to continue if they see little interest in the project. Hence, it can be claimed that crowdfunding offers potential benefits to founders, even beyond capital (Mollick, 2014).

Although crowdfunding has become popular for the last ten years, actually the idea is not a novel approach as a financing option. In the famous case of the Statue of Liberty in 1884, in order to overcome the financing problem of constructing the statue in New York, Joseph Pulitzer (publisher of *New York World*) made an open call to *New York World* readers to make donations. A total of 125,000 readers donated more than $100,000 in total, and they had their names cited in the newspaper, as a reward. As another reward, Pulitzer also offered model statues: 5 dollars for a 12-inch model and 1 dollar for a 6-inch model (Herve & Schwienbacher, 2018). Later, in 21st century, crowdfunding has become popular especially in the arts and creativity-based industries such as recorded music, films, and video games. For years, Sellaband, founded in 2006 as a music-only platform, has dominated the crowdfunding market, but subsequently Kickstarter, founded in 2009 as a broader creative-projects platform, has become more popular (Agrawal, Catalini, & Goldfarb, 2014).

Although information digitalization era and the rise of web 2.0 have played an important role in the spread of crowdfunding, the first online crowdfunding projects did not occur through online portals that are specialized on crowdfunding. For example, British software company Trampoline System was launched after a successful crowdfunding campaign via its own web page by some entrepreneurs (Belleflamme et al., 2013). They raised £1 million to fund their project. The first online crowdfunding portal is considered to be Artist Share, a US firm founded in early 2000s. This portal has facilitated artists to fund their projects with small contributions from their fans. With the arrival of the online platforms, which are mentioned above, the processes of crowdfunding projects have been standardized and these projects have begun to reach higher number of individuals. Thus, crowdfunding portals have spread globally.

In the rest of the chapter, functioning of the crowdfunding will be explained firstly, followed by the discussion of different types of crowdfunding and comparison of them to traditional financing alternatives. Before the final remarks, a brief information about the status and volume of crowdfunding in different countries will be summarized.

2 Types of Crowdfunding

Crowdfunding may be categorized based on the nature of the consideration received. The consideration of the funders when supporting the crowdfunding campaign can either be monetary or non-monetary in nature. Monetary considerations include expecting a stake in the business or share in its profits, or interest income on the capital provided. Investment-based crowdfunding and lending-based crowdfunding are types of crowdfunding including those considerations. Invoice trading, involving the disposal of unsettled invoices, is also seen as a type of crowdfunding with monetary considerations. These three types are often regarded as forms of financial technology (Fin Tech) because of their proximity to the financial markets. Funders may also have non-monetary considerations in the form of products or services like in reward-based crowdfunding, or funders may have no direct and measurable considerations for the investment like in donation-based crowdfunding (Dietrich & Amrein, 2017).

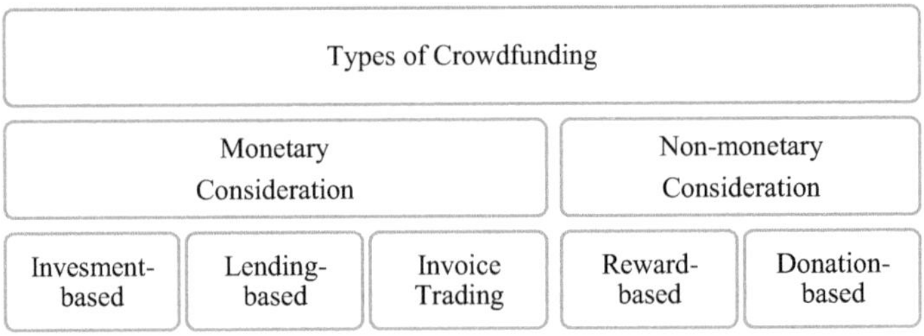

Fig. 13.1: Types of Crowdfunding Based on the Considerations of Funders.
Source: Dietrich & Amrein, 2017, p. 3

a Investment-Based Crowdfunding

In investment-based crowdfunding, funders receive securities of the founder in exchange for the funds provided. The securities offered by the founder may be equity shares, debt securities, or contractual instruments (EC, 2016).

If the project owners sell small ownership stakes of their firm, in return for funding they receive, it is called equity crowdfunding and the dominant model observed in investment-based crowdfunding is this type. In equity crowdfunding, funders become shareholders in the business, and this type is subject to strict regulations, because it involves the public offering of financial securities (Heminway & Hoffman, 2010). Equity crowdfunding is considered to be significantly different than other types of crowdfunding in terms of the risk and return characteristics of it. The risk level of equity crowdfunding is higher; thus funders expect a potential financial return on their investments. Moreover, they face large information asymmetries while evaluating the founders (Mochkabadi & Volkmann, 2018).

Because of a fraud risk, the existence of regulations for equity crowdfunding is essential for its development (Dushnitsky et al., 2016). Information disclosure about the project founders and their business activities, maximum investment limits for each funder, and maximum crowdfunding raising limits in a given time for the founders are generally required by equity crowdfunding regulations. Equity crowdfunding was firstly adopted in the UK, and the first equity crowdfunding platform is Crowdcube (Viña & Black, 2017). Even though the United States was not the first country to adopt equity crowdfunding, it was the first one to propose regulations about equity crowdfunding in 2012, with the Jumpstart Our Business Start ups (JOBS) Act. However, this act was not implemented until 2016 by the US Securities and Exchange Commission. Many countries, such as

Italy, France, Germany, Belgium, the United Kingdom, and Austria, followed these steps, by implementing similar regulations on equity crowdfunding (Hornuf & Schwienbacher, 2017).

Real estate crowd investing is also a part of the investment-based crowdfunding. The funders may choose debt or equity investments in real estate crowdfunding. In debt investments, loans provided by the funders are linked to a specific property, and secured by this property until repaid. If the funders choose equity investments, they purchase shares of a limited liability company which invests in a limited partnership holding the actual property (Schweizer & Zhou, 2017). Thus, funders become co-owners of a property in real estate crowdfunding. Here, co-ownership involves purchasing a percentage of an existing tenanted property, and funders take a stake in the rental income of the property (Dietrich & Amrein, 2017).

b Lending-Based Crowdfunding

In this approach, funding occurs as a loan. Founders borrow money from the crowd with a pre-determined payback amount and period (Chan & Patel, 2018). Therefore, the funder expects a return on the capital invested for the project and the investment decision depends on achieving this financial return. In some cases, investors may prefer only the return of the principal, without any interest, due to being interested only in the promotion of the social good, rather than a financial investment. France, the United Kingdom, and a few other countries plan to regulate this type of crowdfunding, similar to the regulations on equity crowdfunding. According to Zhang and Liu (2012), Prosper project, which offered to pay the principal with a fixed interest, is an example to lending-based crowdfunding.

Lending-based crowdfunding contains some risks for the funders. Different platforms and loans involve a higher risk than holding the cash on deposit. The reason behind is that lending-based crowdfunding is not a liquid investment. Thus, it may not always be possible for funders to cash their investment in quickly, or for as much money as they paid (Llobera, Hernando & Piera, 2016).

c Invoice Trading

Invoice trading is also a type of crowdfunding with monetary considerations, in which funders purchase unsettled business invoices at a discount, and they receive a return consisting of the difference between what they pay for the invoices and the amounts stated on the invoices themselves (Dietrich & Amrein, 2017). This type is in fact a form of asset-based financing, and typical investors are institutions and high net worth individuals (EC, 2016). An example of a web-based invoice trading platform is Market invoice which is based in the United Kingdom, and this platform is regarded as the largest invoice trading platform (Dorfleitner, Rad, & Weber, 2017).

d Reward-Based Crowdfunding

Funders receive different types of rewards in exchange for funding the project, in this approach. This type of crowdfunding offers tangible, but non-financial, benefits for the financial contributions of the funders (Kuppuswamy & Bayus, 2017). The most common reward is gaining the priority to reach the project's output before everyone else, or having the chance of buying the output at a discounted price. Entrepreneurial projects, such as producing a consumer product like hardware or software, select this type of crowdfunding method more often. This type of reward leads the funder to make a consumption decision as well, while making an investment decision. Funders also act as consumers during the process; hence the investment decision is primarily affected by the utility, which will be derived by the consumption of the promised product (Schwienbacher, 2018). Other reward alternatives are: being credited, opportunity to meet the project owners, and receiving souvenirs. Kickstarter platform, which is known as the world's largest reward-based crowdfunding platform, only allows for this crowdfunding model (Mollick, 2014). The famous case of the "Pebble Smartwatch" crowdfunding project is a typical example of reward-based crowdfunding. Eric Migicovsky, the inventor of the watch, launched a campaign in Kickstarter to raise $100,000, which he required for tooling the equipment to move from his prototype to a small production run. It took only two hours for him to raise the required capital; moreover, he raised more than $10 million from 68,929 people just in 37 days until he closed his campaign (Agrawal, Catalini, & Goldfarb, 2014).

This type of crowdfunding generally offers an advanced subscription to a business that has not yet been established, but it can also be used for mature businesses (Rechtman & O'Callaghan, 2014). The most important societal advantage of reward-based crowdfunding is considered as the low barriers to entry for both funders and founders, because anyone with an internet connection has the opportunity to raise funds for their projects or to fund projects through this approach (Kim & Hann, 2013).

e Donation-Based Crowdfunding

In this model, funders basically do not expect any return for their donations, thus they become philanthropists. Funds are raised collectively, to help charitable causes. In this type of crowdfunding, the main aim is improving public life by supporting social and environmental deficiencies. The funders of this type expect not a financial return but social return, which provides them a satisfaction of witnessing the projects conducted successfully (Bassani, Marinelli, & Vismara, 2018). The pioneer donation-based crowdfunding platform is "GoFundMe", which was launched in 2010, with examples ranging from local organizations set up for a Little League team's travel expenses to a championship tournament (Freedman & Nutting, 2015). Another good example for this type is Just Giving, which was funded by funders' donations without expecting any reward or financial return (Smith et al., 2014).

3 Functioning of the Crowdfunding and Comparison to Traditional Financing Alternatives

Entrepreneurs generally use the crowdfunding alternative during the beginning stage of their project or business life cycle. Similar to the funds coming from family, friends, and professional investors, crowdfunding funds the initial stages of a project, as well. Due to information asymmetry problems, start-ups and new players usually prefer crowdfunding option to the other traditional financing options.

To bring the individuals, who are willing to provide the funds, and the project owners looking for funds to finance their projects together, online crowdfunding platforms play the intermediate role in between them. Costs of searching and matching for both sides decrease with the intermediate role of these platforms (Evans, 2011). Unlike banks, venture capital investors, or angel investors, these platforms do not collect any information about any parties. Platforms only bring the two sides of the market together, by playing the intermediation role. Avoiding collecting any information also leads the costs to be reduced (Hornuf and Schwienbacher, 2016). The intermediation role of the platforms helps them to extract value for themselves. According to Giudici et al. (2012), some of the platforms charge the project owners with an average of 7 % of the total funds raised, but some of them do not prefer this kind of charging option. Some platforms choose to receive the commission only when the target level funding is reached. In exchange for the commission, platforms offer services, such as outsourcing of proprietary services to other platforms, legal support and involvement in contracts, analysis of campaign timeframes and access, usage of escrow accounts, and management of payment methods.

Crowdfunding platforms are not identical; they differ in some aspects. Some of the platforms contain all types of crowdfunding, whereas others specialize just in a few categories. Platforms also differ in terms of the target funding levels: while some of the platforms have the "all or nothing funding model", which stipulates the target level to be met, other platforms may prefer "keep it all funding model", that allows all funding to be kept no matter if the target is achieved or not. Nevertheless, there are also platforms which offer both options to the project founders (Cumming et al., 2016).

Although most of the projects aim to collect small amount of capital, mainly around or under $1,000, there has been an increase in the number of projects that target much higher amount. The timeline for collecting capital is finite, usually a short period. The project owner creates a webpage (which is considered as a campaign) on a crowdfunding portal, and this page should contain information about the purpose of the project and the specific outcomes by using the contributed funds. Entrepreneurs' time and resources consumed during this campaign may be interpreted as upfront cost (Babich, Tsoukalas, & Marinesi, 2017). The project's webpage also shows the current funding status of the project, the funding level target, number of days remaining for contributions, and people who chose to contribute to the project. A funder may choose to contribute the project financially, or comment on the projects. In exchange for this financial contribution, funder may receive a reward, equity, buying priority, certificate, etc. In contrast to the professional investors, who guide how to develop the project, the crowd has the option to give direct feedback on the project. Hence, the crowd/funders may also become the final consumers of the project output.

To reach large numbers of funders and to attract sufficient financial support, founders also broadcast their project on social media channels by using the sharing links to social media offered by most of the crowdfunding platforms. Most widely used social media channels for this purpose are especially Facebook and Twitter. According to Borst, Moser, and Ferguson (2018), usage of social media has a positive effect on crowdfunding success by adding an economic value to the crowdfunding effort.

The most crucial aspect of crowdfunding is that it is an alternative venture capital investment (Schwienbacher & Larralde, 2010). In crowdfunding, a large number of people contribute a small amount of money to the project through online platforms, in contrast to the traditional financing options, in which a few professional investors (such as banks, venture capital funds, angel investors) choose to invest a huge amount of money on the project. There are two important differences between crowdfunding and traditional financing of new businesses. In crowdfunding, financing is provided by the relatively small contributions of many individuals. Additionally, potential funders have an opportunity to observe the level of support from other project backers before making their own decision. This indicates that social information has an important role in crowdfunding process (Kuppuswamy & Bayus, 2017). At the same time, online crowdfunding markets have reduced the transactions costs for participants. Moreover, they facilitated the unbundling of resources and expertise. In traditional finance setting, financial institutions, venture capitalists, and business angels provide both the financial resources and their expertise in evaluating and managing risk. However, in crowdfunding markets funders are providing only the financial resources, not the expertise (Kim & Viswanathan, 2018).

Despite these differences, Mollick (2013) has found that, signals of quality used by venture capitalists to assess the viability of new businesses are also used by crowd funders. But his findings also revealed that crowdfunding seems to avoid some biases pervasive in venture capital funding, meaning that crowdfunding is more democratically distributed (Mollick, 2013).

Exit from the investment is an important phenomenon for venture capital firms; hence a well-developed stock market, which will allow those firms to exit an entrepreneurial firm through an initial public offering (IPO), is crucial for venture capital financing model. Exit opportunities for crowd investors are rather restricted, because entrepreneurial firms financed with crowdfunding is generally too small for an IPO (Hornuf & Schwienbacher, 2015).

4 Crowdfunding in Different Countries

The roots of the modern and digitised form of crowdfunding goes back to the beginning of this century. But the US crowdfunding platforms have pioneered the market from 2005 onwards, and crowdfunding has started to gain a momentum in Europe especially in the UK, Germany, and the Netherlands after 2010 (Gierczak, Bretschneider, Haas, Blohm, & Leimeister, 2016). It is claimed that there are over 1,300 online platforms worldwide (Rau, 2017). These platforms are considered to have a $140 billion financial volume by 2015. Only in 2015, Kickstarter has raised over $2 billion from 9.7 million people, for funding around 95,000 ideas only in the USA. This amount has reached to almost $3 billion, gathered by 12.7 million people in 2017. By 2018, the most successfully completed Kickstarter projects in terms of the money raised have been Pebble Time ($20,34 million), Coolest Cooler ($13,29 million), and Peeble 2, Time 2 ($12,78 million) (Statista, 2018).

Together with the increase in its popularity among entrepreneurs and investors, the amount of money raised by crowdfunding platforms has been increasing each year. The platforms raised $6.1 billion in 2013, $16.2 billion in 2014, and $34.4 billion (figure includes around $25 billion in P2P lending) in

2015, almost doubling the amount each year (Massolution, 2015). While $17.2 billion of this amount was raised by North American crowdfunding platforms, $10.5 billion was raised by Asian platforms, and $6.5 billion was raised by European crowdfunding platforms (Fundly, 2019). According to Massolution (2015), global volume of funds raised by lending-based crowdfunding is $25 billion, $2.85 billion by donation-based crowdfunding, $2.68 billion by reward-based crowdfunding, and $2.56 billion by equity-based crowdfunding. As of 2018, equity crowdfunding is the most invested model in the USA, and leading equity crowdfunding platform in the USA is Wefunder (Statista, 2018).

The Crowd Data Center (2018) reports that the USA had the most fully funded crowdfunding projects (15,148) in 2018. Second was the UK with 3,921 projects, Canada is in third rank with 1,380 projects, Australia is the fourth country with 564 projects, and Germany is in fifth rank with 459 projects. The USA also raised the biggest amount in terms of fully funded projects, over $556 million, the UK raised the second most with almost $62 million, Canada third with $38 million, Denmark fourth with $29 million, and China raised the fifth highest amount with $24 million, in 2018. It is worth to note that alternative finance market grew by 312 % only in 2015, in China (Businessweekly, 2017). Crowdfunding industry in China raised RMB 11,42 billion in the same year. Among the 415 crowdfunding platforms in China (315 platforms in 2015), 207 of them were reward-based platforms, 131 were equity-based platforms (Chen et al., 2018).

Compared to the USA, European crowdfunding sector is a more heterogeneous market with a high level of diversity across different platforms. Some of the member countries in European Union have a special regulation for crowdfunding, but some do not have such a regulation. In fact, there are some member countries in which there are little or no crowdfunding market (e.g., Croatia, Cyprus, Hungary). However, in some countries like France, Italy, and the UK, regulations specific to crowdfunding have boosted the crowdfunding market. In order to boost the crowdfunding market further, some member states, such as Belgium and France, have established specific tax incentives in favor of crowdfunding. In nearly all of the member countries of the EU, except Sweden, licencing or registration is required to establish and operate crowdfunding platforms. In Sweden, no licence is required for equity-based crowdfunding platforms, but a licence is required for lending-based platforms (EU, 2017). Nonetheless, a crucial difference between the EU and the USA should be mentioned. Although legislation for equity crowdfunding (with JOBS Act) was introduced in the USA in 2012, this Act was not enforced until 2016. Meanwhile lending and equity crowdfunding platforms have already been operating for many years in the EU.

Wardrop et al. (2015) reports that crowdfunding activity in Europe increased by 151 % in 2014, and 92 % in 2015. The UK is the largest market (more than 80 % of the market volume) in terms of crowdfunding in the EU at the moment, followed by France, Germany, the Netherlands, and Finland. In 2015, lending-based crowdfunding accounted for 50 % of the market volume in the EU. Equity- and reward-based crowdfunding each cover 15 % of the total volume, whereas donation-based crowdfunding accounts 2 % of the EU market. In the UK, equity and reward-based crowdfunding account 7.6 % and 1.3 % of the market. Also in the UK, an estimated 20 % of all early-stage equity investments occurred through equity crowdfunding platforms in 2015 (Beauhurst, 2017).

Although crowdfunding is considered largely as a developed-world phenomenon, it also has a high potential to stimulate innovation and create jobs in developing economies. According to World Bank (2013), there are up to 344 million potential funders in developing economies, who have a potential to make small crowdfunding investments in community businesses. Those funders are assumed to have the ability to deploy up to $96 billion a year by 2025 in crowdfunding investments. China has the greatest potential, followed by East Asia, Central Europe, Latin America/the Caribbean, and the MENA region (Worldbank, 2013).

Crowdfunding is expected to grow on an average of 29 % between 2018 and 2022 (Statista, 2018). Short et al. (2017) report that the World Bank estimates the volume of crowdfunding to reach $300 billion by 2025, and most of this volume to be allocated to loan-based crowdfunding.

Conclusions

Crowdfunding seems to have a promising potential as an alternative financing model for entrepreneurs. Even though it is not a new phenomenon, online crowdfunding transactions have not started before the beginning of 2000s. Up to now, a tremendous development is observed in its volume and popularity. Moreover, different types of crowdfunding offer entrepreneurs and funders various options for financing and investing. For example, reward-based crowdfunding is more suitable for project owners in creative industries; however, investment-based crowdfunding seems more appropriate for SMEs.

A critical issue in crowdfunding is that an entrepreneur has to provide a lot of crucial information about his/her project or business on the webpage, to be able to inform the potential funders and receive their contributions, which in turn increases the risk of the project or the business idea being replicated. In order to reduce this level of risk, a platform must take the necessary actions, so that a possible fraud case to affect the industry's future may be eliminated. As a matter of fact, legal infrastructure and regulations play an important role in the elimination of such a risk factor, especially in investment based crowdfunding model. As mentioned before, most of the countries proceeded in regulating the legal environment; however, developing countries seem to be a little behind the developed countries in terms of legal regulations. Considering the financial problems of entrepreneurs in developing countries and importance of solving the financing problems of them for their economies, those countries would pay more attention to take actions which will contribute to the development of crowdfunding.

References

Agrawal, A., Catalini, C. and Goldfarb, A. (2014). Some Simple Economics of Crowdfunding. *NBER/Innovation Policy and the Economy, 14*(1), 63–97.

Babich, V., Tsoukalas, G. and Marinesi, S. (2017). *Does Crowdfunding Benefit Entrepreneurs and Venture Capital Investors? Georgetown McDonough School of Business Research Paper; The Wharton School research paper.* SSRN.

Bassani, G., Marinelli, N. and Vismara, S. (2018). Crowdfunding in Healthcare. *The Journal of Technology Transfer*, 1–21. doi:10.1007/s10961-018-9663-7

Bayus, B. L. (2013). Crowdsourcing new product ideas over time: An analysis of the Dell IdeaStorm community. *Management science, 59*(1), 226–244.

Beauhurst. (2017). *The Deal: Equity Investment in the UK 2017.*

Belleflamme P., Lambert T. and Schwienbacher, A. (2011). *Crowdfunding: Tapping the Right Crowd, Center for Operations Research and Econometrics.* Belgium: Louvain-la-Nouve.

Belleflamme, P., Lambert, T. and Schwienbacher, A. (2013). Individual Crowdfunding Practices. *Venture Capital: An International Journal of Entrepreneurial Finance*, 15(4-Special Issue), 313–333.

Borst, I., Moser, C. and Ferguson, J. (2018). From Friendfunding to Crowdfunding: Relevance of Relationships, Social Media and Platform Activities to Crowdfunding Performance. *New Media & Society, 20*(4), 1396–1414.

Chan, C. R., Park, H. D., Patel, P. and Gomulya, D. (2018). Reward-based Crowdfunding Success: Decomposition of the Project, Product Category, Entrepreneur, and Location Effects. *Venture Capital:An International Journal of Entrepreneurial Finance, 20*(3), 285–307.

Chen Z., Wang H. and Yuan X. (2018). Statistic Analysis of China's Crowdfunding Industry. In: Wang J., Xu H., Ma J., Zhang Y., Chen Z. (eds) *Financing from Masses*. Singapore: Springer.

Cumming, D. J., Leboeuf, G. and Schwienbacher, A. (2016). Crowdfunding Models: Keep-it-all vs. All-or-nothing. *SSRN Electronic Journal.* 1-41 https://papers.ssrn.com/sol3/papers.cfm?abstract_id=2447567

Dietrich, A. and Amrein, S. (2017). *Crowdfunding Monitoring Switzerland 2017.* Institute of Financial Services Zug IFZ: Switzerland.

Dushnitsky, G., Guerini, M., Piva, E. and Rossi-Lamastra, C. (2016). Crowdfunding in Europe: Determinants of Platform Creation across Countries. *California Management Review*, 58(2), 44–71.

Dorfleitner, G., Rad, J. and Weber, M. (2017). Pricing in the Online Invoice Trading Market: First Empirical Evidence. *Economics Letters* (161), 56–61.

EC. (2016). *Crowdfunding in the EU Capital Markets Union.* Brussels: European Commission.

EU. (2017). *Identifying Market and Regulatory Obstacles to Cross-border Development of Crowdfunding in the EU.* European Commission. European Union, 2017

Evans, D. S., Schmalensee, R., Noel, M. D., Chang, H. H., & Garcia-Swartz, D. D. (2011). Platform economics: Essays on multi-sided businesses. *PLATFORM ECONOMICS: ESSAYS ON MULTI-SIDED BUSINESSES*, David S. Evans, ed., Competition Policy International.

Fershtman, C. and Gandal, N. (2011). A Brief Survey of the Economics of Open Source Software. *CEPR Discussion Paper, No.* 8434.

Fundly (2019). Regional Crowdfunding Statistics. Available at: https://blog.fundly.com/crowdfunding-statistics/#regional

Freedman, D. M. and Nutting, M. R. (2015). A Brief History of Crowdfunding. Retrieved from https://www.freedman-chicago.com/ec4i/History-of-Crowdfunding.pdf

Gierczak, M. M., Bretschneider, U., Haas, P., Blohm, I. and Leimeister, J. M. (2016). Crowdfunding: Outlining the New Era of Fundraising. In O. G. Dennis Brüntje, *Crowdfunding in Europe: State of the Art in Theory and Practice* (pp. 7–24). Springer International Publishing. Cham.

Giudici, G., Nava, R., Rossi-Lamastra, C. and Verecondo, C. (2012). Crowdfunding: The New Frontier for Financing Entrepreneurship?.*SSRN 2157429*

Heminway, J. and Hoffman, S. (2010). Proceed at Your Peril: Crowdfunding and the Securities Act of 1933. *Tenn. L. Rev. 78-879.*

Herve, F. and Schwienbacher, A. (2018). Crowdfunding and Innovation. *Journal of Economic Surveys*, 32(5) 1514–1530.

Hornuf, L. and Schwienbacher, A. (2015). Crowdinvesting – Angel Investing For the Masses? In C. Mason, & H. Landstrom, *Handbook of Research on Venture Capital: Volume 3. Business Angels.* Edward Elgar. Cheltenham, UK.

Hornuf, L., & Schwienbacher, A. (2016). Portal design and funding dynamics in equity crowdfunding. *URl:* http://www.em-lyon.com/minisiteen/content/download/169415/6656834/file/Hornuf, 20.(Accessed Date: 18.01.2019)

Hornuf, L. and Schwienbacher, A. (2017). Should Securities Regulation Promote Equity Crowdfunding? *Small Business Economics*, *49*(3), 579–593.

Investors Boosted by New Global Crowdfunding Index (2017, April 24). Retrieved from: https://www.businessweekly.co.uk/news/financial/investors-boosted-new-global-crowdfunding-index

Kim, K. and Hann, I.-H. (2013). Does Crowdfunding Democratize Access to Capital? A Geographical Analysis. *SSRN Electronic Journal*. doi:10.2139/ssrn.2334590

Kim, K. and Viswanathan, S. (2018). *The Experts in the Crowd: The Role of Reputable Investors in a Crowdfunding Market*. Retrieved from SSRN: https://ssrn.com/abstract=2258243

Kuppuswamy, V. and Bayus, B. L. (2017). Crowdfunding Creative Ideas: The Dynamics of Project Backers in Kickstarter. In L. H. Douglas Cumming, *The Economics of Crowdfunding: Startups, Portals and Investor Behavior* (pp. 151–182). Palgrave Macmillan.Doi. 10.1007/978-3-319-66119-3,

Llobera, J. M., Hernando, J. R. and Piera, D. T. (2016). Loan-Based Crowdfunding Investment as an Alternative Vehicle for Channelling Institutional and Personal Savings: The Collaborative Economy. *International Journal of Advances in Management and Economics*, *5*(6), 57-71.

Massolution (2015). 2015CF: The Crowdfund Industry Report. Available at: http://www.smv.gob.pe/Biblioteca/temp/catalogacion/C8789.pdf

Mochkabadi, K. and Volkmann, C. K. (2018). Equity Crowdfunding: A Systematic Review of the Literature. *Small Business Economics*, 1-44. doi:10.1007/s11187-018-0081-x

Mollick, Ethan R., Swept Away by the Crowd? Crowdfunding, Venture Capital, and the Selection of Entrepreneurs (March 25, 2013). Available at SSRN: https://ssrn.com/abstract=2239204 or http://dx.doi.org/10.2139/ssrn.2239204

Mollick, E. (2014). The Dynamics of Crowdfunding: An Exploratory Study. *Journal of Business Venturing*, *29*, 1–16.

.

Rau, P. R. (2017). Law, Trust, and the Development of Crowdfunding. *SSRN Electronic Journal*. http://dx.doi.org/10.2139/ssrn.2989056

Rechtman, Y. and O'Callaghan, S. (2014). Understanding the Basics of Crowdfunding. *The CPA Journal*, 84(11), 30–33.

Schweizer, D. and Zhou, T. (2017). Do Principles Pay in Real Estate Crowdfunding? *The Journal of Portfolio Management Special Real Estate Issue*, *43*(6), 120–137.

Schwienbacher, A. (2018). Entrepreneurial Risk-Taking in Crowdfunding Campaigns. *Small Business Economics, 51*, 843–859.

Schwienbacher, A., & Larralde, B. (2010). Crowdfunding of small entrepreneurial ventures. *Handbook of entrepreneurial finance, Oxford University Press, Forthcoming.*

Short, J. C., Ketchen, D. J., McKenny, A. F., Allison, T. H. and Ireland, R. D. (2017). Research on Crowdfunding: Reviewing the (Very Recent) Past and Celebrating the Present. *Entrepreneurship Theory and Practice*, 41(2), 149–160.

Smith, S., Windmeijer, F. and Wright, E. (2014). Peer Effects in Charitable Giving: Evidence from the (Running) Field. *The Economic Journal*, 125(June), 1053–1071.

Statista (2018). Crowdfunding - Statistics and Facts. Available at: https://www.statista.com/topics/1283/crowdfunding/

The Crowd Data Center (2018). Stats and Analytics. Available at: http://www.thecrowdfundingcenter.com/data/

Turan, S. S. (2015). Financial Innovation-Crowdfunding: Friend or Foe?. *Procedia-Social and Behavioral Sciences, 195*, 353–362.

Wardrop, R., Zhang, B., Rau R. and Gray M. (2015). Moving Mainstream: The European Alternative Finance Benchmarking Report. Available at: http://ec.europa.eu/finance/generalpolicy/docs/crowdfunding/150304-presentations-ecsf_en.pdf

Worldbank (2013). *Crowdfunding's Potential for the Developing World.* Washington, DC: infoDev, Finance and Private Sector Development Department.

Zhang, J., & Liu, P. (2012). Rational herding in microloan markets. *Management science, 58*(5), 892–912.

Ozan Gülhan and Alban Hetemi

14 Consequences of Money Laundering: An Audit and Governance Perspective

Highlights: The main purpose of this chapter is to explore the importance and role of audit, governance and controls on Anti-Money Laundering (AML) Compliance Program, especially for Financial Institutions (FI), in order to mitigate and prevent risks of money laundering phenomenon. The audit, as a mechanism of risk management, historically played an important role to maintain a robust AML Compliance Program. Establishing a compliance culture into the overall structure of a financial institution is critical to the development of an effective AML Compliance Program.

Keywords: Audit, Anti-Money Laundering, Compliance Program, quality assurance, assessment, effects of money laundering

Introduction

The money laundering is a worldwide phenomenon which has started being treated since the beginning of deregulation of financial markets, where such a deregulation has made the countries more vulnerable to this subject. In particular, in today's world the capital and fund movement takes place within seconds and with the usage of this high technology the money laundering process accelerates.

Nowadays, in the global market, free movement of capital between various countries enabled through the usage of a high technology (electronic banking) allow money launderers to move their funds (of a criminal origin) to different countries in order to conceal the origin of funds. Apart from the use of traditional ways of money laundering through the bank or other business activities, currently, due to the development of financial markets, various financial instruments (financial derivative instruments) are used in order to hide the origin of funds.

Taken into account all of these consequences international bodies such as FATF issues international standards to combat this phenomenon. Additionally, increasing international co-operation in the field of anti-money laundering and cross-border have given powers to international organizations to recommend mitigating measures, standards and principles and in order to apply such standards in practice to fight the money laundering phenomenon.

2 Money Laundering at a Glance

Money laundering is a global problem and no country is immune to this global phenomenon. Today, we are living in a world of international controls and mechanisms to combat money laundering. From practice it has been proved that money laundering has a negative effect on a country, both, economic and social aspects. Money laundering, among other effects, also effects economic growth and through it other aspects such as: the increase of crime and corruption, the country's reputation risk, social costs, and so on. Based on regulations and laws, but also standards and international recommendations, countries are obliged to establish anti-money laundering mechanism.

3 Definitions and Organizations

Money laundering refers to the process through which criminals and their counterparts tend to hide the origin of criminal income (trafficking in human beings, drugs, fraud, prostitution, etc.) through the financial system, through banking or other sectors. Simply put, money laundering is the process of making money dirty to look clean.

The money laundering process is commonly defined as involving three stages: the placement, the layering, and the integration stage.

In the initial – or placement – stage of money laundering, the launderer introduces his illegal profits into the financial system. This might be done by breaking up large amounts of cash into less suspicious smaller sums that are then deposited directly into a bank account, or by purchasing a series of monetary instruments (cheques, money orders, etc.) that are then collected and deposited into accounts at another location.

After the funds have entered the financial system, the second – *or layering* – stage takes place. In this phase, the launderer engages in a series of conversions or movements of the funds to distance them from their source. The funds might be channeled through the purchase and sale of investment instruments, or the launderer might simply wire the funds through a series of accounts at various banks across the globe. This use of widely scattered accounts for laundering is especially prevalent in those jurisdictions that do not co-operate in anti-money laundering investigations. In some instances, the launderer might disguise the transfers as payments for goods or services, thus giving them a legitimate appearance.

Having successfully processed his criminal profits through the first two phases, the launderer then moves them to the third stage – *integration* – in which the funds re-enter the legitimate economy. The launderer might choose to invest the funds in real estate, luxury assets, or business ventures.

Tab. 14.1: International Organizations Related to Anti-Money Laundering

Organization	Explanation
Financial Action Task Force – FATF	International organization issuing recommendations for improving national legal systems, enhancing the role of the financial sector and intensifying cooperation in the fight against money laundering.
The Basel Committee on Banking Supervision	International organization issuing principles for banks in order to combat money laundering.
European Union	The EU is issuing Directives specifically for preventing the use of the financial system for the purpose of money laundering. As of today five Directives are published.
Egmont Group of Financial Intelligence Units	Egmont Group is a united body of 159 Financial Intelligence Units (FIUs). The purpose of this group is to provide a forum for the FIUs from all over the world to improve co-operation in the fight against money laundering and terrorist financing.
The Wolfsberg Group	The Wolfsberg Group is an association of 11 global banks. The main aim is to prepare and implement best practices for anti-money laundering policies.
The World Bank (WB)and International Monetary Fund (IMF)	WB and IMF are supporting the efforts of FATF in addressing the resistance of certain nations to joining the international battle against money laundering.

Source: Information is obtained from the respective websites of the listed institutions

Money laundering is global phenomenon and is in the focus of different organizations and initiatives worldwide. Some of these organizations which are contributing to combat and prevent money laundering are given in Tab. 14.1.

3.1 Country Ratings and Effects of Money Laundering

Money laundering cripples country economies, distorts foreign direct investments as well as economic growth, and harms citizens around the globe. MONEYVAL Annual Report 2017 estimated the amount of money laundered worldwide range from $500 billion to a staggering $1 trillion, with disastrous effects on the global economy, especially on vulnerable, developing economies.

There is no "zero" risk of money laundering in any country. This is understandable by referring to such assessment as Basel AML Index as well as MONEYVAL reports or other international assessment on money laundering. For example, the Basel AML Index shows an increase in the minimum risk score, from 1.78 in 2017 to 2.57 in 2018, which means that the risks of money

Tab. 14.2: Countries as per Risk Score for Money Laundering

Country	Risk Score 2017	Risk Score 2018	Change in Score 2017–2018
Finland	1.78	2.57	0.80
Estonia	2.73	2.73	0.00
Lithuania	3.67	3.12	-0.55
New Zealand	3.03	3.20	0.17
Macedonia	4.09	3.33	-0.76
Bulgaria	3.84	3.53	-0.31
Slovenia*	2.78	3.75	0.97
Sweden*	3.40	3.75	0.35
Croatia	4.11	3.83	-0.28
Israel	3.59	3.84	0.24

Source: Basel AML Index 2018 (https://index.baselgovernance.org)

Tab. 14.3: Top 10 Countries with the Greatest Improvements in Risk Score

Country	Risk Score 2017	Risk Score 2018	Change in Score 2017–2018
Trinidad and Tobago*	6.75	5.25	-1.50
Tanzania	7.86	6.71	-1.15
Bolivia	7.13	6.02	-1.11
Ghana*	6.33	5.32	-1.01
Grenada	5.05	4.20	-0.85
Montenegro	4.76	3.95	-0.81
Brazil	5.76	4.96	-0.80
Macedonia	4.09	3.33	-0.76
Venezuela	6.44	5.69	-0.75
St. Vincent and the Grenadines	5.22	4.46	-0.75

Source: Basel AML Index 2018 (https://index.baselgovernance.org)

laundering are increased. Between 2017 and 2018, Latvia, Iceland, Denmark, and Poland left the list of top 10 low-risk countries and Lithuania, Macedonia, Bulgaria, and Croatia joined it. Tab. 14.2 presents such changes.

The 10 countries with the greatest improvements in risk score in the Basel AML Index 2018 are presented in Tab. 14.3.

Tab. 14.4 presented the effects of money laundering in the economy by effecting different macroeconomic variables.

Tab. 14.4: Effects of Money Laundering

Effect Subject	**Effect Mechanism**	**Literature**
Consumption	Money laundering distorts the consumption since the money has been transferred from the victim to the criminal, the latter will consume/use the money in a way different from how it was consumed earlier. Moreover, money laundering itself involves the purchase of assets, such as real estate, jewellery, gold/silver, artwork, and other luxury products because these assets give the money launderer the opportunity to conceal huge amounts of illegal money, without causing suspicion.	Walker (1995), Bartlett (2002)
Investments and savings	The impact of money laundering on investment is negative, where this is primarily from the fact that in their selection to invest, launderers focus on those investments that are less likely to be investigated than to maximize returns on investments. Money can be moved from countries with good economic policies and higher rates of return to countries with poor economic policies and low return rates. This implies that global capital is invested less optimally than would be the case in the absence of money. Money laundering redirects income from large savers to small ones or from sound investments to those risky, low-quality investments.	Fullerton and Karayannis (1994), Tanzi (1997), Quirk (1997), McDonell (1998 and 2001), Bartlett (2002)
Prices	Money launderers invest their dirty money in various projects in order to conceal the criminal and illegal origin of their money. As a result, they are willing to pay much higher prices than the real value of the property. They are willing to pay for special property more than their current value, thus causing artificial price increases.	Keh (1996)
Competition	Money launderers operate with a business and use additional illegal funds to subsidize that business; it gives them a competitive advantage over legitimate businesses to the point where they will drive them out of business.	Arlacchi & Ryle (1986), Walker (1995), Unger Busuioc (2007)
Import and Export	Money laundering activities can bring about a distortion of the country's imports and exports. It has been highlighted that money launderers tend to buy luxury goods and goods. Consequently, this will be problematic for the country's balance of payments. Importing such luxury goods does not generate any domestic economic activity or employment, and these affect domestic prices, reducing the profitability of domestic enterprises.	Baker (1999), Bartlett (2002)

(*continued on next page*)

Tab. 14.4: (continued)

Effect Subject	Effect Mechanism	Literature
Growth	Through money laundering activities, funds have been redirected from sound and risky projects to high-risk ones, from productive to non-productive investments, and crime and corruption are alleviated, then economic growth can be effected. When a particular industry or industry is no longer attractive to money launderers, they tend to simply abandon it, potentially causing these sectors to suffer serious damage to their economies.	Quirk (1997b), Tanzi (1997), Walker (1999), McDowell &Novis (2001), Bartlett (2002), Ferwerda and Bosma (2005), Hetemi, Gulhan et al. (2018)
Employment	Money laundering effects production reductions and rising unemployment because resources are shifted from money launderers to high-productivity sectors (manufacturing jobs that generate jobs) in sterile sectors (investment in artistic works, gold jewellery, etc.) which do not generate jobs.	Walker (1995)
Money and foreign exchange	Money laundering also affects the money demand. According to the IMF, a 10 % increase in crime leads to a 6 % reduction in total money demand. A 10 % increase in crime will discourage demand for the respective country currency by just 10 %. Money laundering can thus have a negative impact on demand for money, exchange rate and interest rates. Traditionally, money laundering would bring a rise in demand for money, but this trend has recently been inverse because of changes in money laundering methods from cash and through the banking system to non-cash instruments and barters.	Quirk (1997a), Tanzi (1997)
Interest rates	An increase in the exchange rate is associated with a reduction in exports and an incentive for imports, while an expansion of the monetary base would lead to an increase in prices. In addition, interest rate is affected because launderers invest their funds more in projects, least likely to be discovered by law enforcement institutions rather than those that bring high rates of return.	Tanzi (1996), Walker (1999), McDonell (1998) McDowell (2001), Boorman and Ingves (2001)
Capital flow	Money launderers can channel their funds of criminal origin to countries or financial institutions, which do not have strict rules. This can undoubtedly lead to capital outflows from countries with sound economic policies and higher return rates to countries with more efficient policies and low return rates.	Tanzi (1996), Keh (1996)

Tab. 14.4: (continued)

Effect Subject	**Effect Mechanism**	**Literature**
Foreign Direct Investments	Once a country's trading and financial systems are perceived as under the influence of criminal elements, this could endanger the reputation of the jurisdiction and undermine investor confidence. It is perceived as a weak regulatory environment and a tax haven, the respective country will always stimulate the capital of an illegal nature and considerable benefits may be derived, especially if the money were invested directly in the economy and not simply the country of transit for such unlawful capital.	Boorman and Ingves (2001)
Financial sector	Money laundering process is carried out in large amounts; this affects the solvency and liquidity of the banking sector and also compromises the banking stability. Money laundering behavior and economic choices are less predictable than those of conventional investors. Consequently, financial institutions or groups of such institutions may make wrong policy choices about the percentage of assets they need to hold liquid and, as a result, become incapable of satisfying unexpected demands for solvency and/or collapse.	McDowell (2001), Alldridge (2001), McDonell (1997)
Reputation	The impact of money laundering in the financial sector harms financial institution employees and the trust of clients is fundamental to the growth of sound financial institutions. Due to the perceived risk of fraud and corruption related to money laundering, economic agents will choose to avoid such institutions and develop their business elsewhere.	McDonell (1997), Bartlett (2002)
Corruption	This starts with a real effect, and if it is successful, money launderers will expand and corrupt other professionals (i.e., lawyers, bankers, accountants), and public officials responsible for financial market regulation. Money laundering activities can corrupt certain parts of the financial system and undermine banks' governance.	Alldridge (2001), Keh (1996), Quirk (1997)
Crime	Money laundering can alleviate crime because it provides criminal organizations with funds that are legitimate, which funds they can use to subsidize, diversify, and expand. The other side of the coin is that both the criminal and terrorist organizations and those which bear the costs of money laundering will tend to be 'natural' to be located elsewhere than where the rules were adopted.	Levi (2002), Masciandaro (2004)

4 AML Risk Assessment

Lately, legal framework to prevent and combat money laundering has become more risk focused, by requiring financial institutions to understand the risks they may face based on their business model and strategy. A risk management mechanism framework and a robust AML Risk Assessment tool of this framework has become a key priority. The AML Risk Assessment is the base/source of new scenarios to be designed by financial institutions in order to mitigate new risks identified. As such, the AML Risk Assessment shall include identifiable risk matrix, thus providing the most effective levels of AML Compliance and ability to identify, analyse report, and prevent money laundering.

4.1 Content and Methodology

The AML Risk Assessment shall present a full survey of financial institutions' situation regarding the exposure to the risk of money laundering. Subsequently, this assessment identifies the specific risk attached to clients, products and services, countries, and channels. The associated risk shall then be categorized and assessed in order to prioritize the respective preventive measures and mitigate all risks associated with money laundering. According to the Wolfsberg Group, a

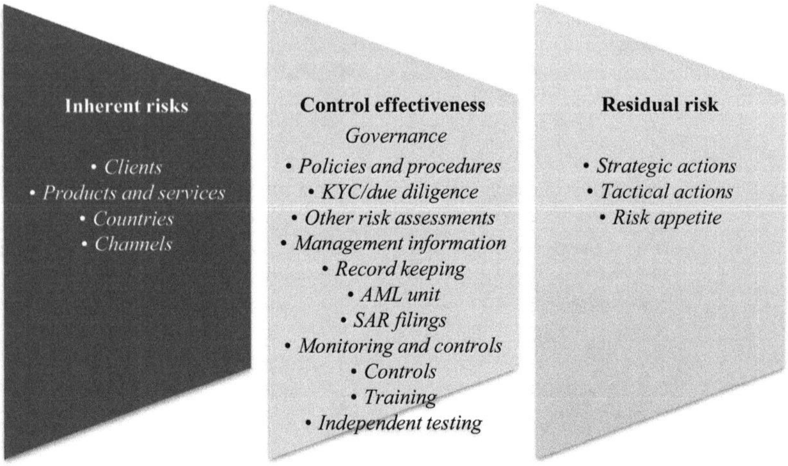

Fig. 14.1: Risk Assessment Methodology. Source: *Wolfsberg Group's FAQ on Risk Assessment*

three-phased approach can be adopted in order to undertake a risk assessment. Fig. 14.1 illustrates the inherent risks, control effectiveness, and residual risks.

First step while conducting AML Risk Assessment is to determine inherent risk and the exposure to money laundering risks. The risks can vary from one financial institution to another one and must be defined in a risk-based approach and is a key point for the overall AML Risk Assessment.

Second step is the evaluation of internal controls/safeguards. In this step it is evaluated the effectiveness of internal control mechanism and they need to be mapped versus these risks identified.

Third step is determining the residual risk. As such, once the inherent risks are identified and determined as well as the effectiveness of internal control mechanism has been evaluated, the residual risk can be determined. Based on the residual risk the financial institutions may enhance existing measures they have in place or accept risks as the case can be.

The identification of risk factors shall mainly rely on empirical data sourced from typology analysis of cases that have occurred in financial institutions. But, it shall also take into consideration risk factors identified in typology reports from relevant external sources (government bodies, international organizations, research papers, media reports, etc.).

4.2 Client Risk Assessment

The assessment of risks associated with the clients of financial institutions is based on number of client type, ownership, industry, activity, profession and/or business, alongside other factors, such as the length of a client relationship. Some factors that may impact risk score of clients are: country residence, country of activity, sector of activity, presence of PEP, financial incidents, cross-border flows, usage sensitive products, country of incorporation, sector sensitivity, Ultimate Beneficial Owner (UBO) residence, date of creation (for legal entities). The following categories can be used to stratify the client base and to identify aspects of client risk: client type, ownership, industry, activity, profession and/or business. Based on these factors each client type is assigned a risk score, depending upon the expected amount of risk each type carries. The data may be utilized to determine what % of each client types are classified according to the risk score, e.g., low risk versus high risk, medium risk versus high risk, in order to determine the overall inherent client risk.

4.3 Products and Services Risk Assessment

The assessment of risks associated with the products and services of financial institutions is based on empirical evidence from the analysis of Suspicious

Activity Reports (SARs), filed by the financial institutions within a period of time (e.g., the past three years) and according to the following methodology.

The frequency of transaction types and product types involved in all SARs of the past three years is measured against the overall number of SARs during this period. To assess, the resulting rates are to be interpreted as the probability of occurrence of a certain type in an SAR. The following threshold values can be applied:

- < 4.99 % = Low Risk
- 5–9.99 % = Medium Risk
- > 10 % = High Risk

Product types or transaction types present in more than 10 % of all SARs are considered to be of higher risk.

4.4 Country Risk Assessment

The Worldwide Governance Indicators (WGI) of the World Bank and the Financial Secrecy Index (FSI) of the Tax Justice Network will be taken into account to assess a country's exposure to risks of money laundering and other illicit financial flows in addition to more traditional information sources like the Corruption Perception Index (CPI) of Transparency International. In addition to the quantitative assessment, a qualitative analysis of the general money laundering and terrorist financing risk environment will be included into the financial institutions risk profile. The qualitative part shall assess the overall framework and general situation for the financial institutions' country of operation and is rather descriptive.

4.5 Channels Risk Assessment

The reasoning behind the assessment of service channel risk is slightly different. Here, the classification is based on the level of anonymity that these channels offer when servicing the customer. The level of anonymity of service channels refers merely to the servicing of customer after initial identification. Here, for instance, the risk of identify fraud is deemed higher when servicing a client through e-banking than servicing a customer face-to-face over the counter. Based on the Wolfsberg Group's FAQ on Risk Assessment channels/servicing should be assessed whether, and to what extent, the method of account origination or account servicing, such as non-face-to-face account opening or the involvement of third parties, including intermediaries, could increase the inherent money laundering risk.

4.6 Control Effectiveness

After the first step of assessment, determining of the inherent risks, internal controls mechanism must be evaluated to define how effectively they offset the overall risks. Controls are essential mechanisms to mitigate risks identified. Different controls apply to different activities performed within the financial institutions and will be performed by different bodies (e.g., Front Office, Compliance, Audit).

4.7 Residual Risk Assessment

In order to determine the residual risk on the basis of the factors defined above, it is necessary to screen the respective risks against all mitigating measures in place. However, some of the mitigating measures applied bear a higher mitigating potential than other mitigating measures applied.

The financial institutions deem mitigating measures to be central for managing the risks associated with money laundering, terrorist financing, and other acts punishable by law. These include the presence of Compliance Officer (CO) who serves as the Know Your Client (KYC) Policy owner and coordinator of all AML and Counter Financing of Terrorism (CFT) activities, an implemented KYC principle, and well-defined Customer Due Diligence (CDD) procedures/policies which govern client information and risk categorization as well as regular awareness raising and AML training.

When assessing the residual risk from the probability of occurrence and the efficiency of the measures, the methodology/matrix can be used (Tab. 14.5).

4.8 Deriving Circumstantial Evidence from the AML Risk Assessment

In order to derive circumstantial evidence from the AML Risk Assessment, which can be applied by an IT-based monitoring system, all results of the above described risk measuring model must be taken into consideration. Based on the risk profile of financial institutions, certain indicators are applied to monitor transactions that address the specific risks in the financial institutions. They are reflected in the AML risk profiles for the financial institutions and their results are being analyzed to determine their effectiveness.

Further, all data of SAR are evaluated to establish the risk profile of the financial institutions. This provides to the financial institutions with clues for necessary adjustments of the individual monitoring scenarios.

Tab. 14.5: Matrix of Risk Assessment Methodology

Probability of Occurrence	Efficiency of Measures	Residual Risk
Low	**Low**	**Low**
Low	Medium	Low
Low	High	Low
Medium	Low	Medium
Medium	Medium	Medium
Medium	High	Low
High	Low	High
High	Medium	Medium
High	High	Medium

5 Establishing and Auditing AML Structures in Financial Institutions

The establishment of AML structures has great importance for financial institutions. In this context, the establishment of a transparent, accountable structure in financial institutions will provide easiness during the inspections to be made by the authorities as well as the detection of the sources having the nature of the crime.

To create a proper setup at least below-mentioned topics have to be defined and audited in any financial institution:

- Know Your Customer (KYC)
- Anti-Money Laundering and Counter Financing of Terrorism (AML/CFT)
- International Financial Sanctions (IFS)
- Trainings
- Internal Rule Defining and Record Keeping

5.1 Establishing AML Structures

As mentioned above, an appropriate AML system has five main pillars. These five topics are evaluated in following subchapters.

Know Your Customer

Know Your Customer (KYC) is a process that institutions gather different types of information about the clients in order to ensure that services are not misused. This process starts with the entering to the business relation and continues until

Tab. 14.6: KYC Information

Client's identification (ID, address document, other related documents)
Politically exposed person presence
Client's financials
Ultimate beneficiary owners' identification (direct/indirect ownership exceeds 25 %)
Other related persons documents
Screening against sanctions and PEP lists
Client's position (e.g., director, owner)
Sector of activity
Countries of activity
Income, wealth
Products and transactions
Information checks in public and other sources

Tab. 14.7: Client Segmentation

Corporates and Non-profit Organizations
Corporates
Small and Medium Businesses
Non-profit Private Sector
Financial Institutions
Banks
Insurance Companies
Other Financial Sector
Public Sector
Individuals
Private Clients
Retail Clients

the termination of the relation. KYC information should be updated periodically according to client's risk level. In general in practice these frequencies are 1 year for High-Risk, 3 years for Medium-Risk, and 5 years for Low-Risk clients. In addition to that institutions can define more risk levels to differentiate the client classes (for example: Very High Risk – 6 months). Risk level of clients is defined according to different factors (refer Tab. 14.8).

While performing KYC of any client at least the information listed in Tab. 14.6 should be gathered. Information checks in public and other sources (Google, Name-checker tools, local and international lists, PEP lists) are also important for defining risk levels. Any confirmed adverse or bad news about the

Tab. 14.8: Factors Affecting the Risk Level

Portfolio officers' opinion
Bad news in public/other sources
Country of incorporation
Country residence
Date of foundation
Countries of activity (sensitive countries)
Sector sensitivity and activity
Cross-border flows
Complex shareholder structure
Ultimate beneficial owner residence
Presence of PEP
Transactional profile (risky or sensitive product usage, risky or sensitive transactions performed)
Other events (changes during the business relationship that may affect risk level)

client should increase the risk level, and this change will also change the review frequency.

Client's risk levels and documentation need are affected from different factors which are related to business nature. First of all, segment of the customer should be defined according to the groups mentioned in Tab. 14.7.

There are other factors which are affecting the risk level of the clients according to the information gathered from the client. Some of those factors are given in Tab. 14.8.

In order to include these factors, financial institutions may create a scoring matrix for all segments. Moreover, institutions should define sensitive countries, risky sectors, and acceptable cross-border levels according to their risk appetite. After onboarding the client, financial institution should assign the client to correct segment and define the risk level and review frequency consistent with the documents taken from the client.

While the business relationship is ongoing, KYC process is ongoing according to the review frequency and any triggering events in time. When the relation is terminated, it is important who requested to end the relation. If the client requests the termination, financial institution should give the best effort to finish the KYC process to be sure there is no suspicion about past transactions of the client. On the other hand, if financial institution is willing to terminate it should be make sure that termination conditions are fulfilled.

International Financial Sanctions – IFS

The main component of a proper AML structure is definitely international financial sanctions. In order to protect institutions from fines because of sanctions, organizations need to make sure about if enough resources are allocated related to sanctions. First action should be taken is integration of all local and international sanction lists into screening and filtering systems. In addition to integration timing is also an important aspect; lists should be integrated on a timely manner. Second, organizations have to screen customer databases including all related parties. Whenever there is an update in the lists, alerts will be analyzed in timely manner and appropriate actions should be taken.

Anti-Money Laundering and Counter-Financing of Terrorism

After onboarding and fulfilling all the requirements related to documentation, screening, and filtering, next stage is monitoring the transactions of the clients. Organizations generally use package solutions (monitoring tools) to monitor clients' unusual transactions. For detecting unusual transactions all typologies should be in a related tool. Some examples of unusual transactions are given below:

- Using private account for depositing business turnover/income or making transfers for business purposes
- Depositing under reporting limit or under approval limit
- Activity does not match the profile (for example: unemployed/housewife making frequent deposits or retired/student with high turnover)
- Frequent transfers to different parties without documentation or description like "personal transfer" or "borrowing"
- High amount of withdrawals with no description/reason
- No declaration of on source of funds
- Activity is gambling or betting
- Refusing to collaborate/give information about a suspicion
- Receiving money from high-risk countries
- Receiving money as donations through NGOs

Institutions must ensure regulators that all typologies are covered in their monitoring tool with different scenarios. Identifying the alerts is another important issue about the AML setup. Employees should be vigilant to understand and differentiate if the alerts are suspicious or falsely positive. In case of any suspicious activity detected in clients' accounts, organizations should define clear rules to

Tab. 14.9: AML Trainings

Trainings According to Experience		
Experience Level	**Position**	**Frequency**
Newcomers	All	1 time
1–5 Years	All	Semiannually new trainings/ refreshments
5 and more	All	Annual new trainings/ refreshments
Trainings According to Risk Exposure		
Risk Exposure Level	**Position**	**Frequency**
Low	Nonbusiness line officers and managers	Annual new trainings/ refreshments
Medium		Semiannually new trainings/ refreshments
High	Compliance officers, portfolio officers, business line managers	Quarterly new trainings/ refreshments

treat the alert and/or submit Suspicious Activity/Transaction Reports to local Financial Intelligence Units.

Trainings

Training has a paramount importance related to establish appropriate AML structures. Since the function is technical and needs human intervention, all staff needs to be trained continuously. Trainings must be compulsory for all staff. However, they may be differentiated according to how much the staff will be exposed to AML risks. The trainings would be separated according to experience and position (exposure to the risk) which are presented in Tab. 14.9.

Internal Rule Defining and Record Keeping

Policy and procedure implementation is another important component of AML structures; different internals rules should be set in order to ensure all the risks related to the function is covered. In this context, all related five related pillars of AML structure has to have different policy and procedures. Financial institutions have at least below-mentioned (Tab. 14.10) rules related to AML:

Tab. 14.10: AML Policy/Procedures

Subject	Internal Documentation
KYC	KYC General Policy KYC Segment Policies
AML	AML General Policy AML Alert Treatment Policy
IFS	IFS General Policy IFS Alert Treatment Policy
Trainings	Trainings General Policy
Internal Rule Defining and Record Keeping	Policy/Procedure Publish Policy Record Keeping Policy

In addition to the internal rule definition local regulations foresees different periods for record keeping. These periods are generally defined as 5, 7, or 10 years. From this perspective institutions ensure that all records related to AML are kept in archive for the period defined by the local regulator.

5.2 Auditing AML Structures

Establishing AML setup is the first phase to fulfill requirements of regulators and protecting institutions from criminal funds and activities. Second phase is to control the structure and improve the quality. Since most of the processes need human intervention, operational errors are always possible. To avoid these mistakes and improve the quality within the same structure, controls/audits need to be constructed and performed. Auditing AML setup is one of the best ways to see if the structure and control plan are appropriate, and if there are any deficiencies. Achieving these goals can be a challenge due to the complexities of conducting the audit review itself. This part will give a general overview to supervise this function in order to improve the quality and fulfil the regulatory expectations, to allocate right resources and expertise.

To create proper controls at least below-mentioned topics (Tab. 14.11) are to be audited in any financial institution.

Tab. 14.11: AML Controls

Control	Control Name	Control Structure	Frequency
KYC	Risk Level Controls	Sample based on at least 10 clients (five for onboarding and five for review) from each segment should be checked if they are assigned to correct risk levels.	Quarterly
	Recertification Frequency Controls	Sample based at least on 10 clients (five for onboarding and five for review) from each segment should be checked if review frequency assigned correctly.	Quarterly
	Documentation Controls/Transactional Profile/Portfolio Assessment	Sample based at least on 10 clients from each segment should be checked if all documents are collected, transactional profile in place and portfolio assessment is in clients' file.	Quarterly
	Decision Controls	Sample based at least on 10 clients from each segment should be checked if decision for different risk levels is done in correct level (high risk – compliance function, other risk levels – business functions).	Quarterly
	Termination Controls	Sample based at least on five termination-decided clients from each segment should be checked, if termination is done in line with decision.	Quarterly
AML/ CFT	Detecting Unusual Transactions	Sample based on 10 transactions/ transaction groups defined in scenarios should be checked if they created alert in monitoring tool.	Quarterly
	Investigation of Unusual Transactions – UT which are not correct	Sample based on 10 false positive alerts should be checked if they closed properly and related documentation criteria met.	Quarterly
	Investigation of Unusual Transactions – UT which are correct	Sample based on 10 suspicious alerts should be checked if they closed properly and SAR reported to local FIU.[a]	Quarterly
	Scenario Appropriateness Controls/Typology Coverage	Annually all scenarios defined in the local tool will be compared with local FIU typologies if all of them are covered.	Annually
	Fund/Cash Transfer Controls	Annually fund/cash control thresholds will be checked if they are consistent with institutions' business structure.	Annually

Tab. 14.11: (continued)

Control	Control Name	Control Structure	Frequency
IFS	International List Upload Controls	Quarterly filtering/screening tools will be checked if all international lists are uploaded on a timely manner.	Quarterly
	Local List Upload Controls	Quarterly filtering/screening tools will be checked if all local lists are uploaded on a timely manner.	Quarterly
	Screening of Clients	Quarterly client filtering should be checked if all new clients screened and old clients against the new lists.	Quarterly
	Hit Controls	Quarterly filtering/screening hits should be checked if they are treated according to policies.	Quarterly
Trainings	Training Requirement Controls	Annually trainings will be controlled if requirements from regulators are met.	Annually
	Training Assignment Controls	Semiannually trainings will be controlled if assignments are done to correct group of staff.	Semiannually
	Training Completeness	Quarterly training completeness levels will be controlled if satisfactory levels are met.	Quarterly
Internal Rule Defining and Record Keeping	Internal Procedure Controls	Control should be performed if all policy procedures are in place and they are not expired.	Annually
	Record Keeping Controls	Control should be performed if records are archived in line with regulation.	Annually

[a] Due to confidentiality defined in some countries, such controls can be performed by a person designated within the AML function in order to limit the access of other staff to SAR/STR/UT.

Conclusion

Money laundering refers to the process through which criminals and their counterparts tend to hide the origin of criminal income through the financial system, respectively banking sector or through any other business sector.

Establishing AML Compliance Program is crucial for financial institutions; however, it is not enough, because it must be audited and evaluated. The AML Compliance Program has to be audited on a regular basis to ensure its effectiveness. The audit has to be independent and responsible staff should report directly to the board of directors or to any designated board committee (e.g., audit committees). Auditors must have necessary experience and be sufficiently qualified to ensure that their findings and conclusions are reliable and in line with audit international best practice.

Money laundering has potentially devastating economic, security, and social consequences. The role of financial institutions is crucial to combat and prevent such phenomenon. Money laundering phenomenon can occur in any country, and it has significant economic and social consequences for each country and particularly to those countries that have emerging markets and countries with fragile financial systems, respectively banking sector. The negative impacts of money laundering tend to be magnified in these markets because they tend to have less stable financial systems, a lack of banking regulations, and effective law enforcement. As such international bodies like FATF, Egmont Group, Wolfsberg Group, etc., issues international standards to combat this phenomenon. Moreover, strengthening of international co-operation in the field of anti-money laundering and cross-border has given powers to international organizations to recommend mitigating measures, standards, and principles and applying them in practice in order to prevent and combat money laundering and other financial crimes.

Governance, audit, and controls on AML are crucial mechanisms to prevent money laundering and related crimes. Performing such controls on a regular basis helps financial institutions to identify new risks and mitigate them properly. Additionally, the AML Risk assessment is a robust mechanism that contributes to mitigate risks and enhance the current measures in place as deemed necessary.

As conclusion the role of audit, governance, control structure, and AML set ups in financial institutions protect financial institution itself as well as the country where these financial institutions are operating in.

References

Alldridge, P. (2001). The Moral Limits of the Crime of Money Laundering. *Buffalo Criminal Law Review*, *5*(1), 279–319.

Arlacchi, P. and Ryle, M. (1986). Mafia Business: The Mafia Ethic and the Spirit of Capitalism (Vol. 3, p. 4). London: Verso.

Boorman, J. and Ingves, S. (2001). Financial System Abuse, Financial Crime and Money Laundering-Background Paper. Washington: IMF.

Baker, R. W. (1999). The Biggest Loophole in the Free-Market System. *Washington Quarterly*, *22*(4), 27–46.

Bartlett, B.L. 2002. The Negative Effects of Money Laundering on Economic Development. *Asian Development Bank Regional Technical Assistance Project No*, 5967.

Ferwerda, J. and Bosma, Z. S. (2005). The Effect of Money Laundering on Economic Growth. *Utrecht University School of Economics: paper for applied economics research course.*

Fullerton, D. and Karayannis, M. (1994). Tax Evasion and the Allocation of Capital. *Journal of Public Economics*, *55*(2), 257–278.

Hetemi, A., Merovci, S. and Gulhan, O. (2018). Consequences of Money Laundering on Economic Growth – The Case of Kosovo and Its Trade Partners. *Acta Universitatis Danubius. Œconomica*, *14*(3).

Keh, D. I. (1996). Drug Money in a Changing World: Economic Reform and Criminal Finance. In *UNDCP Technical series* (No. 4, p. 22). UNDCP. New York

Levi, M. (2002). Money laundering and its regulation. *The Annals of the American Academy of Political and Social Science*, *582*(1), 181–194.

Masciandaro, D. (2004). Combating Black Money: Money Laundering and Terrorism Finance, International Cooperation and the G8 Role.

McDonell, R. (1997). An Overview of the Global Money Laundering Problem, International Anti-Money Laundering Standards and the World of the Financial Action Task Force. In *Delivered at the International Conference on Global Drugs Law.*

McDonell, R. (1998). Money Laundering Methodologies and International and Regional Counter-Measures. In *A Conference Convened by the Australian Institute of Criminology, Sydney* (pp. 7–8).

McDowell, J. and Novis, G. (2001). The Consequences of Money Laundering and Financial Crime. *Economic Perspectives*, *6*(2), 6–10.

Quirk, P. J. (1997a). Macroeconomic İmplications of Money Laundering. *Trends in Organized Crime*, *2*(3), 10–14.

Quirk, P.J. (1997b). Money Laundering: Muddying the Macro-Economy. *Finance and Development*, *34*(1), p.7.

Tanzi, V. (1996). *Money Laundering and the International Financial System* (No. 96/55). International Monetary Fund.

Tanzi, V. (1997). Macroeconomic İmplications of Money Laundering. *Responding to Money Laundering, International Perspectives*, pp. 91–104.

Unger, B. and Busuioc, E. M. (2007). *The Scale and İmpacts of Money Laundering.* Edward Elgar Publishing. Cheltenham, UK.

Walker, J. (1999). How Big is Global Money Laundering? *Journal of Money Laundering Control*, *3*(1), 25–37.

Walker, J. R. and Walker, J. (1995). *Estimates of the Extent of Money Laundering in and through Australia*. John Walker Consulting Services. USA.*Web site related links*: EU, World Bank, International Monetary Fund, Council of Europe, FATF, Egmont Group, Wolfsberg Group, and Bank for International Settlements, Transparency International, Basel Governance Index.

Yasemin Dumrul and Zerrin Kılıçarslan

15 The Relationship between Exchange Rates and Interest Rates: The Case of Turkey

Highlights: With the liberalization of international capital movements, capital flows started to move between countries due to differences in interest rates. Especially, short-term foreign capital flows are shifting from economies with low interest rates to economies with high interest rates. However, depending on the changes in interest rates, there may be positive or negative changes in the exchange rate. In this study, the relationship between interest rates and exchange rates has been theoretically and empirically revealed. In this study, which is aimed to examine the relationship between exchange rate and interest rate, Johansen, Fully Modified Least Squares (FMOLS), Dynamic Ordinary Least Squares (DOLS), and Canonical Cointegrating Regression (CCR) methods were applied for the 1987–2017 period in Turkey. According to the results of the empirical analysis, there is a long-term and negative relationship between exchange rate and interest rate. In other words, an increase in the interest rate leads to a decrease in the exchange rate.

Keywords: Interest rate, Exchange rate, Cointegration tests, Turkey

Introduction

With the liberalization of international capital movements, capital flows started to move between countries due to differences in interest rates. With the liberalization of the capital movements, the economic units, which have a surplus of savings in developed countries, tried to obtain maximum returns by evaluating their savings in developing countries where interest rates are higher (Saraçoğlu, Kuzu and Kocaoğlu, 2015: 78). Especially, short-term foreign capital flows are shifting from economies with low interest rates to economies with high interest rates in order to benefit from the arbitrage opportunity that will be created by the interest rate difference (Aslan, Terzi and Sıampan, 2014: 16; Doğan, Afsal, Aydın and Gürbüz, 2017: 1426). In particular, countries that have difficulty in paying their external debts countries encourage the entry of funds into their countries by increasing interest rates and thus ensuring that capital is influential on exchange rates (Aslan, et al. 2014: 17).

There is no consensus on the direction of the relationship between the interest rate and the exchange rate in the literature. Changes in interest rates may affect the exchange rate in two ways, either negative or positive. Usually, the most common situation is that interest rates have a negative effect on exchange rates.

The increase in interest rates in a country leads both domestic investors and foreign investors to sell their foreign currency or foreign currency assets and to move towards domestic investment instruments and domestic currency. Thus, the demand for national currency is increasing. With increasing demand for national currency, foreign exchange supply increases, national currency gains value, and exchange rate falls. On the other hand, the fall in interest rates causes demand to shift from domestic assets to foreign assets. Thus, the demand for foreign currency increases, the domestic currency loses value, and the exchange rate rises (Gül, Ekinci and Özer, 2007: 24). In such cases, investors demand domestic investment instruments until interest rate parity is ensured (Karacan, 2010: 73).

Interest rates are also positively affected by the exchange rate. In the long run, a positive relationship is observed between exchange rates and nominal interest rate differences due to changes in expected inflation rates. The increase in nominal interest rates leads to an increase in expected inflation. If the inflation rate in a country is expected to be higher than in other countries, the exchange rate will rise and the value of the country will lose value, assuming that other conditions do not change (Ökte, 2011: 232).

This study aims to analyze the relationship between exchange rate and interest rate theoretically and empirically. In the second section of the study, the theoretical framework will be presented. In the third section, the applied literature related to the previous studies in this field will be included. The fourth section describes the data and method of application to be made on Turkey. In the fifth section, the results of the application will be included. In the last section, results and evaluations of the study will be presented.

2 Theoretical Framework

The relationship between interest rates and exchange rates has been discussed in various theoretical models of international economics. In this study, the relationship between interest rate and exchange rate will be taken into consideration in floating exchange rate.

The first approach to be addressed is *the Mundell-Fleming approach*, which tries to explain the exchange rates under the assumption of full capital mobility. In this approach, international capital movements are included in the Keynesian incomes approach. In full capital mobility and flexible exchange rate system, contractionary monetary policy application increases domestic interest rates and foreign capital inflow into the country. National money demand of foreign investors causes the exchange rate to fall (Öztürk and Bayraktar, 2010:166–167). This model predicts a negative relationship between interest rate and exchange rate (Andrieş, Căpraru, Ihnatov and Tiwari, 2017: 263; Sı, Lı, Chang and Baı, 2018: 6).

Another approach that explains the relationship between interest rate and exchange rate is *the Uncovered Interest Parity (UIP) approach*, also known as the Open Fisher or the International Fisher Effect. This approach shows that the nominal interest rate differences between the two countries should be equal to the expected change in the exchange rate (Ray, 2012: 236). According to this approach, investors borrow in low interest rate currencies and invest in currencies that provide high interest rates. However, they do not take any protective measures against the exchange rate risk (Yalçıner, 2012: 187, 192). According to this approach, where there are no capital controls and limitations (full capital mobility), no transaction costs or taxes, and investors do not demand any risk premiums, the values of the countries' currencies vary according to the differences in interest rates. In other words, according to this approach, the currency of a country with a high interest rate depreciates by the difference of interest rate and the currency of a country with a low interest rate appreciates by the difference of interest (Güney and Tunalı, 2017: 37). As a result, according to this approach, there is a negative relationship between the interest rate and the exchange rate.

Portfolio equilibrium models also indicate a negative relationship between the exchange rate and the interest rate. Accordingly, the differences in interest rates cause the investors to reorganize their portfolios. The increase in domestic interest rates increases the demand of interest-earning assets. Thus the exchange rate falls and that country's currency appreciates (Andrieş, et al., 2017: 263). Keeping the interest rate low also changes the portfolio preferences in favor of foreign currency assets. This creates pressure on exchange rates and will lead to an increase in inflation due to the transition effect from exchange rate to price (Gül et al., 2007: 23). However, with the decline in interest rates, profit opportunities are disappearing and the capital can suddenly leave the country. As a result, the exchange rate will rise and the national currency will depreciate (Sı et al., 2018:6).

Another approach that explains the relationship between exchange rate and interest rate is the *Monetarist Approach*. This approach is divided into a sticky price model called Keynesian theory and a flexible price model called Chicago theory (Frankel, 1979: 610). In the sticky price model, it is suggested that there is a negative relationship between the exchange rate and the nominal interest rate difference between countries in the short term under the assumption of stickiness of prices. In this approach, changes in nominal interest rates reflect changes in contractionary monetary policy. If the domestic interest rate increases according to the foreign interest rate, domestic money supply will meet the domestic money demand without a decrease in prices. This increase in interest rate will cause capital inflow into the country and the national currency will appreciate (Dülger and Cin, 2002: 50; Frankel, 1979: 610). In the flexible price model developed by Frankel (1976) and Bilson (1978), it is suggested that there is a positive relationship between the exchange rate and the nominal interest rate difference between countries under the assumption that prices are full flexible and that capital is full free. According to this approach, changes in the nominal interest rate will reflect the change in the expected inflation rate. The increase in domestic interest rate in relation to foreign interest rate will lead to a decrease in the demand for national currency and an increase in inflation. Thus, the national currency will depreciate (Frankel, 1979: 610).

In addition to these approaches, the relationship between the exchange rate and the interest rate can be explained by *the real interest rate difference theory* proposed by Frankel (1979), which combines the flexible price model with the sticky price model. According to the real interest rate difference theory, the reason of the exchange rate movements is the real interest differences between the countries (Frankel 1979: 610–611). According to Frankel (1979), the exchange rate is determined by the difference in the demand for money (relative money demand or supply), the difference in income (relative income), the difference in interest rates (relative interest rate), and the difference between the inflation rates (relative inflation rate) of the two countries (Frankel, 1979: 612). According to Frankel (1979), in economies with high and variable inflation rates, a flexible price monetary approach should be used. However, in economies with low and stable inflation rates, a monetary price with a sticky price should be used. In the economies with moderate inflation, it is stated that, apart from these two approaches, real interest rate differences approach will give realistic results. According to Frankel (1979), the exchange rates may deviate from the equilibrium value. According to the theory, there is a negative relationship between the exchange rates and the nominal interest rate differences in the short term. Accordingly, the implementation of a contractionary monetary policy leads to an increase in interest rates and capital inflows to the country in the short term. This will lead to a decrease in the exchange rate and the appreciation of the national currency. In the long run, a positive relationship exists between exchange rates and nominal interest rate differences due to the changes in expected inflation rates. If the inflation rate in a country is expected to be higher than in other countries, ceteris paribus, the exchange rate will rise and the national currency will depreciate. If the inflation rate is expected to be less than in other countries, the exchange rate falls and the national currency will appreciate (Ökte, 2011: 232).

3 Applied Literature

In the applied literature, different results were found about the direction of the relationship between interest rate and exchange rate. In Tab. 15.1, the applied literature summary related to the interest rate and exchange rate relationship is presented.

Tab. 15.1: Applied Literature Summary of the Relationship between Interest Rate and Exchange Rate

Author	**Period/Country**	**Method**	**Results**
Sı et al.(2018)	1996M1–2015M9 BRICS countries	Wavelet Analysis	Long-run; $IR \uparrow \rightarrow EXC \uparrow$ (South Africa, Russia) $EXC \uparrow \rightarrow IR \uparrow$ (China) $EXC \leftrightarrow IR$ (India, Brazil)
Andrieş et al. (2017)	1999:02–2014:12 Romania	Wavelet-based analysis	Short-run; $IR \uparrow \rightarrow EXC \downarrow$ Long-run; $IR \uparrow \rightarrow EXC \uparrow$
Demirgil and Karaca (2017)	2009–2016 Turkey	ARDL	$EXC \uparrow \rightarrow IR \uparrow$
Sekmen and Ravanoğlu (2017)	2005:05–2017:06 Kazakhistan	VAR Analysis	$EXC \leftrightarrow IR$
Saraç and Karagöz (2016)	2003:02–2015:08 Turkey	Frequency domain Granger causality test	$EXC - IR$
Shastri and Shastri (2016)	1996 Q1–2014 Q4 India	Johansen Juselius and Gregory Hansen cointegration tests	$EXC - IR$
Hacker, Karlsson, and Månsson (2014)	1999–2009 Sweden	Granger causality	$IR \rightarrow EXC$
Wilson and Sheefeni (2014)	1993:Q1–2012:Q4 Namibia	VAR Analysis	$IR \uparrow \rightarrow EXC \uparrow$
Kayhan, Bayat, and Uğur (2013)	1993:03–2011:07 BRIC-T Countries	Nonlinear Granger causality	All countries (short-run): $EXC \uparrow \rightarrow IR \downarrow$ China (long-run): $IR \rightarrow EXC$
Gül et al. (2007)	1984–2006 Turkey	Granger causality	$EXC \rightarrow IR$

(*continued on next page*)

Author	Period/Country	Method	Results
Dash (2004)	1993:04–2003:03 1995:07–2003:3 India	Cointegration, ECM, Impulse Response Analysis	$IR \uparrow \rightarrow EXC \downarrow$
Dekle, Hsiao, and Wang (2002)	1997–1998 Korea, Malaysia, Thailand	VAR Analysis	$IR \uparrow \rightarrow EXC \downarrow$
Gümüş (2002)	1993W41–1994W52 Turkey	ECM	$IR \uparrow \rightarrow EXC \uparrow$

Note:→one directional causality; ↔bi-directional causality, ↑→in case of increase, ↑increase, ↓ decrease, – no causality
Source: Created by the authors.

In the applied literature the differences occur depending on which interest rates the countries take into account (nominal or real interest rates; short- or long-term interest rates, etc.), which country or country group is included in the analysis (developed or developing country), what type of exchange rate regime the countries adopt, the period covered, and the method used (short term, long term) (Andrieş, et al. 2017: 263).

4 Data and Econometric Methodology

We use annual data for Turkey from 1987–2017. In this study, deposit interest rate variable is used as interest rate and real effective exchange rate as exchange rate variable. The deposit interest rate data were obtained from the International Monetary Fund (IMF – International Financial Statistics) and the real effective exchange rate data from the Bruegel database. Both the exchange rate and interest rate variables are included in the analysis by taking logarithms. This study examines how the interest rate affects the exchange rate. Therefore, in Equation 1, the predicted model is as shown below:

$$EXC_t = \alpha + \beta_1 IR_t + \varepsilon_t \tag{1}$$

where the EXC denotes the real effective exchange rate, the IR interest rate and ε_t the error term.

In the study, firstly, the stability of the variables used in the model in equality (1) should be tested. If the variance of a variable does not change over time and depends on the distance between two periods, this variable is expressed as stationary. According to Granger and Newbold (1974), in the case of non-stationary series, a spurious regression problem may occur. In

Tab. 15.2: Unit Root Test Results

Variable	ADF		P-P		KPSS	
	Level	First Difference	Level	First Difference	Level	First Difference
LEXC	-1.859144 (-.963972)	-7.351452 (-2.967767)	-1.792197 (-2.963972)	-7.326515 (-2.967767)	0.625927 (0.463000)	0.201244 (0.463000)
LIR	-0.436767 (-2.963972)	-6.198883 (-2.967767)	-0.422854 (-2.963972)	-6.162590 (-2.967767)	0.568927 (0.463000)	0.311596 (0.463000)

Source: Calculated by the authors.

this case, the result obtained by regression analysis does not reflect the actual relationship. Regression analysis with non-stationary time series reflects the real relationship only if there is a cointegration relationship between these series (Gujarati, 1999: 713–726). Thus, unit root tests are used to determine the unit root states or stationary of the variables used in the studies. In this study, Augmented Dickey-Fuller (1981) (ADF), Phillips and Perron (1988) (P-P), and Kwiatkowski, Phillips, Schmidt and Shin (KPSS) (1992) unit root tests were used as unit root tests. The results of the unit root test are as shown in Tab. 15.2.

In the ADF and PP unit root tests, the null hypothesis that the variables have a unit root is tested. In the KPSS unit root test, the null hypothesis that the variables are stationary is tested. According to the results of ADF, P-P, and KPSS unit root test, the null hypothesis is rejected and the alternative hypothesis is accepted. Therefore, the results obtained from all three-unit root tests show that the first difference of the variables discussed in this study is I (1).

After unit root tests are performed, cointegration tests can be applied to reveal the long-term relationship between variables. In this study, Johansen cointegration test was used because the variables were stationary in the first differences. Indeed, according to Johansen (1988), the series to be included in the analysis should be equally stationary. The results of the Johansen cointegration test are presented in Tab. 15.3.

As can be seen from Tab. 15.3, the Johansen cointegration test, along with the characteristic roots called eigenvalue, reflects trace and maximum eigenvalue (Max-Eigen) test statistics and their critical table values. As a result of the analysis, it was concluded that there is at least one cointegrated vector among the variables. In this case, it can be said that there is a long-term relationship between exchange rate and interest rate.

Tab. 15.3: Johansen Cointegration Test Results

Trace Test Results				
Hypothesized No. of CE(s)	**Eigenvalue**	**Trace Statistic**	**Critical Value 0,05**	**Prob.**
None *	0.479457	20.31380	15.49471	0.0087
At most 1	0.094691	2.685941	3.841466	0.1012
Maximum Eigenvalue Test Results				
Hypothesized No. of CE(s)	**Eigenvalue**	**Max-Eigen Statistic**	**Critical Value 0.05**	**Prob.**
None *	0.479457	17.62786	14.26460	0.0142
At most 1	0.094691	2.685941	3.841466	0.1012

Source: Calculated by the authors.

Long-term coefficients of the variables can be obtained after the long-term relationship between interest rate and exchange rate variables have been established. In order to obtain these coefficients, FMOLS (Fully Modified Ordinary Least Square) developed by Phillips and Hansen (1990), DOLS (Dynamic Ordinary Least Square) developed by Stock and Watson (1993), and CCR (Canonical Cointegrating Regression) developed by Park (1992) methods were used. These tests are valid under the assumption that the variables discussed are stationary at first differences and that there is a cointegration relationship between the variables. The FMOLS method is an effective estimator for the elimination of deviations due to the successive correlation between the independent variables and the error term. The DOLS method is an effective estimator for eliminating deviations from the endogeneity problem between the independent variables and the error term.

The CCR method is an estimator used to eliminate deviations from the traditional OLS (Ordinary Least Square) method (Nazlıoğlu, 2010: 99).The test results of these three methods are given in Tab. 15.4.

As can be seen in Tab. 15.4, according to FMOLS, DOLS, and CCR results, there is a long-term negative relationship between interest rate and exchange rate. According to the results of FMOLS, DOLS, and CCR tests, in Turkey, a 1 % increase in interest rates causes the exchange rate to decrease of, respectively, 0.25 %, 0.26 %, and 0.25 %. The fact that the coefficients obtained from these three tests were very close to each other showed that the results obtained in the tests were consistent. In addition, the results obtained from all three tests were statistically significant at the significance level of 1 %.

Tab. 15.4: FMOLS, DOLS, and CCR Test Results

Dependent Variable: LEXC		LIR	C
FMOLS	Coefficient	-0.253358	5.236294
	t-statistic	-7.333490	41.92732
	Probability	0.0000	0.0000
	R-squared	0.747770	
	Adjusted R-squared	0.738761	
DOLS	Coefficient	-0.263985	5.294531
	t-statistic	-8.122713	44.28298
	Probability	0.0000	0.0000
	R-squared	0.841934	
	Adjusted R-squared	0.814445	
CCR	Coefficient	-0.252901	-7.187820
	t-statistic	5.234178	40.82413
	Probability	0.0000	0.0000
	R-squared	0.747380	
	Adjusted R-squared	0.738358	

Source: Calculated by the authors.

Conclusions

The relationship between interest rates and exchange rates has long been the subject of theoretical and empirical studies. There is no consensus on the direction of the relationship between the interest rate and the exchange rate in the literature. The effects of the changes in interest rates on the exchange rate and the size of this effect play an important role in determining the monetary policies to be implemented. In this study, a theoretical relationship between interest rates and exchange rates, in the framework of various theoretical economic models are explained and made an empirical application to Turkey.

This study aimed to investigate the relationship between the exchange rate and interest rate in Turkey during the period 1987–2017. Johansen, FMOLS, DOLS, and CCR methods were used in this framework. According to the results of the analysis, although there is a long-term relationship between the exchange rate and the interest rate, the interest rate affects the exchange rate negatively. In other words, an increase in the interest rate leads to a decrease in the exchange rate. Therefore, by taking this relationship into consideration, policy makers can determine appropriate interest policies. The asymmetric impact of the changes in interest rates on the exchange rate can be examined for future studies.

References

Andrieş, A. M., Căpraru, B., Ihnatov, I. and Tiwari, A.K. (2017). The Relationship between Exchange Rates and Interest Rates in a Small Open Emerging Economy: The Case of Romania. *Economic Modelling*, 67: 261–274.

Aslan, N., Terzi, N. and Sıampan, E. (2014). Türkiye'de Kısa Vadeli Sermaye Hareketlerinin Ekonomik Büyüme ve Reel Döviz Kuru İle İlişkisi. *Finansal Araştırmalar ve Çalışmalar Dergisi* 5(10): 15–32.

Bilson, J. F. (1978). The Monetary Approach to the Exchange Rate: Some Empirical Evidence. *Staff Papers, 25*(1), 48–75.

Dash, P. (2004). The Relationship between Interest Rate and Exchange Rate in India. *Sixth Annual Conference on Money and Finance in the Indian Economy*, March 25–27, Mumbai. http:www.igidr.ac.in/conf/money/mfc_6/mfc_06/dash.doc (Access Date: 07.09.2018)

Dekle, R., Hsiao, C. and Wang, S. (2002). High Interest Rates and Exchange Rate Stabilization in Korea, Malaysia and Thailand: An Empirical Investigation of the Traditional and Revisionist Views. *Review of International Economics* 10(1): 64–78.

Dickey, D. A. and Fuller, W. A. (1981). Likelihood Ratio Statistics for Autoregressive Time Series with a Unit Root. *Econometrica* 49: 1057–1072.

Doğan, İ., Afsal, M. Ş., Aydın, S. and Gürbüz, S. (2017). Faiz Oranları ve Döviz Kuru Dönemsel Analizi; Türkiye Örneği. *International Journal of Academic Value Studies* 3(13): 199–205.

Dülger, F. and Cin, M. F. (2002). Türkiye'de Döviz Kuru Dinamiklerinin Belirlenmesinde Parasalcı Yaklaşım ve Eşbütünleşme Yöntemiyle Sınama. *ODTÜ GelişmeDergisi* 29(1–2): 47–68.

Frankel, J. A. (1976). A Monetary Approach to the Exchange Rate: Doctrinal Aspects and Empirical Evidence. *Scandinavian Journal of Economics* 78(2): 200–204.

Frankel, J. A. (1979). On the Mark: A Theory of Floating Exchange Rates Based on Real Interest Differentials. *The American Economic Review* 69(4): 610–622.

Gül, E., Ekinci, A. and Özer, M. (2007). Türkiye'de Faiz Oranları ve Döviz Kuru Arasındaki Nedensellik İlişkisi: 1984–2006. *İktisat, İşletme ve Finans Dergisi* 22(251): 21–31.

Gümüş, İ. (2002). Effects of the Interest Rate Defense on Exchange Rates during the 1994 Crisis in Turkey. *TCMB Working Paper*, No: 14.

Güney, A. and Tunalı, H. (2017). Faiz Oranı Paritesi Yaklaşımı Üzerine Bir Değerlendirme. *Journal of Academic Researches and Studies* 9(16): 35–48.

Granger, C.W.J. and Newbold, P. (1974). Spurious Regressions in Economics. *Journal of Econometrics* 2(2): 111–120.

Granger, Gujarati, D.N. (1999). *Temel Ekonometri*, (Çev. Ü. Enesen & G.G. Enesen). İstanbul: Literatür Yayınları.

Hacker, R. S., Karlsson, H. K. and Månsson K. (2014). An Investigation of the Causal Relations between Exchange Rates and Interest Rate Differentials Using Wavelets. *International Review of Economics & Finance* 29: 321–329.

Johansen, S. (1988). Statistical Analysis of Co-Integrating Vectors. *Journal of Economic Dynamics and Control* 12(2–3): 231–254.

Karacan, R. (2010). Faiz, Döviz Kuru İlişkisinin Makroekonomik Performansa Etkisi Üzerine Bir Değerlendirme. *Kocaeli Üniversitesi Sosyal Bilimler Enstitüsü Dergisi* 20(2): 72–92.

Kayhan, S., Bayat, T. and Uğur, A. (2013). Interest Rates and Exchange Rate Relationship in BRIC-T Countries. *Ege Academic Review* 13(2): 227–236.

Kwiatkowski, D., Phillips, P. C. B., Schmidt, P. and Shin, Y. (1992). Testing the Null Hypothesis of Stationarity Against the Alternative of a Unit Root. *Journal of Econometrics* 54: 159–178.

Nazlıoğlu, Ş. (2010). *Makro İktisat Politikalarının Tarım Sektörü Üzerindeki Etkileri: Gelişmiş ve Gelişmekte Olan Ülkeler İçin Bir Karşılaştırma*. Yayınlanmamış Doktora Tezi. Kayseri: Erciyes Üniversitesi.

Ökte, K. S. (2011). "Ödemeler Dengesine Parasal Yaklaşım: Bir İnceleme". *Elektronik Sosyal Bilimler Dergisi* 10(35): 221–236.

Öztürk, N. and Bayraktar, Y. (2010). Döviz Kurlarını Açıklamaya Yönelik Yeni Yaklaşımlar. *Cumhuriyet Üniversitesi İktisadi ve İdari Bilimler Dergisi* 11(1): 157–191.

Park, J. Y. (1992). "Can on İcalcointegrating Regressions". *Econometrica* 60: 119–143.

Phillips, P. C. B. and Perron, P. (1988). "Testing for a Unit Root in a Time Series Regression". *Biometrika* 75(2): 335–346.

Phillips, P.C.B. and Hansen, B. E. (1990). "Statistical İnference in İnstrumental Variables Regression with I(1) Processes". *Review of Economic Studies* 57: 99–125.

Ray, S. (2012). Testing the Validity of Uncovered Interest Rate Parity in India. *Advances in Applied Economics and Finance* 1(4): 236–246.

Saraç, T. B. and Karagöz, K. (2016). Impact of Short-term Interest Rate on Exchange Rate: The Case of Turkey. *Procedia Economics and Finance* 38: 195–202.

Saraçoğlu, M., Kuzu, M. and Kocaoğlu, F. (2015). Türkiye Ekonomisinde Sermaye Hareketleri, Döviz Kuru, Enflasyon ve Faiz Arasındaki Etkileşimlerin Küresel Ekonomi Politik Çerçevesinde Analizi. *Gazi Journal of Economics and Business* 1(2): 75–110.

Sekmen, F. and Ravanoğlu, G. A. (2017). Faiz Haddi ve Para Arzının Döviz Kuru Üzerine Etkisi: Kazakistan. *Manas Journal of Social Studies* 6(4): 333–342.

Shastri, S. and Shastri, S. (2016). Exchange Rate Interest Rate Linkages in India: An Empirical Investigation. *Journal of Financial Economic Policy* 8(4): 443–457.

Si, D. K., Lı, X.-L., Chang, T. and Baı, L. (2018). Co-Movement and Causality between Nominal Exchange Rates and Interest Rate Differentials in BRICS Countries: A Wavelet Analysis. *Romanian Journal of Economic Forecasting* 21(1): 5–19.

Stock, J.H. and Watson, M. W. (1993). A Simple Estimator of Cointegrating Vectors in Higher Order Integrated Systems. *Econometrica* 61: 783–820.

Wilson, L. and Sheefeni, J. P. S. (2014). The Relationship between Interest Rate and Exchange Rate in Namibia. *Journal of Emerging Issues in Economics, Finance and Banking* 3(1): 947–961.

Yalçıner, K. (2012). *Uluslararası Finansman*. Ankara: Detay Yayıncılık.

Sefer Uçak, A. Gamze Aytekin and Özlem Kuvat

16 Inflation-Exchange Rate Relationship: The Case of Turkey

Highlights: The Purpose of the study; transition strategy to the Central Bank's inflation targeting since 2002 in Turkey together is to examine the inflation and exchange rate relations. In this strategy, the most important control instruments of the CBRT are interest rates and exchange rates. Because of Turkey is dependent on imports energy and intermediate goods, the loss of value in exchange rates, causing an increase in producer prices of imported input costs, is creating inflationary effect. The transition effect of exchange rates is partially reflected in domestic prices in countries with low import dependency, whereas in countries with high import dependency in energy and production it is almost completely reflected. In the study, 2003-2017 between years, econometric relationship between inflation and the exchange rate is tested in Turkey. According to ARDL analysis, inflation and exchange rate variables are cointegrated in the long run. The 1 % change in exchange rates increases inflation by 1.13 %, and these variables act together in the long run. Thus, the transition effect appears to be quite high in Turkey during the period mentioned, and the CBRT should take measures to prevent currency depreciation for price stability.

Keywords: Inflation, exchange rate, transition effect, ARDL bound test

Introduction

Increases in exchange rates in the countries that are growing based on imports have a negative impact on the country's economy. Depreciation losses in exchange rates cause an inflationary effect as countries increase their import input costs and producer prices. In particular, the depreciation losses in exchange rates in countries dependent on imports in energy and intermediate goods, such as Turkey, cause an increase in domestic price level, i.e., inflation. Since 2002, the CBRT (Central Bank of the Republic of Turkey) has been trying to control inflation through the inflation targeting strategy and the exchange rate and interest rate mechanism. This chapter explores the relationship between inflation and exchange rates which were examined in Turkey between 2003–2017 years. As a result of the cointegration analysis, cointegration was detected between the series. According to the causality analysis, a one-way causality relationship between exchange rates and inflation was determined in Turkey during the aforesaid period.

2 Inflation and Exchange Rate Relationship

The theoretical relationship between inflation and exchange rate was first proposed by Dornbusch (1976). Dornbusch explained the theoretical relationship between the two variables through concepts such as market density, import level, import substitution, and domestic production channels. He underlined that fluctuations in exchange rates in an open economy affected domestic prices on both intermediate and final goods. Moreover, he argued that the uncertainties caused by the fluctuations in the exchange rate would affect the price makers and would lead to an increase in domestic prices.

Svensson (2000) stated that the exchange rate affects inflation through three channels.

First of all, the exchange rate changes affect the demand for domestic goods and imported goods due to the relative prices between domestic and imported goods. Therefore, the exchange rate change indirectly affects inflation through net exports.

Secondly, the exchange rate change directly affects the Consumer Price Index by increasing the prices of imported final products. Therefore, according to Svensson (2000), this second effect affects inflation in a much shorter period than the first effect.

Thirdly, it stated that the wages over the consumer price index increases caused by the exchange rate, and the change in the exchange rate, increased the inflation by changing the asset prices with the effect on expectations.

The reflection of the exchange rates on the general level of prices for the countries that are dependent on imports and especially on developing economic growth causes inflation to increase. This reflection effect basically occurs in two ways.

The first is the reflection of changes in the exchange rate on the prices of imported products and services. The second effect is that changes in prices of imported goods and services affect the transition to consumer and producer prices. If the exchange rates increase at a certain rate (loss of value of national currency), then the transition effect is complete if the export goods are at the same rate as the foreign goods and the import goods are at the same rate as the national currency. If the exchange rate increases, the export goods prices are lower and the imported goods are less expensive, the transition effect will be partial (Seyidoğlu, 2013: 473). It is also directly related to the monetary policy strategy implemented by the central bank. Factors affecting the relationship between exchange rate, import cost, and inflation can be listed as follows (Işık, et al. 2004: 238):

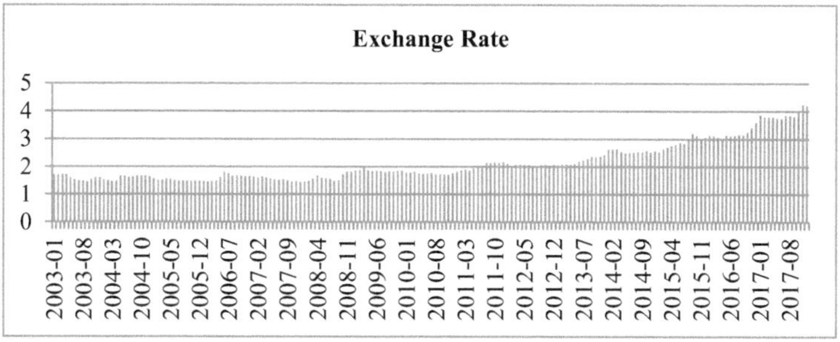

Fig. 16.1: Exchange Rates Change. Source: CBT, EVDS: Access: 20.05.2018

- Expected permanent loss of value in national currency by markets,
- Energy costs (oil, natural gas) and price increases rate in imported goods,
- The openness of the economy (capital movements),
- Total demand,
- The effects of fiscal policy.

The depreciation of the national currency will cause an increasing effect on domestic prices, along with these basic factors: price increases in imported inputs, inflation expectations, and increasing production costs (Gül and Aykut, 2006; Ekinci et al., 2006: 93).

3 Causes and Sources of Inflation in Turkey

CBRT has tried to control inflation with its implicit inflation targeting since 2002 and with its explicit inflation targeting strategy since 2006. However, the supply shocks experienced have had difficulty meeting the inflation target due to the volatility in the global crisis and exchange rates. The course of exchange rates in Turkey between 2003 and 2017 is given in Fig. 16.1 and the course of inflation is given in Fig. 16.2.

In the aforementioned years, the increase in the CPI index based on 2003=100 was realized as 212 % in spite of the appreciation increase of 144 % in exchange rates. According to these results, the effect of the appreciation increase in exchange rates (depreciation losses in TL) on the transition to inflation is more complete than partial. Thus, exchange rates are one of the main causes of inflation in Turkey.

As of 2017, approximately $233 billion of total imports were $33 billion in investment of capital goods imports (14.1 %), raw materials and intermediate

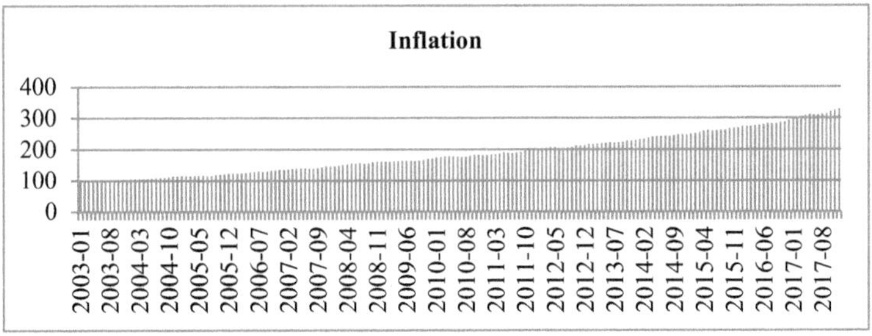

Fig. 16.2: Inflation Change. Source: CBT, EVDS: Access: 20.05.2018

goods imports were $171 billion (73.4 %), and consumer goods imports were $28 billion (12.01 %). Oil and natural gas imports expressed as confidential data of approximately $20.7 billion in raw material imports are conspicuous. Therefore, the Turkish economy, which grew by 7.4 % in real terms in 2017, is an inevitable result of the growth of 17.6 % of imports. The growth of the Turkish economy is dependent on imports. The main reasons for this are: intermediate goods and especially energy (8.9 %) depend on external dependency and high value-added product imports (13 %) (TSI, Foreign Trade Statistics).

In the Turkish economy, where growth is dependent on imports, the volatility in foreign exchange rates will inevitably be reflected in the producer and consumer prices. With the strict monetary policy measures implemented by the central bank in the fight against inflation, total demand is reduced and inflation is being tackled, but it is partially waived from growth.

Increases in foreign exchange rates in import-based growth countries have a negative impact on the country's economy. Therefore, ensuring a stable structure of exchange rates for Turkey's economy, the consumption of individuals and organizations will have a positive effect on production and investment decisions. Depreciation losses in exchange rates cause an inflationary effect as countries increase their import input costs and producer prices. The depreciation losses in foreign exchange rates in countries dependent on imports, especially in energy and intermediate goods, such as Turkey, cause an increase in inflation.

4 Related Literature

The literature summary examining the changes in foreign currency exchange rates in Turkey's import and export prices due to internal reflection is given in Tab. 16.1. Overall the work carried out in Turkey, exchange losses in the value of the reflection inflation are seen to be close to full rather than partial. Among the main reasons for this are the growth and import growth and dependence on imports and exports (although changing on a sectoral basis).

In the studies, it is seen that the effect of the transition effect in exchange rates is originating from imports and that the 1 % depreciation of the exchange rates in the long term is almost equal to the inflation. According to the results of causality, it was found that the general trend was one-way towards inflation from exchange rates. According to these results, exchange rates are one of the main causes of inflation in Turkey.

5 Empirical Analysis

5.1 Variables and Set of Data

In this study, the relationship between exchange rate and inflation in the period 2003:01–2017:12, which can be obtained for Turkey, was examined with a monthly time series. The exchange rate and inflation data covering the period of interest were compiled from EVDS database statistics. ER data were obtained with the participation of 50 % of the dollar and Euro, and the data were evaluated with the index data which was taken as a basis in 2013.

The logarithm of the series is taken and since the series are monthly, they are seasonally adjusted with seasonal correction. Monthly Seasonally Adjusted Logarithmic Exchange Rate Euro-Dollar Average 2003 Index (ER) and Monthly Seasonally Adjusted Logarithmic Inflation Rate 2003 Index (INF) were used as variables. Time path change views of the variables are given in Figs. 16.3 and 16.4.

In Figs. 16.3 and 16.4, ER and INF graphs indicate an increasing trend. There is no scattering around a certain value. Descriptive statistics for the variables are presented in Tab. 16.2.

According to the descriptive statistics, the mean of the ER variable was 0.71 for median measurements, while the median was 0.61, and the mean and median for the INF variable was 5.17. The variance measure was 1.07 for the ER variable and 1.24 for the INF variable.

5.2 Methodology and Findings

In order to understand the long-term feature of a time series, it is necessary to first determine whether the process has changed over time and determine the extent of the effect of previous period values on the series. If the property of a process changes over time, the serial is not stationary. In a stationary time series, the difference between the two successive values occurs from the time interval and is not due to the time. If the series is not stationary, fake regression occurs.

Tab. 16.1: Summary Literature on the Causes and Sources of Inflation

Writer	*Release Year*	*Period*	*Methodology*	*Result*
Leigh D. and Rossi M.	*2002*	*1994–2002*	*VAR model*	As a result of the study, it was revealed that one point change in exchange rates reflected a wholesale price index as 0.60 and as a consumer price 0.45 points.
Telatar F. and Telatar E.	*2003*	*1995–2000*	*Granger Causality*	A causality relationship from exchange rate variability to inflation has been established.
Bayraktutan Y. and Arslan İ.	*2003*	*1980–2000*	*Granger Causality*	In this study, it was found that there was a significant and negative relationship between the exchange rate and the import volume, and a significant and negative relationship between the inflation rate and the import volume.
Işık N., Acar D., Işık H.	*2006*	*1982–2003*	*Co-integration Analysis*	In the case of a 1 % increase in exchange rates, it has been determined that inflation will increase by 0.9 %.
Gül E. and Ekinci A.	*2006*	*1990–2006*	*Granger Causality Analysis*	The causality relationship between exchange rate and inflation has been shown to be one-way from exchange rate to inflation.
Sever E. and Mızrak Z.	*2007*	*1987–2006*	*VAR model*	It has been concluded that inflation and interest rate response is higher in the changes in exchange rates.
Volkan A., Saatçioğlu C. and Korap L.	*2007*	*1994:04–2002: 122003: 01–06:12*	*VAR*	The effect of depreciation losses on exchange rates in the 2003 period on inflation has decreased compared to post-2003. The decline in the exchange rate pass-through on domestic prices corresponds to a 25 % decline in CPI inflation after 2003.

Tab. 16.1: (continued)

Writer	*Release Year*	*Period*	*Methodology*	*Result*
Büyükakın F. C. and Turkish A.	*2009*	*1990--2007*	*VAR model*	It has been concluded that the exchange rate variability in terms of inflation is an important indicator of the changes in inflation and that monetary transfer has shown that the exchange rate channel operates effectively in the economy.
Selim S. and Güven E.	*2014*	*1990–2012*	*Granger Causality*	The result is that the real effective foreign exchange rate affects the CPI.
Ergin A.	*2015*	*2005–2014*	*VAR model*	In the study, which examines the passivity of the exchange rate on inflation, export and import prices, it is observed that the effect on the general level of domestic prices was mainly realized through the import channel.
Alptekin V., Yılmaz K. Ç. and Taş T.	*2016*	*2005–2015*	*VAR model*	In the study, it was observed that the response of consumer prices to a unit shock in exchange rates was lower than the response of producer prices.
Ekinci E. B. M. M., Alhan A. and Ergor Z. B.	*2016*	*2010–2015*	*R Programming Language – Nonparametric regression*	It has been determined that the inflation and exchange rate announced the interest rate of 93 %.
Petek A. and Çelik A.	*2017*	*1990–2015*	*VAR Analysis*	In the study, it was determined that there was a one-way relationship between CPI and exports to imports. In addition, it has been observed that there is a one-way relationship between exchange rates and import and export.

(continued on next page)

Tab. 16.1: (continued)

Writer	*Release Year*	*Period*	*Methodology*	*Result*
Bulut Ş.	*2017*	*2001–2017*	*VAR model*	In the study, one-way causality from the exchange rate to the general level of prices has been found in the long term, whereas in the short term one-way causality from the general level of prices to the exchange rates has been obtained. In addition, it was concluded that an increase of 1 % in the exchange rate basket was increasing inflation by 0.92 %.
Bozdağlıoğlu E. Y. Y. and Yılmaz M.	*2017*	*1994–2014*	*VAR Model*	There is a short-term causality relationship from the nominal exchange rate to inflation. Inflation is affected by these increases.
Akgül I. and Özdemir S.	*2018*	*2003–2016*	*Dicks-Panchenko Causality Test*	While there was bidirectional causality between inflation and interest rates in the 2003–2011 period, this relationship was eliminated after the break in 2011. In addition, after 2008, the causality from exchange rate to inflation has emerged.

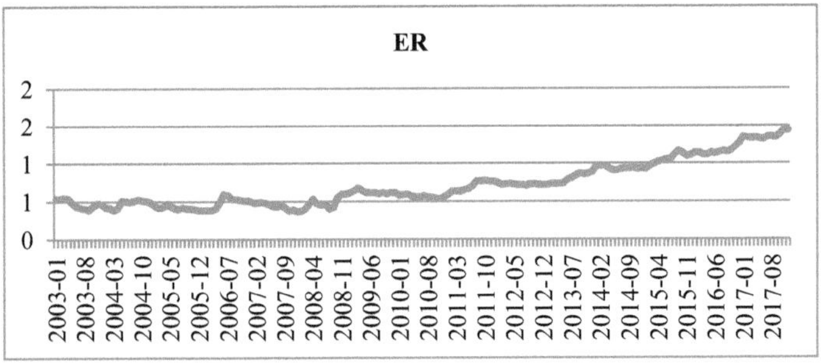

Fig. 16.3: Exchange Rate Change. Source: CBT, EVDS: Access: 20.05.2018

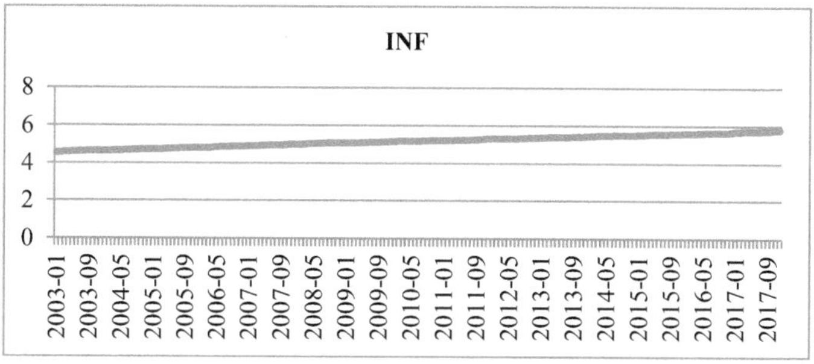

Fig. 16.4: Inflation Change. Source: CBT, EVDS: Access: 20.05.2018

Tab. 16.2: Descriptive Statistics

	ER	INF
Mean	0.710409	5.173200
Median	0.613611	5.178659
Maximum	1.439448	5.790963
Minimum	0.364454	4.546650
Std. Dev.	0.289430	0.346001
Skewness	0.860000	-0.034261
Kurtosis	2.652743	1.865148

Therefore, in order to understand the time-path process of the series, the relationship between Y_t and Y_{t-1} should be estimated. The most common method developed for testing stasis is the unit Root Test. Tests such as expanded Dickey-Fuller (ADF), Phillips-Perron (PP), Kwiatkowski, Philips, Schmidt, Shin (KPSS), and Zivot and Andrews (ZA) can be applied for unit root test (Dickey and Fuller, 1979; Phillips and Perron 1988, Kwiatkowski, Philips, Schmidt and Shin 1992; Zivot and Andrews, 2002; Kutler, 2007: 284; Dikmen, 2012: 309).

In the study, ADF, PP, and KPSS tests, which did not examine the structural break for the stability of the variables, were applied as Model A considering the ZA constant for structural fracture analysis.[1] The results of these tests are given in Tab. 16.3. According to the table, the ER and INF series are not stable at the level compared with critical values at 5 % meaning levels as a result of the ADF, PP, and KPSS unit root test. As a result of the difference, both variables are stable

1 The analysis was performed with E-views 9.0 package program.

Tab. 16.3: ADF-PP-KPSS-ZA Test Results

			ADF	PP	KPSS	ZA
ER	Level	t	-2.021871[2]*	-1.827452 [5]	0.383927 [10]*	-3.379368 [2]*
		Prob.	0.5850**	0.6874**		0.015568
	1. Differences	t	-10.45861 [1]*	-9.526868 [10]	0.213618	-10.91740 [1]*
		Prob.	0.000**	0.000**		0.05
INF	Level	t	-3.315552 [1]*	-3.371890 [6]	0.213618 [10]*	-3.427052[4]*
		Prob.	0.0671**	0.0585**		0.017
	1. Differences	t	-8.408843 [3]*	-12.03487 [19]	0.107816*** [12] (LM-stat.)	-7.054403 [4]*
		Prob.	0.000**	0.000**		0.005**
	Critical Value	%1	-4.010740	-4.010143	0.216000	-5.34
		%5	-3.435413	-3.435125	0.146000	-4.93
		%10	-3.141734	-3.141565	0.119000	-4.58

* Gives appropriate change with lag lengths. The Akaike knowledge criterion in the ADF test is Newey-West Bandwidth for Barlett kernel in PP and KPSS tests.
** If the probability value for ADF and PP is greater than 0.05, H_0 hypothesis (H_0: series is not stationary) is accepted, the series is not stationary. If the probability is less than 0.05, the H_0 hypothesis is rejected, the series is stationary.
*** When the LM statistic value calculated for KPSS is less than the critical value of 1 %, the H_0 hypothesis (H_0 : serial stasis) is accepted, and the series is stationary.

at 1 %, 5 %, and 10 % significance levels, and ER and INF are I (1) series. The breakdown in the ER series was in the fourth month of 2009, while the break in the INF series was realized at the eleventh month of 2008.

According to the results of the test, both series are I (1) and series are stationary. An ARDL bound test was used to investigate the relationship between variables. Paseran et al. (2001) suggested that the relationship between long-term relationship and short-term causality can be investigated by the ARDL method. The results obtained with this method are more effective and neutral than the results of the classic cointegration methods. In addition, better results can be obtained in small samples with no longer periods of time (Paseran et al., 2001; Koçak, 2014: 68).

5.3 Investigation of Cointegration Relationship and Long-Term Analysis

The econometric model established for the case where inflation is an independent variable is given in Equation 1, and the econometric model established

Tab. 16.4: F Bound Test

Model 1: F Value	26.93530	k=1
Model 2: F Value	3.041618	k=1
Significance Level	Lower Critical-Limit	Upper Critical-Limit
10 %	3.02	3.51
5 %	3.62	4.16
2.5 %	4.18	4.79
1 %	4.94	5.58

for the situation where the exchange rate is an independent variable is given in Equation 2. The coefficients α_1 and $\beta_1$are expected to be positive.

$$Model\ 1: \quad INF_t = \alpha_0 + \alpha_1 ER_t + \varepsilon_t \tag{1}$$

$$Model\ 2: \quad ER_t = \beta_0 + \beta_1 INF_t + \varepsilon_t \tag{2}$$

When testing ARDL models, the bound test is performed to determine whether there is a cointegration relationship. In this study, the F frontier test (Wald test) was applied and the established hypotheses are as follows:

Model 1: H0: $\alpha_3 = \alpha_4 = 0$ No Co-integration.
H1:$\alpha_3 \neq \alpha_4 \neq 0$ There is Co-integration.

Model 2: H0: 3 $\beta_3 = \beta_4 = 0$ No Co-integration.
H1:$\beta_3 \neq \beta_4 \neq 0$ There is Co-integration.

As a result of the bound test, it is seen that the test statistic for Model 1 (26.9) is above the lower and upper limit values according to the different significance levels, but for the Model 2, the test statistic value (3.0) can only cross the lower limit at the level of 10 % significance level. Therefore, according to Model 1, the H_0 hypothesis that there is no cointegration relationship between INF and ER variables was rejected. The obtained values are given in Tab. 16.4.

In this context, the ARDL format of Model 1 is given in Equation 3 below. The long-term and short-term relationships between the ARDL and the INF variable and the ER variable that is thought to influence it can be determined. The appropriate latency level is (2.1). The model based on the estimation of the model ARDL (2, 1) is given in Equation 4 and the coefficient values are given in Tab. 16.5. When the probability values are taken into consideration, it is observed that the coefficients are significant.

Tab. 16.5: Results of the ARDL (2.1) model

Variable	Coefficients	Standard Error	t-statistic	Possibility
INF (-1)	1.137289	0.072800	15.62209	0.0000
INF(-2)	-0.143348	0.072276	-1.983353	0.0489
ER	0.051367	0.013008	3.948896	0.0001
ER(-1)	-0.044486	0.013081	-3.400832	0.0008
C	0.032121	0.012261	2.619675	0.0096

Diagnostic Tests
There is no autocorrelation in χ^2_{BG} 0,781 (0.4543>0.05)
There is no variance change in χ^2_{BPG} 1.886 (0.1148>0.05)
There is normality in χ^2_{JB} 2.25 (0.32>0.05)

$$\Delta \mathrm{INF_t} = \alpha_0 + \sum_{i=1}^{m} \alpha_{1i} \Delta \mathrm{INF_{t-i}} + \sum_{i=1}^{m} \alpha_{2i} \Delta \mathrm{ER_{t-i}} + \alpha_3 \mathrm{INF}_{t-1} + \alpha_4 \mathrm{ER}_{t-1} + u_t \tag{3}$$

$$INF_t = \alpha_0 + \sum_{i=1}^{m} \alpha_{1i} INF_{t-i} + \sum_{i=0}^{m} \alpha_{2i} ER_{t-i} + u_t \tag{4}$$

The long-term slope term for the ARDL (2.1) model and the fixed term were found to be significant. The model is given in Equation 5.

INF=5.301168+ 1.135557* ER
$t_{hes(}$12.209147)(5.119302) (5)
P(0.0000)(0.0000)

In this case, it can be said that the long-term effect of ER on INF is significant and positive. A 1 % change in the ER ratio will provide a change of 1.13 % on the INF.

5.4 Testing Stability of Coefficients

The CUSUM and CUSUMQ graphs were examined in order to examine the stability of long-term coefficients for all observation periods. In these graphs, since the blue lines were in the red band range (for 5 % significance level) indicating the upper and lower limit, the parameters were significant and the coefficients were stable. These results indicate that Turkey is committed in the long-term INF function of variables established by the ER model. The CUSUM graph is shown in Fig. 16.5 and the CUSUMQ graph is given in Fig. 16.6.

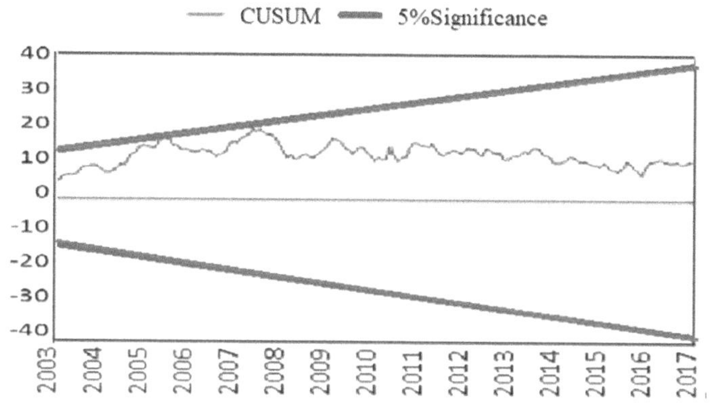

Fig. 16.5: Stability Test CUSUM Graph

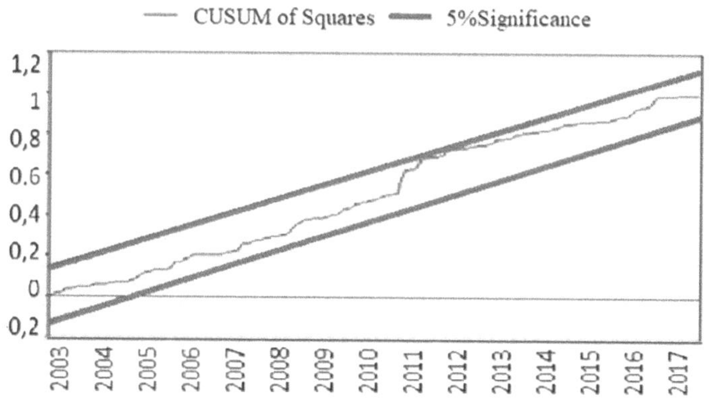

Fig. 16.6: Stability Test CUSUMQ Graph

5.5 Short-Term Analysis and Error Correction Model

The series must be cointegrated before the error correction model can be applied. The error correction model examines whether the effects of the shocks they encounter in the long run are temporary or not, and how long they will be eliminated. If the equation of error correction ECT_{t-1} (*CointEq (-1)*) value is significant, how much of the variability in a period in the dependent variable is corrected in the other period can be explained. In addition, this coefficient is expected to be negative to ensure the stability of the model. The negative sign here indicates a short-term imbalance towards the equilibrium for long term (Yıldırtan, 2011: 248).

Tab. 16.6: ECM Error Correction Model for ARDL (2.1)

Variance	Coefficient	Standard Error	t-statistic	Possibility
Δ (INF)(-1)	0.143348	0.071739	1.998190	0.0473
Δ (ER)	0.051367	0.012595	4.078344	0.0001
$ECT_{(t-1)}$	-0.006059	0.000670	-9.041021	0.0000

In this study, ARDL error correction model (ECM) equation which is established to investigate the short-term relationship mechanism between ER and INF variables is given in Equation 6 and the results are given in Tab. 16.6. Here Δ is the difference operator.

$$\Delta\, INF_t = \alpha_0 + \sum_{i=1}^{m} \alpha_{1\mathrm{i}} \Delta\, \mathrm{INF}_{\mathrm{t-i}} + \sum_{i=0}^{n} \alpha_{2\mathrm{i}} \Delta\, \mathrm{ER}_{\mathrm{t-i}} + \delta ECT_{\mathrm{t-1}} + e_t \tag{6}$$

As given in the table, the coefficient of the varianceECT_{t-1} was obtained as -0.006059. As this value is negative, the error corrector mechanism is running and the deviation is reduced.Δ (INF (-1)) and Δ(ER) is statistically significant, since the probability value is <0.05. Also the short-term effect of ER on the INF variable can be said to be positive and significant.

Conclusion

The changes in the exchange rates cause changes in the domestic price levels due to various effects. The direction of this change is as much as the loss of exchange rates of domestic prices in developing countries and especially countries with high import dependency. The transition effect of the exchange rates is partially reflected in domestic prices in countries with low import dependency, whereas in countries with a high dependency on energy and production imports it is seen full. The impact of exchange rates on inflation in Turkey is quite high with key factors such as high energy dependency and import dependency on exports.

In this study, the relationship between exchange rate and inflation in the period between 2003:01–2017:12 was examined by monthly time series. As a result of the unit root tests, the series were stationary at the same degree. Since it provides an advantageous way for short-term analysis, the ARDL model was chosen to investigate the existence of co-integration. According to the results of the ARDL model bound test, INF and ER variables act cooperatively in a long term. The effect of the ER variable on the INF variable is positive and significant according to the long-term and short-term coefficients. The 1 % change in the

ER variable increases the INF value by 1.13 %, and these variables move together in the long term. According to the results of the error correction model, the coefficient of ECT_{t-1} is negative and statistically significant.

According to these results, the transition effect in Turkey is quite high. In order to achieve price stability, which is the main objective of the Central Bank, it is necessary to check exchange rates. Therefore, implementation of tight monetary policies should be continued, imports dependence should be reduced, foreign capital inflows should be encouraged, and indigenousness production rates should be increased in production. Measures to be taken against structural phenomena in the economy and money management will be able to prepare the environment for the domestic prices to have a stronger structure against the short-term shocks and long-term effect of the exchange rate.

References

Akgül, I. and Özdemir, S. (2018). Enflasyon-Faiz Oranı ve Enflasyon-Döviz Kuru İkilemi: GEG Programı Döneminde Türkiye Gerçeği. *Ege Akademik Bakış*, 18(1), 153–166.

Alptekin, V., Yılmaz, K. Ç. and Taş, T. (2016). Döviz Kurundan Fiyatlara Geçiş Etkisi: Türkiye Örneği. *Selçuk Üniversitesi Sosyal Bilimler Enstitüsü Dergisi*, 35, 1–9.

Bayraktutan, Y. and Arslan, İ. (2003). Türkiye'de Döviz Kuru, İthalat ve Enflasyon İlişkisi: Ekonometrik Analiz (1980–2000). *Afyon Kocatepe Üniversitesi İİBF Dergisi*, 5(2), 89–104.

Bozdağlıoğlu, E. Y. and Yılmaz, M. (2017). Türkiye'de Enflasyon Ve Döviz Kuru İlişkisi: 1994–2014 Yılları Arası Bir İnceleme. *Bitlis Eren Üniversitesi İktisadi ve İdari Bilimler Fakültesi Akademik İzdüşüm Dergisi*, 2(3), 1–20.

Bulut, Ş. (2018). Fiyatlar Genel Düzeyi İle Döviz Kuru Arasındaki Eşbütünleşme ve Nedensellik İlişkisi: Türkiye Örneği. *Aydın İktisat Fakültesi Dergisi*, 2(1).

Büyükakın, F, C. and Türk, A. (2009). Parasal Aktarım Mekanizması: Türkiye'de Döviz Kuru Kanalının VAR Analizi. *Dokuz Eylül Üniversitesi İktisadi ve İdari Bilimler Fakültesi Dergisi*, 24(1), 171–198.

Dickey, D. A. and Fuller. W. A. (1979). Distribution of the Estimators for Autoregressive Time Series with a Unit Root. *Journal of the American Statistical Association*, 74.366a, 427–431.

Dikmen, N. (2012). *Ekonometri Temel Kavramlar ve Uygulamalar*. Dora Yayınevi. Bursa

Dornbusch, R. (1976). Expectations and Exchange Rate Dynamics. *The Journal of Political Economy*, 84(6), 1161–1176.

Ekinci, E. B. M., Alhan, A. and Ergör, Z. B. (2016). Parametrik Olmayan Regresyon Analizi: Faiz oranı, Enflasyon ve Döviz Kuru Arasındaki İlişkinin İncelenmesi Örneği. *Bankacılık ve Sigortacılık Araştırmaları Dergisi*, 2(9).

Ergin, A. (2015). Döviz Kuru Enflasyon Arasındaki Geçiş Etkisi: Türkiye Örneği. *Niğde Üniversitesi İktisadi ve İdari Bilimler Fakültesi*, 8(3), 13–29.

Gül, E. and Aykut, E. (2006). Türkiye'de Enflasyon ve Döviz Kuru Arasındaki Nedensellik İlişkisi: 1984-2003. *Anadolu Üniversitesi Sosyal Bilimler Dergisi*, 6(1), 91–106.

Işık, N, Acar, D. and Işık, H. (2004). Enflasyon ve Döviz Kuru İlişkisi: Bir Eşbütünleşme Analizi. *Süleyman Demirel Üniversitesi İktisadi ve İdari Bilimler Fakültesi Dergisi*, 9(2).

Koçak, E. (2014). Türkiye'de Çevresel Kuznets Eğrisi Hipotezinin Geçerliliği: ARDL Sınır Testi Yaklaşımı. *İşletme Ve İktisat Çalışmaları Dergisi*, 2(3), 62–73.

Kutlar, A. (2007). *Ekonometriye Giriş*. Nobel Yayın Dağıtım. Ankara.

Kwiatkowski, D., Schmidt P. and Shin Y. (1992). Testing the Null Hypothesis of Stationarity Against the Alternative of a Unit Root. *Journal of Econometrics*, 54(1–3), 159–178.

Leigh, D. and Rossi, M. (2002). Exchange Rate Pass- Through in Turkey. *IMF Working Paper*, https://www.imf.org/external/pubs/ft/wp/2002/wp02204.pdf. Access date: 02.07.2018.

Mamak Ekinci, E., Alhan, A. and Ergör, Z. (2016). Parametrik Olmayan Regresyon Analizi: Faiz oranı, Enflasyon ve Döviz Kuru Arasındaki İlişkinin İncelenmesi Örneği. *Bankacılık ve Sigortacılık Araştırmaları Dergisi*, 2 (9), 28–37.

Pesaran, M. H, Yongcheol S. and Richard J. S. (2001). Bounds Testing Approaches to the Analysis of Level Relationships. *Journal of Applied Econometrics*, 16(3), 289–326.

Petek, A. and Çelik, A. (2017). Türkiye'de Enflasyon, Döviz Kuru, İhracat ve İthalat Arasındaki İlişkinin Ekonometrik Analizi (1990–2015). *Finans Politik & Ekonomik Yorumlar*; İstanbul, 54(626), 69–87.

Phillips, P.C B. and Perron, P. (1988). Testing For a Unit Root in Time Series Regression. Biométrika, 75(2), 335–346.

Selim, S. and Güven, E. (2014). Türkiye'de Enflasyon, Döviz Kuru ve İşsizlik Arasındaki İlişkinin Ekonometrik Analizi, *Ekonomik ve Sosyal Araştırmalar Dergisi*, 10(1), 79–204.

Sever, E. and Mızrak, Z. (2007). Döviz Kuru, Enflasyon ve Faiz Oranı Arasındaki İlişkiler: Türkiye Uygulaması. *Sosyal Ekonomik Araştırmalar Dergisi*, 7(13), 264–283.

Seyidoğlu, H. (2013). *Uluslararası İktisat-Teori Politika ve Uygulama*. İstanbul: Güzem Can Yayınları.

Svensson, L.E.O. (2000). Open-Economy Inflation Targeting. *Journal of International Economics*, 50 (1),155–183.

Telatar, F. and Telatar, E. (2003), The Relationship Between Inflation and Different Sources of Inflation Uncertainty in Turkey. *Applied Economic Letters*, 10(7).

CBRT, The Central Bank of the Republic of Turkey, EVDS, Electronic Data Delivery System, https://evds2.tcmb.gov.tr/index.php?/evds/serieMarket Accessed: 20.05.2018.

TSI, Turkish Statistical Institute Foreign Trade Statistics, (Turkish Statistical Institute, Foreign Trade Statistics), http://www.tuik.gov.tr/PreTablo.do?alt_id=1046 Accessed: 02.07.2018.

Volkan, A., Saatçioğlu, C. and Korap, L. (2007). Impact of Exchange Rate Changes on Domestic Inflation: The Turkish Experience (No. 2007/6). Discussion Paper, *Turkish Economic Association.*

Yıldırtan, D. Ç. (2011). *E-Views Uygulamalı Temel Ekonometri: Makro Ekonomik Verilerle*. Türkmen Kitabevi. İstanbul.

Zivot, E. and Andrews, D. W. K. (2002). Further Evidence on the Great Crash, the Oil-Price Shock and the Unit-Root Hypothesis. *Journal of Business & Economic Statistics*, 20(1), 25–44.

Levent Korap

17 Theoretical Modeling Basis of TL/US Dollar Exchange Rate: An Econometric Practice

Highlights: In this chapter, TL/US dollar exchange rate is examined by using quarterly frequency data for the observation period of 2005Q4–2017Q4. Monetary model exchange rate determination mechanism has been introduced in a theoretical approach, and multivariate ARDL bounds testing has been applied to the data for estimation purposes. The findings indicate that the monetary exchange rate has a cointegrated relationship consistent with the fundamentals of economic theory. While the monetary exchange rate is in a positive interaction with the relative money supply, an increase in the relative real income level results in the appreciation of the national currency against the US dollar. Furthermore, as a priori assumed, a positive relationship has been found between the monetary exchange rate and the expected inflation rate variable.

Keywords: Foreign exchange rate, economic fundamentals, expected inflation, bounds testing, Turkish economy

Introduction

Determination of exchange rates and the exchange rate policies applied for stabilization purposes constitute one of the most controversial issues of interest in contemporaneous economics literature, which allows the researchers to easily implement the developments in econometrics. Such a phenomenon has a great importance for both developed and developing countries since policy makers tend to canalize use of exchange rate to gain an ex ante designed macroeconomic growth performance as well as to break the inertial nature of prices dominated in the economy in fighting inflation. Thus, investigation of the long-run course of exchange rates enables researchers to examine efficiency of the discretionary policies and to extract expected consequences of policy implementations based on exchange rate determination. In this line, modeling the determinants of exchange rate for a developing country would help researchers conduct empirical investigations for testing the coherence of international macroeconomic theories such as purchasing power parity (PPP) and uncovered interest parity (UIP) as well as theories explaining the determination of exchange rates assuming open economy conditions.

Following the seminal paper of Meese and Rogoff (1983), many papers have been attributed to modeling the behavior of exchange rates so as to see whether monetary fundamentals are able to explain the long-run course and the short-run dynamics of exchange rates. These include, for example, MacDonald and Taylor (1993); McNown and Wallace (1994); MacDonald and Marsh (1997); Cheung and Chinn (1998); Mark and Sul (2001); Rapach and Wohar (2004); Abhyankar, Sarno, and Valente (2005); Karfakis (2006); Chin, Azali, and Matthews (2007); Shylajan, Sereejesh, and Suresh (2011); and Afat, Gómez-Puig, and Sosvilla-Rivero (2015), and try to describe the power of the exchange rate determination models against each other. At the extent they produce more accurate estimates, models have been accepted to be superior when compared with the others. Studies yielded by Telatar and Kazdağli (1998), Bahmani-Oskooee and Kara (2000), Dülger and Cin (2002), Civcir (2003; 2004), Yazgan (2003), Erlat (2003), Ozdemir (2004), and Uz and Ketenci (2010) give some estimations for the Turkish economy.

In this study, the monetary model of exchange rate determination is tested for the TL/US dollar exchange rate. For this purpose, in the next section, a hypothetical model is considered in the light of economic literature, and this model is extended briefly to include inflationary expectations. In the third section, the data and time series properties are specified, and a methodological explanation for estimation process is given in the fourth section. The fifth section deals with multivariate time series estimation, and applies to an econometric attempt. The sixth section summarizes the main results and concludes the chapter.

2 Model Construction

Following Neely and Sarno (2002) we begin our analysis by examining the flexible price monetary model (FPMM). Model is constructed in line with the assumptions based on the quantity theory of money (QTM) and the purchasing power parity (PPP) relating the changes in price level and exchange rate to the money supply changes. McNown and Wallace (1994) relate this feature of the model to having more information content than the PPP in determining foreign exchange rates under the presence of stable monetary demand in the economy. For the domestic and foreign money markets, consider the following equilibrium conditions:

$$money_t = price_t + \gamma_1 income_t + \gamma_2 interest_t \tag{1}$$

$$money_t^f = price_t^f + \gamma_1^f income_t^f + \gamma_2^f interest_t^f \tag{2}$$

In Equation 1 $money_t$, $price_t$,$income_t$, and $interest_t$ represent the domestic money supply, the general price level, the real income level, and the interest rate, respectively, in any $t$observation period. The magnitudes other than the interest rate are expressed in natural logarithmic terms, while the interest rate is expressed in own linear form. Equition 2 includes the identical foreign variables under money market equilibrium. The coefficients $\gamma_1$and $\gamma_2$indicate the positive constants used for income elasticity of demand for money and interest rate semi-elasticity, respectively.

The second assumption taken into account in the construction of FPMM is the validity of the absolute PPP. In this case, prices in two currencies will tend to be equalized through exchange rate movements resulting from the arbitrage conditions of the goods market:

$$er_t = price_t - price_t^f \tag{3}$$

In Equation 3, the expression of er_trespresents the domestic price of foreign currency, i.e., nominal exchange rate, in natural logarithms. Subtracting Equation 2 from Equation 1, solving for $\left(price_t - price_t^f\right)$ and inserting the result into Equation 3 yield the FPMM of nominal exchange rate determination:

$$er_t = \left(money_t - money_t^f\right) - \left(\gamma_1 income_t - \gamma_1^f income_t^f\right) + \left(\gamma_2 interest_t - \gamma_2^f interest_t^f\right) \tag{4}$$

Let us assume as a simplifying assumption for the ease of applying to the modern time series estimation techniques that the income elasticities and interest rate semi-elasticities of money demand equal of each other for the home and foreign countries:

$$er_t = \left(money_t - money_t^f\right) - \gamma_1\left(income_t - income_t^f\right) + \gamma_2\left(interest_t - interest_t^f\right) \tag{5}$$

Following Karfakis (2003), expectations can also be introduced in Equation 5. The nominal interest rate can be represented by the sum of real interest rate $(rint_t)$ and the expected inflation $(expinf_t)$:

$$interest_t = rint_t + expinf_t \tag{6}$$

$$interest_t^f = rint_t^f + expinf_t^f \tag{7}$$

In a similar way to the simplification in Equation 5 for the ease of applying to the contemporaneous time series estimation techniques, let us assume that domestic and foreign real interest rates tend to be equalized, and rearrange exchange rate determination model in Equation 9 by utilizing Equation 8:

$$interest_t - interest_t^f = expinf_t - expinf_t^f \tag{8}$$

$$er_t = \left(money_t - money_t^f\right) - \gamma_1\left(income_t - income_t^f\right) + \gamma_3\left(expinf_t - expinf_t^f\right) \tag{9}$$

In line with this model specification, we expect a positive relationship between nominal exchange rate and relative money supply and a negative relationship between relative income level and nominal exchange rate. Thus, the larger the home relative to the foreign money supply the larger would be the nominal exchange rate, and the larger the home relative to the foreign real income level the lower would be the nominal exchange rate. As for the sign of the relative expected inflation, since an increase in expected inflation decreases the demand for money and increases demand for domestic and foreign assets, we expect that an increase in expected relative inflation would lead to a depreciation of domestic currency.

3 Data and Time Series Properties

In this study, it is aimed to estimate the exchange rate determination model specified by Equation 9 for the Turkish economy. The sample period using quarterly frequency data is determined as 2005Q4–2017Q4. The reason of employing the starting period as 2005Q4 is that from this period on the Central Bank of the Republic of Turkey (TCMB) changes the definition of money supplies and calculates them as the sum of domestic currency–based deposits and foreign currency–based deposits in terms of domestic currency in the banking system.

For the monetary exchange rate variable(er_t), the Turkish lira (TL)/US dollar is taken into consideration. In this study, the broad money supply indicators have been used for the Turkish and the US economies respresented by the sum of currency in circulation, demand and time deposits in the banking system, repurchase agreements (REPO), money market funds, and the total value of securities issued all expressed in the form of M3 money supply($money_t$).

A 2010: 100 based index is considered for the monetary aggregates. For the real income aggregate ($income_t$), the gross domestic income data calculated in the form of chained volume index has been used, and for this purpose, the

Tab. 17.1: Lee-Strazicich (2003) unit root test: Two internal refraction

Variables	Model: Crash	Model: Break	Inference
er_t	-2.42	-5.27	$I(1)$
Δer_t	-5.76	-6.48	$I(0)$
$money_t$	-1.80	-6.31	$I(0)$ or $I(1)$
$\Delta money_t$	-5.64	-6.86	$I(0)$
$income_t$	-2.39	-5.69	$I(1)$
$\Delta income_t$	-3.65	-8.38	$I(0)$
$expinf_t$	-2.83	-6.27	$I(0)$ or $I(1)$
$\Delta expinf_t$	-12, 89	-15, 65	$I(0)$
Critical value	5 %	-3.56	-6.18

Source: Calculated by the Author

base years for the Turkish and the US economies are 2009 and 2012, respectively. The expected inflation rate variable $(expinf_t)$ based on consumer price index (cpi) is represented by quarterly inflation rates occuring in the period $(t + 1)$ with the base year 2015 for the Turkish and the US economies, and calculated as $(\ln cpi_{t+1} - \ln cpi_t)$ where $\ln$is the natural logarithm operator. The data for the variables examined in the study have been compiled from the electronic data delivery system of the Organization for Economic Cooperation and Development (OECD) (https://stats.oecd.org/, access date: 06.12.2018), and the natural logarithm operator is used for all the variables considered.

In the paper, before the model estimation process the unit root knowledge of the variables are tried to be examined. For this purpose, a contemporaneous unit root testing method proposed by Lee and Strazicich (2003) allowing endogenous break points in the estimation process has been applied to the data. The test results based on the H_0 assumption that the variable has a unit root with break are reported in Tab. 17.1.Δ represents the different processor. The table gives the smallest test statistics (tau) of Lee-Strazicich (2003) under two possible multiple breaks. The estimation findings take into account structural break at an unknown date in the selected sample. The maximum lag length assumed for the tests has been determined as 5. According to the unit root estimation findings, the monetary exchange rate and relative income level variables have a first degree integrated structure, while the level forms of relative money supply and the relative expected inflation rate variables are found in the form of $I(0)$ or $I(1)$, and thus yield some contradictory results as for the unit root model used. In line with these findings, for the estimation of model in Equation 9, the autoregressive distributed lag bounds testing approach as a contemporaneous times series estimation process has been applied to the data.

4 Autoregressive Distributed Lag (*ARDL*) Bounds Testing Approach

We find in the former section that the variables have different orders to be integrated. Therefore, we cannot apply to the single equation Engle and Granger (1987) approach or maximum likelihood-based Johansen (1995) multivariate cointegration techniques under an autoregressive (*VAR*)framework (Göktaş, 2005). Instead of these approaches, let us follow the methodologies developed in Pesaran et al. (2001). These estimation techniques, namely autoregressive distribued lag (ARDL) bounds testing procedures, can allow us to consider $I(0)$ and $I(1)$ variables together in a cointegrating equation. Let us consider the following vector error correction model presentation:

$$\Delta Y_t = \mu + \lambda Y_{t-1} + \sum_{j=1}^{p-1} \gamma_j \Delta Y_{t-j} + \varepsilon_t \tag{10}$$

In Equation 10, $Y_t = [y_t x_t]'$ is defined as the variable vector. $\mu = [\mu_y \mu_x]'$ is a vector of constant terms and Δ=(1 – L) indicates the difference operator. The vector of error terms is assumed to satisfy $\varepsilon_t = \left[\varepsilon_y \varepsilon_x\right]' \sim N(0, \Omega)$, with a zero mean, normal distribution, and constant variance. λ indicates the long-run multiplier matrix and γ is the short-run reaction matrix.

$$\lambda = \begin{bmatrix} \lambda_{yy}\lambda_{yx} \\ \lambda_{xy}\lambda_{xx} \end{bmatrix} = -\left(I - \sum_{j=1}^{p} \phi_j\right) \tag{11}$$

$$\gamma_j = \begin{bmatrix} \gamma_{yy,j}\gamma_{yx,j} \\ \gamma_{xy,j}\gamma_{xx,j} \end{bmatrix} = -\sum_{k=j+1}^{p} \phi_k \tag{12}$$

I is an identity matrix and φ_j is the vector autoregression model coefficient matrix. The diagonal elements of matrix λ are left unrestricted. Such a case allows for the possibility that the time series used can be either I(0) or I(1). For instance, $\lambda_{yy} = 0$ would imply that the variable y is I(1) and $\lambda_{yy} < 0$ would imply that the variable is I(0). One of the non-diagonal elements of the long run multiplier matrix, λ_{yx} or λ_{xy}, can take zero-value.

The bounds testing co-integration approach, considering the above-explained methodology, enables researchers to use variables in testing single co-integrating relationship among the variables, no matter they are I(0) or I(1). In light of these explanations, we can write the possible co-integration relationship as follows:

$$\Delta y_t = \alpha + \varphi y_{t-1} + \delta x_{t-1} + \omega \Delta x_t + \sum\nolimits_{j=1}^{p-1} \beta_{P,j} \Delta y_{t-j} + \sum\nolimits_{j=1}^{q-1} \beta_{x,j} \Delta x_{t-j} + u_t \tag{13}$$

In Equation 13, $\varphi$and δ are the long-term multiplier coefficients, while Δy_{t-j} and Δx_{t-j} express the short-term dynamic structure of our error correction model. The bounds testing approach requires the ordinary least squares (OLS) estimation of Equation 13 with or without trend component, and then we must test the absence of a long-term relationship between the level values of y_t and x_t by use of the *F*-statistics in line with the below hypotheses:

$$H_0 : \varphi = 0, \delta = 0$$

$$H_1 : \varphi \neq 0, \delta \neq 0 \tag{14}$$

In Equation 14, the rejection of H_0 hypothesis by the standart *F*- (or Wald-) tests leads to the acceptance of H_1 hypothesis and indicates a long run equilibrium relationship between the variables. The statistics such estimated, then, are compared with the non-standard distributed asymptotic critical value bounds reported in Pesaran et al. (2001). If estimated *F*-statistic falls outside of the critical value bounds, we can definitely infer whether or not there exists a co-integrating relationship between the variables, regardless of the order of integration of the variables. In this case, if *F*-statistic exceeds its respective upper critical values, this means rejection of the null hypothesis of no cointegration between the variables. If *F*-statistic is found below the lower critical value bounds, we cannot reject nonexistence of a cointegrating relationship. If estimated statistic lies between the bounds, we cannot make any conclusive inference as to the existence of a possible cointegrating relationship and need to know the order of integration of the underlying regressors.

In addition to this estimation procedure, if we find that the value of the *t*-statistic of the one-period lagged coefficient of the dependent variable (ϕ) in Equation 13 is greater than the critical values reported by Pesaran et al. (2001), this would also reflect the existence of a co-integrating relationship between the variables in the model. ARDL-based bounds testing approach is also able to yield consistent long run coefficient estimators even in small samples.

5 Bounds Testing Estimation Results

As a next step, the *ARDL* bounds testing cointegration and error correction modeling approaches have been used to examine the validity of the economic modeling issues constructed in the former sections. For this purpose, several *ARDL* models considering the maximum lag number as 4 for both dependent and independent variables have been estimated by using Akaike information criterion. It should be noted that the number of models estimated is 500.

In the case of no deterministic component or of only the constant coefficient used as deterministic component restricted in the long-term equation, the $ARDL\,(1,3,3,2)$ model is determined as the appropriate model that minimizes the information criterion. When the constant coefficient and the trend is assumed together as the deterministic component, the $ARDL\,(1,4,3,2)$ model is chosen by the information criteria. The existence of a cointegrated economic relationship which depends on the deterministic component assumptions considered is presented in Tab. 17.2.

Following Pesaran and Shin (1998), standard errors related to the probability values have been obtained by the Delta method. Five percent significance level has been considered for the F-statistic I(0) and I(1) critical values. The statistical probability values of the variables have been presented to the readers in[]:

The analysis of long-term equations in level values reveals that there is a co-integrated relationship between the variables for all the models estimated, regardless of the deterministic component assumptions restricted to the equations. In all the models, we can observe that estimation results of the F-statistics exceed the upper critical values, and thus, infer that there exists a cointegrating relationship between the time series in the level form, without considering whether they are I(0) or I(1). Moreover, in the models where the constant coefficient or the trend component is not restricted into the long-term level equation although they are included in the conditional error correction model, t-statistics result in a value in absolute terms higher than the critical values. The models generally yield similar variable coefficients. In all the models, the model in which the constant term as the only deterministic component is allowed in the conditional error correction model while it is not restricted to the long-term level equation, i.e., unrestricted constant and no trend equation, has been found with the highest F-statistic. Thus, from now on, the analysis will be carried out with this model. The equation related to the estimated cointegrated relationship is reported below:

$$\begin{array}{llll} er_t = 1.11 * money_t & - 0.36 * income_t & + 0.47 * expinf_t & \\ Prob. \quad [0.00] & [0.00] & [0.03] & (15) \end{array}$$

The findings in Equation 15 support the exchange rate determination mechanism specified in Equation 9. Monetary exchange rate and the relative money supply has a positive relationship, while relative income level and monetary exchange rate is estimated in a negative relationship. Furthermore, all coefficients have a statistical significance in acceptable levels. Thus, following Karfakis (2006),

Tab. 17.2: Long-term equation in level values and bounds testing

ARDL $(1, 3, 3, 2)$ *model*
No constant and no trend

$er_t = 1.53 * money_t - 0.31 * income_t + 0.55 * expinf_t$
Prob. [0.00] [0.00] [0.02]

F–Bounds test $I(0) I(1)$
$F - stat. 8.745\% 2.45 3.63$

t–Bounds test $t - stat. - 3.905\% - 1.95 - 3.33$

ARDL $(1, 3, 3, 2)$ *model*
Restricted constant and no trend

$er_t = 1.11 * money_t - 0.36 * income_t + 0.47 * expinf_t + 2.40$
Prob. [0.00] [0.00] [0.03] [0.13]

F–Bounds test $I(0) I(1)$
$F - stat. 8.235\% 2.79 3.67$

ARDL $(1, 3, 3, 2)$ *model*

Unrestricted constant and no trend

$er_t = 1.11 * money_t - 0.36 * income_t + 0.47 * expinf_t$
prob. [0.00] [0.00] [0.03]

F–Bounds test $I(0) I(1)$
$F - stat. 9.275\% 3.23 4.35$

t–Bounds test $t - stat. - 4.035\% - 2.86 - 3.78$

ARDL $(1, 4, 3, 2)$ *model*
Unrestricted constant and resrtricted trend
$er_t = 1.64 * money_t - 0.49 * income_t + 0.55 * expinf_t - 0.12 * trend$
prob. [0.01] [0.11] [0.09] [0.22]

F–Bounds test $I(0) I(1)$
$F - stat. 9.195\% 3.38 4.23$

(continued on next page)

Appendix (continued)

ARDL $(1,4,3,2)$ *model*

Unrestricted constant and unrestricted trend

$er_t = 1.64 * money_t - 0.49 * income_t + 0.55 * expinf_t$

prob. [0.01] [0.11] [0.09]

F–Bounds test $I(0)I(1)$

$F - stat.$7.975%4.015.07

t–Bounds test$t - stat.$ – 2.405% – 3.41 – 4.16

Source: Calculated by the Author

in the long-term a positive monetary shock has a permanent increase on the exchange rate level value, and an increase in the relative income level will also lead to the appreciation of the national currency against the US dollar. Karfakis attributes this result to that policy decisions increasing economic growth would result in a stronger national currency.

At the same time, with a significant sign and in line with our a priori expectations, the relative expected inflation rate variable has a positive sign. Under the long-term stationary equilibrium conditions, a positive relative expected inflation, as expected, will cause the national currency to depreciate against the US dollar. Although the statistical significance level varies, obtaining similar findings as for the coefficient values and the signs in case of considering different deterministic component assumptions tend to increase the reliability of the estimation results in the sample period. Although different deterministic component assumptions can be taken into account, the statistical significance level may vary, and similar findings in terms of coefficient size and sign are used to increase the reliability of the estimation results during the sample period. When the findings of the estimated econometric model are evaluated in general, it is observed that strong support has been given to the theoretical exchange rate determination model hypothesized in the second section above. The model diagnostics test knowledge is presented in Tab. 17.3.

$\chi^2_{SC}(1)$ and$\chi^2_{SC}(4)$are the first and fourth order Breusch-Godfrey error terms Lagrange multiplier test F-statistics under the assumtion of no serial correlation, *Nor*is the Jarque-Bera normality statistic under the assumption that error terms are distributed normally, and *Het*is the Breusch-Pagan-Godfrey heteroskedasticity test *F*-statistic under the assumption of constant variance.

Tab. 17.3: Diagnosis (diagnostic) information

χ^2_{SC} (1)	χ^2_{SC} (4)	*Nor*	*Het*
0.12 (0.73)	0.57 (0.69)	1.90 (0.39)	1.22 (0.31)

Source: Calculated by the Author

Tab. 17.4: Conditional error correction regression for the ***ARDL*** **(1, 3, 3, 2)**model

Dependent Variables: d				
Variables	**Coefficient**	**Std. Err.**	**t-statistics**	**Prob.**
$d(money)_t$	1.70	0.35	4.28	0.00
$d(money)_{t-2}$	0.78	0.36	2.16	0.04
$d(income)_t$	-0.70	0.31	-2.26	0.03
$d(income)_{t-2}$	-1.23	0.30	-4.06	0.00
$d(expinf)_t$	2.09	1.26	1.67	0.10
$d(expinf)_{t-1}$	-3.01	1.41	-2.13	0.04
EC_{t-1}	-0.21	0.03	-6.17	0.00
C	0.50	0.08	5.92	0.00
$Adj.R^2$	0.61			
$Durbin - Watsonstat$	1.83			

Source: Calculated by the Author

The related probability values are given in parantheses. Examination of Tab. 17.3 does not bring out any diagnostic problem, and indicates that the error terms structure of the model estimated has a white noise framewrok. The short-term error correction equation for this model is reported in Tab. 17.4 with the statistically significant coefficients.

Tab. 17.4 indicates that approximately 21 % of deviations from the long-term equilibrium relationship disappear during one period. In other words, the equilibrium conditions of the exchange rate determination model tend to be restored in nearly five observation periods. The relative money supply and relative income level variables seem to carry on the long-term properties estimated in the *ARDL* model.

Conclusion

Approaches to the determination of exchange rates in line with economic theoretical foundations can provide an important information content to researchers by combining some contemporary monetary theories and monetary market equilibrium conditions that reveal the conditions of equilibrium in commodity and asset markets. This study aimed to investigate the mechanism of exchange rate determination under the conditions of the Turkish economy. A sticky price exchange rate determination model has been estimated in the light of the developments in contemporary time series econometrics. Our estimation results as for the TL/US dollar exchange rate has indcated that the exchange rate has been determined in a multi-variable structure in accordance with the theoretical basis. In a statistically significant way, the monetary exchange rate has a positive relationship and the real income level has a negative relationship with the nomainal exchange rate. On the other hand, the expected relative inflation rate positively affects the monetary exchange rate under the long-term stationary equilibrium conditions. Therefore, a positive relative inflation differential will cause national currency to depreciate against the US dollar.[1] These findings indicate that the monetary exchange rate should not be used as a policy tool in the long term considering the foreign exchange market equilibrium conditions. In other words, in the case that policy makers try to use monetary exchange rate as a policy tool in the long-term, the desired policy outcomes cannot possibly be obtained, since the exchange rate is determined in line with theoretical bases.

In this study, whether the estimation findings are sensitive to changes in the sample period should be tested with subsequent studies. In this sense, the studies that will test the validity of both the purchasing power parity and the uncovered interest rate parity in the economy will be complementary to this study.

References

Abhyankar, A., Sarno, L. and Valente, G. (2005). Exchange Rates and Fundamentals: Evidence on the Economic Value of Predictability. *Journal of International Economics*, 66, 325–48.

Afat, D., Gómez-Puig, M. and Sosvilla-Rivero, S. (2015). The Failure of the Monetary Model of Exchange Rate Determination. *Applied Economics*, 47(43), 4607–629.

Bahmani-Oskooee, M. and Kara, O. (2000). Exchange Rate Overshooting in Turkey. *Economics Letters*, 68, 89–93.

Cheung, Y.-W. and Chinn, M. D. (1998). Integration, Cointegration and the Forecast Consistency of Structural Exchange Rate Models. *Journal of International Money and Finance*, 17, 813–30.

1 Relevant readers can apply to Sarno and Taylor (2003) for a more comprehensive investigation of exchange rate determination mechanism.

Chin, L., Azali, M. and Matthews, K.G. (2007). The Monetary Approach to Echange Rate Determination for Malaysi. *Applied Financial Economics Letters*, 3(2), 91–4.

Civcir, İ. (2003). The Monetary Models of the Turkish Lira/U.S. Dollar Exchange Rate: Long-Run Relationships, Short-Run Dynamics and Forecasting. *Eastern European Economics*, 41(6), 43–63.

Civcir, İ. (2004). The Long-Run Validity of the Monetary Exchange Rate Model for a High İnflation Country and Misalignment: The Case of Turkey. *Emerging Markets Finance and Trade*, 40(4), 84–100.

Engle, R. F. and Granger, C. W. J. (1987). Co-integration and Error Correction: Representation, Estimation and Testing. *Econometrica*, 55, 251–76.

Erlat, H. (2003). The Nature of Persistence in Turkish Real Exchange Rates. *Emerging Markets Finance and Trade*, 39(2), 70–97.

Göktaş, Ö. (2005). *Teorik ve Uygulamalı Zaman Serileri Analizi*. İstanbul: Beşir Kitabevi. https://stats.oecd.org/, erişim tarihi: 06.12.2018.

Johansen, S. (1995). *Likelihood-based Inference in Cointegrated Vector Autoregressive Models*. Oxford: Oxford University Press.

Karfakis, C. (2003). Exchange Rate Determinationduring Hyperinflation: The Case of the Romanian lei. *Applied Financial Economics*, 13, 473–76.

Karfakis, C. (2006). Is There an Empirical Link between the Dollar Price of the Euro and the Monetary Fundamentals? *Applied Financial Economics*, 16, 973–80.

Lee, J. and Strazicizh, M. C. (2003). Minimum Lagrange Multiplier Unit Root Test with Two Structural Breaks. *The Review of Economics and Statistics*, 85(4), 1082–089.

MacDonald, R. and Marsh, I.W. (1997). On Fundamentals and Exchange Rates: A Casselian Perspective. *Review of Economics and Statistics*, 79(4), 655–64.

MacDonald, R. and Taylor, M. P. (1993). The Monetary Approach to the Exchange Rate: Rational Expectations, Long-Run Equilibrium, and Forecasting. *IMF Staff Papers*, 40(1), 89–107.

Mark, N.C. and Sul, D. (2001). Nominal Exchange Rates and Monetary Fundamentals Evidence from a Small Post-Bretton Woods Panel. *Journal of International Economics*, 53, 29–52.

McNown, R. and Wallace, M. S. (1994). Cointegration Tests of the Monetary Exchange Rate Model for Three High-İnflation Economies. *Journal of Money, Credit and Banking*, 26(3), 396–411.

Meese, R. A. and Rogoff, K. (1983). Empirical Exchange Rate Models of the Seventies: Do They Fit Out of Sample? *Journal of International Economics*, 14(1–2), 3–24.

Neely, C.J. and Sarno, L. (2002). How Well Do Monetary Fundamentals Forecast Exchange Rates? *FRB of St. Louis Review*, September/October, 51–74.

Ozdemir, Z.A. (2004). Mean Reversion in Real Exchange Rate: Empirical Evidence from Turkey, 1980–1999. *METU Studies in Development*, 31, 243–65.

Pesaran, M.H. and Shin, Y. (1998). An Autoregressive Distributed-Lag Modelling Approach to Cointegration Analysis. *Econometric Society Monographs*, 31: 371–413.

Pesaran, M.H., Shin, Y. and Smith, R.J. (2001). Bounds Testing Approaches to the Analysis of Level Relationships. *Journal of Applied Econometrics*, 16, 289–326.

Rapach, D.E. and Wohar, M.E. (2004). Testing the Monetary Model of Exchange Rate Determination: A Closer Look at Panels. *Journal of International Money and Finance*, 23, 867–95.

Sarno, L. and Taylor, M. P. (2003). *The Economics of Exchange Rates*. Cambridge, UK: Cambridge University Press.

Shylajan, C.S., Sereejesh, S. and Suresh, K.G. (2011). Rupee-Dollar Exchange Rate and Macroeconomic Fundamentals: An Empirical Analysis Using Flexible-Price Monetary Model. *Journal of International Business and Economy*, 12(2), 89–105.

Telatar, E. and Kazdagli, H. (1998). Re-examine the Long-Run Purchasing Power Parity Hypothesis for a High İnflation Country: The Case of Turkey. *Applied Economics Letters*, 5, 51–3.

Uz, İ. and Ketenci, N. (2010). Exchange Rate Determination: Monetary Approach in the New EU Members and Turkey. *Applied Economics Letters*, 17(10), 963–67.

Yazgan, M.E. (2003). The Purchasing Power Parity Hypothesis for a High İnflation Country: A Re-Examination of the Case of Turkey. *Applied Economics Letters*, 10(3), 143–47.

Burçay Yaşar Akçalı

18 Testing of Overconfidence Hypothesis in Borsa Istanbul

Highlights: The first part of this chapter included studies on the overconfidence hypothesis and the existence of this hypothesis, the relationship between stock returns and transaction volume. Then, the methodologies of Toda-Yamamoto causality test were explained. Finally, empirical findings have been presented on the data set and on the existence of the overconfidence hypothesis both on the market and on the sectoral basis of the Borsa Istanbul.

Keywords: Overconfidence hypothesis, Toda-Yomamoto, BIST100

Introduction

In traditional finance theory, it is accepted that people behave rationally, do not repeat the same mistakes, follow the new information, update their expectations correctly, and choose the investment that gives them the highest benefit by taking into account the return-risk ratios; in other words, they act in accordance with the expected benefit theory. The idea that investor psychology might play a role in the formation of stock prices was first introduced by Kahneman and Tversky (1979), and the expectation theory as an alternative to the expected benefit theory was developed. In this theory, it is argued that people give different weight levels to gains and losses at different levels of probability, and that the perceived risk should be taken into account instead of the expected risk, and it is argued that the decisions taken by people are the ones that are best satisfied, not maximizing benefit. On the other hand, it is also stated that irrational behaviors are not temporary, but are systematically affecting investors and showing continuity.

While the traditional financial approach advocates the Efficient Markets Hypothesis (EMH), the behavioral finance approach advocates the Overreaction Hypothesis. According to the EMH, investors react to the information that reaches the market, so that they can act rationally. When there is a new flow of information coming to the market, there will be no upward and downward trends in prices, and no reversal movements will occur because the stock prices will change right, fast, and exactly. In the overreaction hypothesis, investors who make decisions in the face of intense and rapid information flow in the financial markets are forced to use simplifying ways to accelerate the decision-making phase. In such a case, irrational decisions will emerge as the information possessed will be used more narrow-scoped. On the other hand, all investors are not equal in terms of knowledge and experience. In the overreaction hypothesis, investors react more to the market than they should have to know about the most striking information, causing the stock prices to move away from their real values, but then realizing their fault and making corrections in the opposite direction to the prices.

Because individuals are dissent from rationality, the market tends to deviate from the existing activity based on knowledge. While people are making investment decisions, they want to avoid risks, optimize their preferences, and diversify their portfolios, but the research shows that they cannot do this in practice. There are various psychological biases that cause people to dissent from rationalism. They are divided into three as heuristic, cognitive biases, and emotional biases. *Heuristic* means that people choose a short cut to make decisions; *cognitive biases* mean that people deceive themselves, and *emotional biases* mean that people make emotional judgments. As a result of psychological biases, investors are able to keep losing shares for a long time (fear of grief) and while losing their shares, show herd behavior with the motivation to act together, perform extremely safe and overly optimistic frequently and adversely, connect emotionally to the shares they are familiar with, react extremely or inadequately and seek support for their own beliefs, and tend to refuse the noncommittal information (Döm, 2003; Özçam, 2006; Yaşar Akçalı, 2018).

In the studies conducted, there is much evidence that people show variability and errors in their decisions due to systematic and irrational tendencies. This situation, which is also defined as an illusion, is not limited to only uneducated and non-intelligent people, and it is suggested that it affects all sections of society with an incomprehensible consistency and continuity (Hanson and Kysar, 1999: 635–642).

When making decisions, investors are not only affected by economic or financial indicators, by the way in which they perceive their own inner worlds, experiences, and opportunities. This view contradicts the traditional finance theory and constitutes the subject of behavioral finance. Human nature and behavior are more complex than traditional finance theory. The disciplines such as psychology and sociology also reveal the necessity of more realistic theories explaining the process of making economic and financial decisions.

In the process of making investment decisions, various behavioral finance models have been developed under the assumption that investors may be affected by psychological prejudices. According to the overconfidence hypothesis, which is expressed as a cognitive bias, an investor tends to have overconfidence in himself/herself, linking his/her market earnings to his/her own ability and knowledge, and then he/she processes more in the further period. Hence, the overconfidence hypothesis suggests that there is a causal relationship from the stock return to transaction volume. In this study, it is aimed to determine the validity of the overconfidence hypothesis in Borsa İstanbul (BIST) on the basis of market and sector. In this respect, the relationship between the yield and the transaction volume, which is shown among the reasons of the overconfidence hypothesis, has been examined by using the Toda-Yamamoto Causality Test on a total of 12 indexes selected during the period of 16.11.2009–25.01.2019 in the BIST.

According to the results obtained from the study, a relationship could not be determined from the yield on the BIST 30 and BIST 100 index on a market basis, while a causality relation was found from the yield to the transaction volume in the BIST ALL index. This result points to the existence of the overconfidence hypothesis in the entire BIST index, while the existence of the overconfidence hypothesis in the BIST 30 and BIST 100 indices has not been achieved. On the sectoral basis, while there was no causality relation between the BIST Financials, BIST Insurance, BIST REIT Indices, the volume of transaction towards BIST; BIST Service, BIST Chemistry, BIST Metal, BIST Industry, and BIST Technology indices, causality relationship was determined from yield to transaction volume. This result shows that the overconfidence hypothesis is not valid in the indices related to the financial sector, while it points to the existence of the overconfidence hypothesis in other indices of the sector.

2 Overconfidence Hypothesis

The theory of Overconfidence was first proposed by Daniel, Hirshleifer, and Subrahmanyam (1998). Overconfidence refers to the investor's confidence in the private information he or she has, and causes one to connect his or her successes to his or her knowledge, and to bind his or her failures to external factors (e.g., bad luck). The continuity of this situation causes people not to see their own faults and exaggerate their achievements (Cunningham, 2002: 18).

Cognitive psychology generally advocates that people have overconfidence. Psychological findings indicate that overconfidence shows people with excessive predictability and risks because of their knowledge. This information is an important factor in putting forward a person's exaggeration. For example, in a study conducted in Sweden, 80% of drivers suggest that they are better drivers than the average. Individuals tend to posess overconfidence not only in their driving skills or responses to general questions but also in financial decisions. In a survey among active investors, more than half of the investors expressed their ability to over average (Moore, Kurtzberg, Fox and Sometimesman, 1999: 97).

There are three factors that trigger excessive trust. These are: *self-attribution bias*, *illusion of knowledge* and *illusion of control*. Self-attribution bias attributes the success of individuals to their natural abilities and/or foresight; failures are attributed to external factors such as failure (Döm, 2003: 62–67). If individuals succeed in their investments, this will increase their confidence in themselves, even if it is due to luck or the overall trend of the market. The illusion of knowledge is that as individuals increase their knowledge about a subject, they think that their predictions will increase the accuracy. However, the fact that some of the information can be misleading, that most investors do not have the training or the skills to interpret the information, and that individuals tend to interpret the information they obtain according to their previous beliefs and opinions may always lead to the misunderstanding of the fact that more information brings the individual closer to the correct prediction. The illusion of control is the belief that although it is impossible for the human body to actually control it, it can control the results of an event or at least affect the results. These three factors trigger and nourish the tendency of overconfidence (Döm, 2003: 63).

People believe that they will not make mistakes by relying on their own skills and experience. At the same time, overconfident people, rather than acting from a model that has already emerged when making their investments, define a short-term model and consider it to be a long-term future model. Such trends can be seen in all investors, from individual investors to international fund managers. EMH argues that these irrational tendencies will be eliminated by rational investors. In reality, however, it is often observed that these irrational tendencies of investors are followed by other investors. This usually occurs when the fund managers are concerned about measuring their performance against other fund managers, in which they are competing, and they act as non-rational individual investors, not judging by real values.

In the financial sense, overconfidence can be defined as the fact that an investor has more confidence in his or her knowledge than all investors in the market have and that he or she tends to consolidate his or her faith. Instead of information owned by all investors on the market, an investor who is inclined to rely more on the information they collect and information learned from the inside, and who takes advantage of his/her capabilities, tends to believe that he/she can control the results of the transactions he/she will perform and to feel more overconfident. The overconfidence on investors' own capabilities and knowledge can cause them to take more trades while reducing the perceived risk, and if the result of the decision has been successful recently, they may tend to make more active and speculative trading decisions by thinking that the success will continue. Of course, when an investor starts investing for the first time, he or she will not be inclined to overconfidence in his or her skills, and this confidence will be shaped over time according to his or her financial success or failure. Investors' financial success increases their self-overconfidence, while this increase in overconfidence leads investors to do more by following more aggressive investment strategies (Gervais and Odean, 2001: 1–2). In addition, Hens (2003) argues that 75 % of investors who have a tendency to overconfidence find themselves smarter than an average investor and therefore play an important role in the increase in transaction volume by performing more trades.

3 Literature Review

When the literature on the role of the overconfidence hypothesis in the stock market is examined, it was concluded that in general, the investors in the overconfidence trend tied their gains to their own ability and knowledge, and accordingly, they traded more in the further period. The following is a list of the studies that examine the relationship between the return and the transaction volume of the overconfidence hypothesis and test it in different time frames and in different markets:

Odean (1998) examined the relationship between overconfidence and transaction volume, market depth and volatility, and found that investors' overconfidence in themselves increased the transaction volume and deepened the market. According to Odean, investors with a tendency to overconfidence will pursue an aggressive portfolio strategy based on the information they have acquired, while market makers will perform new transactions to deepen the market. On the other hand, the presence of a large number of overconfidence investors will cause the market to have an under reaction to publicly disclosed information, and a high reaction to noises. Although the transaction volume increases and the market deepens, investors who are overconfident will make transactions based on noises rather than information, and incorrectly estimated prices will cause the market to become more volatile.

In the study where stocks traded in NYSE, AMEX, and NASDAQ between 1987 and 1993, Barber and Odean (1999) found that investors who have a tendency to overconfidence in the daily closing prices had a lower return even though they traded more. People do more transactions when they are overconfident, and when dealing costs are taken into account, they reduce their return on transactions. In other words, overconfidence brings along many transactions and wrong investment decisions. Another result obtained from the study is that men are 45% more active than women.

Gervais and Odean (2001) suggested that investors tend to present overconfidence due to their success. They found that the investors with overconfidence tend to increase the transaction volume, in other words, they attributed the positive returns obtained by the investors to their own knowledge and skills, thus increasing the transaction volume by making more transactions in the following period. Investors with a tendency to be overconfident will tend to process as a result of every signal that reaches them, and then there will be noise rather than knowledge in the market. Traders who are transacting in line with noise will increase volatility in prices. In addition, the researchers claimed that the overconfidence tendency was mostly exhibited by investors who are at the beginning of their investment careers, and that the investors' experience increased and that they were away from the overconfidence trend.

Chuang and Lee (2006) attempted to show the reflection of the different effects of the overconfidence on the investors in the market by using the weekly series of daily data of all companies traded at least 4 years in NYSE and AMEX in 1963–2001 period. The researchers found that the increase in the yield of the result of the causality test increased the transaction volume, the investors who obtained a positive return of self-confidence in the subsequent periods as a result of the increase in their confidence. In addition, researchers found that the over-reliance trend led to an increase in volatility in prices, and found that investors perceived the risks of their stocks lower than they were, and that they were turning to more risky investments. According to the findings, high stock returns bring high transaction volume and then more active transactions. In addition, investors have been found to have traded more aggressively in the bull market than in the bear market.

Statman, Thorley, and Vorkink (2006) investigated the relationship between overconfidence and transaction volume with vector autoregressive model and impact response analyses and examined the stocks traded in NYSE/Amex between 1962 and 2002 on daily closing values. According to the findings, it was concluded that high transaction volume was realized in the period following high yields and the success of investment strategy increased the overconfidence trend.

Lin (2005) examined investor behavior to test whether there is a case of overconfidence in the Taiwan market. It has only found that there is overconfidence in the bull market and then more aggressive investments and excessive volatility. Chou and Wang (2011) tested the overconfidence hypothesis on the Taiwan Stock Exchange with data from 2001 to 2006. According to the findings obtained, a positive correlation was found between past yields and the volume of transactions in the following period.

Glaser and Weber (2009) also examined the relationship between past positive yields and transaction volume. As a result of the study conducted on the German stock exchange between 1997 and 2001, they argue that investors attributed to their high portfolio earnings bias and that this situation resulted in overconfidence tendency and an important reason for the increase in transaction volume.

The first work in Turkey was done by Korkmaz and Çelik (2007). Between the years 1995 and 2006, they examined the closing price and volume range of 114 firms traded on the ISE and the overconfidence hypothesis on the behavior of investors. According to the results of the causal test applied, investors with overconfidence do more transaction after their yields and are more active in the market where their income is realized. In addition, due to the investors' tendency to overconfidence, it was investigated whether over-transaction resulted in volatility in the index and concluded that overconfidence resulted in volatility, albeit weak.

Otluoğlu (2009), according to the results of the study carried out between 2001 and 2009 in order to determine whether the overconfidence behavior was exhibited by investors in ISE, the increase in the yield in the ISE 30 index was identified as the Granger reason for the increase in the transaction volume. It has been concluded that individuals gain more confidence in their own abilities as a result of their return on their investments and consequently they make more purchases. According to EGARCH and TGARCH analysis, volatility of the market is not due to overconfidence behavior.

In order to test the existence of hypothesis of overconfidence in the ISE, in Bolaman's (2011) study conducted between 1991 and 2011, a positive causality result was obtained from the return to processing volume as predicted by the hypothesis of overconfidence. However, it is stated that conditional volatility does not increase with the transaction volume resulting from overconfidence.

Horasan and Bozkurt (2016) tried to explain the volume of transactions in the Borsa Istanbul by taking advantage of the least-squares method and behavioral error types with overconfidence, optimism, excessive pessimism, and rational expectation in their analysis between 1995 and 2014, covering a total of 19 years. The study concluded that the irrational behavior of the investors operating in the BIST and the overconfidence on them have a significant impact on the transaction volume and that this behavior has a positive reaction. It has also been concluded that the BIST is active in weak form.

4 Econometric Method

If an investor is overconfident, he/she can connect his/her market earnings to his/her own share selection and knowledge, and accordingly, he/she can take more transaction in the following period. Therefore, the overconfidence hypothesis suggests that there is a causal relationship between stock return and transaction volume (Chuang and Lee, 2006). For this purpose, the hypothesis established in the study will be as follows:

H_1: Market return (or loss), overconfident investor causes the investor to transact more (or less) in the next period.

Toda-Yamamoto causality analysis was preferred as the method of the study. Toda and Yamamoto (1995) showed that this test has an asymptotic chi-square (χ^2) distribution with k degree of freedom, regardless of whether the corresponding series is stationary, stationary or concentric around the trend. Another contribution of this test is that no pre-tests are needed to determine unit root and cointegration properties. This minimizes the risk associated with the use of the relevant method and the misinterpretation of the integration degree of the series. On the other hand, since it is applied to the level values of the series, the loss of information resulting from the difference is also prevented.

In Toda-Yamamoto approach, the predicted VAR (k+dmax) model is defined as follows:

$$y_t = \delta_1 + \sum_{i=1}^{k+d\max} \alpha_{1i} y_{t-i} + \sum_{j=1}^{k+d\max} \beta_{1j} x_{t-j} + \varepsilon_{1t}$$

$$x_t = \delta_2 + \sum_{i=1}^{k+d\max} \alpha_{2i} x_{t-i} + \sum_{j=1}^{k+d\max} \beta_{2j} y_{t-j} + \varepsilon_{2t}$$

Here k indicates the appropriate lag length, dmax is the largest of the variable degrees of integration in the system. In addition, error terms e_{1t} and e_{2t} are assumed to have a zero mean and fixed covariance matrix. Toda-Yamamoto extended Granger analysis is a two-step method: in the first phase of the VAR model, which gives fairly sensitive results to the latency length, optimal latency (K) and maximum integration levels of variables in the model (DMAX) are determined by unit root tests with knowledge criteria such as AIC and SIC. After determining the optimal lag length (k) of the VAR model in the Toda-Yamamoto causality test and the maximum stochasticity (dmax) of the studied series, a VAR model (k + dmax) is estimated by the seemingly unrelated regression method. In order to determine the existence of the mutual causality relationship between variables, the hypothesis h_0:a_1i=0 and H_0:a_2i=0 is tested using the modified Wald test statistic using χ^2. If the calculated MWALD test statistic is greater than the K degree of freedom table, the abovementioned hypotheses are rejected.

Tab. 18.1: BIST Market Indices Descriptive Statistics Regarding Transaction Volume and Yield Series

	BIST All Volume	BIST 100 Volume	BIST 30 Volume	BIST All Return	BIST 100 Return	BIST 30 Return
Mean	883,000,000	690,000,000	460,000,000	0.032853	0.032044	0.031947
Median	790,000,000	631,000,000	425,000,000	0.093987	0.085589	0.069883
Maximum	2,920,000,000	2,590,000,000	2,020,000,000	6.880583	6.895168	6.965161
Minimum	141,000,000	96,940,000	54,740,000	-11.05002	-11.06379	-10.90195
Standard Deviation	367,000,000	286,000,000	197,000,000	1.370876	1.416057	1.503334
Skewness	1.39	1.53	1.99	-0.595921	-0.516553	-0.385688
Kurtosis	5.33	6.87	10.63	7.133137	6.639081	5.868224
Jarque-Bera	1268.53	2342.80	7151.44	1784.798	1380.34	850.9293
Probability	0.00	0.00	0.00	0.00	0.00	0.00
Observations	2315	2315	2315	2315	2315	2315

Source: Created by the Author

4.1 Data Sets and Empirical Findings

In this study where the hypothesis of overconfidence in the market and sector is analyzed in Stock Market Istanbul (BIST), indices calculated by BIST with different qualities are used in order to enable investors to follow the movements in the market.

Three market indices as market indices: BIST 30 (XU030), BIST 100 (XU100), and BIST National whole (XUTUM-ALL).

In sector indices, BIST Bank (XBANK), BIST Financial (XUMAL), BIST Insurance (XSGRT), BIST Real Estate Investment Trust (XGMYO-REIT), BIST Services (XUHIZ), BIST Chemical, Petroleum and Plastic (XKMYA), BIST Simple Metals (Metal Main-XMANA), BIST Industrial (XUSIN) and BIST Technology (XUTEK), a total of 9 sector index was used.

The logarithmic yield series and logarithmic transaction volume data obtained from the daily closing prices series of the indices covering the period of 16.11.2009–25.01.2019 (2315 data) were used. The data were obtained from "investing.com".

When we look at the descriptive statistics of the BIST All, BIST 100, and BIST 30 market indices, yield and transaction volume data for the period 16.11.2009–25.01.2019 are given in Tab. 18.1. On average, BIST Whole Index is 883 Million TL, BIST 100 Index is 690 Million TL, BIST 30 Index has 460 Million TL. The yield of the indices was close to each other and was realized as 0.032. According

Tab. 18.2: BIST Sector Indexes Descriptive Statistics Regarding Transaction Volume Series

	BIST Financial	BIST Industry	BIST Bank	BIST Service	BIST Metal	BIST REIT	BIST Chemistry	BIST Technology	BIST Insurance
Mean	0.018793	0.05197	0.00900	0.036201	0.065668	0.00198	0.064759	0.092484	0.044825
Median	0.043457	0.126175	-0.0030	0.096532	0.110375	0.05628	0.131863	0.11289	0.066981
Maximum	7.715099	6.45512	9.47814	6.203447	9.211918	8.46530	7.405138	9.124733	31.09416
Minimun	-11.29466	-11.4009	-11.861	-9.69925	-10.6221	-10.399	-9.369942	-15.15178	-30.11389
Standard Deviation	1.676659	1.217644	1.98663	1.237752	1.744071	1.54914	1.501542	1.734273	1.534254
Skewness	-0.348269	-1.00987	-0.2580	-0.64400	-0.39072	-0.5457	-0.506785	-0.641789	-0.083737
Kurtosis	5.551385	10.70575	5.25415	6.935663	5.72101	7.48353	6.359452	10.2676	141.6652
Jarque-Bera	674.7001	6121.05	515.809	1654.108	773.0706	2053.91	1187.715	5253.656	1854706
Probability	0.00	0.00	0.00	0.00	0.00	0.00	0.00	0.00	0.00
Obsservations	2315	2315	2315	2315	2315	2315	2315	2315	2315

Source: Created by the Author

to the skewness, kurtosis, and Jarque-Bera test statistics, it can be said that the series did not conform to a normal distribution and showed typical financial time series characteristics.

When the descriptive statistics of BIST sector indices transaction volume data for the period 16.11.2009–25.01.2019 are given in Tab. 18.2, the sector index with the highest transaction volume on the average is BIST Financial Index with the trading volume of 455 Million TL and the second index is BIST Industrial Index. So these are followed by BIST Bank, BIST Service, BIST Metal, BIST REIT, BIST Chemistry, BIST Technology, and finally BIST Insurance index. According to the skewness, kurtosis, and Jarque-Bera test statistics, it can be said that the series did not conform to a normal distribution and showed typical financial time series characteristics.

When the descriptive statistics of the BIST sector yield series for the period 16.11.2009–25.01.2019 are given in Tab. 18.3 is analyzed. We see that BIST Technology index is observed in the index with the highest yield and the second index is the BIST Metal index with 0.092, followed by BIST Chemistry, BIST Industrial, BIST Insurance, BIST Service, BIST Financial, BIST Bank, and BIST REIT index, respectively. According to the skewness, kurtosis, and Jarque-Bera test statistics, it can be said that the series did not conform to a normal distribution and showed typical financial time series characteristics.

Fig. 18.1 shows the logarithmic yield and logarithmic transaction volume charts for some indices included in the study. It is observed that indices from the graphs are distributed at a certain average and thus they are stable.

According to the ADF stasis test results in Tab. 18.4, it was concluded that the BIST Industrial Index transaction volume was 5 %; the BIST Insurance index transaction volume was 10 %; and all other variables were stable at the level of 1 % significance.

Tabs. 18.5 and 18.6 shows the results of the Toda-Yamamoto causality test, which is used to test the relationship between the indices used in the study and from the transaction volume to yield. A causal relationship between the yield and the transaction volume as a result of the test constitutes evidence of the existence of an overconfidence hypothesis in the market or index.

Tab. 18.5 shows the results of the Toda-Yamamoto test in which causality relationship was investigated from BIST market indices yields to the transaction volume. According to the test results, 10 % confidence level, BIST 30 and BIST 100 index for the transaction volume of the yield was not determined, while a causality relationship between BIST and the transaction volume of the yield was determined in the whole index. This result points to the existence of the overconfidence hypothesis in the BIST index, while the existence of the overconfidence

Tab. 18.3: BIST Sector Indices Descriptive Statistics of Logarithmic Return Series

	BIST Financial	BIST Industry	BIST Bank	BIST Service	BIST Metal	BIST REIT	BIST Chemistry	BIST Technology	BIST Insurance
Mean	455,000,00	276,000,00	232,000,00	141,000,0	73,828,27	70,707,60	42,448,981	11,882,458	5,741,639
Median	423,000,00	223,000,00	210,000,00	109,000,0	58,420,00	59,300,00	34,300,000	8,530,000	2,500,000
Maximum	1,550,000,	1,300,000,0	1,310,000,0	606,000,0	536,000,0	543,000,0	485,000,000	99,080,000	204,000,000
Minimum	70,190,000	37,860,000	21,430,000	17,320,00	8,240,000	5,590,000	4,150,000	1,180,000	30,000
Standard Deviation	169,000,00	153,000,00	119,000,00	91,344,78	49,737,06	46,901,49	30,563,348	10,333,442	10,208,200
Skewness	1.50	1.86	2.64	1.37	2.04	1.93	3.81	2.836657	7.52
Kurtosis	7.50	8.21	16.14	4.65	9.92	10.40	37.72	14.32301	102.98
Jarque-Bera	2822.52	3952.77	19334.83	986.55	6218.31	6732.30	121914.20	15471.62	985957.80
Probability	0.00	0.00	0.00	0.00	0.00	0.00	0.00	0.00	0.00
Observations	2315	2315	2315	2315	2315	2315	2315	2315	2315

Source: Created by the Author

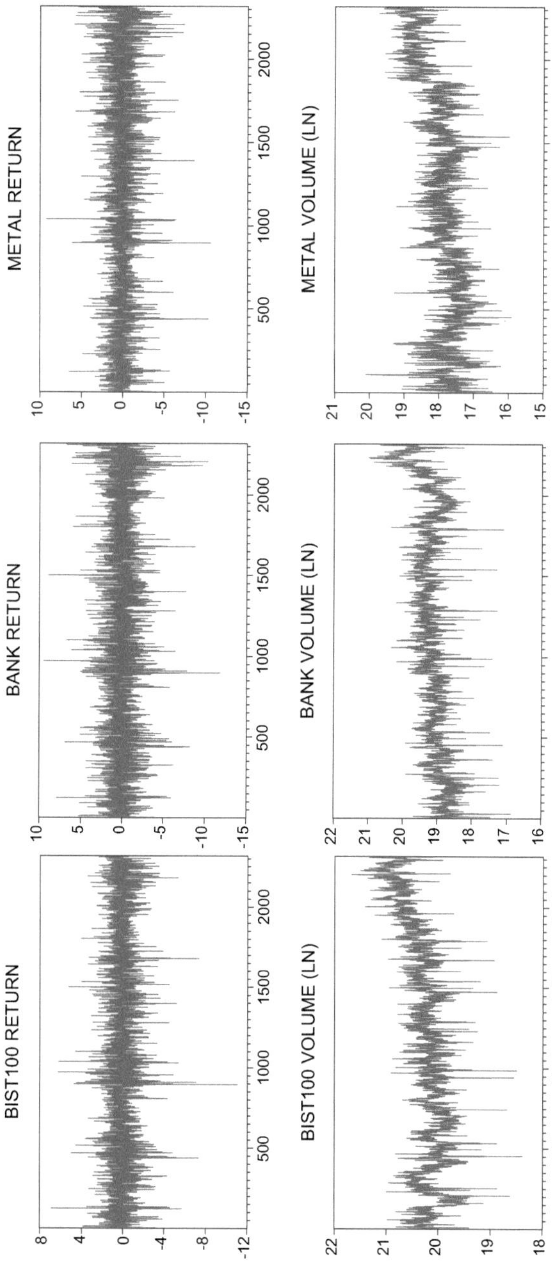

Fig. 18.1: Graphs of Some Indices

Tab. 18.4: ADF Unit Root Test Results *

	BIST ALL		**BIST 100**		**BIST 30**		**BIST financial**	
	Return	**Transaction Volume**	**Return**	**Transaction Volume**	**Return**	**Transaction Volume**	**Return**	**Transaction Volume**
ADF test statistic	-19,64	-4.38	-19,61	-5.32	-48,94	-6.49	-49,17	-6.06
Prob. value	0.0000	0.0023	0.0000	0.0000	0.0000	0.0000	0.0000	0.0000
	BIST Industry		**BIST Bank**		**BIST Service**		**BIST Metal**	
	Return	**Transaction Volume**	**Return**	**Transaction Volume**	**Return**	**Transaction Volume**	**Return**	**Transaction Volume**
ADF test statistic	-15,61	-3.59	-49,42	-6.00	-47,36	-6.28	-12,81	-5.15
Prob. value	0.0000	0.0304	0.0000	0.0000	0.0000	0.0000	0.0000	0.0001
	BIST REIT		**BIST Chemistry**		**BIST Technology**		**BIST Insurance**	
	Return	**Transaction Volume**	**Return**	**Transaction Volume**	**Return**	**Transaction Volume**	**Return**	**Transaction Volume**
ADF test statistic	-48,01	-4.7139	-21,94	-4.2940	-35,66	-5.5192	-54,99	-3.1804
Prob. value	0.0000	0.0006	0.0000	0.0032	0.0000	0.0000	0.0000	0.0886

*The ADF test has been applied to models and levels containing trend and intercept. AIC information criterion was used.
Source: Created by the Author

Tab. 18.5: Toda-Yamamoto Causality Test Results for BIST Market Indices

BIST Market Indices	Modeling	Lag Length	Wald Test Chi-Square Test IST.	Chi-Square Value Table	Relation
BIST 30	Volume = *f* (YIELD)	5	4.2400	9.2363	No
BIST 100	Volume = *f* (YIELD)	5	9.0593	9.2363	No
BIST ALL	Volume = *f* (YIELD)	5	20.0065*	9.2363	**Exist**

*It is seen according to 10 % significance level. Optimal lag length is determined by AIC criterion, k+d=VAR lag length + stability degree; (because series is stationary, only lag length is obtained).
Source: Created by the Author

Tab. 18.6: Toda-Yamamoto Causality Test Results for BIST Sector Indices

BIST Sector Indices	Modeling	Lag Length	Wald Test Chi-Square Test IST.	Chi-Square Value Table	Relation
BIST Banks	Volume=*f*(YIELD)	5	5.7407	9.2364	No
BIST Financial	Volume=*f*(YIELD)	5	2.9145	9.2364	No
BIST Insurance	Volume=*f*(YIELD)	15	10.3408	22.3071	No
BIST Real Estate Investment Trust	Volume=*f*(YIELD)	13	12.8237	19.8119	No
BIST Service	Volume=*f*(YIELD)	6	17.4021*	10.6446	Exist
BIST Chemical, Petroleum & Plastic	Volume=*f*(YIELD)	10	49.5929*	15.9872	Exist
BIST Basic Metals	Volume=*f*(YIELD)	12	20.9102*	18.5493	Exist
BIST Industry	Volume=*f*(YIELD)	10	60.0114*	15.9872	Exist
BIST Technology	Volume=*f*(YIELD)	8	24.2842*	13.3616	Exist

*It is seen according to 10 % significance level. Optimal lag length is determined by AIC criterion, k+d=VAR lag length + stability degree; - (because series is stationary, only lag length is obtained)
Source: Created by the Author

hypothesis in the BIST 30 index and the BIST 100 index cannot be reached, even if there are multiple limits. The reason for reaching a different result from the study of Otluoğlu (2009) for the BIST 30 Index is thought to have originated from the periods studied since the said study also included the 2001 crisis period.

Tab. 18.6 shows the results of the Toda-Yamamoto test, which investigated causality relationship between BIST sector yields index and transaction volume.

According to the results obtained from the test, at the 10 % confidence level, there was not determined causal relationship between the yield and the transaction volume in BIST Banks, BIST Financial, BIST Insurance, and BIST REIT Indices; in the remaining BIST Service, BIST Chemistry, BIST Metal, BIST Industry, and BIST Technology indices, the causality relationship from the yield to the transaction volume was determined. This result shows that the overconfidence hypothesis is not valid in BIST Banks, BIST Financial, BIST Insurance, and BIST REIT indices, which are more related to the financial sector, while the overconfidence hypothesis exists in the rest of the indices.

Conclusion

Models created within the framework of behavioral finance theory, which explores the effects of psychological prejudices on investors, have been developed to explain the findings that traditional finance theory cannot adequately explain. Psychological prejudices is constituted by the heuristic, cognitive biases, and emotional biases that individuals use to solve complex problems in daily life in a practical way. These biases are either caused by the way individuals process information and organize it or affect emotions when recording information. The behaviors of individuals who tend to exhibit such biases will move away from rationality and will affect the investment decisions of individuals. According to the overconfidence hypothesis, which is expressed as a cognitive bias, an investor tends to have overconfidence in himself/herself, linking his/her market earnings to his/her own ability and knowledge, and then he/she processes more in the further period. Therefore, the overconfidence hypothesis suggests that there is a causality relationship from the stock return to transaction volume.

In this study, covering the period of 16.11.2009–25.01.2019, the overconfidence hypothesis was analyzed both on a market and sectoral basis in Borsa Istanbul with the Toda-Yamamoto Test. Within the scope of the research, the relationship between the yield and volume shown among the reasons for overconfidence trend is examined.

According to the test results, in the market based, BIST 30 and BIST 100 index for the transaction volume of the yield was not determined, while a causality relationship between BIST ALL and the transaction volume of the yield was determined. This result points to the existence of the overconfidence hypothesis in the BIST index, while the existence of the overconfidence hypothesis in the BIST 30 index and the BIST 100 index cannot be reached. On the sectoral basis, while there was no causality relation between the BIST Financials, BIST Insurance, BIST REIT Indices, the volume of transaction towards BIST; BIST Service, BIST

Chemistry, BIST Metal, BIST Industry, and BIST Technology indices, causality relationship was determined from yield to transaction volume. This result shows that the overconfidence hypothesis is not valid in BIST Banks, BIST Financial, BIST Insurance, and BIST REIT indices, which are more related to the financial sector, while the overconfidence hypothesis exists in the rest of the indices.

The fact that there is no overconfidence hypothesis in indexes related to finance sector indicates that investors who invest in these indices act more rationally than overconfidence and noise and act more information based. In other indices, it is concluded that investors tend to be overconfident and increase the transaction volume in this trend. It is considered that it would be beneficial for investors to act by evaluating these findings in the investment decisions of financial market actors.

References

Barber, B. M. and Odean, T. (1999). The Courage of Misguided Convictions. *Financial Analysts Journal*, 55(6), 41–55.

Bolaman, Ö. (2011). *Behavioral Finance: Overconfidence Hypothesis and Evidences from Istanbul Stock Exchange*. Dokuz Eylül University, Social Sciences Institute, Unpublished Master Thesis.

Chou, R. K. and Wang, Y. Y. (2011). A Test of the Different Implications of the Overconfidence and Disposition Hypotheses. *Journal of Banking & Finance*, 35(8), 2037–2046.

Chuang, W. I. and Lee, B. S. (2006). An Empirical Evaluation of the Overconfidence Hypothesis. *Journal of Banking & Finance*, 30(9), 2489–2515.

Cunningham, L. A. (2002). Behavioral Finance and Investor Governance, *Washington & Lee Law Review*, C. LIX, 2002, http://ssrn.com/abstract=255778.

Daniel, K., Hirshleifer, D. and Subrahmanyam, A. (1998). Investor Psychology and Security Market Under and Overreactions. *Journal of Finance*, C.LIII, 53 (6), 1839–1845.

Döm, S. (2003). *Yatırımcı Psikolojisi*. Değişim Kitabevi, İstanbul.

Gervais, S. and Odean, T. (2001). Learning to Be Overconfident. *The Review of Financial Studies*, 14(1), 1–27.

Glaser, M. and Weber, M. (2009). Which Past Retuns Affect Trading Volume. *Journal of Financial Markets*, 12, 1–31.

Hanson, J. D. and Kysar D. A. (1999). Taking Behavioralism Seriously: The Problem of Market Manipulation. *New York University Law Review*. 74–630.

Hens, T. (2003). A Rough Guide to Behavioral and Evolutionary Finance, Erişim Tarihi: 01.02.2019, http://www.evolutionaryfinance.ch/pr/Behavioral%20and%20Evolutionary%20Finance-English.pdf

Horasan, M. and Bozkurt, R. (2016). Davranışsal Finansın Borsa İstanbul İşlem Hacmi Üzerine Etkilerine Yönelik Bir Çalışma. *Yönetim ve Ekonomi Araştırmaları Dergisi*, 14(1), 23–36. Retrieved From Http://Dergipark.Gov.Tr/Yead/Issue/21831/234662

Kahneman, D. and Tversky, A. (1979). Prospect Theory: An Analysis of Decision under Risk. *Econometrica*, C.XLVII(2).

Korkmaz, T. and Çelik, E. İ. (2007). Davranışsal Finans Modellerinden Aşırı Güven Hipotezinin Geçerliliği: İMKB'de Bir Uygulama. *İktisat İşletme ve Finans Dergisi*, 22(261), 137–154.

Lin, M. C. (2005). Returns and Investor Behavior in Taiwan: Does Overconfidence Explain This Relationship?. *Review of Pacific Basin Financial Markets and Policies*, 8(03), 405–446.

Moore, D. A, Kurtzberg, T. R., Fox, C. R. and Bazerman, M. H. (1999). Positive İllusions and Forecasting Errors in Mutual Fund Investment Decisions. *Organizational Behavior and Human Decision Processes*, C.79(2).

Odean, T. (1998). Volume, Volatility, Price and Profit When All Traders Are Above Average. *The Journal of Finance*, 53(6), 1887–1934.

Oltuoğlu, E. (2009). *Davranışsal Finans Çerçevesinde Aşırı Güven Hipotezinin Test Edilmesi: İMKB'de bir Uygulama*. İstanbul Üniversitesi, Sosyal Bilimler Enstitüsü, Yayınlanmamış Yüksek Lisans Tezi

Özçam, M. (2006). Yatırımcı Eğitimi: Dünya Uygulamaları ve Türkiye için Öneriler. *Sermaye Piyasası Kurulu Araştırma Raporu.*

Statman, M., Thorley, S. and Vorkink, K. (2006). Investor Overconfidence and Trading Volume. *The Review of Financial Studies*, 19(4), 1531–1565. https://doi.org/10.1093/rfs/hhj032

Toda, H. Y. and Yamamoto, T. (1995). Statistical Inference in Vector Autoregressions with Possbly Integrated Process. *Journal of Econometrics*, 66, 225–250.

Yaşar Akçalı, B. (2018). Davranışsal Finans ve Fiyat Köpüğü Olgusu: Fiyat Köpüğüyle İlgili Mevsimsel Birim Kök Araştırması. *Filiz Kitabevi*, İstanbul, pp. 78–89.

M. Kenan Terzioğlu

19 Long Memory Model: BIST 100 Index

Highlights: Ignoring the nonlinear structure of the price movements in financial markets can lead to false investment decisions by creating misleading results. In the context of the study, long memory is tested in stock index using integrated GARCH, integrated exponential GARCH, fractional integrated GARCH, and fractional integrated EGARCH models to characterize volatility. It is concluded that, since the long-term dependence in BIST 100 volatility is best defined by the fractional integrated process, the shock to the optimal forecast of future conditional variance is distributed at a slow hyperbolic rate.

Keywords: Long memory, volatility, FIGARCH, FIEGARCH

Introduction

The volatility in stock markets changes over time and shows a positive serial correlation. The temporary change in financial market volatility can be modeled by the autoregressive conditional heteroscedasticity (ARCH) model classification introduced by Engle (1982). Generalized ARCH (GARCH) and exponential GARCH (EGARCH) model structures are used to characterize high-frequency financial market volatility in determining the time-dependent variation observed in conditional variances (Bollerslev, 1986; Nelson, 1991). The mean-reverting process with slowly hyperbolic rate of the autocorrelation function associated with return and volatility is called long memory in return and volatility. Although the change in volatility is not a coincidence, GARCH models cannot handle long memory. Long memory dynamics indicate the presence of nonlinear relationships between mean and variance. A shock to conditional variance is important in the optimal forecast of variance for all future times in the integrated GARCH (IGARCH) model introduced by Engle and Bollerslev (1986). Therefore, from the perspective of forecast, the difference between the covariance stationary GARCH and the IGARCH model is representative of the difference between the processes I (0) and I (1) for the conditional mean. However, the distinction between time series I (0) or I (1) for the conditional mean may be narrow. Therefore, instead of short-memory models, parametric methods such as fractional integrated GARCH (FIGARCH), which take into account long-term memory, have been developed.

Long-term memory (d) provides better results in risk-return measurement, while the entire future cannot be forecast (Mandelbrot and Hudson, 2004). The

ARMA process has a short-memory because the autocorrelations of a stationary and reversible autoregressive moving average model (ARMA) process are geometrically reduced in the form of $|\rho_j| \leq cm^{-k}\rho_j$. Since the process has long-term memory when the result of $\lim_{n\to\infty} \sum |\rho_j|$ is not infinite for y_t discrete time series and ρ_j autocorrelation function, fractional integrated processes have long-term memory. y_t process is integrated with the (d), where L is a lag operator, in which it can be shown as $(1-L)^d y_t = u_t$. While 0 <d <0.5, the autocorrelation of the process decreases hyperbolically and the process has long-term memory (Baillie, 1996). Additional flexibility is achieved by permitting the fractional arrangement of integration as in the models of l (d) class (Hosking, 1981). In contrast to the series I(0) time series in which shocks are reduced at exponential rate, or the series I(1) without mean-reverting, the distribution of shocks is in hyperbolic ratio in the I(d) time series with 0<d<1. This generalization is important in the modeling of long-term economic events (Baillie, Chung and Tieslau, 1996). By generalizing the standard ARIMA models to fractional integrated ARFIMA models, flexibility in modeling long-term dependence in conditional variances can be achieved (Baillie, Bollerslev and Mikkelsen, 1996). Similar to the ARFIMA model class for the conditional mean, the shock to the conditional variance in the FIGARCH model is temporarily as the effect in the forecast of the future conditional variance disappears by decreasing the hyperbolic ratio.

Crato and Lima (1994) emphasize the existence of long-term memory in high-frequency series. Bollerslev and Mikkelsen (1996) examine the characteristics of the financial market volatility with the fractional integrated EGARCH (FIEGARCH) model. Comte and Renault (1998) emphasize that the volatility process is not only stochastic but also long-term memory. Lobato and Savin (1998) show that there is no evidence for the existence of long-term memory in returns, but there is long-term memory in the return frames. Cavalcante and Assaf (2004) state that there is no long-term memory feature in yields but there is long-term memory in volatility. Diebold and Inoue (2001) demonstrate the relationship between long-term memory and regime change. Kirman and Tevssière (2002) show that the first conditional moments of the financial time series can produce long-term memory properties. Granger and Hyung (2004) indicate that long-term memory is due to structural breaks in the series.

In the experimental studies on long-term memory, stock markets come to the fore. Blasco and Santamaria (1996) emphasize that there is no long-term memory capability in the Spanish stock markets. Resende and Teixeira (2002) indicate that there is no long-term memory capability in the Brazilian stock markets. Tolvi (2003) concludes that three of the 16 OECD countries' stock markets have long-term memory characteristics. Caporale and Gil-Alan (2004) indicate that the S&P 500 index shows long-term memory characteristics. Aygören (2008) tests the fractal in BIST. Ural and Demireli (2009) emphasize the existence of long-term memory. Kasman et al. (2009) show the existence of long-term memory in the return series of some countries. Çevik and Erdoğan (2009) show that long-term memory exists in stocks considering the structural break in the banking sector. Ural and Küçüközmen (2011) conclude that the S&P500, FTSE100, DAX, CAC40, and ISE100 stock markets have dual long-term memory properties. Yalama et al. (2011) stated that there is no long-term memory effect in spot market returns but long-term memory in both spot and future volatility. Çevik (2012) states that Turkish stock markets have long-term memory characteristics. Bhattacharya and Bhattacharya (2012) emphasize that the selected indices have long-term memory properties in their volatility. Günay (2014) shows the existence of long-term memory effect. Balıbey and Türkyılmaz (2016) show that structural changes in volatility are not statistically significant in long-term memory in the return volatility.

In the scope of the study, the existence of long memory effect and volatility in BIST-100 stock market index as well as the existence of both asymmetry and leverage effect within the scope of established models are investigated. In the first part of the study, after giving general information about the subject, the second part gives information about FIGARCH and FIEGARCH model structures. The third section examines the significance of long-term existence in the conditional variance of the volatility estimated using different models for the Daily BIS-100 index during the period 02.11.1987–31.01.2019. In the last section, the findings are included.

2 Model Structure

The fractional integrated GARCH (FIGARCH) model, a parametric method which is an extension of the ARFIMA used to model long-term memory in returns and determine the long-term memory in volatility, takes into account the existence of the resistivity in the volatility of the financial time series. Similar to the ARIMA model, where$0 < \beta_1 < 1$ and $\varepsilon_t = z_t h_t^{1/2}$,

$$h_t = \alpha_0 + \beta_1 h_{t-1} + (1 - \beta_1)\,\varepsilon_t^2 \tag{1}$$

shows the finite resistance of conditional variance to a shock in the return squares for the IGARCH model. Since the volatility process is mean-reverting, it is accepted that IGARCH model is restrictive (Tayefi and Ramanathan, 2012). FIGARCH model allows the integration coefficient to take values between 0 and

1 (Baillie et al., 1996). While $v_t = \varepsilon_t^2 - \sigma_t^2$, $c_1(d) = d$ and $c_2(d) = \frac{1}{2}d(1-d)$ and ε_t^2's conditional variance shown as

$$h_t = \frac{w}{[1-\beta(L)]} + \left[1 - \frac{\phi(L)}{[1-\beta(L)]}(1-L)^2\right]\varepsilon_t^2 \tag{2}$$

and fractional difference processor defined as

$$(1-L)^d = \sum_{k=0}^{\infty} \frac{\Gamma(d+1)L^k}{\Gamma(k+1)\Gamma(d-k+1} = 1 - \sum_{k=1}^{\infty} c_k(d)L^k \tag{3}$$

then, for 0 <*d*< 1 FIGARCH (p,d,q) model can be obtained as

$$\phi(L)(1-L)^d\varepsilon_t^2 = w + [1-\beta(L)]v_t \tag{4}$$

FIGARCH model is reduced to a standard GARCH (p,q) model while d = 0 and to a IGARCH model for d = 1 (Liu and Shieh, 2007). The infinite expansion of the gamma function used in the fractional difference processor indicates a slow hyperbolic reduction rate for the coefficients of lagged-squared returns, showing that the impulse-response weights are robust (Maheu, 2005). Due to the fact that asymmetric effects of shocks cannot be evaluated with FIGARCH model, using $g(z_t) = \theta(z_t) + \gamma[|z_t| - E|z_t|]$ and $Inh_t = w + \phi(L)^{-1}(1-L)^d[1+\alpha(L)]g(z_{t-1})$
FIEGARCH (p, d, q) model can be shown as

$$\phi(L)(1-L)^d Inh_t = \beta_0 + \sum_{i=1}^{q} \beta_i|x_{t-i}| + \gamma_i x_{t-i} \tag{5}$$

The FIEGARCH model (p,d,q) transforms to the EGARCH model in the case of d = 0 and to IEGARCH in the case of d = 1 (Bollerslev and Mikkelsen, 1996).

3 Long-Term Memory in the Stock Market

Most of the GARCH-type methods in modeling of temporary change in stock market volatility reveal that the process of volatility is permanent and not covariance-stationary (Bollerslev, et al., 1994). Nevertheless, the fractional integrated variance model provides additional flexibility to reveal long-term dependencies in the volatility process. Within the scope of the study, 7813 observations, which consist of daily prices in the BIST-100 stock index covering the periods 02.11.1987–31.01.2019, are used. Daily returns are obtained by taking first-order

Tab. 19.1: Descriptive Statistics of BIST-100 Return Series

Mean	Maximum	Minimum	Standard Deviation	Skewness	Kurtosis	J-B (Prob)	Obs.
0.1218	21.7107	-19.9785	2.5377	0.0350	4.9922	8115.00 (0.0000)	7813

logarithmic differences and multiplying by 100. Tab. 19.1 shows the descriptive statistics of the return series.

Non-continuous transactions in the stocks that constitute the index may cause a significant series dependence on the index returns (Lo and MacKinlay, 1990). An AR model is performed for the mean of the models estimated to be taken into account for serial dependence. Return variance tends to be higher in the weekend and post-holiday periods where the transaction does not take place, whereas the increase is proportionally less than the length of the non-transaction period (French and Roll, 1986). To get this effect, an N_t indicator variable indicating the number of days of inactivity between days t and t -1 is added to the conditional variance equations. The ARCH-LM test shows the existence of significant ARCH effects in standard errors. Ljung-Box (Q and Q^2) statistics provide evidence regarding to the long-term memory characteristics in the squared return series.

Tab. 19.2 shows the estimation of the AR-FIGARCH (1, d, 1) model since the traditional ARCH-type models expressing exponential decay or infinite persistence can be over-restrictive. The estimated fractional difference parameter, $\hat{d}$, is statistically different from both 0 and 1. In respect of AIC selection criteria, FIGARCH model is strongly preferred according to IGARCH model. In the volatility process, the shock disappears in the estimated state while the decrease occurs at a slow hyperbolic rate. It can be stated that the effect of shocks in variance slowly decreases and eventually disappears. Since the long memory (d) parameter for FIGARCH and FIEGARCH models are significantly different from zero, the volatility has a long memory process. In addition, it can be said from the Ljung-Box statistic that the return series are independent and identically distributed (i.i.d). At the same time, the asymmetry term is statistically significant. It can be said that negative shocks cause a higher rate of return volatility than positive shocks. Stock volatility tends to be proportionally higher in negative shocks compared to positive shocks. EGARCH model structure is used to take the asymmetry effect into consideration and the asymmetrical relationship between volatility change and past returns is found statistically significant.

Tab. 19.2: Stock Return Models

	IGARCH	FIGARCH	IEGARCH	FIEGARH
α_0	0.1060797701*	0.110723024*	-0.44068145**	-0.439902196**
α_1	0.0693945469**	0.070996975*	0.16980154*	0.170083365**
α_2	0.0022487189**	-0.001667105 **	0.11022990*	0.110074158**
α_3	0.0038900701**	0.003970565*	0.34975979**	0.349460007**
ω	0.0378291785**	-0.077413459 **	1.73364233	1.735475043
δ	0.4112416119*	0.427318286**	-0.33333333**	-0.333147999 *
φ_1	1.0000000000	0.163589457*	1.00000000	-0.016472225
φ_2	0.0845611765*		-0.01248545 **	
β	0.9175291630*	0.372549283**		
θ			-1.18757019 **	-1.186997390 **
γ			0.31788911 **	0.318107404**
ψ			-0.68154208 *	-1.917083827
d		0.355294766 **		0.087356800**

*, **, and *** indicate significance levels of 10 %, 5 %, and 1 %, respectively.

Conclusion

In the context of the study, the long memory features, asymmetric effects, and structural changes of BIST-100 index volatility have been evaluated, and it is concluded that there are long memory features in BIST-100 volatility. The conditional variance of the index is best modeled by the fractional integrated process. A more flexible fractional integrated EGARCH model class can be used to characterize long-term dependencies in BIST-100 stock market volatility. In addition, it is observed that the effects of shocks on volatility are asymmetrical and the leverage effect occurs in the short-run.

References

Aygören, H. (2008). İstanbul Menkul Kıymetler Borsasının Fractal Analizi. *Dokuz Eylül Üniversitesi İktisadi ve İdari Bilimler Fakültesi Dergisi*, 23(1).

Baillie, R. T., Bollerslev, T. and Mikkelsen, H. O. (1996). Fractionally Integrated Generalized Autoregressive Conditional Heteroskedasticity. *Journal of Econometrics*, 74(1), 3–30.

Baillie, R. T., Chung, C. F. and Tieslau, M. A. (1996). Analysing Inflation by the Fractionally Integrated ARFIMA–GARCH Model. *Journal of Applied Econometrics*, 11(1), 23–40.

Balıbey, M. and Turkyılmaz, S.(2016). An Empırıcal Investıgatıon of Asymmetrıc Long Memory and Structural Breaks in the Volatılıty of Turkısh Stock Market. *International Journal of Business Quantitative Economics and Applied Management Research*, 3(1)

Bhattacharya, S. N. and Bhattacharya, M. (2012). Long Memory in Stock Returns: A Study of Emerging Markets. *Iranian Journal of Management Studies*, 5(2), 67–88.

Blasco IV, N. and Santamaria, R. (1996). Testing Memory Patterns in the Spanish Stock Market. *Applied Financial Economics*, 6(5), 401–411.

Bollerslev, T. (1986). Generalized autoregressive conditional heteroskedasticity. *Journal of econometrics, 31*(3), 307–327.

Bollerslev, T., Engle, R. F. and Nelson, D. B. (1994). ARCH Models. Handbook of Econometrics, 4, 2959–3038.

Bollerslev, T. and Mikkelsen, H. O. (1996). Modeling and Pricing Long Memory in Stock Market Volatility. *Journal of Econometrics*, 73(1), 151–184.

Caporale, G. M. and Gil-Alana, L. A. (2004). Fractional Cointegration and Tests of Present Value Models. *Review of Financial Economics*, 13(3), 245–258.

Cavalcante, J. and Assaf, A. (2004). Long Range Dependence in the Returns and Volatility of the Brazilian Stock Market. *European Review of Economics and Finance*, 3(5), 22.

Comte, F. and Renault, E. (1998). Long Memory in Continuous-Time Stochastic Volatility Models. *Mathematical Finance*, 8(4), 291–323.

Crato, N. and de Lima, P. J. (1994). Long-Range Dependence in the Conditional Variance of Stock Returns. *Economics Letters*, 45(3), 281–285.

Çevik, E. İ. (2012). İstanbul Menkul Kıymetler Borsası'nda Etkin Piyasa Hipotezinin Uzun Hafıza Modelleri İle Analizi: Sektörel Bazda Bir İnceleme. *Journal of Yasar University*, 7(26).

Çevik, E. İ. and Erdoğan, S. (2009). Bankacılık Sektörü Hisse Senedi Piyasasının Etkinliği: Yapısal Kırılma ve Güçlü Hafıza. *Doğuş Üniversitesi Dergisi*, 10 (1), 26–40.

Diebold, F. X. and Inoue, A. (2001). Long Memory and Regime Switching. *Journal of Econometrics*, 105(1), 131–159.

Engle, R. F. (1982). Autoregressive Conditional Heteroscedasticity with Estimates of the Variance of United Kingdom Inflation. *Econometrica: Journal of the Econometric Society*, 50 (4), 987–1007.

Engle, R. F. and Bollerslev, T. (1986). Modelling the Persistence of Conditional Variances. *Econometric Reviews*, 5(1), 1–50.

French, K. R. and Roll, R. (1986). Stock Return Variances: The Arrival of Information and the Reaction of Traders. *Journal of Financial Economics*, 17(1), 5–26.

Granger, C. W. and Hyung, N. (2004). Occasional Structural Breaks and Long Memory with an Application to the S&P 500 Absolute Stock Returns. *Journal of Empirical Finance*, 11(3), 399–421.

Günay, S. (2014). Yapısal Kırılmalar Dahilinde Bist-100 Endeksi Volatilitesinin Uzun Dönemli Bellek Analizi. *Journal of Yasar University*, 9(36).

Hosking, J. R. M. (1981). Fractional Differencing. Biometrika 68 165–176. *Mathematical Reviews (MathSciNet): MR614953 Zentralblatt MATH*, 464.

Kasman, S., Turgutlu, E. and Ayhan, A. D. (2009). Long Memory in Stock Returns: Evidence from the Major Emerging Central European Stock Markets. *Applied Economics Letters*, 16(17), 1763–1768.

Kirman, A. and Teyssiere, G. (2002). Microeconomic Models for Long Memory in the Volatility of Financial Time Series. *Studies in Nonlinear Dynamics & Econometrics*, 5(4).

Liu, S. M. and Shieh, S. J. (2007). Long Memory in Volatility of T-Bond Futures Markets: A Value-at Ris Approach. *The Journal of Human Resource and Adult Learning*, 3(2), 225–233.

Lo, A. W. and MacKinlay, A. C. (1990). When Are Contrarian Profits due to Stock Market Overreaction?. *The Review of Financial Studies*, 3(2), 175–205.

Lobato, I. N. and Savin, N. E. (1998). Real and Spurious Long-Memory Properties of Stock-Market Data. *Journal of Business & Economic Statistics*, 16(3), 261–268.

Maheu, J. (2005). Can GARCH Models Capture Long-Range Dependence?. *Studies in Nonlinear Dynamics & Econometrics*, 9(4).

Mandelbrot, B., & Hudson, R. 2004. The misbehavior of markets: A fractal view of risk, ruin, and reward. New York: Basic Books

Nelson, D. B. (1991). Conditional Heteroskedasticity in Asset Returns: A New Approach. *Econometrica: Journal of the Econometric Society*, 59 (2), 347–370.

Resende, M. and Teixeira, N. (2002). Permanent Structural Changes in the Brazilian Economy and Long Memory: A Stock Market Perspective. *Applied Economics Letters*, 9(6), 373–375.

Tayefi, M. and Ramanathan, T. V. (2012). An Overview of FIGARCH and Related Time Series Models. *Austrian Journal of Statistics*, 41(3), 175–196.

Tolvi, J. (2003). Long Memory in a Small Stock Market. *Economics Bulletin*, 7(3), 1–13.

Ural, M. and Demireli, E. (2009). Hurst Üstel Katsayisi Araciliğiyla Fractal Yapi Analizi ve İMKB'de Bir Uygulama. *Atatürk Üniversitesi Iktisadi ve Idari Bilimler Dergisi*, 23(2), 243–255.

Ural, M. and Küçüközmen, C. C. (2011). Analyzing the Dual Long Memory in Stock Market Returns/Borsa Endeks Getirilerinde Ikili Uzun Hafiza Analizi. *Ege Akademik Bakis*, 11, 19.

Yalama, A., Celik, S. and Sevil, G. (2011). Long Memory in Stock Markets: Empirical Study on Spot and Future Markets in Turkey. *In International Conference-Las Vegas*.

Mehmet Özer

20 Underpricing in Initial Public Offerings: Turkey, 2011–2013[1]

Highlights: In this study, the factors affecting short-term returns were analyzed. The presence of investors holding 5 % or more of the public offering, the number of foreign investors participating in the public offering, and the issue-specific characteristics such as public offering revenue have a positive and statistically significant effect on the second day, the first week, and the first month adjusted returns, including the first day adjusted returns. On the other hand, the firm-specific asset size has a negative and statistically significant effect on short-term returns. The debt-liability ratio has a negative effect on short-term returns.

Keywords: Initial Public Offering, underpricing, short-term return

Introduction

The pricing of initial public offerings is one of the most important topics of the finance literature, and there is a consensus that initial public offerings are underpriced. The fact that the public offering price is below the closing price of the first day means that the share is initially underpriced. On the other hand, due to the fact that there is a 10 % price margin on the stock market for each trading session, low pricing will be better to evaluate not only on the first day's returns but also on the second day, the first week, the first month, and also the first three months. In other words, short-term returns of up to three months will be used to examine the pricing behavior of initial public offerings. Moreover, the investigation of underpricing in terms of only by different markets will not be as descriptive as we want. Therefore, it is necessary to identify explanatory variables that cause underpricing in a market. It is possible to identify these explanatory variables under three groups as company-specific, issue-specific, and market-specific explanatory variables. The company-specific variables can be defined as the total asset size, the ratio of short and long-term liabilities to the total liabilities, the size of equity, and the financial structure of the company, as well as the characteristics such as the age of the company and the sector in which it operates. It is possible to list the characteristics of the issue in the following

1 This study was derived from Mehmet ÖZER's Capital Market Board of Turkey Expertise Thesis (2015).

way: total Initial Public Offering (IPO) revenue, the number of domestic and foreign investors participating in the public offering, the method of public offering, whether there is an investor with a share of more than 5 % of the public offering or not, the reliability of intermediary institution. Finally, market-specific explanatory variables are the short-and long-term trend of the market, the nature of the market traded, and the volatility of the market. The pricing of initial public offerings is one of the most important topics of the finance literature, and there is a consensus that initial public offerings are underpriced. If public offering price is below the closing price of the first day, then the share publicly offered is underpriced. In other words, the concept of underpricing is used for a very short term. In Stoll and Curley (1970), Logue (1973), Reilly (1973), and Ibbotson (1975) are the first studies that showed that the public offering price is below the first-day closing price. Tab. 20.1 summarizes the studies of underpricing analysis for different countries.

As can be seen from Tab. 20.1, although underpricing differs from country to country and time zone, it is a phenomenon encountered in all markets. For this reason, there are too many theoretical and empirical studies that try to determine the causes of underpricing in initial public offerings. Brau and Fawcett (2006) collect the possible causes of underpricing in initial public offerings under eight headings:

1) *Asymmetric information between the investor and the issuer: Because the investor has more information about the market, the effort to integrate with the customers in the purchase side with minimum effort.*
2) *Asymmetric information between the issuer and potential investors: lower price propositions due to investors' perception of uncertainty about the future.*
3) *Asymmetric information between investors who are informed and uninformed: Informed investors prefer lower price for counterparty risk perception.*
4) *To be seen as a method of protection from potential legal conflicts which may be encountered by the issuers in the future.*
5) *The market is seen as a tool in terms of its operability: underpricing can increase demand by domino effect, decrease market cost in other market transactions, attract investors' attention due to the rise in the first day, increase the post-public supply trading volume.*
6) *Expanding the investor base: underpricing can increase the investor base, increasing the share's liquidity, and increasing the company's transparency of the investor base.*
7) *Investment companies want to provide their support in the next public offering by providing high returns to potential good customers.*

Tab. 20.1: Summary of Short-Term Underpricing (DF) Literature

Study	Country	Time Period	Number of Companies	Underpricing Amount(%)
Aggarwal, Leal, and Hernandez (1993)	Mexico	1987–1990	44	2,8
Aggarval and Kunz (1994)	Switzerland	1983–1989	103	35,8
Cassia, Giudici, Paleari, and Radondi (2004)	Italy	1985–2001	182	19,3
Chi and Padgett (2005)	China	1996–2000	668	129,2
Cigerza and Procianoy (2007)	Brazil	2004–2006	29	7,1
Dowson (1987)	Hong Kong	1978–1983	21	13,8
Dowson (1987)	Malesia	1978–1987	21	166,7
Eijgenhuijsen and Van der Valk (1997)	Argentina	1991–1994	20	4,4
Ghosh (2004)	India	1993–2001	1842	95
How (2000)	-Australia	1979–1990	130	107,2
Jakobsen and Sorensen (2000)	Denmark	1984–1992	76	3,9
Krinsky, Kim, and Lee (1992)	Korea	1985–1990	275	79
Koh and Walter (1989)	Singapore	1973–1987	66	27,2
Peter (2007)	Sri Lanka	1996–2000	30	57,2
Ritter and Welch (2002)	USA	1980–2001	6249	18,8

8) *Issuers do not care about pricing because the funds they have obtained are already high*

In these explanations, the most analyzed approaches are models based on asymmetric knowledge. Rock (1986) argued that some investors have more knowledge than all actors in the market, and proposed the theory of the Winner's Curse. Because of the information set they have, they do not bid on high priced IPOs, but shift their demands to underpriced IPOs. Other investors, on the other hand, tend to offer more offerings to proportionally high-priced public offerings as they bid on all IPOs. Because other investors are facing more losses, there is a set of investors who stop bidding on initial public offerings in the long term. This leads to the inability of investors with a large set of information to generate sufficient demand for all IPOs, and ultimately, the systematic majority of initial public offerings are underpriced.

Welch (1989) claims that it is important to achieve an increase in the price of shares to attract publicly traded companies, new entrepreneurs and funders to the company, and therefore IPOs are underpriced, since they believe that underpricing will help the company to realize its future plans. Jagadesh, Weinstein, and Welch (1993) showed that the first-day yields and the returns after the first day had the same effect on the company's future funding.

Benveniste and Spindt (1989) suggested that sale via book building within a price range method is important in terms of intermediary institutions to gather information from the dominant investors in the process. In this method, the lowest and highest prices are determined for the shares to be offered to the public, and discussions are made with potential investors about investment decisions. If there is sufficient demand, the price of the IPO is determined higher than it should be, and if low demand is received, it is determined lower. However, even in the event of high demand, underpricing can be made to provide potential investors with a short-term return. This is the logic behind why public offerings are generally made at low prices. However, although this method is appropriate to explain moderate underpricing, it is insufficient to explain low prices up to 50 %.

The common feature of all underpricing theories based on the asymmetric information mentioned above and not mentioned here is that the increase in asymmetric information degree will increase the degree of underpricing. According to these models, when asymmetric information is eliminated, underpricing is completely eliminated, as well.

On the other hand, even if there is symmetric information in the market, there are also models that claim that underpricing will be maintained for different reasons. Tinic (1988), Hughes and Thakor (1992) argue that companies offer their shares to public offer underpricing to reduce their legal obligations and risks. According to these authors, a share of a company that is offered to the public of $ 20 and whose real value is $ 30 is suggested to be less likely to face legal disputes than a share of $ 30 to the public. However, Drake and Vetsuypens (1993) have shown that IPOs with lower underpricing rates are more likely to face legal disputes.

Boehmer and Fishe (2001) suggested that the volume of transactions after the initial public offering was higher, and therefore, the intermediary institution, which mediated the public offerings, had a higher transaction fee. This theory, however, claims that underpricing benefits the intermediary institution that mediates the public, not the company that shares its shares.

Summary information on the studies made for the Turkish markets regarding the underpricing of initial public offerings is shown in Tab. 20.2.

Tab. 20.2: Summary of Short-Term Underpricing Literature on Turkey

Study	Time Period	Number of Companies	Underpricing Amount
Aydoğan and Yıldırım (1991)	1989–1991	33	1,2
Akkaşoğlu (1992)	1990–1991	35	12,5
Erdem (1993)	1989–1992	64	18,8
Kıymaz (2000)	1990–1996	163	13,1
Aktaş, Aydoğan and Karan (2003)	1992–2000	190	9,2
Özden (2005)	1990–1997	134	7,1
Bildik and Yılmaz (2006)	1990–2000	244	5,9
Küçükkocaoğlu (2008)	1993–2005	217	9,6
Eraydın (2008)	1999–2007	88	7,3
Daştan (2008)	2004–2007	25	5,8
Çelik and Sağlam (2011)	1993–2006	40	11,3

Among the studies in Tab. 20.2, except Aydoğan and Yıldırım (1991), they found the underpricing rate to be statistically significant. Tab. 20.1 shows strong evidence that underpricing is a reality for developed and developing countries, while Tab. 20.1 shows that this fact is also true for Turkey.

2 Data Set

In this study, as seen in Tab. 20.3, 71 companies offered to the public in the stock exchange between 2011 and 2013 within the scope of public offering mobilization were used. Information about the markets and years in which these companies are offered to the public is shown in Tab. 20.3.

On the other hand, the summary information on the issues such as the age of the companies that make their first public offering during the mentioned period, and the public opening rate after the public offering are also included in Tab. 20.4.

3 Method, Analysis, and Results

In any regression analysis, the structure of the equation to be estimated using the Ordinary Least Squares method can be expressed as follows in its most general form.

Tab. 20.3: Market-Year Offered to the Public

Market	2011	2012	2013	Total
Star Market	4	3	3	10
Main Market	18	12	3	33
Emerging Companies Market (ECM)	2	10	9	21
Collective and Structured Products Market (CSPM)	2	2	3	7
Total	26	27	18	71

Source: http://www.spk.gov.tr/Sayfa/AltSayfa/895

Tab. 20.4: Age of Companies and Demand Collection-Time to Start Trading

	Mean	Std. Deviation	Min.	Max.
Age	14,02	9,83	2	48
Free Float Rate	27,82	9,55	5,34	50
Demand Collection-Time to Start Trading (Day)	4,72	1,91	1	12

Source: https://www.borsaistanbul.com/en/data/data/equity-market-data (25.06.2015)

$$Y = X\alpha + \varepsilon$$

In the above equation, Y is a dependent variable and represents n * 1 the column matrix; X represents n * k dimensional matrix with the k independent variable, α represents the coefficients of the independent variables, and k * 1 represents the column matrix; ε shows the n * 1 dimensional error terms where the Gauss-Markov assumptions are satisfied. Dependent variables will be cumulative returns adjusted according to the first-day, second-day, 1-week, and 1-month market returns and gross abnormal returns on the first day. It is possible to aggregate these explanatory variables under three groups, represented by the X Matrix, as company-specific, public offering-specific, and market-specific explanatory variables. Company-specific factors may be the factors that define the financial structure of the firm such as total asset size, the ratio of short- and long-term liabilities to total liabilities, equity size, revenue, as well as characteristics such as the age of the firm and the sector in which it operates. It is possible to list the characteristics of the public offering in the following way: total IPO revenue, the number of domestic and foreign investors participating to the public offering, the method of public offering, whether there exists an investor with a share

Tab. 20.5: The Effects of Issue-Specific Properties on Underpricing

	Adjusted First Day Returns	Adjusted Second Day Returns	Adjusted First Week Returns	Adjusted First Month Returns
d %5	3.481*	6.123**	13.98***	11.50*
	(1.73)	(2.07)	(3.23)	(1.93)
ml	-2.917	-7.457**	-10.64**	-25.00
	(-1.17)	(-2.13)	(-2.04)	(-1.54)
m2	2.465	0.294	-3.931	-22.21
	(0.94)	(0.09)	(-0.94)	(-1.53)
ipo_income	-2.470**	-3.489**	-5.782***	-4.054
	(-2.29)	(-2.30)	(-2.74)	(-1.38)
Investment Agency	0.968	3.105	3.541	7.537*
	(0.60)	(1.28)	(1.01)	(1.70)
foreigninvnmb	0.0180***	0.0161***	0.00650**	0.0332***
	(9.35)	(4.96)	(2.02)	(6.77)
_c	41.36**	57.17**	95.37**	76.21
	(2.09)	(2.02)	(2.45)	(1.26)
R^2	0.230	0.233	0.255	0.184

*The parentheses are t-statistics. Significance Level: * $p < 0.1$, ** $p < 0.05$, *** $p < 0.01$*

of more than 5 % or not, the reliability of the public intermediary institution. Finally, market-specific explanatory variables are the short-and long-term trend of the market, the nature of the market traded, and the volatility of the market.

The results of the regression analysis are shown in Tab. 20.5 where the first-day, second-day, first-week and first-month adjusted returns of companies presented to the public between 2011 and 2013 are dependent variables and the following characteristics of the public are used as independent variables. Independent variables:

***d* 5 %**: *Dummy variable taking value 1 if there exists an investor who has a share of 5 % or more of the IPO, 0 otherwise.*

m1: *Dummy variable showing that the public offering has been done with a capital increase only.*

m2: *Dummy variable showing the public offerings with capital increase and joint sale.*

IPOrevenue: *Logarithm of income from IPO.*

Intermediary Institution: *The variable in which investment institutions are divided into three groups according to their qualifications and activities in the*

capital market 1 = Large intermediary institutions, 2 = Medium-size intermediary institutions, 3 = Small intermediary institutions.
foreigninvnmb *The number of foreign investors participating in the public offering.*

As can be seen from Tab. 20.5, where we analyze the impact of issue-specific characteristics on short-term returns (underpricing), the presence of investors holding 5 % or more of the public offering has a positive and statistically significant effect on the second day, the first week and the first month returns, including adjusted returns. In fact, this variable was included in the analysis to test the validity of Rock's (1986) theory of "Winner's Curse". According to the aforementioned theory, since large investors have a broader set of information, they not only participate in underpriced public offerings but also keep the number of shares they buy from these IPOs high. On the other hand, while the majority of the institutional investors occupies 70 % of the total capitalization of the Stock Exchange, foreign investors, which constitute only 15 % of the total transaction volume, are wider and have a tendency to position the market in line with foreign investors' operations; it requires the inclusion of the number of foreign investors in the analysis. Note that the coefficient of the variable is statistically significant in the first day, the first two days, the first week and the first-month yields are dependent variables, and in almost all of them are statistically significant at even 1 %. Both coefficients of the existence of investors who have 5 % or more shares that are issued and the number of foreign investors being statistically significant indicates that Rock's Winner's Curse Theory also applies to public offerings held in different markets in Turkey between 2011 and 2013.

We have classified the intermediary institutions into three groups according to their qualifications: the big and qualified ones take the value of 1, medium-sized takes the value 2, and small intermediary institutions takes the value 3. Although the coefficient of the "intermediary institution" variable is positive as expected, it is statistically significant only on the first month of the income. The reason why the coefficient of this variable is expected to be positive is that investment firms that have relatively low reputation in the market are implicitly under taking underpricing (short-term positive return) to attract investors to the public offering they are intermediating. Boehmer and Fishe (2001) suggested that the volume of transactions after the initial public offering was higher, and therefore, the intermediary institutions, which mediated the public offerings, had a higher transaction fee. The reason for the statistically significant effect of this variable on the monthly adjusted cumulative returns is that small intermediary institutions may wish to extend the time to lower pricing to increase the transaction volume in a relatively long period, such as 1 month, rather than waiting for investors to increase the transaction volume in a very short period.

While the dummy variable (m1) for public offerings only with the capital increase was statistically significant and negative in regressions were adjusted cumulative returns on the second day and the first week were dependent variables, it is not significant in first day and first month returns. On the other hand, the dummy variable (m2) for both capital increase and public offerings through the existing shares of shareholders is not statistically significant for all short-term returns.

Habib and Ljungqvist (1998) showed that as the IPO revenue increased, the dilution effect would also increase and therefore there was a negative relationship between the IPO revenue and the short-term yield. As can be seen from the table, there is a negative relationship between the IPO revenue and the first day, the second day, the first week, and the first-month yields.

The independent variables included in Tab. 20.6 that examine the impact of firm-specific characteristics on short-term returns are:

ln_currentass: *Natural logarithm of the current assets.*
ln_assets: *Natural logarithm of the total assets.*
ratfixasstotalass: *The ratio of fixed assets to the total assets.*
debtliabilitiesratio*: The ratio of short- and long-term debts to the total liabilities.*
findebtpassiveratio*: The ratio of total short- and long-term financial liabilities to the total liabilities.*

As can be seen from Tab. 20.6, there is a decrease in short-term returns as the asset aggregate and debt-liability ratio increases. Ghosh (2004) and Deb and Marisetyy (2010) showed that there was a negative correlation between short-term returns and total asset size for initial IPOs in India. Similarly, Kıymaz from studies conducted in Turkey (2000) also revealed that there is a negative relationship between firm sizes with short-term returns. Since larger firms have a more transparent structure than smaller firms before the public offering, it is thought that the firms' values are correctly estimated by both investors and intermediary institutions, and therefore underpricing tendency is reduced.

On the other hand, before the IPO, small firms use various methods (such as valuation of their tangible assets) in order to reach higher equity, thus reducing the debt-to-liability ratio, which means that companies with relatively high debt-liability ratios are larger. In this context, the reason why the aforementioned variable affects the first day and second day returns in a negative and statistically significant way may be the reason explained above.

The last and most important factor, that we think, affects short-term returns is the markets where companies that are offered to the public are traded. In this context, mc1, mc2, mc3, and mc4 are the dummy variables representing the

Tab. 20.6: Effects of Firm-Specific Characteristics on Short-Term Returns

	Adjusted First Day Returns	Adjusted Second Day Returns	Adjusted First Week Returns	Adjusted First Month Returns
ln_currentass	2.068	4.101	5.452	4.426
	(1.08)	(1.45)	(1.16)	(0.64)
ln_assets	-2.931*	-5.517**	-7.556*	-6.989
	(-1.73)	(-2.07)	(-1.72)	(-1.10)
ratfixasstotalass	1.251	7.687	15.45	9.759
	(0.19)	(0.78)	(0.97)	(0.41)
debtliabilitiesratio	-10.72**	-15.55*	-15.34	-14.89
	(-2.10)	(-1.98)	(-1.27)	(-0.91)
findebtpassiveratio	-1.011	0.718	3.346	-5.980
	(-0.20)	(0.09)	(0.38)	(-0.47)
cons	27.16**	39.69**	50.69**	65.63*
	(2.25)	(2.26)	(2.07)	(1.96)
R^2	0.121	0.116	0.0847	0.0548

market of the issue, Main Market, Star Market, ECM, and the CSPM, respectively (Tab. 20.7).

When we look the Tab. 20.7, we can see that the results are consistent with that of previously founded with t-statistics. The raw abnormal first day returns, adjusted first day, second day, first week, and first month returns are statistically significant at any significance level (1 %, 5 %, and 10 %). On the other hand, in the same period, the average of the first day-adjusted returns for 33 companies offered to the public in the Main Market was 7, 43 %. The average of cumulative returns adjusted according to the second day, first week, and first-month market returns of these Main Market companies is 10.74 %, 14.00 %, and 18.29 %, respectively. In the Emerging Companies Market, the underpricing rate for companies offered to the public is less, and the average of the adjusted returns on the first day was 3.74 %. The increasing trend seen in the Main Market is also the case for the ECM, while the average of the second day, first week, and first month yields are 5.26 %, 9.46 %, and 10.19 %, respectively. As can be seen from these results, the main driving reason for reaching the underpricing result in the analysis that includes all of the IPOs during the period of 2011–2013, is the statistically significant underpricing for the 54 companies traded in the Main Market and ECM.

Tab. 20.7: Effects of the Trading Market on Short-Term Returns[a]

	Adjusted First Day Returns	Adjusted Second Day Returns	Adjusted First Week Returns	Adjusted First Month Returns
mc1	0.922	0.0127	-2.051	-3.705
	(0.35)	(0.00)	(-0.75)	(-0.99)
mc2	7.429***	10.74***	14.01**	18.29**
	(4.20)	(3.89)	(3.36)	(3.26)
mc3	3.740**	5.265*	9.456**	10.19**
	(2.22)	(1.98)	(2.30)	(2.01)
mc4	1.041	0.772	2.987	2.417
	(0.60)	(0.35)	(0.61)	(0.45)
R^2	0.291	0.271	0.241	0.227

*Parentheses are T statistics. Significance level: * p<0.1, ** p<0.05, *** p<0.01*

[a] Since four markets and four dummy variables are existing, when the four dummy variables are included in the regression analysis with a constant term, the coefficients cannot be predicted due to the perfect multicollinearity. Therefore, a regression without a constant term is run.

Conclusion

The shares of the companies with many different economic and institutional structures are listed in Borsa Istanbul A.Ş. In four different markets such as Star Market, Main Market, Emerging Companies Market, and Collective and Structured Product Market, it is necessary to analyze the pricing behavior of the IPOs and their subsequent performances by the markets they are traded. The averages of the first day raw abnormal returns and the cumulative returns adjusted for market returns on the first day, second day, first week and first month are analyzed by using the complete data set consisting of public offerings performed between 2011 and 2013 without market distinction. While statistically significant (with low pricing), the analysis taking into account the market being traded, the returns mentioned in the public market in the Main Market and ECM are statistically significant, whereas in the public market in Star Market and CUBE, it is statistically insignificant. However, in the analysis carried out by taking into account the market in which the issue was done, the yields mentioned above are only statistically significant for the IPOs in the Main Market and in the ECM, and the mentioned yields are statistically insignificant for the public offerings in the Yıldız Market and the CSPM.

The presence of investors holding 5 % or more of the public offering, the number of foreign investors participating in the public offering, and the issue-specific characteristics such as public offering revenue have a positive and statistically significant effect on the second day, the first week, and the first month adjusted returns, including the first day adjusted returns. Both coefficients of the existence of investors who have 5 % or more share that are issued and the number of foreign investors being statistically significant indicates that Rock's Winner's Curse Theory also applies to public offerings held in different markets in Turkey between 2011 and 2013. On the other hand, one of the firm-specific characteristics asset size has a negative and statistically significant effect on short-term returns. Since larger firms have a more transparent structure than smaller firms before the public offering, it is thought that the firms' values are correctly estimated by both investors and intermediary institutions, and therefore underpricing tendency is reduced. The debt-liability ratio has a negative and statistically significant effect on short-term returns. Before the public offering, the use of various methods (such as valuation of tangible fixed assets) in order to show the equity of small companies higher decreases the debt-liability ratio and therefore leads to the relatively high debt-liability ratio of relatively large companies. This situation is thought to cause the coefficient of the variable to be negative.

References

Aggarwal R., R. Leal and Hernandez, F. (1993). The Aftermarket Performance of IPOs in Latin America. *Financial Management*, Cilt 22.1, 42–53. Doi: 10.2307/3665964

Aggarwal, R and Kunz, R. M. (1994). Why İnitial Public Offerings are Underpriced: Evidence from Switzerland. *Journal of Banking and Finance,* 18, 705–723. Doi: 10.1016/0378-4266(93)00016-I.

Akkaşoğlu, A. (1992). *Pricing of Initial Public Offerings*. Master Tezi. Bilkent Üniversitesi, Ankara.

Aktas, R., M. B. Karan and Aydogan, K. (2003). Forecasting Short Run Performance of İnitial Public Offerings in the Istanbul Stock Exchange. *Journal of Entrepreneurial Finance and Business Ventures*, 8.1, 69–85. https://digitalcommons.pepperdine.edu/jef/vol8/iss1/5.

Aydoğan, K and Yıldırım, J. (1991). İlk Kez Halka Arz Edilen Senetlerin Fiyat Performansı. *Üçüncü İzmir İktisat Kongresi İçin Yapılmış Yayınlanmamış Çalışma*. Bilkent Üniversitesi. Ankara.

Benveniste, L. M. and Spindt, P. A. (1989). How Investment Bankers Determine the Offer Price and Allocation of New Issues. *Journal of Financial Economics*, 24, 343–361. Doi: 10.1016/0304-405X(89)90051-2.

Bildik, R. and Yılmaz, M. K. (2006). The Market Performance of Initial Public Offerings in the İstanbul Stock Exchange. *BDDK Bankacılık ve Finansal Piyasalar*, 2, 49–77. https://papers.ssrn.com/sol3/papers.cfm?abstract_id=952526.

Boehmer, E. and Fishe, P. R. (2001). Equilibrium Rationing in İnitial Public Offerings of Equity. *University of Miami Working Paper.* https://papers.ssrn.com/sol3/papers.cfm?abstract_id=273610.

Brau, J. C. and Fawcett, S. (2006). Initial Public Offerings: An Analysis of Theory and Practise. *The Journal of Finance.* LXI.1, 399–436. 006. Doi: 10.1111/j.1540-6261.2006.00840.

Cassia, L. Giudici, G., Paleari, S., & Redondi, R. (2004). IPO Underpricing in Italy. *Applied Financial Economics*, 14(3), 179–194. DOI: 10.1080/0960310042000187333

Çelik, A.E. and Sağlam, G.Y. (2011). İMKB'de Düşük Fiyatlandırma ve Aracılık Türü, Arz Yılı, Aracı Kurum Etkileri Üzerine Bir Araştırma. *Doğuş Üniversitesi Dergisi*, 12.2, 289–303. http://openaccess.dogus.edu.tr/handle/11376/249

Chi, J. and Padgett, C. (2005). Short-Run Underpricing and İts Characteristics in Chinese İnitial Public Offering (IPO) Markets. *Research in International Business and Finance*, 19.1, 71–93. D.

Cigerza, G. C. and Procianoy, J. L. (2007). Ipos İn Emerging Markets: A Comparison of Brazil, India and China. Working Paper. https://papers.ssrn.com/Sol3/papers.cfm?abstract_id=968300

Deb, S.S. and Merisetty, V.B. (2010). Information Content of IPO Grading. *Journal of Banking and Finance*, 34, 2294–2305. Doi: 10.1016/j.jbankfin.2010.02.018.

Dowson, S.M. (1987). Secondary Stock Market Performance of İnitial Public Offers, Hong Kong, Singapore and Malaysia: 1978–1984. *Journal of Business Finance and Accounting*, 14.1, 65–76. Doi: 10.1111/j.1468-5957.1987.tb00529.

Drake, P. D. and Vetsuypens M. R. (1993). IPO Underpricing and İnsurance against Legal Liability. *Financial Management*, 22, 64–73. Doi: 10.2307/3665966.

Eijgenhuijsen, H. and Van Der Valk R. (1997). Initial Public Offerings in Mexico and Argentina. *Serie Research Memoranda 0009 Free University Amsterdam, Faculty of Economics, Business Administration and Econometrics.* https://ideas.repec.org/p/vua/wpaper/1997-9.html.

Eraydın, K. (2008). *The Underpricing and Long Run Performance of Inıtıal Public Offerings. Master Tezi.* Lund University School of Economics and Management.

Erdem, H. (1993). *A Study on the Price Behaviour of Initial Public Offerings.* Master Tezi, Boğaziçi Üniversitesi. İstanbul.

Ghosh, S. (2004). Revisiting IPO Underpricing in India. *Working Paper.* https://papers.ssrn.com/sol3/papers.cfm?abstract_id=703501.

Habib, M.A. and Ljungqvist A.P. (2001). Underpricing and Entrepreneurial Wealth Losses in IPOs: Theory and Evidence. *Review of Financial Studies*, 14.2, 433–458. Doi: 10.1093/rfs/14.2.433.

How, J. C. Y. (2000). Initial and Long-Run Performance of Mining IPOs in Australia. *Australian Journal of Management*, 25.1, 95–118. Doi: 10.1177/031289620002500107.

Hughes, P. J. and Thakor A. V. (1992). Litigation Risk, İntermediation, and the Underpricing of İnitial Public Offerings. *Review of Financial Studies*, 5, 709–742. doi: 10.1093/rfs/5.4.709.

Ibbotson, R. G. (1975). Price Performance of Common Stock New İssues. *Journal of Financial Economics*, 2, 235–72. Doi: 10.1016/0304-405X(75)90015.

Ibbotson, R. G. and Jaffe J.F. (1975). The Hot Issue Market. *Journal of Finance*, 30.4, 1027–1043. doi: 10.1111/j.1540-6261.1975.tb01019.

Jakobsen, J. and Sorensen O. (2000). Decomposing and Testing Long-Run Returns with an Application to İnitial Public Offerings in Denmark. *Department of Finance Copenhagen Business School*, WP 2000–2. http://www.forskningsdatabasen.dk/en/catalog/2397931373.

Kıymaz, H. (2000). The İnitial and Aftermarket Performance of Ipos in an Emerging Market: Evidence from Istanbul Stock Exchange. *Journal of Multinational Financial Management*, 10, 213–227. doi: 10.1016/S1042-444X(99)00027-4.

Koh, F. and Walter, T. (1989). A Direct Test of Rock's Model of the Pricing of Unseasoned İssues. *Journal of Financial Economics*, 23, 251–272. Doi: 10.1016/0304-405X(89)90058-5.

Küçükkocaoğlu, G. (2008). Underpricing in Turkey: A Comparison of the IPO Methods. *International Research Journal of Finance and Economics*, 13, 162–182. http://www.baskent.edu.tr/~gurayk/kisiselipounderpricing.pdf

Ljungqvıst, A.P. and Wilhelm, W.J. (2003). IPO Pricing in the Dot-Com Bubble. *Journal of Finance*, 58, 723–752. Doi: 10.1111/1540-6261.00543.

Logue, D. E. (1973). On the Pricing of Unseasoned Equity İssues: 1965–1969. *Journal of Financial and Quantitative Analysis*, 8, 91–103. Doi: 10.2307/2329751.

Özden, O. E. (2005). The Initial and Long-Run Price Performance of İnitial Public Offerings: The Turkish Experience 1990–1997. *Journal of Social Science Research*. University of Texas.

Peter, S. (2007). Performance of İnitial Public Offerings and Privatized Offers. Evidence from a Developing Country. *Managerial Finance*, 33, 798–809. https://www.emeraldinsight.com/doi/abs/10.1108/03074350710779241.

Reilly, F. K. (1973). Further Evidence on Short-Run Results for New İssues İnvestors. *Journal of Financial and Quantitative Analysis*, 8, 83–90. Doi: 10.2307/2329750.

Ritter, J. R. and Welch I. (2002). A Review of IPO Activity, Pricing, and Allocations. *The Journal of Finance*, LVII.4, 1795–1828. Doi: 10.1111/1540-6261.00478.

Rock, K. (1986). Why New İssues Are Underpriced. *Journal of Financial Economics*, 15, 187–212. Doi: 10.1016/0304-405X(86)90054-1.

Stoll, H. R. and Curley, A. J. (1970). Small Business and the New İssues Market for Equities. *Journal of Financial and Quantitative Analysis*, 5, 309–322. Doi: 10.2307/2329998.

Tınıç, S. (1988). Anotomy of Initial Public Offerings of Common Stocks. *The Journal of Finance*, 43.4, 789–822. Doi: 10.1111/j.1540-6261.1988.tb02606.

Welch, I. (1989). Seasoned Offerings, İmitation Costs, and the Underpricing of İnitial Public Offerings. *Journal of Finance*, 44, 421–450. Doi: 10.1111/j.1540-6261.1989.tb05064.

Berna Serener

21 Dividend Policy Studies in Turkey

Highlights: The Stock Exchange in Turkey began its operations in Istanbul in 1986. Since its inception, several articles have been written on the dividend policies of firms. The purpose of this paper is to present a literature review on the dividend policy studies of the firms listed on the Borsa Istanbul. Furthermore, this paper aims to identify any research gaps that need to be addressed in the future. This paper categorizes the dividend policy of Turkish firms listed on the Borsa Istanbul into six groups: price and volume reactions of dividends and right issues, dividend policy studies, determinants of dividend policy, international studies, ownership structure and dividend policy, and corporate governance and dividend policy.

Keywords: Dividend policy, Turkey, Market reactions, laws, determinants

Introduction

In their influential paper, Miller and Modigliani (1961) argued that dividend policy is irrelevant, and thus has no effect on firm value. The productiveness of a firm has a greater impact on a firm's value than its dividend policy. On the contrary, the stock exchange in Turkey is relatively new. The Istanbul Stock Exchange (ISE) was founded in 1986 and subsequently renamed as Borsa Istanbul (BI) in 2013. To the best of the author's knowledge, Aydogan and Muradoglu (1998) published the first empirical paper on the dividend policy of firms listed on the stock market in Turkey.

Turkey has a "bank-centered financial system" (Al-Najjar and Kilincarslan, 2017). The Turkish market was described as underdeveloped in 2003 (Aivazian, Booth and Cleary, 2003a). Large families own holding companies and banks. Controlled by families, business groups borrow from a bank within the group. During the early years of the Istanbul Stock Exchange, dividend policy was not important for Turkish firms. Firms followed unstable dividend policies where volatility in earnings led to unstable current dividend payments.

Regulations influencing the dividend policy of public firms have changed over the years. From 1982 to 1994, distribution of 50 % of the earnings as cash dividends was mandatory in order to protect the rights of minority shareholders (Adaoglu, 1999). During this period, firms gathered their cash dividends back by issuing rights issues at the same time as cash dividends (Adaoglu, 1999). Between 1981 and 1990, a high mean payout ratio of 60 % was recorded (Yilmaz, 2003).

Tab. 21.1: Price and Volume Reactions of Dividends and Right Issues

Year	Author(s)	Sample size	Year	Author(s)	Sample size
1998	Aydogan and Muradoglu	109 stock dividend-right offerings	2010	Yilmaz and Selcuk	184 dividend announcements
2003	Muradoglu and Aydogan	516 stock dividend-right offerings.	2011	Gunalp, Kadioglu, and Kilic	429 cash dividend announcements
2003	Batchelor and Orakcioglu	110 cash dividend, stock dividend and right offerings	2015	Kadioglu, Telceken, and Ocal	902 cash dividend announcements
2006	Yilmaz and Gulay	602 cash dividends			

In 1995, the mandatory dividend distribution was abolished and firms were allowed to choose between cash and stock dividends (Al-Najjar and Kilincarslan, 2018). In 2003, a compulsory dividend policy was introduced requiring firms to pay a minimum of 20 % in dividends. However, firms had the freedom of choice between cash dividends and stock dividends (Al-Najjar and Kilincarslan, 2018). In 2004, the mandatory minimum dividend payment was 30 %. For the period from 2006 to 2008, the ratio was 20 %. In 2009, firms were granted the freedom to make a decision on their dividend policies (Al-Najjar and Kilincarslan, 2018).

The aim of this chapter is to review the literature in Turkey and to shed light on the research gaps where further research is needed. A search has been conducted on the Taylor and Francis, Emerald, Springer, Elsevier, and Scopus databases for dividend policy studies in Turkey. Only articles written in English are included in this chapter. The literature review consists of six sections: price and volume reactions of dividends and right issues, dividend policy studies, determinants of dividend policy, international studies, ownership structure and dividend policy, and corporate governance and dividend policy.

2 Literature Review

2.1 Price and Volume Reactions of Dividends and Right Issues

A summary of studies written on price and volume reactions of dividends and rights issues is shown in Tab. 21.1. Aydogan and Muradoglu (1998) analyzed how the stock prices reacted to the announcement and the implementation of stock dividends and rights for the period from 1988 to 1993. A total of 109 events were analyzed using an event study methodology. During the first period from

1988 to 1990, securities were thinly traded and the market was not transparent in Turkey. As a result, price reactions to stock dividends and right offerings were positive at the time of the board meeting. During the second period from 1991 to 1993, the abnormal returns disappeared at the declaration date and the actual payment date of stock dividends and rights issues as the market became efficient. Using 110 events from 1990 to 1994, Batchelor and Orakcioglu (2003) analyzed the influence of stock dividends on share prices in the Istanbul Stock Exchange using a GARCH model. The authors summarized that markets did not react to stock dividend payments. The stock prices rose after an increase in dividends, or vice-versa. Using 513 events, Muradoglu and Aydogan (2003) investigated how the stock market responded to stock dividends and rights offerings by using three sub-periods: 1988–1989, 1990–1992, and 1993–1994. Abnormal returns and higher trading volumes were only detected during 1993 and 1994. The authors concluded that this was because of two reasons. First, the investors could track the market better as the financial information disclosed was improved. Second, the mix of investors changed as small investors entered the market. Stock prices were volatile both on the day and the day after the stock dividend was paid. Yilmaz and Gulay (2006) investigated how cash dividend payments affect stock prices and volumes in Istanbul Stock Exchange. A total of 602 cash dividends were examined for the period of 1995–2003. It was found that stock prices increased prior to the payment of cash dividends, whereas prices decreased on the ex-dividend day and continued falling after the payment. Trading volume, on the other hand, increased before the dividends were paid, but was stable once the dividends were paid. The authors concluded that the effects of cash dividends on stock prices and trading volumes were different. Small companies with high dividend payout ratios exhibited greater price and volume reactions. Therefore, profitable investment opportunities were available for investors around the ex-dividend date. Yilmaz and Selcuk (2010) analyzed how the stock market responded to changes in dividend announcements. Cumulative abnormal returns were calculated for 184 dividend announcements for the period between 2005 and 2008. Using an event window of three days, the results showed that stock prices rose when dividends were increased. When dividends decreased, the stock prices also decreased. The stock market did not respond when dividends were stable. The results provide evidence for the signaling hypothesis in Turkey. Gunalp, Kadioglu, and Kilic (2011) evaluated the announcement of 429 cash dividends on stock prices in Turkey using a panel regression method. For the period of 2003–2009, following the announcement date, an inverse relationship between cash dividends paid per share and abnormal stock returns was detected. Dividends were taxed more than the

Tab. 21.2: Dividend Policy Studies

Year	Author(s)	Sample size	Year	Author(s)	Sample size
1999	Adaoglu	1317 companies	2016	Kadioglu and Ocal	123 companies
2000	Adaoglu	776 companies	2017	Kadioglu and Yilmaz	227 companies
2003	Yilmaz	n/a	2017	Al-Najjar and Kilinarslan	264 companies
2008	Adaoglu	144 companies	2017	Kilincarslan	80 companies
2008	Albayrak and Pekkaya	65 companies	2018	Baker, Kilincarslan, and Arslan	126 companies
2010	Kirkulak and Kurt	n/a	2018	Baker and Kilincarslan	216 companies

n/a: Not available

capital gains in Turkey. Therefore, shareholders sold their stocks upon hearing the news regarding the cash dividend payment. Therefore, the stock market reaction to cash dividend announcements provides evidence for the tax clientele hypothesis. Gunalp et al. (2011) argued that information is not discharged before the dividends are announced, and thus the markets are becoming more efficient over time in Turkey. Using a panel regression method, Kadioglu, Telceken, and Ocal (2015) researched the reaction of the stock market to 902 cash dividend announcements for a longer period of time, namely 2003–2015. The results concur with the results of Gunalp et al. (2011).

2.2 Dividend Policy Studies

A summary of dividend policy studies is shown in Tab. 21.2. Adaoglu (1999) studied how the changes in the regulations affected the dividend policy of companies listed on the Istanbul Stock Exchange from 1990 to 1997. Until 1995, companies trading on the Istanbul Stock Exchange were legally required to pay a minimum of 50 % cash dividends from profits. In 1995, the change in regulations offered the companies the flexibility to adopt their dividend policies according to their needs. According to Adaoglu (1999) cash dividend payout ratios decreased after the regulator changed. Until 1994, there were no differences in cash dividend policies among different industries. After 1994, however, upon the change of the regulation, cash dividend policies started to differ among different industries. Adaoglu (1999) argued that corporations issued rights at the same time as cash dividends in order to gather the distributed cash dividends back. Net dividend payouts (cash dividends – right issues) were almost zero for banks and very low for manufacturing corporations. Adaoglu (2000) used two different periods, namely from 1985–1994 and 1995–1997, to analyze the stability of dividend policies of ISE corporations. Adaoglu (2000) concluded that cash dividend policies were not only unstable during the period from 1985 to 1994 when 50% dividend payments were mandatory, but also during the period of 1995–1997 where firms had flexible dividend policies. Moreover, the earnings of a company were the main determinant of the cash dividends to be distributed. After the regulatory change, dividend payout ratios became lower, and the number of firms discontinuing making dividend payments decreased. Adaoglu (2008) observed a decrease in the number of cash dividend payers, but an increase in the dividend concentration during the period 1985–2006. Furthermore, the payment of dividends was higher in industries with high market capitalization. The mandatory dividend policy regulation that was put into effect in 2003 did not change the dividend payout ratios of the firms. Albayrak and Pekkaya (2008) investigated how dividend policies of firms affected stock prices. The authors concluded that both the current and previous years' dividends were important factors in determining the dividend policies of firms during 2004–2006.

Kirkulak and Kurt (2010) posited that income, concentration of dividends, the percentage of dividend payers, and the amount of dividends decreased for the firms on the Istanbul Stock Exchange during the period from 1991 to 2006. According to Kirkulak and Kurt (2010), financial crises and current earnings of firms affected the dividend policy of firms. Firms preferred dividend elimination to decreasing dividend payments. When firms continued to pay dividends, they made the effort to increase dividend payments in the following years. Kadioglu and Ocal (2016) examined whether there was a relationship between changes in dividends and the future profitability of firms. By using data for the period of 2004–2014, the researchers proved that changes in dividends did not impact any changes in future earnings. Thus, dividend signaling theory does not hold in Turkey, and dividends are not a sign of the future profitability of forms. Kadioglu and Yilmaz (2017) checked and proved the validity of the free cash flow hypothesis for the period of 2008–2014. The free cash flow hypothesis states that "rather than paying dividends, managers use free cash flow to invest in projects with negative net present value" (Kadioglu and Yilmaz, 2017). Using data from 227 companies in a panel regression, Kadioglu and Yilmaz (2017) found an inverse relationship between dividends paid and free cash flow.

Kilincarslan (2017) examined the behavior of 80 cash dividend paying firms during 2009–2016. The results revealed that firms take current income and previous dividend payments into account while shaping their cash dividend policies. Kilincarslan (2017) argued that firms adopt steady dividend policies after the abolishment of mandatory dividend payments and have a long-term goal in setting dividend payout ratios. Firms adjust their dividend payments to the targeted payout rations in the long run. Income, leverage, growth rate, and firm size affect dividend payments in Turkey. Al-Najjar and Kilincarslan (2017) examined the consequence of the changing regulations on cash dividend payments after 2003 for the period of 2003–2012. Litner's partial adjustment model and a logit model were used to determine the relationship between financial attributes and the probability of dividend payments. The results suggested that the factors affecting the dividend payments in the Istanbul Stock Exchange and Litner's model are identical. It was found that firms in Turkey determined payout ratios in the long run and altered their cash dividends by moderately smoothing dividends. During 2003–2012, even though dividend policies in Turkey were more volatile compared to the firms in the US market, Turkish firms followed steady dividend policies. Concentration of ownership structure influenced dividend payments and dividend smoothing as well. Profitability, maturity, and firm's size positively affected the distribution of cash dividends. Investment opportunities and leverage negatively affected cash dividends. Baker, Kilincarslan, and Arsal's (2018) study was unique. First, unlike its counterparts, it used a survey method. Second, the authors tested the validity of ten dividend policy theories. A questionnaire consisting of 55 questions was collected from 57 dividend-paying firms listed on the Borsa Istanbul. The results provided evidence for "Linter's partial adjustment model", "signaling theory", "catering hypothesis", "firm life cycle hypothesis", and "bird-in-the-hand hypothesis". The findings did not show evidence for "the agency cost theory", "substitution model of dividends", "tax-related explanations", "transaction cost theory", and "residual dividend policy". Baker and Kilincarslan (2018) researched the opinions of managers of firms that do not pay dividends. The findings revealed that firms do not pay dividends because of a lack of cash, availability of growth opportunities, low income, and the cost of obtaining debt. Although taxes are not an important factor while setting a no dividend policy, shareholders' wishes are important. Young and small firms with abundant growth opportunities and low income have the tendency not to pay cash dividends (Baker and Kilincarslan, 2018). Shareholders holding large amounts of stock, high debt ratio, and growth possibilities negatively impact cash dividend payments. According to Baker and Kilincarslan (2018), between 1990 and 2002, the dividend policies of the firms listed on the Istanbul Stock Exchange significantly differed from those of the firms in developed countries. Although the ranking of an industry by using cash dividend ratio did not change

Tab. 21.3: Determinants of Dividend Policy

Year	Author(s)	Sample size	Year	Author(s)	Sample size
2015a	Kuzucu	38companies	2017	Takmaz	283 companies
2015b	Kuzucu	142 companies	2018	Bostanci, Kadiogluand Sayilgan	106 companies
2017	Kisava and John	n/a	2018	Al-Najjar and Kilincarslan	264 companies

n/a: Not available

radically during 1990–2002, the trend was not steady. Changes in an economy affected the financial sector more than other sectors. Net cash dividends (cash dividends – rights) decreased after 1995 (Tab. 21.2).

2.3 Determinants of Dividend Policy

Several studies have been conducted on the determinants of dividend policy in Turkey (Tab. 21.3). Unlike other studies, Kuzucu (2015a) employed a survey method to investigate the opinions of financial managers for 38 firms. Kuzucu (2015a) aimed to compare the dividend policies of Turkish firms with those of European and English firms. The results indicated that cash dividends and earnings are positively correlated. According to managers in Turkey, attainable changes in profitability, steadiness, and the amount of future earnings and intention to distribute earnings are the major determinants of dividend payments. Similar to the European and English firms, profitability is the most critical factor determining dividend policy in Turkey. Using panel data for the time period 2006–2013, Kuzucu (2015b) posited that firms with larger size, older age, and higher price/earnings ratios pay higher dividends. Firms with higher debt ratios, faster growth rate, and higher financial profit pay lower dividends. The results support the maturity hypothesis in Turkey. In other words, mature firms experience more difficulties finding profitably projects compared to young firms and prefer to use idle resources for paying dividends. Kuzucu's research (2015b) supported the bird-in-the-hand and signaling hypothesis. Kisava and John (2017) used data from 2005 to 2016 and concluded that the size of a firm, financial profitability, net income, leverage, and earnings retained within the company are the determinants of dividend policy.

For the period of 2003–2015, Takmaz (2017) used logit regression methodology and data from nonfinancial nonutility companies to determine the factors affecting dividend payments in Turkey. Takmaz (2017) summarized that as the profitability and maturity of a firm increases, dividend payout ratios increase. On the other hand, higher debt ratios decrease dividend payout ratios for the companies. Ownership structure and liquidity of a firm, however, have no effect on dividend policy. Bostanci, Kadioglu, and Sayilgan (2018) utilized dynamic panel data methodology and data from the Borsa Istanbul for the period 2009–2015. Market capitalization was used as a proxy for the size, and it was found that profitability (net profit/equity), liquidity, market value/book value, and past years' dividend payments positively affect the dividend payout ratios. Maturity, the amount of family control and the debt ratio had no effect on the dividend payout ratios. Al-Najjar and Kilincarslan (2016) investigated the factors affecting dividend policy after 2003. From 2003 onwards, Turkey adopted reforms in compliance with the International Monetary Fund's agreement.

Al-Najjar and Kilincarslan (2016) used logit and tobit models and demonstrated that the financial profitability, maturity, and size of a firm have a positive influence on the dividend payments. The leverage and growth rate of a company negatively affect a firm's dividend policy. After 2003, "business risk", "free cash flow", "liquidity", and "asset tangibility" had no effect on the dividend policies of Turkish firms (Al-Najjar and Kilincarslan, 2016). Furthermore, after 2003 in Turkey, it was observed that the factors affecting the dividend decisions of Turkish firms have strong similarities to the dividend policies of firms in developed countries.

2.4 International Studies

International studies have used data from many countries along with Turkey to investigate dividend policies. La Porta, Lopez-de-Silanes, Shleifera, and Vishny (2000) tested the validity of the outcome agency model of dividends and the substitute agency model of dividends in 33 countries including Turkey. The outcome model claims that companies make dividend payments because minority shareholders force companies to pay cash. Therefore, the higher the rights of minority shareholders, the higher is the dividend payout ratio. The substitution agency model of dividends posits that insiders who are concerned with issuing new shares in the future pay dividends as they want to be recognized for acting in a positive manner towards the minority shareholders. Data from 4,000 companies were used. The countries were divided into two groups: civil law countries and common law countries. Turkey was included in the civil law countries group. It was proven that the dividend payout ratios of common law countries are higher than civil law countries, because La Porta et al. (2000) claimed that "common law countries have stronger shareholder protection than civil law countries". La Porta et al. (2000) asserted that dividends to cash flow ratios and dividends to sales ratios of common law countries are statistically significantly higher than civil law countries. Mature firms in common law countries pay higher dividends because when there are growth opportunities, dividend payments can be postponed, as the minority shareholders are well protected. In common law countries where the minority shareholders' protection is high, mature firms have a higher dividend to cash flow, dividend to earnings, and dividend to sales ratios. In summary, the findings of the study supported the outcome model of agency problems.

Aivazian, Booth, and Cleary (2003a) compared and contrasted the dividend policies of emerging market countries with the dividend policy of the USA for the period between 1981 and 1990. The countries studied were Korea, India, Malaysia, Thailand, Zimbabwe, Jordan, Pakistan, and Turkey. It was found that although emerging markets had greater financial restrictions, the factors affecting the dividend policies of the emerging countries and the USA were the same. Profitability measured as the return on assets and the market to book ratio had a positive impact on dividend payment ratios. Tangibility of assets and high leverage had a negative impact on dividend payment ratios. The results provided validity for the residual cash flow theory of dividends. Financial leverage negatively affected dividend payments. Although emerging market countries were found to be different in terms of dividend policies, in general they had higher dividend payout ratios relative to the US firms.

Aivazian, Booth, and Cleary (2003b) compared the dividend policies of eight emerging countries (Korea, India, Malaysia, Thailand, Zimbabwe, Jordan, Pakistan, and Turkey) with the USA during 1980–1990. Two hypotheses were tested: substitute hypothesis and complement hypothesis. The substitute hypothesis states that dividends are used as a means to "substitute for direct communication with the external investors". Dividend policies among countries vary because of diverse structures. For instance, in countries where capital markets function effectively, dividends are important. In contrast, in a bank-centered financial system, the payment of stable dividends is not important. The complement hypothesis claims that dividends promote an environment in which agency and information problems are controlled. The findings stated that in the emerging countries studied, dividends were more volatile compared to the USA. Therefore, forecasting dividend changes is more difficult in these countries. Current dividends are better determinants than past dividends in the USA compared to the emerging markets. The Litner model is not valid in emerging countries. The research findings provided support for the substitute hypothesis. Operating in a bank-centered financial system, dividend policies in emerging countries cannot be used to forecast future earnings and to decrease agency costs.

Tab. 21.4: International Studies on Dividend Policy

Year	Author(s)	Sample size	Year	Author(s)	Sample size
2000	La Porta, Lopez-de-Silanes, Shleifer, and Vishny	33 countries	2003b	Aivazian, Booth, and Cleary	9 countries
2003a	Aivazian, Booth, and Cleary	9 countries	2004	Mitton	19 countries

Tab. 21.5: Ownership Structure and Dividend Policy

Year	Author(s)	Sample size(s)	Year	Author	Sample size
2017	Al-Najjar and Kilincarslan	264 companies	2000	Yurtoglu	257 companies

Mitton (2004) investigated the relationship between corporate governance and dividend policy by using data from 19 countries including Turkey. It was found that corporate governance and dividend payout ratios are positively related only when investors are protected by law. The relationship between corporate governance and firm profitability is also positive. However, growth opportunities available for a firm and dividend payouts are negatively related.

2.5 Ownership Structure and Dividend Policy

Al-Najjar and Kilincarslan (2017) explored the relationship between ownership variables and the dividend policy of firms (Tab. 21.5). Specifically, the impact of family involvement via stock possession and board membership on dividend payment was examined. Furthermore, the impact of minority stockholders and block holders of non-family members (international investors, national financial institutions, and the government) on dividend payments was investigated. The results showed that the higher the international and government ownership, the lower are the dividends paid. Ownership variables negatively affect dividend payments. Yurtoglu (2000) proved that the higher the ownership concentration, the lower the dividend payout ratios.

2.6 Corporate Governance and Dividend Policy

Tab. 21.6 summarized the studies on corporate governance and dividend policy in Turkey. Gurbuz, Aybars, and Kutlu (2010) assessed how corporate governance

Tab. 21.6: Corporate Governance and Dividend Policy

Year	Author(s)	Sample size	Year	Author	Sample size
2010	Gurbuz, Aybars, and Kutlu	164 companies	2015	Aydin and Cavdar	19 companies

affects the financial performance of firms in Turkey using 164 firms for the period of 2005–2008. The results revealed that there is a positive relationship between corporate governance and financial firms. Aydin and Cavdar (2015) found an insignificant relationship between corporate governance and dividend policy among 19 firms in Borsa Istanbul during 2007–2014. Aydin and Cavdar (2015) also found a positive relationship between foreign ownership, firm size, and dividend policy. Furthermore, the study concluded that ownership concentration, managerial ownership, and return on equity are negatively related.

Conclusion

Tabs. 21.1 to 21.6 summarize the studies conducted in Turkey. First, Turkish researchers concentrated on writing empirical papers only on Turkey. Non-Turkish researchers, on the other hand, compared Turkey with a group of other countries (Tab. 21.4). International studies are now outdated as the last article was written by Mitton (2004). There is a need to collaborate with researchers from other countries to conduct international studies comparing the dividend policies of Turkish firms with the firms in Europe, Asia, and the Middle East.

Second, the majority of studies have used time series data. Only a limited number of studies have used the survey method (Baker and Kilincarslan, 2018; Baker, Kilincarslan and Arsal, 2018; Kuzucu, 2015b). More studies should be performed using a survey method. Moreover, studies using questionnaires have generally asked for the opinions of managers or employees. Research can be done on investors' opinions on dividend policies in Turkey.

Third, Turkish laws governing dividend policies have changed many times over the years. Adaoglu (1998) compared the dividend policies during 1985–1994 and 1995–1997. Hence, a research opportunity exists to compare the effect of changing regulations on dividend policy.

Fourth, the reaction of the stock market when dividends change has not been analyzed by any researchers.

Fifth, the relationships of corporate governance and ownership structure with the dividend policy have only been examined by a few researchers (Tab. 21.5 and 21.6), indicating that there is a need to conduct further studies on these subjects.

References

Adaoglu, C. (1999). Regulation Influence on the Dividend Policy of the Istanbul Stock Exchange (ISE) Corporations. *ISE Review*, 3(11), 1–19.

Adaoglu, C. (2000). Instability in the Dividend Policy of the Istanbul Stock Exchange (ISE) Corporations: Evidence from an Emerging Market. *Emerging Markets Review*, 1(3), 252–270.

Adaoglu, C. (2008). Dividend Policy of the ISE Industrial Corporations: The Evidence Revisited (1986–2007). *BDDK Bankacilik ve Finansal Piyasalar*, 2(2), 113–135.

Aivazian, V., Booth, L. and Cleary, S. (2003a). Do Emerging Market Firms Follow Different Divined Policies from U.S. Firms?. *The Journal of Financial Research*, 26(3), 371–387.

Aivazian, V., Booth, L. and Cleary, S. (2003b). Dividend Policy and the Organization of Capital Markets. *Journal of Multinational Financial Management*, 13(2), 102–121.

Albayrak, A.S. and Pekkaya, M. (2008). Examining the Relationship between Price of Equity and Dividend Policy of Firms Operate in Service and Industry Sectors of ISE. *Selcuk Universitesi Sosyal Bilimler Meslek Yuksekokulu Dergisi*, 11(1–2), 137–156.

Al-Najjar, B. and Kilincarslan, E. (2016). The Effect of Ownership Structure on Dividend Policy: Evidence from Turkey. *Corporate Governance*, 16(1), 135–161.

Al-Najjar, B. and Kilincarslan, E. (2017). Corporate Dividend Decisions and Dividend Smoothing. *International Journal of Managerial Finance*, 13(3), 304–331.

Aydin, A.D. and Cavdar, S.C. (2015). Corporate Governance and Dividend Policy: An Empirical Analysis from Borsa Istanbul Corporate Governance İndex. *Accounting and Finance Research*, 4(3), 66–76.

Aydogan, K. and Muradoglu, G. (1998). Do Markets Learn from Experience? Price Reaction to Stock Dividends in the Turkish Market. *Applied Financial Economics*, 8(1), 41–49.

Baker, H. K., Kilincarslan, E. and Arsal, A.H. (2018). Dividend Policy in Turkey: Survey Evidence from Borsa Istanbul Firms, *Global Finance Journal*, 35, 43–57.

Baker, H.K. and Kilincarslan, E. (2018). Why Companies Do Not Pay Cash Dividends: The Turkish Experience. *Global Finance Journal*, 1–18.

Batchelor, R. and Orakcioglu, I. (2003). Event-Related GARCH: The Impact of Stock Dividends in Turkey. *Applied Financial Economics*, 13(4), 295–307.

Bostanci, F., Kadioglu, E. and Sayilgan, G. (2018). Determinants of Dividend Payout Decisions: A Dynamic Panel Data Analysis of Turkish Stock Market. *International Journal of Financial Studies*, 6(93), 1–16.

Gunalp, B., Kadioglu, E. and Kilic, S. (2011). The Announcement Effect of Cash Dividend on Share Prices and the Tax Clientele Effect: Evidence from Turkish Capital Markets. *Paper Presented at the Euroconference.* DOI: 10.13140/RG.2.1.2980.4400.

Gurbuz, A.O., Aybars, A. and Kutlu, O. (2010). Corporate Governance and Financial Performance with a Perspective on Institutional Ownership: Empirical Evidence from Turkey. *Journal of Applied Management Accounting Research*, 8(2), 21–37.

Kadioglu, E. and Ocal, N. (2016). Dividend Changes and Future Profitability: Evidence from the Turkish Stock Market. *International Journal of Economics and Finance*, 8(3), 196–205.

Kadioglu, E., Telceken, N. and Ocal, N. (2015). Market Reaction to Dividend Announcement: Evidence from Turkish Stock market. *International Business Research*, 8(9), 83–94.

Kadioglu, E. and Yilmaz, E.A. (2017). Is the Free Cash Flow Hypothesis Valid in Turkey? *Borsa Istanbul Review*, 17(2), 111–116.

Kılınçarslan, E. (2017). Cash Dividend Payments: A Study of Financial Sector in Turkey. *Bankacılık ve Sigortacılık Araştırmaları Dergisi*, 2(11), 92–117.

Kirkulak, B. and Kurt, G. (2010). Are Dividends Disappearing or Shrinking? Evidence from the Istanbul Stock Exchange. *Emerging Markets Finance & Trade*, 46(2), 38–52.

Kisava, Z. and John, F.M. (2017). Determinants of Dividends Payout and Policy Used in Emerging Economies: Evidence from Turkey. *Business and Economic Research*, 7(2), 362–374.

Kuzucu, N. (2015a). A Survey of Managerial Perspective on Corporate Dividend Policy: Evidence from Turkish Listed Firms. *International Journal of Research in Business and Social Sciences*, 4(2), 1–19

Kuzucu, N. (2015b). Determinants of Dividend Policy: A Panel Data Analysis of Turkish Listed Firms. *International Journal of Business and Management*, 10(11), 149–160.

La Porta, R., Lopez-de-Silanes, F., Shleifer, A., & Vishny, R. (2000). Investor protection and corporate governance. *Journal of financial economics, 58*(1–2), 3–27.

Miller, M.H. and Modigliani, F. (1961). Dividend Policy, Growth and the Valuation of Shares. *Journal of Business*, 40(4), 1031.1051.

Mitton, T. (2004). Corporate Governance and Dividend Policy in Emerging Markets. *Emerging Markets Review*, 5(4), 409–426.

Muradoglu, G. and Aydogan, K. (2003). Trends in Market Reactions: Stock Dividends and Rights Offerings at Istanbul Stock Exchange. *The European Journal of Finance*, 9(1), 41–60.

Najjar-Al, B. and Kilincarlsan, E. (2018). Revisiting Firm-Specific Determinants of Dividend Policy: Evidence from Turkey. *Economic Issues*, 23(Part 1), 3–34.

Takmaz, S. (2017). Dividend Policy Drivers in Turkish Listed Firms. *International Journal of Academic Value Studies*, 3(16), 40–52.

Yılmaz, M. K.,(2003) Hisse Senetleri İMKB'de İşlem Gören Şirketlerin Temettü Politikaları Üzerine Bir Analiz: Nakit Temettü-Sektör Davranışı İlişkisi, İMKB Dergisi, Sayı: 25–26.

Yilmaz, A.A. and Selcuk, E.A. (2010). Information Content of Dividends: Evidence from Istanbul Stock Exchange. *International Business Research*, 3(3), 126–132.

Yilmaz, M.K. and Gulay, G. (2006). Dividend Policies and Price-Volume Reactions to Cash Dividends on the Stock Market: Evidence from the Istanbul Stock Exchange. *Emerging Markets Finance and Trade*, 42(4), 19–49.

Yurtoglu, B.B. (2000). Ownership, Control and Performance of Turkish Listed Firms. *Empirica*, 27 (2), 193–222.

Yurtoglu, B. (2003). *Corporate Governance and Implications for Minority Shareholders in Turkey* (Turkish Economic Association Discussion Paper 2003/7 website: https://core.ac.uk/download/pdf/6379628.pdf)

List of Figures

List of Tables